The theme of this volume is challenging both in its scale and in its scope. Its purpose is to take account of the state of research and writing on the symbiotic relationship between banking, trade and industry and the state during the rise and expansion of capitalism, and to compare and assess the results in order to widen current perspectives. Topics range from the origins of banking in the Middle Ages, through the influence of banks in leading industrial economies as well as in 'latecomer' economies, to the expansion of banking in America and Asia.

The volume has been edited in connection with the session 'Banking, Trade and Industry in Europe, America and Asia (XIII–XX Centuries)' at the 18th International Congress of Historical Sciences, Montreal, 1995.

Banking, trade and industry

Banking, trade and industry

Europe, America and Asia from the thirteenth to the twentieth century

---

EDITED BY

ALICE TEICHOVA
Honorary Fellow of Girton College, Cambridge

GINETTE KURGAN-VAN HENTENRYK
Professor of History, Free University of Brussels

AND DIETER ZIEGLER
Reader in Economic History, University of Bielefeld

CAMBRIDGE
UNIVERSITY PRESS

PUBLISHED BY THE PRESS SYNDICATE OF THE UNIVERSITY OF CAMBRIDGE
The Pitt Building, Trumpington Street, Cambridge CB2 1RP, United Kingdom

CAMBRIDGE UNIVERSITY PRESS
The Edinburgh Building, Cambridge CB2 2RU, United Kingdom
40 West 20th Street, New York, NY 10011–4211, USA
10 Stamford Road, Oakleigh, Melbourne 3166, Australia

First published 1997

Printed in the United Kingdom at the University Press, Cambridge

Typeset in Baskerville 11/13 pt

*A catalogue record for this book is available from
the British Library*

Library of Congress cataloguing in publication data

Banking, trade and industry: Europe, America and Asia from the
thirteenth to the twentieth century / edited by Alice Teichova,
Ginette Kurgan-van Hentenryk and Dieter Ziegler.
          p.   cm.
Edited in connection with the session, 'Banking, Trade, and
Industry in Europe, America and Asia (XIII–XX Centuries)' at the
18th International Congress of Historical Sciences, Montreal, 1995.
ISBN 0 521 57361 0
1. Banks and banking – History – Congresses. I. Teichova, Alice.
II. Kurgan-van Hentenryk, G. III. Ziegler, Dieter.
HG1551.B296   1997
332.1'09 – dc20   96–22566   CIP

ISBN 0 521 57361 0 hardback

WD

Contents

Notes on contributors

DAVID ABULAFIA is Reader in Mediterranean History at Cambridge University, and a Fellow of Gonville and Caius College. His books on medieval Italian and Catalan trade include *The Two Italies* (1977) and *A Mediterranean Emporium* (1994). His current interests lie mainly in fifteenth-century southern Italy.

PAOLA AVALLONE is researcher of the Institute of Studies on the Economy of Southern Italy in the Modern Age – Italian National Council of Research. She teaches business history at the Istituto Universitario Navale of Naples. Her publications include *Stato e Banchi Pubblici a Napoli a metá del '700. Il Banco del Poveri: una svolta* (1995). She is currently working on economic crime in Neapolitan public banks and on commercial circuits in southern Italy in the seventeenth and eighteenth centuries.

H. V. BOWEN is Lecturer in Economic and Social History at the University of Leicester. He has written widely on eighteenth-century British economic, imperial and political history, and his books include *Revenue and Reform: The Indian Problem in British Politics, 1757–1773* (1991) and *Elites, Enterprise and the Making of the British Overseas Empire, 1688–1775* (1996). He is currently working on an economic history of the English East India Company between 1750 and 1830.

ERIC BUSSIÈRE is Professor of Modern Economic History at the University of Artois. His main fields of interest are history of French investment banks and of European integration. His publications include *Paribas, Europe and the World (1872–1992)* (1992).

YOUSSEF CASSIS teaches economic history at the University of Geneva and is a Visiting Research Fellow at the Business History Unit, the London School of Economics and Political Science. He is joint editor, with Philip Cottrell, of *Financial History Review*. He is the author of *City Bankers 1890–1914* (1994), and joint editor, with F. Crouzet and T. Gourvish, of *Management and Business in Britain and France. The Age of the Corporate Economy* (1995). He is currently completing a study of big business in twentieth-century Europe.

P. L. COTTRELL is Professor of Economic and Social History at the University of Leicester. He writes on modern financial history, as with a contribution to R. Roberts and D. Kynaston (eds.), *The Bank of England. Money, Power and Influence 1694–1994* (1995), and currently is co-editor of *Financial History Review*.

LUIGI DE ROSA is Professor of Economic History at the Free International University in Social Sciences (LUISS) of Rome. He is author of books and articles including *History of the Bank of Rome*, 2 vols. (1982–3), and *History of the Bank of Naples*, 4 vols. (1989–92). At present he is working on the history of the Italian banking system since Unification.

ELENA FRANGAKIS-SYRETT is Professor of History at Queens College, the City University of New York. She is the author of books and articles on eighteenth- and nineteenth-century European–Ottoman commercial relations, including *The Commerce of Smyrna in the Eighteenth Century, 1700–1820* (1992). She is currently working on the role of European banks in the economic development of the Ottoman Empire and on the penetration and impact of Western capital in the Near East in the nineteenth and early twentieth centuries.

MONTSERRAT GÁRATE OJANGUREN is Professor of Business History at País Vasco University, Bilbao. Her publications include *Comercio Ultramarino e Illustración: La Real Compañía de La Habana (1740–1845)* (1994). Her research is concerned with the influence of funds from Spanish America on Spanish industrialization, and also with the configuration of financial circuits, especially through London and Paris.

KANJI ISHII is Professor of Economics at the University of Tokyo. He is author of *Nihonkeizaishi (Economic History of Japan)* (1991) and *Kindainihon to Igirisushihon (Modern Japan and British Capital)* (1984). At present he is working on the history of the Industrial Revolution in Japan.

GINETTE KURGAN-VAN HENTENRYK is Professor of History at Université Libre de Bruxelles. She is author of books and articles on economic and social history including *A History of European Banking* (with R. Bogaert and H. Van der Wee) (1994). Currently she is editing a *Dictionary of Belgian Business* and publishes a collective biography of managers of the Société Générale (nineteenth and twentieth centuries).

HÅKAN LINDGREN is Professor of Economic History and attached to the Institute for Research in Economic History (EHF) at the Stockholm School of Economics. Among his publications are *Corporate Growth. The Swedish Match Industry in its Global Setting* (1979), and *Active Ownership: Investor and the Wallenberg Group* (1994). At present he is working within a research programme on 'The Role of Savings and Savings Banks in 150 Years of Economic Development'.

CARLOS MARICHAL is Professor of History at the Centro de Estudios Históricos, El Colegio de México. He received his PhD from Harvard University in 1977. He is author of *A Century of Debt Crisis in Latin America: from Independence to the Great Depression 1820–1930* (1989). As John Simon Guggenheim Fellow he is working on a history of banking in Latin America.

SHIZUYA NISHIMURA obtained his PhD from the University of London in 1969. He is Professor Emeritus at Hosei University, Tokyo, and currently Visiting Fellow at Clare Hall, Cambridge University. He is the author of books and articles, including *The Decline of Inland Bills of Exchange in the London Money Market 1855–1913* (1971) and 'The French Provincial Banks, the Banque de France, and Bill Finance, 1890–1913', in *Economic History Review*, 48, 3 (August 1995). At present he is working on the history of international banking in China.

MICHAEL NORTH is Professor of Modern History at Ernst-Moritz-Arndt-University in Greifswald. His publications include *Kunst und Kommerz im Goldenen Zeitalter* (1992) (forthcoming in English at Yale University Press), *Das Geld und seine Geschichte* (1994) and *Von Aktie bis Zoll* (1995). Currently he is working on comparative history of economy, culture and society (1400–1900).

ANDRÉS M. REGALSKY is Professor of History at the Universidad de Lujan and the Instituto Di Tella, Buenos Aires. He is the author of

'Foreign Capital, Local Interests and Railway Development in Argentina', *Journal of Latin American Studies*, 21, 3 (1989) and many other articles on foreign capital and financial history in Argentina. At present he is working on banking history and financial elites before 1930.

LARRY SCHWEIKART is Professor of History at the University of Dayton, USA. He has written many articles on finance and national defence and security and published *Banking in the American South* (1987) and co-authored *Banking in the American West* with Lynne Pierson Doti (1991). At present he is working on a textbook history of entrepreneurs in America.

ROBERT C. H. SWEENY is Associate Professor of History at the Memorial University, Newfoundland. He lives with Elizabeth-Anne Malischewsky and their daughter Charlotte in St John's, Newfoundland. His numerous publications focus on the history of capitalism in Canada. Currently he is conducting research on pre-industrial Montreal.

ALICE TEICHOVA is Emeritus Professor of Economic History at the University of East Anglia, Norwich, Honorary Fellow of Girton College, Cambridge University, and Senior Research Associate of the London School of Economics and Political Science. Her interests concern economic history and international relations of the twentieth century. Her publications include *Mezinárodní kapitál a Československo v letech 1918–1938* (*International Capital and Czechoslovakia 1918–1938*) (1994) and 'International Finance 1929–1939', in Wilfried Feldenkirchen, Frauke Schönert-Röhlt and Günther Schulz (eds.), *Wirtschaft Gesellschaft Unternehmen* (1995).

GABRIEL TORTELLA is Professor of Economic History at the Universidad de Alcalá, Alcalá de Henares, Madrid. He currently is President of the International Economic Association. His numerous publications include *El desarollo de la España contemporánea. Historia económica de los siglos XIX y XX* (1994). His research interests concern economic change, banking and monetary history and human capital in Europe.

HERMAN VAN DER WEE is Emeritus Professor of Social and Economic History at the University of Louvain (Belgium). He is author of several books and articles including *La Banque Nationale de Belgique et l'histoire monétaire entre les deux guerres mondiales* (1975) and, as co-author, *A History of European Banking* (1994). He is currently writing a book on the history of the *Société Générale de Belgique, 1822–1997*, and a chapter in the *Cambridge History of European Textiles*.

ANDREI YUDANOV is Professor of Economic Theory at the Financial Academy under the Government of Russia, Moscow. He is the author of *Big Business and Business Cycle* (1989) and *Competition: Theory and Practice* (1996). His current research deals with problems of the impact of competition on economic development.

DIETER ZIEGLER is Reader in Economic History at the University of Bielefeld, Germany. He is Book Review Editor of *Financial History Review*. His publications include *Central Bank, Peripheral Industry. The Bank of England in the Provinces, 1826–1913* (1990) and *Das Korsett der 'Alten Dame'. Die Geschäftspolitik der Bank of England 1844–1913* (1990). His current research is concerned with comparative history of private banking.

Acknowledgements

The editors wish to express their gratitude to the funding institutions, above all the Royal Historical Society, the British Academy and the Austrian Federal Ministry of Science and Research, which enabled the organizers and authors to participate in the work of the Congress. They also extend their warm thanks to William Davies of Cambridge University Press for his support and assistance.

1 Introduction

Alice Teichova, Ginette Kurgan-van Hentenryk and Dieter Ziegler

---

This volume explores the symbiotic relationships between banking, trade and industry and the state during the rise and expansion of capitalism, and seeks to compare and assess the results in order to widen current perspectives. The chronological dimension of its twenty-one contributions spans eight centuries and the geographical dimension extends across four continents.

Banking and trade in the pre-industrial era

The cradle of modern banking stood in the northern Italian cities. In this context David Abulafia traces the protracted process of the emancipation of banking from long-distance trade. The scope of early banking operations ranged from the pawnbroker who concentrated on small loans, often aimed at peasants or artisans in need of short-term credit, to the collectors of papal taxes who transmitted funds from the northern outposts of Christian Europe to Rome. In order to circumvent the ecclesiastical prohibition of usury, which restrained the money-lender from living exclusively off the charging of interest, the business of banking was conducted in the context of trading. Such exchange transactions were tolerated by the Church as they were generally regarded as non-usurious. The primary objective of the larger banking businesses was therefore neither deposit taking nor the provision of local

1

credit but exchanges and transfers. Abulafia, by concentrating on fourteenth- and fifteenth-century Florence, concluded that modern ideas of investing into production or of competitiveness cannot be fully applied to these early banking companies, whose success was built on a network of family connections and trust rather than on rules set by an anonymous market.

It may be doubted whether pre-industrial Europe was an economic entity but there can be little doubt that the commercial centres connecting the Mediterranean, the Baltic and the North Sea took shape along European trade routes from the late Middle Ages. As the 'first mover' in the development of banking the Italian cities fell behind, late medieval Italian banking techniques were successfully adapted to their local environment in other European cities. As the centre of gravity of commercial activity shifted from the Mediterranean to the Atlantic and north-western Europe, new banking techniques spread to those regions with which the commercial centres were connected by long-distance trade. Geneva lost its position as a leading financial centre to Lyons as early as the mid-fifteenth century, and Bruges to Antwerp about half a century later. Antwerp and Amsterdam in turn were unable to keep their leading position as they failed to develop a modern discount and issuing banking system. The decline of the Amsterdam financial market is not as yet fully understood; however, the hypothesis of 'institutional ponderousness' advanced by Herman Van der Wee in the case of Amsterdam might more generally explain the regional discontinuity in the development of banking.

Antwerp bankers developed the practice of endorsement and modern discount during the sixteenth century, which was an out-standing technical innovation and decisively stimulated the transferability and negotiability of commercial paper. This innovation was only fully exploited in Amsterdam, where many Antwerp bankers had immigrated. To limit the speculative activities of the immigrated bankers the Amsterdam authorities in 1609 founded a public deposit and clearing bank: the Amsterdamsche Wisselbank. This bank turned out to be an enormous success. Van der Wee stresses that it must not be regarded as a particular banking innovation as its business did not significantly differ from banking practices introduced by the Italian bankers and elaborated in Bruges and Antwerp. Nevertheless, the Wisselbank was a cornerstone of Amsterdam's position as the leading financial centre of the seventeenth and early eighteenth centuries: it refined the banking techniques, which it had copied, concentrating all accounts in a single bank; its own seemingly unshakeable solvency enhanced the trust in these accounts.

The spread of banking techniques along the established medieval trade routes is analysed in detail by Paola Avallone, Youssef Cassis, Michael North and Herman Van der Wee. In southern Italy and Naples public banks, descending from charitable institutions, became of overall importance as they functioned as main lenders to the governments of the Kingdom and of the City of Naples but also provided services to the public, such as opening saving accounts, lending money on collateral and issuing paper documents which were used both as credit and as means of payment. By accepting the public banks' *fedi di credito* for tax payments the government helped to ensure that these documents were widely accepted instead of metal currency.

A major innovation introduced by some of the public banks, such as the Neapolitan public banks and the Stockholms Banco, was paper money. Although the issuing of bank notes in Sweden had been prohibited after the failure of the Stockholms Banco, deposit receipts issued by the Riksbank soon became a substitute, and by 1726 the *transportsedlar* were accepted as legal tender by the state for tax payments. By the mid-century confidence in this medium of exchange had already become so great that neither suspension nor resumption of the notes' convertibility into coin seriously undermined monetary stability.

Spain's history exemplifies a case of declining commercial and financial centres. In almost all the main commercial centres of the Kingdoms of Aragon and Castile bankers had been established by the late Middle Ages, and by the sixteenth century Spain had become the very centre of the emerging world market. Gabriel Tortella observes, in the seventeenth century, 'a sharp cleavage between the early modern and the modern periods in the field of banking'. The Sevillian bankers, in particular, who were closely linked to the chaotic finances of the Spanish crown were prevented from developing a banking system appropriate to the needs of the rising commercial capitalism of the seventeenth and eighteenth centuries. Persistent budget deficits and lack of respect for legal rules and the market mechanism stymied private business. This helps to explain why Spain was unable to keep its leading position in the emerging world market. The same is true for the demise of the bankers of southern Germany, who had been closely related to the Spanish crown and consequently were brought down by the Spanish state bankruptcies of 1557, 1575 and 1607.

The state did not always play a retarding role in the development of banking, as the Spanish case might suggest. Indeed, the public bank was created by governmental (or rather municipal) authorities. Although most of these deposit and clearing or note issuing agencies finally proved unable to adapt to the needs of modern industrial capitalism, they can be seen as the forerunners of the modern central bank.

One important exception is the Swedish Riksbank. Its predecessor, the Stockholms Banco had not only combined deposit and credit functions but also became the first note issuing bank in Europe. Although Håkan Lindgren rejects the term 'central bank' as an anachronism for the early Riksbank, which had been founded in 1668 by the Swedish Parliament when the Stockholms Banco had to close its doors; learning the lesson of its failed predecessor and dividing the giro from the credit function, it gradually took on embryonic central banking functions in the course of the eighteenth century. The fact that all Scandinavian countries had founded public and semi-public banks by the eighteenth and early nineteenth centuries can be attributed to the example of the Riksbank, in particular to its successful introduction of paper money in a specie-scarce economy.

The other major exception, the Bank of England, was in fact no public bank, but privately owned by the merchant elite of the City of London. However, the Bank was developed and protected by a state which became financially dependent upon it. The British national debt and the taxation system withstood the early modern wars and crises (including the French Revolutionary and Napoleonic Wars) so that the Bank was able to develop, by trial and error while fairly independent from state control, both its commercial activities and – closely related to the latter – its early central banking strategies. It was, however, the state which forced the Bank of England to extend its activities as the backbone of the London finance market to the English provinces, where the Industrial Revolution was taking place. This 'crisis-induced reaction by the state', as Huw Bowen and Philip Cottrell described it, paved the way to turn the Bank of London into a national central bank. The final step in the establishment of the modern banking system was the creation of a note issuing agency: in 1694 the Bank of England was founded and in 1707 it was granted the right to issue bank notes. Although the founding of the Bank was in the first place motivated by the state's demand for a government banker, it was relatively free to develop its commercial business of bullion purchases, note issuing and discounting, and with it the Bank became the backbone of the emerging financial centre of the world.

Outside Europe – with the exception of North America – the development of banking techniques was connected with the European trading and financial network in early modern times. Montserrat Gárate analyses the development of payment and clearing transactions between Europe, Spain and the Spanish colonies in Latin America in the eighteenth century. The export of manufactured goods from different parts of Europe to the Latin American colonies created the demand for a means of payment which was not only payable in Spain, but in all major European commercial centres and the Atlantic ports. Drafts payable in Bordeaux, Paris, London or Amsterdam were successfully introduced and eased the development of the triangular export trade between Europe, Spain and the Latin American colonies.

These innovations hardly touched the domestic colonial economies. In the early period the abundance of precious metals in Latin America discouraged the development of more sophisticated means of payment. Some important merchant banking houses appeared in the colonial centres during the heyday of the triangular export trade with Europe, but they did not develop an intra-colonial banking infrastructure. When the colonies had become independent in the early nineteenth century and the strong links to the European economies were in danger of being cut a large majority of the Latin American merchant banking houses decided to transfer their businesses to one of the European centres with which they had already close contact, apart from Spain, mostly with Bordeaux, Paris and London.

From the viewpoint of world trade this Euro-centric approach has brought a greater understanding of banking in the imperialist period; however, it has tended to neglect indigenous economic development in former colonial areas. Recent research on banking in non-European countries has not primarily been concerned with its impact on industrialization but has emphasized its influence on political, social, national and institutional development. Thus Carlos Marichal characterizes the bank as a key institutional innovation not necessarily linked to industrialization but connected with the agro- and mineral-export economies of Latin America. From the second half of the nineteenth century the dominant role in political and administrative modernization and in the evolution of state structures was played by powerful government banks in Argentina, Brazil, Chile, Mexico and Peru. In these countries, he postulates, the banking revolution preceded the industrial revolution. This is borne out by Andrés Regalsky's account of

Argentina when he also stresses that the banking system supported agrarian rather than industrial capitalism.

From the very beginning of European settlement the situation in North America was different, since it lacked the precious metals of the Spanish colonies. The British and French colonies relied on coin shipped from Europe, and as the colonial societies grew other forms of money had to be introduced. Already in the second half of the seventeenth century the British colonial legislature was empowered to print paper money in order to finance military expeditions against the French, and in the mid-eighteenth century the government of Nova Scotia – followed by other colonial governments – issued treasury notes for the same reason. The British government, however, was concerned and prohibited the issue of treasury bills and restricted colonial note issue. According to Larry Schweikart these restrictions 'provided one of several economic irritations that contributed to the American Revolution'. The impact of independence in North America furthered the development of banking. As early as 1782 the Continental Congress permitted the establishment of the first chartered bank in North America. Established in Philadelphia to support the credit of the young nation it issued paper money convertible in gold and silver, and despite the unfavourable circumstances it proved to be a success. Its example was soon followed by other banks, and by 1800 there were more than thirty commercial banks, among them the First Bank of the United States, chartered by the Congress of the United States in 1791. As in Britain the foundations had been laid for backing the early stages of industrialization in the US; in Schweikart's words, 'financial intermediaries played a key role in supplying credit to antebellum American industrial and commercial development'.

The role of banks in the process of industrialization

The growth of banking in England in the second half of the eighteenth century cannot be interpreted simply as a reaction to the needs of the first industrializing nation. In the nineteenth century London was still the world centre of commercial capitalism and its banking mechanism was only marginally attuned to industrialization. Banking in the English provinces and in Scotland developed as a reaction to the inadequate provision of means of payment by the Bank of England and of short-term credit by the London money market.

Historians agree that in the early period when industrialists relied mainly on their own resources the English banking system was permissive in the sense of neither actively promoting nor restricting new investment but accommodating all credit-worthy borrowers. With the quickening pace of economic and technological change and the increasing capital intensity of industry, however, the parochial character of banks in the provinces came into conflict with the rising demand for credit. Practically until the turn of the century, the banks supplied their local economy by refinancing through the London money market. Growing dependence on their London correspondents and the long-term effect of the crisis of 1878 led to the transformation of the independent provincial banks into branches of the London-based deposit banks.

In Belgium the Société Générale's investment in industry resulted from illiquidity of its short-term debtors during the 1830s crisis. To avoid a crash, the Société Générale required its customers to transform their firms into joint-stock companies and convert their bills into shares which were kept in its portfolio. Concurrently the new Belgian state's decision to build a railway system stimulated investment banking. Banks financed industry by short-term loans which mostly became revolving credits and were generally converted into stock. The crisis of 1848 revealed the weaknesses of the system: when the banks were unable to get capital from the market they were overwhelmed by non-liquid assets; in the crisis of 1848, they lost their issuing privilege and part of their discount business. During the following twenty years the Société Générale operated as a *banque d'affaires*. From the 1870s it started commercial banking and at the end of the century mixed banking was the dominant feature of the Belgian financial market.

The centralized French state developed a centralized banking system with Paris at its centre only slowly, as described by Eric Bussière. Apart from the fact that the Banque de France had already been created in 1800, the breakthrough for a modern banking system only came with the building of the railway network in the mid-nineteenth century and was facilitated by the Saint-Simonian belief of the banking pioneers. Around 1860 a new generation of banks was created, among them the famous Crédit Mobilier. Although this bank was a model for a whole generation of banking, it finally failed, because it proved unable to cope with the illiquid nature of long-term engagements in industry and transport. Investment banking was abandoned and from the 1880s the banking system *à la française* was established with two types of banks: the deposit banks specialized in collecting public savings and lending short-term to industry and commerce; and the *banques d'affaire* which applied the resources of the *haute banque* to capital market operations, such as foreign government loans and public utilities.

The third quarter of the nineteenth century was the decisive period when the structure of the German banking system was shaped. Unlike France, however, investment banking in Germany did not fail, but was successfully extended by the first joint-stock banks, which had been modelled on the Crédit Mobilier. During these decades the banks gradually moved from funding railways to financing industry. This was facilitated by their current account and overdraft business best attuned to the financial needs of industry and commerce. In this context Dieter Ziegler points out that the relative success of the German universal banking system before 1914 depended on the holding of a relatively large guarantee capital and, also, on the central bank's *de facto* liquidity guarantee for fundamentally sound banking houses whose assets were temporarily unavailable. When in the 1920s the banks operated on a much smaller capital basis and when in 1931 the Reichsbank was not prepared to step in as a lender of last resort, the whole system collapsed and was rebuilt only by massive state intervention. A similar pattern can be observed in the revival of Italian banking. As Luigi De Rosa argues, banking reappeared in Italy during the catching-up process of industrialization in the nineteenth century. It was largely modelled on an adaptation of the Crédit Mobilier system, strongly influenced by German and, to a lesser extent, by Swiss banks. Italian banking in the first half of the twentieth century followed the path from universal banking to total state control of the financial system under Mussolini's Fascist dictatorship.

In Switzerland the banking system was also influenced by the Crédit Mobilier model. By the mid-nineteenth century it was dominated by small local and cantonal banks, on the one hand, and by influential, internationally oriented private banking dynasties in Geneva and Basle, on the other. When this banking structure proved inadequate to cope with the new demands of large investment projects, such as railways, joint-stock banks were founded. This is discussed by Youssef Cassis who mentions the non-economic reason for the establishment of the Crédit Suisse partly as a nationalist reaction to prevent foreign control of the country's railway network; the spectacular success of this bank finally induced the Basle bankers to overcome their institutional ponderousness. When the Basler Handelsbank and the Basler Bankverein were founded Zurich had already overtaken Basle as the predominant financial centre of Switzerland. As in all universal banking systems current account credit became prominent as a means of financing domestic industry and the Swiss banks were, at the same time, prepared to undertake capital market transactions. The great banks were engaged in Swiss-based finance companies which made direct investments in both domestic and foreign capital intensive ventures of the so-called Second Industrial Revolution, particularly the electrical industry and electricity supply.

According to Alice Teichova it was in the Habsburg Monarchy where the symbiosis of banking and industry was to be found in its purest form. Most typically this was expressed by the foundation in 1855 of the K.k. privilegierte Österreichische Credit-Anstalt für Handel und Gewerbe as a joint-stock bank on the pattern of the Paris Pereire brothers' Crédit Mobilier but adapted to Austrian conditions. Before the Great War eight leading Vienna banks had secured strategic positions in most branches of industry and their influence reached to all the empire's territories. After the break-up of the Habsburg Monarchy they found themselves suddenly standing at the head of multinational diversified concerns. Their efforts in defending their leadership in central Europe were eventually unsuccessful. The tradition of universal banking continued unbroken in the successor states. However, except for Czechoslovakia, insufficient domestic resources, liquidity problems and debt crises characterized the interwar period. Without a 'lender of the last resort' universal banks were unable to cope with the world economic crisis of the 1930s. It marked an end to the form of mixed banking that had functioned in central Europe since the 1880s.

An example of the long-term success of the Crédit Mobilier model in banking is Sweden. Unlike the other continental European investment banks, which were not authorized to issue bank notes, commercial banking in Sweden was started by note issuing banks. After the turn of the century when the major institutional obstacle, the prohibition of share ownership, was removed the full adoption of universal banking was completed. Lindgren concluded that, although the Swedish banks had been *de jure* deposit banks, by the turn of the century they had become *de facto* universal banks which took on the 'missionary role' which Alexander Gerschenkron had attributed to latecomer economies of the first generation. The comparison between the patterns of industrialization of the four Scandinavian countries – Finland, Sweden, Denmark and Norway – can be seen as an acid test for the role and importance of banking for industrialization in general. Diverse legal and institutional environments had created differently structured financial systems. Lindgren argues that each Scandinavian country developed the financial system most suitable to its economy.

By the turn of the century the leading European banks, above all of Britain, France and Germany, were a powerful force in developing capitalism in relatively economically backward countries. Elena Frangakis-Syrett emphasizes the involvement of the leading European banks in the Ottoman Empire's finances, in the construction of its railways and in investment in public utilities. Foreign influence was decisive in the Imperial Ottoman Bank and a cluster of foreign, especially French and German, banks dominated the Empire's banking sector at the same time as the domestic disorganized financial sector consisted mainly of merchants lending to small-scale enterprise and to rural borrowers.

The prevalent assumption of the unequal relationship between indigenous and foreign banks is tested and disputed by Shizuya Nishimura in the case of China. He substantiates that there existed a true division of labour between the operations of international and native banks: the former specialized in foreign exchange business and services to European and Japanese residents in China and they were also the bankers of the Chinese government until 1905 when the Bank of China was founded; the latter, the *chien chuangs*, were closely connected with their Chinese clients. These native banks were protected by barriers of language and traditional techniques from foreign penetration. This raises the question how far China's traditional economy was penetrated by Western and Japanese imperialist business.

Mature banking systems

A market-oriented financial system is characterized by a high degree of division of functions through specialized financial institutions – including banks, financial markets and market intermediaries. In a bank-oriented financial system savings are largely directly transferred from those who generate them to those wishing to use them by the intermediation of banks. Thus Britain, with her functional specialization, is seen as representing a market-oriented financial system and Germany, with her tradition of universal banking, as a bank-oriented financial system. The merits as well as the 'purity' of the respective systems which matured in the late nineteenth century are controversial.

Critically assessing the British-market-oriented system it was debated whether it had been partly responsible for the poor performance of British industry in the twentieth century, because of an alleged drain of funds overseas. However, in 1929/30 the official (Macmillan) Committee on Finance and Industry reported that most financial needs of the British economy were met satisfactorily, but difficulties were experienced by smaller and medium-sized businesses in raising capital. This became known as the 'Macmillan Gap'. Contemporary bankers and, increasingly, economic historians argued that it was not the primary task of a bank to become involved in the decision making process of non-bank customers; the maintenance of its liquidity had to be the primary objective of any bank in order to safeguard the interests of depositors. From this point of view the relative decline of British industry seemed not to have been caused by the failure of the market-oriented financial system but due to lack of demand.

The term universal bank does not necessarily mean that a bank-oriented financial system totally lacked any degree of division of functions. In the case of Germany, Dieter Ziegler stresses that the universal bank should not be equated with the great bank (Großbank) and that the banking system should not be narrowed to credit banks only. In Germany, unlike in Britain, the division of labour among various money institutions existed but was not functionally confined to specific groups of customers.

Andrei Yudanov accepts the Gerschenkronian assumption that the ploughing back of profits assisted by bank financing had been unable to industrialize Russia but he dismisses Gerschenkron's state-induced 'Russian pattern'. He finds, however, elements of Gerschenkron's Russian, English and German tripartite model. The 'English pattern' prevailed in the textile industry where neither bank investments nor state financing were of any importance. The 'German pattern' can be detected in the great banks of St Petersburg which provided big industry with current account credits and converted an amassed credit account into stock which was, in case of need, kept in the banks' portfolio. The fragile economic structure of the country often induced the banks directly to intervene both by limiting the managerial autonomy of the individual enterprise and by market regulation through the formation of cartels. As in Austria the Russian bank involvement was largely confined to the biggest and soundest industrial concerns. Foreign investors not only held a large portion of the joint-stock capital issued on behalf of the big industrial and transport concerns, but also of the great banks' capital. The banks can be seen as middlemen between first-class borrowers and the foreign, notably French, capital market. In the post-socialist era the problems are not dissimilar. However, the recipients of bank finance in Russia are no longer the big industrial concerns but commercial firms either engaged in the export of raw materials or the import and domestic marketing of consumer goods. The banks concentrate on these commercial firms because the economy in transition makes any investment with a longer-term gestation period an extremely risky business. As profits from commercial transactions are short term and reaped directly, the banks channel their funds there and enterprises of all other types are virtually deprived of any credit resources.

In contrast, the multifarious structure of the Japanese banking system can be seen as one major reason for the most successful example of a follower economy in the twentieth century. Kanji Ishii rejects the revisionist view, which played down the role of banking (including the Bank of Japan) in the period of high economic growth between the Wars. He accepts the orthodox view of the decisive role of bank finance for the whole period from the late nineteenth century to the 1970s but stresses the importance of the public financial institutions from the early twentieth century onwards. These extra-market financial institutions were responsible for the bulk of all long-term investments in Japanese industry in the 1950s. A further strong point in the Japanese financial system was the Bank of Japan. Although the central bank did not normally fund industrial concerns directly, from the late nineteenth century until 1973 it supported financial institutions which granted loans to industrial enterprises, such as city banks, regional banks, trust banks and others. Against the revisionists' claim that the most important objective of central bank monetary policy had been the stability of the currency, Ishii insists that apart from the depression of the 1920s the Bank of Japan had always supplied the strategic industries with growth money. It was only after the inflationary period of 1973–4 that price stability became the primary objective of monetary policy.

It has been maintained that market-oriented systems were less vulnerable to catastrophes because functional specialization limited losses to a particular market segment, while the bank-oriented system was unable to insulate failing market segments. The remarkable stability of the British financial system since the mid-nineteenth century in contrast to the banking crisis of the early 1930s, which affected almost all universal banking systems in central and northern Europe, has frequently been explained by the nature of the system. However, a comparison between the US and the Canadian financial systems, as well as between Italy and Spain, clearly shows that market-oriented systems are not necessarily stable whereas bank-oriented systems have been able to withstand even the crisis of the early 1930s.

The Canadian and Spanish financial systems were only marginally affected by the Great Depression of the early 1930s, and neither can be classified as market-oriented. A major reason for the remarkable stability of the Canadian banking system after the First World War was the concentration process and the development of branch banking. Already after Confederation the concentration process had begun, but normally not by the liquidation of existing banks, rather by their conversion into bank branches. Federal deregulation in 1900 further facilitated the rationalization of banking in Canada, so that by the 1920s an almost nationwide network of bank branches had been established controlled by three distinct financial groups, each centred around one of the big three chartered Montréal banks. Canadian economists and economic historians are sceptical about the arguments advanced by those American colleagues who propose the adoption of a variant of the Canadian system by the US. Greater stability had its price: Canada had long possessed one of the most concentrated corporate structures, but no integrated national economy because of, as Robert Sweeny emphasizes, 'dialectical struggles stemming from the specific social and national relations within the country', which until today have not been pacified. The greater stability of the Canadian system comes at the expense of oligopoly and undue concentration of economic power.

Conclusion

The contributions summarized in this Introduction are revised versions of papers submitted to Session II-16 at the 18th International Congress of Historical Sciences at Montreal (27 August–3 September 1995). They contain an appraisal of what has been accomplished by recent research and writing and show both the common features and the significant differences in the evolution of banking as an integral part of the expansion of capitalism. This was a process which lasted for centuries until two types of a modern banking system had been developed in the industrially advanced economies by the late nineteenth century: the (Anglo-Saxon) market-oriented financial system characterized by a division of functions, and the (central European) bank-oriented financial system characterized by universal banking. The perceived failures and successes of both systems will have to be more extensively empirically examined against the background of political, economic and social change. If such endeavours are encouraged by this volume it will have fulfilled the hopes of the editors and contributors.

PART ONE

Origins of banking: from local to distant markets

2 The impact of Italian banking in the late Middle Ages and the Renaissance, 1300–1500

David Abulafia

Over twenty years ago, when I was undergoing my initiation in research in Italian economic history, I went to cash a cheque drawn on the London bank of Messrs Coutts and Company, founded as recently as 1692, in the marble halls of a great Italian bank situated on the Piazza dei Banchi at Genoa. My own transaction, involving the acceptance of a paper document drawn on an account over a thousand miles away, was itself the lineal descendant of the business transactions carried out in that Piazza and in the other banking centres of medieval Italy seven centuries earlier. But an even stronger reminder of the medieval heritage was provided by the woman in the queue ahead of me, who was apparently cashing her savings of gold coins for modern Italian lire; each one of her coins was carefully assayed by the bank clerk before being accepted. Such images are, of course, deceptive if they are thought to imply that the great banks of medieval Italy inhabited marble halls or possessed staffs of the gigantic size found in modern banks. The Genoese bankers of the thirteenth century operated from small booths containing *banci* or *tabule*, exchange tables, on which transactions were conducted.[1] The magnificent surviving palaces of the Peruzzi or Medici in Florence may say something about the wealth of the great banking families of late medieval Tuscany, but little space within these palaces was given over to banking operations. Besides, the oldest bank in present-day Italy, the Monte dei Paschi di Siena founded in 1472, descends from the pawnbroking office of late fifteenth-century

Siena, and it is to similar origins that other very old banks in Italy, such as the Banco di Napoli, must primarily be traced.

Indeed, any approach to the problem of banking and capitalism in late medieval Italy must contend with several fundamental problems. In the first place, there is the question of definition of terms. The application to late medieval Italy of language that has long been adapted to the needs of a modern industrial economy is unavoidable; but it affects even the use of so basic a term as 'banking', a term which in fact originated in this very period and place. Of the Medici firm a distinguished economic historian has flatly insisted: 'it was not a bank in the modern sense of the term', concerned in the first place with deposits and extended loans;[2] it will be seen in this discussion that I have preferred where possible to employ such terms as 'company' or 'firm' to describe the Florentine banks. The use of the epithet *bancherius* to describe businessmen who specialized in the exchange or handling of money (including deposits) can be found in Genoa as early as the twelfth century, though these individuals, like any Genoese with cash in hand, also invested in trading expeditions and bought or sold cloth. There were certainly several types of money specialist, ranging from the moneylender or pawnbroker who concentrated his attention on small loans, often aimed at peasants or artisans in need of short-term credit, to the collectors of papal taxes, *mercatores camere*, who were able soon after 1200 to transmit funds from England, Ireland, even Scandinavia, as far as Rome.[3] Pawnbrokers, for their part, were intrinsically involved in the running of shops selling a great variety of goods, mostly but not exclusively unredeemed second-hand objects such as metalwork or textiles. Ecclesiastical disapproval of usury meant that it was unusual for a moneylender to live exclusively off the charging of interest, which would need to be masked as part of wider transaction costs.[4] Indeed, exchange transactions were generally regarded as non-usurious on the grounds that exchange rates fluctuated, and the element of uncertainty meant that the banker was not 'buying time' by charging interest at an agreed rate, but was providing a risky service to his clients, for which he could legitimately claim a reward. It was also a widespread, and just about licit, custom in Genoa and elsewhere to agree upon a fictitious settlement date for a loan, subject to the charging of a penalty for breach of contract.[5] The existence of such mechanisms does not prove that the Church had no influence on the development of banking; rather the opposite was the case: bankers were constrained by the law of the Church, and some of their most prestigious operations, such as the handling of the papal account, were the source of little direct profit, but rather of prestige. The pope was a 'loss leader' for those bankers who serviced his account. At the top end of the scale too there is little evidence that individuals or companies concentrated on the handling of money, to the exclusion of other commercial transactions such as the sale of cloth or foodstuffs. The pure banker, in the sense of an individual or group of individuals who lived almost entirely off the profits of exchange transactions, certainly existed in such cities as thirteenth-century Siena, Piacenza or Asti; but it must be stressed that the major banks of the Italian late Middle Ages were much more than banks: commodity transactions, often on a massive scale, as well as investment in wool workshops, not to mention the operation of tax farms, were all part of the range of profit-making activities that made the Bardi and Peruzzi famous in the early fourteenth century and the Medici in the fifteenth.[6]

It is generally agreed that the profits to be made in banking were derived in the first instance from exchange transactions, although claims have been made for the primary role of moneylending rather than moneychanging. Certainly, the importance of exchange facilities grew as the trade routes through France to Flanders became more active; the Champagne fairs became the major centre for exchange dealings in the thirteenth century, and it is increasingly clear that the function of Champagne as a clearing house was facilitated by the growing sophistication of Italian techniques for the transfer of money. Early forms of bill of exchange can be identified by 1200, and particular credit in the development of the banking activities of the fairs must go to the bankers of Asti, Piacenza and other north-west Italian centres, who acted as intermediaries between Genoese or other Italian merchants and the cloth producers of Flanders and northern France. The exchange transactions could and did mask the charging of interest rates, a factor which makes the compilation of tables of exchange rates between medieval currencies an extremely challenging task.[7] There is no need here to examine the full range of options which enabled a Florentine bank to make a loan in Florence in florins and to recover (by means of a notional triangular network of exchanges) capital and interest again in florins, without incurring the wrath of the Church. For the primary objective of the larger banking enterprises was neither deposit taking nor the provision of local credit, but the accumulation of profits through charges on exchanges and transfers. How lucrative this could be is apparent from, say, the profits of the Milan branch of the Medici in 1459 on exchanges conducted with the Geneva fairs: £3,043 13s 4d, or 10% of the gross profits of the branch; but it is also important to note that sales of silks, brocades, English wool, jewellery and belts produced 42% of profits.[8] In other words, the more purely mercantile side of Medici company business was often especially lucrative. It will be seen that the operation of banking business alongside the sale of luxury goods or foodstuffs is a fundamental feature of the great Florentine banks of the late Middle Ages.

Here it is proposed to concentrate on those big Florentine banks, the Bardi, Peruzzi, Medici and so on, between about 1300 and about 1500, that is, between the emergence into clear light of the Peruzzi and the fall of the Medici bank in 1494. This is partly for lack of intensive study of banking in other Italian centres, though good recent work by Edward English has illuminated the banking history of thirteenth-century Siena, and a major study of banking in Venice is expected shortly from Reinhold Mueller.[9] Lucca too has been a focus of attention in the thirteenth and fourteenth centuries, especially at the hands of Thomas Blomquist, while its banking links to England have been studied from the evidence in London by Richard Kaeuper.[10] Indeed, the links between the Italian bankers and the English crown have long been a well-researched theme. Other kingdoms have fared less well: the Italian presence in Spain is best known from sixteenth-century evidence, and much more attention needs to be paid to Genoese and Florentine links with Castile, even after the magisterial opening studies of Federigo Melis.[11] Florentine bankers in southern Italy first became a focus of interest in the work of Georges Yver, way back in 1903, on the basis of a vast body of Neapolitan documentation, now sadly laid waste; but it will be seen that the role of the Florentines in southern Italy is now being re-emphasized in the latest research.[12] Moving later, the activities in fifteenth-century Naples of the Strozzi bankers of Florence are well documented, thanks to the researches of Alfonso Leone;[13] but there are still vast gaps, for instance the lack of a full-scale study of those great rivals to the Medici, the Pazzi. It should be mentioned, however, that pawnbroking in Italy, especially the Jewish loan banks of the late fourteenth and fifteenth centuries, has been closely and effectively analysed in a number of studies; these include a celebrated survey by Léon Poliakov which reveals how intense was the discussion in ecclesiastical circles about the legitimacy of permitting the Jewish *banchieri* to function, and how persistent were Franciscan attempts to establish loan banks which were free of the taint of 'usury'.[14] It is not, though, intended here to dwell long on this predominantly 'down market' type of banking, but rather – for reasons that will rapidly become obvious – on activities related to the exchange of money on an international scale.

Despite these examples of much-valued research, there is a strong impression that the history of early Italian banking has gone into recession. Long favoured in the entourage of *Annales*, the study of the history of trade and banking has given way to the study of the mental world of the merchant. Economic historians of Italy have been anxious, in recent years, to provide a broader analysis of the factors allowing for growth or promoting recession in the much-debated post-Black Death era; it is here that the work of Richard Goldthwaite and John Day has achieved especial significance, and Goldthwaite has also written a characteristically clear and thoughtful essay on the Medici and fifteenth-century capitalism, offering new perspectives on attitudes to competitiveness in the fifteenth century.[15] All the same, it is a surprise to be reminded that many of Armando Sapori's classic studies of early Italian banking date back over fifty years, though they are still much cited; it is actually sixty years since he published his ground-breaking edition of the banking records of the Peruzzi.[16] The pioneering studies of Raymond de Roover, a businessman turned business historian, have established a firm outline of the development of the Medici bank; his full statement of the bank's history was published in 1963,[17] while a preliminary study appeared as far back as 1948.[18] In 1954 he could write: 'In recent years, more progress has been made in the history of banking, perhaps, than in any other field of economic history. Moreover, most of the publications which are responsible for this advance in our knowledge have been devoted to banking in the Middle Ages.'[19] The reality was, in fact, that much of the most striking progress had been made by de Roover himself, and since his death in 1972, and the publication by Julius Kirshner of a collection of de Roover's key articles in 1974, the study of medieval banking has shifted its emphasis, so that the analysis of theories of usury has remained a significant area of research (notably at the hands of Kirshner), while business histories of medieval companies have been rather rare. A major exception, however, is the publication in the autumn of 1994 of Edwin Hunt's study of the Florentine Peruzzi; like de Roover, Hunt approaches his subject from the vantage point of years spent in business, and his work raises important issues concerning the role of banking activities, as such, in the overall business profile of what we are accustomed to call the Florentine banks.[20]

Hunt insists that it is more appropriate to term the Bardi, Peruzzi and Acciaiuoli of fourteenth-century Florence 'super-companies' than banks, in view of the geographical range of their activities, stretching as far afield as England, Spain or the Aegean, and in view of the enormous range of economic activities that they encompassed. If commodity trading was indeed the major preoccupation of the Peruzzi, then the image of the company as simply the Peruzzi Bank is inadequate. Hunt points out that a study limited to Florentine dealings with the English kings or the popes will conclude that the Peruzzi or Bardi were in the first instance bankers or wool merchants; a study that looks closely at their Mediterranean connections will suggest that they were very large general merchants; a study that homes in on Florence will see them as manufacturers as well as traders. Hunt says: 'to focus only upon specific aspects of the businesses produces results like those of the fabled three blind men trying to understand the nature of an elephant'. Nor should it be forgotten that several Florentine banks took care to invest in real estate, whether as a buffer against hard times or, more likely, as a sign that the company was operated by respectable individuals with roots (ancestral or invented) in the countryside. Thus the range of activities was as wide as circumstances allowed, from the purchase of a narwhal's horn to the management of customs taxes in the ports of the Kingdom of Naples. It would be a cardinal error to single out what by modern standards are regarded as banking operations from the full range of business concerns conducted 'in the name of God and profit' by the Florentine bankers. Emphasis will therefore be placed here on the relationship between investment in long-distance trade or in manufacturing and the money side of these companies' business.

It is essential to understand what these companies were not. They were not permanent establishments with plant. Marble halls, it has been seen, were definitely not part of their equipment, which, at its most basic, consisted of their account books, especially the secret account books which survive for the Peruzzi and, later on, the Medici. Although heavily involved in the grain trade out of southern Italy, the Peruzzi possessed neither ships nor wagons nor mules for the transport of these goods, for all these would need to be hired. Even the prime warehouse which they used in Florence was leased for three or four years at a time; though part owned by a member of the Peruzzi family, he was not a partner or employee of the firm. The Peruzzi and their rivals were not permanent in another respect: the companies consisted of short-term partnerships which were periodically renewed (allowing thereby for redistribution of capital shares), though the actual process of dissolution and renewal did not interfere with continuing business.

Cash flow and the management of trade were, of course, indissolubly linked, and it was precisely the careful accounting and substantial assets that these companies possessed that made it possible to operate on a Europe-wide scale, arranging for the long-distance transport of prodigious amounts of wool, cloth and grain; cloth imported for finishing in Florence tied up capital, and even when the cloth was prepared it still had to be re-exported towards consumers in Naples or North Africa. Cash was therefore, as Hunt demonstrates, often immobilized for long periods, and the difficulties faced by the Florentine banks from the 1330s to the great crisis of 1343 are more easily comprehensible in this light.[21] Equally, the growth of the Peruzzi company has to be attributed to a cumulative process whereby the trading profits of the 1280s and 1290s inspired confidence among possible investors. The reorganized company of 1300 raised capital of £124,000, of which £54,000, nearly 44%, had been injected by outsiders; and interest bearing deposits at 7 or 8% attracted still more capital.[22]

Yet it was arguably the political ties of the Florentine banks, or at least of the Florentine city government (just now in constant flux), that did most to establish the Bardi, Peruzzi and Acciaiuoli as the most powerful and wealthiest banks of the Middle Ages, easily surpassing even the fifteenth-century Medici. The divisions within Italy between Guelf and Ghibelline factions, the former broadly pro-papal, and divisions among the Guelfs between so-called White and Black factions, generally served the interests of those Black Guelf banks that identified most strongly with the papal cause, and which were able to sustain the pope's hard-pressed finances at a time of bitter conflict between the Angevin rulers of Naples and the Aragonese kings of Sicily.[23] It was difficult to steer a safe course between the competing monarchs of Naples and Sicily, or between France and England; what is impressive is that the leading Florentine banks were able to maintain important trading ties with rulers constantly at odds with one another, all of whom were desperate for the credit and other financial services that the Bardi and Peruzzi could offer. The Florentines, for their part, were determined to gain privileged access to the grain supplies of southern Italy and Sicily, or to the wool of England; loans to the rulers of these lands lubricated the trade routes, and were justified through the commercial opportunities they created, certainly not through the payment of interest (which was at best negligible).[24] Such loans also provided direct access to the most demanding consumers, who were themselves arbiters of taste for their wealthier subjects; it is likely that sales of fine cloth and other luxury items at the courts of debtor princes were made highly profitable by the insistence on charging inflated prices for luxury goods, as the unstated cost of granting hefty loans. Yet it is not difficult to see that this was also a precarious state of affairs, as events around 1340 began to reveal: close ties to Edward III of England drew the bankers into a financial morass and contributed significantly to the shattering bankruptcies of 1343.[25]

In July 1335 the Peruzzi possessed five agents in England, four in France, four at Avignon, four in Flanders and six in Sicily, but in the Kingdom of Naples they had eleven: six based in Naples and five at the grain exporting station of Barletta.[26] South Italian grain was indeed a major preoccupation of the Peruzzi, as it was for all Florence: the city is said to have been able to feed itself from local supplies for only five months out of twelve in a normal year, during the early fourteenth century, which was a period when there were many famine years too; and the Florentines were active in supplying wheat from Sicilian or Apulian stocks to other areas as well, as far afield at Cilician Armenia.[27] The Acciaiuoli were not far behind the Peruzzi in their close attention to southern Italy, with nine agents at Naples and Barletta in 1341 and three in Sicily; their coverage of northern Europe, though far from negligible, was slighter than that of the Peruzzi; and it is noticeable that the three great banks were not averse to co-operative ventures from the very start, whether in financing cotton shipments from Cyprus to Ancona and Venice, or grain shipments from Sicily to Tunis: they were not exclusively concerned with trade towards Florence, and had good links to leading Catalan shipowners, to Genoese or Venetian cloth-dealers, or to whichever merchant offered the specialities that they needed to conclude an elaborate business deal.[28] They did not assume that they alone had the capacity to see a transaction through from start to finish. In other words, they possessed a range of specific functions in trade and finance, and did not seek to rationalize the conduct of international trade by bringing ancillary commercial activities (such as ship-chandling) under their control; some of these skills were in any case famously tied to other commercial centres such as Barcelona, Venice and Genoa.

Nowhere is this sense of definite, limited objectives truer than in the case of investment in the woollen industry. The Peruzzi and Bardi were active in the export of English wool, whether to Flanders, to feed that region's looms, or, increasingly, towards Italy, where good imitations of Flemish cloth were being produced, especially the Florentine *panni alla francesca*, by the 1330s.[29] Spain and North Africa also featured prominently as sources of wool. But the Peruzzi did not control the process of woollen cloth production once the raw materials had arrived in Florence; an exceptionally elaborate putting-out system was operated by the *lanaiuoli*, relying on artisans who worked at home on the multiple process of cleansing, carding or spinning, dyeing, weaving and finishing. Woollen cloth sold back by *lanaiuoli* could then be distributed along the trade networks dominated by the companies, notably in the Kingdoms of Naples and Sicily.[30] Occasional direct control of wool workshops by the Peruzzi and other banks should not confuse the picture: their investment in the running of a woollen cloth firm was a business opportunity like any other, and if profits failed to meet expectations there was no reason to pursue the project permanently. Of course, there were smaller banks which placed a heavier emphasis on the woollen cloth industry of Florence; the Alberti bank, closely studied by Sapori and de Roover, seems to have grown out of a cloth importing firm, and retained a *bottega della lana* in 1321–3, in which they had invested over £12,000, yet the shop appears to have been liquidated by 1325 before re-emerging a couple of years after that.[31] Thus even those who placed large investments in cloth were not necessarily committed to the unremitting pursuit of that objective, despite its fundamental importance in the Florentine economy. Practical interests, notably profitability, naturally took first place. It would perhaps be true to state that the companies were so well attuned to an economy which throve on putting out, selling, reselling, exchanging that the complex chain of cloth production was not something they would have sought to control from top to bottom. They were simply not monopolists; the idea of in some sense 'rationalizing' the process of industrial production, in an age when factories were to all intents non-existent, had no part in their economic planning. Both in industry and in commerce they were careful to concentrate on the areas of expertise they were known to possess.

The Peruzzi, Bardi and Acciaiuoli gained special strength from the fact that they were in the first instance family operations, but even so they drew on board non-family shareholders (who were even for a time a majority in the Peruzzi company, around 1335).[32] Yet by no means all leading members of the Peruzzi clan were involved with the company. The importance of the extended family in the political and economic life of the Italian urban aristocracy can scarcely be exaggerated. But nearly as important as family ties was the principle of loyalty that bound the staff of the early Florentine companies together, as well as the efficient methods of book-keeping, whether strictly worthy of the title 'double entry' or not, that enabled the central offices to measure the success of the multifarious enterprises in which the company engaged. On this note, it should also be emphasized that the Medici were rather exceptional in maintaining family continuity over a whole century, as a result of a series of genealogical accidents which preserved a single line of inheritance from Giovanni di Bicci at the end of the fourteenth century to Lorenzo il Magnifico at the end of the fifteenth.

As far as it is possible to identify a coherent plan of operations, our evidence is mainly derived from the organizational structure of the great companies: the Bardi, perhaps in view of their size, were particularly ready to allow branch managers extensive discretion, while the smaller Buonaccorsi, number four in the ranking of early fourteenth-century Florentine banks, were rather more tightly managed from the centre.[33] Of the Peruzzi, Hunt says: 'the Florence management centralised *policy* but was prepared to decentralise *execution* within the constraints established by policy.' Decisions had to be made whether a branch would be operated by a partner or a factor, and indeed where it was worthwhile operating a branch of what size. A chairman or *capo* in Florence presided over developments, but it remains unclear how far decisions were made by the *capo* and his close associates on an *ad hoc* basis; this seems most likely, and any idea of a formal company board, meeting regularly in Florence is of course a modern fantasy. Shareholders, rather than lingering in Florence, often travelled as far afield as England to negotiate business and to monitor the performance of branches abroad. In the other direction, Francesco Forzetti, who spent something like forty years as manager in charge of the Palermo branch, was occasionally brought to Florence on business.[34] By the fifteenth century, significant variations can be seen in the overall structure of banks, with the Medici, for instance, operating their branches as notionally independent firms. Indeed Goldthwaite concludes that what was striking by that time was precisely the 'lack of structure' in the banking system: 'their common interests were little served by corporate organisation'. Trust was an essential feature of the operation of any bank, and yet it was based not so much on legally binding documents as upon family relationships and other intimate ties, which could transcend even the bitter political rivalries within the Italian cities or between one city and another. Associated with this was a lack of a genuinely competitive spirit; this was not a mental world Weber or Tawney would perhaps have found it easy to describe.

The principles according to which a banking company should operate were enunciated with supreme clarity in Leon Battista Alberti's *Della Famiglia*, begun in 1432, the work of a highly gifted *uomo universale* who was also a member of a leading banking dynasty:

> Just look at the house of Alberti: as it excels in all professions, so also in this one, pecuniary though it might be, it has flourished in western Europe and in many different parts of the world, always with honesty and integrity; hence we have acquired no little fame among all nations and a pre-eminence not incommensurate with our merits. For in all our business dealings no one was ever found who would permit even the slightest malpractice. We have always observed the greatest simplicity and the plainest truth in every contract; and thus we have come to be recognised as great merchants both in and outside of Italy, in Spain, in the West, in Syria, in Greece, and in all the ports of the world.[35]

Thus the Alberti (in this idealized picture) retained their strong pride in family, and set alongside it an insistence on honesty; together these were the recipe for success, though Leon Battista also had to admit that it was easier to counsel the employment of relatives than to secure their services. As well, the Alberti had taken care to avoid the mushroom growth which had in the end destroyed the Peruzzi and Bardi.[36] It is noticeable that the Medici were not able to draw into the management of their bank significant numbers of their own relatives; nor did the major partners and managers outside the Medici clan succeed much better in drawing in their own relatives. Indeed, it was the quarrelsome, inefficient management of the latter-day Medici bank, and the lack of central control by a *capo* preoccupied with high politics, that fatally eroded the Medici enterprise at the end of the fifteenth century.

There is no need here to reopen the debate on the fall of the Florentine companies in 1343. That they had greatly over-extended themselves is clear, and that a lesson was learned by later banking enterprises emerges from the more modest scale on which their successors, such as the Alberti and eventually the Medici, were content to operate.[37] Glossy royal or papal accounts were seen increasingly as a liability to be avoided where possible, though politics never ceased to intrude: there was no great reason for the Medici to open a glossy new branch in Milan except to foster political ties with Francesco Sforza, duke of Milan, around 1450.[38] This branch was housed in a magnificent palace presented to the Medici by the duke of Milan, adorned with sculptured medallion portraits of the duke and duchess, so that, as Goldthwaite remarks, 'it seemed more suitable for a diplomatic residence than for the working headquarters of a firm'. Indeed, it was arguably neglect of the traditional pursuit of profit which helped bring down the bank in 1494, after decades during which Lorenzo the Magnificent had concentrated his attention on political issues rather than on the family firm.[39]

It would be a mistake to exaggerate the importance of the Medici bank in either Florentine or European affairs. That it was a smaller enterprise than the Peruzzi or Bardi 'super-companies' is well known. Its capital formation in 1451, of 72,000 florins, was not in fact so exceptional: Goldthwaite cites a figure of 53,600 florins for the company of Carlo Strozzi in 1367, and Filippo Strozzi was worth about 70,000 florins when he died in 1491.[40] Indeed, what is more striking than the slight lead obtained by the Medici over other Florentine banks is the large number of banking and trading enterprises overall, so that nearly 140 Florentine firms can be identified operating in late fifteenth-century Lyons. In other words, the Medici were the largest, but not gigantic, fish in a well-stocked and capacious pool. Goldthwaite points out provocatively that 'the history of international banking and commerce in Medicean Florence could be written without so much as mentioning the Medici – and such a study would be a healthy corrective to the current historiographical situation'.[41]

Still, it is the Medici who have attracted the attention of both political and business historians, and their firm will have to be used as an example for want of anything more 'typical'. The Medici display the same diversification into manufacture as so many of the earlier Florentine banks: from 1431, they possessed a wool workshop, opening a second workshop in 1439.[42] This was a period when Florentine woollen manufactures had long passed their peak, and it is not surprising to find them investing also in silk production, acquiring a majority share in what proved a profitable undertaking. In 1441 the two wool shops accounted for one tenth of the assets of the Medici bank, and the silk workshop another tenth. As late as 1491 Lorenzo de'Medici was still prepared to invest in the Florentine wool industry, and it seems that even in the difficult years following his death, French invasion, Medicean exile and revolution under Savonarola profits from the investment accumulated. Demand for silk was particularly healthy in the fifteenth century, and the industry had moved far beyond its early west European base of Lucca; but, whereas Florence had once been master of the woollen industry in Italy, it now had to fight for its place in the silk markets alongside not only Lucca but Genoa and non-Italian centres. The Medici supported not just their own silk workshop but the silk shops of other Florentine entrepreneurs; in 1477 two chests of velvet silk were sent by the Medici to Naples, but none of the silk was actually produced in the Medici workshop.[43] (So too Filippo Strozzi's company was closely involved in the wool trade, and happily bought and sold in transactions with independent workshops, which the firm never sought to monopolize).[44] De Roover concluded that the industrial investments of the Medici 'never yielded more than a small fraction of the total profits derived from business ventures'.[45] Of course, some of the profits of overseas branches were derived from sales of cloth, but the contrast between the profits of the workshops and the profits drawn from banking activities (understood in the widest sense) is striking: between 1397 and 1420 banking and foreign trade produced 143,348 florins, whereas the woolshops produced 8,472 florins, a mere 5.5% of gross profits.[46] Between 1420 and 1435 the revenue from the woolshop accounted for just over 3% of profits; over the next fifteen years, taking the silk shop into account as well, the textile manufacturing arm was producing 10% of profits. Yet these were not negligible sums, and it would be wrong to be misled into ignoring them by over-stressing the massive profits from banking and general trade, which were themselves sizeable at this period.

What was crucial was an ability to adapt to changing economic circumstances, in the aftermath of plague and sudden population loss. Increasingly, there is a tendency to discard the gloomy view of an 'economic depression of the Renaissance' once forcefully presented by Roberto Lopez and Harry Miskimin, and to lay stress on the process of economic reconstruction that characterized the late fourteenth and fifteenth centuries.[47] New economic relationships had to be formed in an age of growing regional specialization; it was also a period in which periodic shortages of specie wreaked havoc in the money markets, especially in regions such as Catalonia where conservative economic policies were generally pursued and innovation came only late. Florence too was caught up in this drastic readjustment, as the shrinking of wool production amply reveals; traditional trading links towards Flanders were compromised by economic difficulties in the Flemish cloth towns, so that they now had little to offer the Florentines in the way of commodities. The bullion famine affected Flanders more, perhaps, than other regions of Europe.[48] Indeed, one effect was the decline of business through Bruges, which would lose its importance as a money market, having already lost its importance as an exchange centre in international trade. Bruges was thus in the long term no more a success story for the Medici than it was for other investors, and the closure of the Bruges office of the Medici bank by Lorenzo de'Medici in 1480 put to an end a history of growing losses.[49]

On the positive side, the lack of heavy dependence on Flanders and England for wool and cloth resulted in a greater diversification of trading enterprises, as Florentines searched for raw materials in areas that had earlier been relatively neglected, such as southern Italy and Spain, both of which were experiencing a massive expansion of wool production. The increasing complexity of international exchanges kept bankers busy, and often in profit, but it also obviated the need for dangerously intimate relations with foreign rulers such as the king of England, who could soak up a perilously high proportion of working capital; a broad portfolio of investments and a broad spread of branches meant that a crisis in the fortunes of one agency did not spell disaster for the entire enterprise, as had occurred in the age of the Bardi and Peruzzi. This process of dispersal meant that no single bank tended to grow disproportionately large, and none was able nor sought to dominate the market in (say) raw wool.

In any case, the Medici found that opportunities for growth were not always as they had anticipated. The successful establishment of the Lyons fairs by Louis XI of France diverted business away from Geneva, and the 1460s saw the Medici reacting carefully to changed circumstances, maintaining offices for a while in both centres, until it became obvious that Lyons was the victor.[50] An early example of failure to make headway is provided by the history of the Naples branch, never itself an important branch, but one which must have seemed, in the light of past Florentine penetration of the region, to hold out promising opportunities; in some years before the liquidation in 1426 the branch made an apparent loss, while political upheaval in the south Italian kingdom made prospects increasingly uncertain. There was a long delay before a Naples office was reopened, in 1471, and here political motives may well have played an important part, with Lorenzo de'Medici hoping to keep an eye on the unpredictable King Ferrante of Naples. If that was the intention, returns were poor indeed, for Ferrante joined the papal conflict with Medicean Florence that followed the Pazzi conspiracy in 1478, and only after a famous visit to the king of Naples did Lorenzo restore peace – and his bank branch. In the meantime Medici assets were confiscated, and the branch continued to be a source of concern even after radical reorganization under the name 'Lorenzo Tornabuoni and Company'.[51] It seems likely that lending to the royal court and the nobility risked going out of control. And here, indeed, is the core of the problem, for after 1479 Lorenzo the Magnificent was determined to maintain cordial relations with Ferrante of Naples. Any losses suffered in Naples were a part payment for the peace of Italy, which was soon to fall apart, with disastrous results not merely for the royal house of Naples but for the Medici and their bank, when the French invaded Italy in 1494–5.[52]

It remains to ask how developments in Italian banking influenced the growth of 'capitalism'. Historians of banking have been understandably reluctant to pursue the term capitalism very far; de Roover used it to indicate primarily the search for profitability. Goldthwaite has rightly stressed the lack of emphasis on competition among firms and the absence of any real preoccupation with the exercise of power, a statement that is strengthened rather than weakened by the gradually declining performance of the Medici bank in the age of Lorenzo il Magnifico. A more elaborate definition, which has been pursued here, would seek to examine the role of the banks in investment in manufacturing, or in other profit-making activities which would result in the mobilization of a significant workforce. Here it is difficult to show that the Florentine banks had a special role. What is striking about them is precisely the way that the Peruzzi and Medici saw investment in cloth workshops as one among many viable business opportunities; but if the viability of the enterprise was called into question, then they were prepared to shift their investments to other types of activity. This largely reflects the fragmented system of cloth production, which in any case was subject to guild intervention. The creation of cloth factories was unthinkable, while the contraction of markets for the fine Florentine cloths of the 1330s necessitated a shift towards investment in silk workshops, in the age of the Medici. But it was not the Medici who were responsible for the expansion of Florentine silk production. Arguably the Bardi and Peruzzi had played a significant role in the provision of English wool, when available, to Florentine looms, but that was only for a brief period, and represented the apogee of an already well-developed woollen cloth industry on which the bankers drew, as merchants seeking to satisfy the needs of foreign consumers, but which they had not really created. This is not to deny their crucial role in servicing the long-distance trade in wool, cloth and grain, and their success in gaining access to the most prestigious, if also the most penurious, purchasers in Europe. The commercial and financial network they created provided an increasingly vital back-up for the trading activities of their fellow-Italians and of native merchants throughout Europe. Thus they did not in fact mould or seek to mould the shape of the European and Mediterranean economy in the late Middle Ages, even though within specific regions, notably England and southern Italy, they helped stimulate production of foodstuffs and raw materials for export. Striking commercial expansion was, indeed, possible without the existence of comparable financial networks, as the example of the German Hansa reveals.[53] But whereas the Baltic and North Sea emerged as a well-integrated set of markets fairly closely co-ordinated by the Hansa, the Mediterranean and western Europe for any number of reasons lacked similar integration and co-ordination. One of the elements that did provide a degree of wider co-ordination was the Italian financial network which, as has been seen, existed not simply to service the specific needs of cities such as Florence, but to provide valuable expertise in the handling of money, the rapid transmission of funds and the bulk purchase of wool, grain and so on. It was the pursuit of these specific skills that was the source of success for the Florentine companies in their heyday.

Notes

1 For the Genoese banks, see Roberto S. Lopez, *La prima crisi della banca in Genova* (Milan, 1956).

2 Richard A. Goldthwaite, 'The Medici Bank and the World of Florentine Capitalism', *Past and Present*, 114 (1987), pp. 3–31.

3 E. Jordan, *De mercatoribus camerae apostolicae saeculo XIII* (Rennes, 1909); W. E. Lunt, *Papal Revenues in the Middle Ages*, 2 vols. (New York, 1934).

4 There is a growing literature on usury; see, e.g., B. Nelson, *The Idea of Usury. From Tribal Brotherhood of Universal Otherhood*, 2nd edn (Chicago, 1969); J. T. Noonan, *The Scholastic Analysis of Usury* (Cambridge, Mass., 1957); J. Le Goff, 'The Usurer and Purgatory', in *The Dawn of Modern Banking*, Center for Medieval and Renaissance Studies, University of California, Los Angeles (New Haven, 1979).

5 See, e.g., David Abulafia, *The Two Italies. Economic Relations between the Norman Kingdom of Sicily and the Northern Communes* (Cambridge, 1977), pp. 272–3.

6 See the incisive comments of Edwin Hunt in his *The Medieval Super-Companies. A Study of the Peruzzi Company of Florence* (Cambridge, 1994).

7 The problem of exchange rates has been raised in a critique by R. Mueller of P. Spufford's exchange tables: 'The Spufford Thesis on Foreign Exchange. The

Evidence of Exchange Rates', *Journal of European Economic History*, 24 (1995), pp. 121–9, as against P. Spufford, W. Wilkinson and S. Tolley, *Handbook of Medieval Exchange*, Royal Historical Society (London, 1986).

8   Raymond de Roover, *The Rise and Decline of the Medici Bank, 1397–1494* (Cambridge, Mass., 1963), p. 266.

9   Edward D. English, *Enterprise and Liability in Sienese Banking, 1230–1350* (Cambridge, Mass., 1988).

10 T. Blomquist, 'The Dawn of Banking in an Italian Commune: Thirteenth-Century Lucca', in *The Dawn of Modern Banking*; R. W. Kaeuper, *Bankers to the Crown. The Riccardi of Lucca and Edward I* (Princeton, N.J., 1973).

11 Melis was ever conscious of the importance of links between Spain and Tuscany. See *inter alia* F. Melis, *Industria e commercio nella Toscana medievale*, ed. M. Tangheroni and B. Dini (Florence, 1989); F. Melis, *I mercanti italiani nell'Europa medievale e rinascimentale*, ed. H. Kellenbenz and L. Frangoni (Florence, 1990); F. Melis, *L'economia fiorentina del Rinascimento*, ed. B. Dini (Florence, 1984); but especially the collected studies in F. Melis, *Mercaderes italianos en España* (Seville, 1976).

12 G. Yver, *Le commerce et les marchands dans l'Italie méridionale au XIIIe et au XIVe siècle* (Paris, 1903).

13 A. Leone, *Il giornale del Banco Strozzi a Napoli (1473)*, Fonti e Documenti per la Storia del Mezzogiorno d'Italia, vol. 7 (Naples, 1981).

14 L. Poliakov, *Jewish Bankers and the Holy See*, transl. M. Kochan (London, 1977).

15 Goldthwaite, 'The Medici Bank'; see also J. Day, *The Medieval Market Economy* (Oxford, 1987), a collection of Day's articles.

16 A. Sapori, *I libri di commercio dei Peruzzi* (Milan, 1934); A. Sapori, *The Italian Merchant in the Middle Ages* (New York, 1970), lacking however, the fine bibliography of the original French edition.

17 De Roover, *Rise and Decline*.

18 Raymond de Roover, *The Medici Bank. Its Organization, Management, Operations and Decline* (New York, 1948).

19 Raymond de Roover, 'New Interpretations of the History of Banking', *Journal of World History*, 2 (1954), p. 38, repr. in Raymond de Roover, *Business, Banking and Economic Thought in Late Medieval and Early Modern Europe*, ed. Julius Kirshner (Chicago, 1974), p. 200; this volume is a collection of de Roover's most important articles.

20 On this, see Hunt, *Medieval Super-Companies*.

21 *Ibid.*, pp. 156–229.

22 *Ibid.*, pp. 128, 259–60.

23 A useful account of these conflicts can be found in E. Léonard, *Les Angevins de Naples* (Paris, 1954), and, for the Catalan-Aragonese in Sicily, see C. Backman, *The Decline and Fall of Medieval Sicily* (Cambridge, 1995); also David Abulafia, 'Southern Italy and the Florentine Economy, 1265–1370', *Economic History Review*, 2nd ser., 33 (1981).

24 For wool, see E. Power, *The Wool Trade in English Medieval History*, ed. M. M. Postan (Oxford, 1941).

25 Hunt revises the classic interpretation of A. Sapori, *La crisi delle compagnie mercantili dei Bardi e dei Peruzzi* (Florence, 1926).

26 Raymond de Roover, 'The Organisation of Trade', in *Cambridge Economic History of Europe*, vol. III (Cambridge, 1963), p. 86, table II.

27 Abulafia, 'Southern Italy', p. 385.

28 For the involvement of the Florentine banks in the grain trade to Tunis, see David Abulafia, 'Catalan Merchants and the Western Mediterranean', *Viator*, 16 (1985),

pp. 233–5; David Abulafia, 'A Tyrrhenian Triangle. Tuscany, Sicily, Tunis, 1276–1300', *Studi di storia economica toscana nel Medioevo e nel Rinascimento in memoria di Federigo Melis*, Biblioteca del Bollettino storico pisano, Collana storica, vol. 33 (Pisa, 1987), pp. 53–75.

29 H. Hoshino, 'The Rise of the Florentine Woollen Industry in the Fourteenth Century', in N. B. Harte and K. G. Ponting (eds.), *Cloth and Clothing in Medieval Europe. Essays in Memory of Professor E. M. Carus-Wilson* (London, 1983), pp. 184–204.

30 Hunt, *Medieval Super-Companies*, pp. 51–7, 67, 170–2.

31 Raymond de Roover, 'The Story of the Alberti Company of Florence, 1302–1348, as Revealed in its Account Books', *Business History Review*, 32 (1958), pp. 14–59, repr. in de Roover, *Business, Banking*, pp. 39–84.

32 Hunt, *Medieval Super-Companies*, pp. 184–5.

33 For the Buonaccorsi, see M. Luzzati, *Giovanni Villani e la compagnia dei Buonaccorsi* (Rome, 1971).

34 On Forzetti, see Abulafia, 'Tyrrhenian Triangle', pp. 70–2.

35 E. Cochrane and J. Kirshner, *The Renaissance*, Readings in Western Civilization, vol. 5 (Chicago, 1986), p. 95.

36 For the early history of this firm, see de Roover, 'The Story of the Alberti Company'.

37 For banking in the era after the fall of the Bardi and Peruzzi, see in particular Y. Renouard, *Les relations des papes d'Avignon et les compagnies commerciales et bancaires de 1316 à 1378* (Paris, 1942); Y. Renouard, *Recherches sur les compagnies commerciales et bancaires utilisées par les papes d'Avignon avant le Grand Schisme* (Paris, 1942); the same author's collected *Etudes d'histoire médiévale*, 2 vols. (Paris, 1968), also offer a great deal of germane material.

38 Goldthwaite, 'The Medici Bank', pp. 29–30.

39 De Roover, *Rise and Decline*, pp. 365–9.

40 Goldthwaite, 'The Medici Bank', p. 16.

41 *Ibid.*, p. 17; cf. Goldthwaite's earlier remarks too, pp. 4–6.

42 De Roover, *Rise and Decline*, pp. 174–89.

43 *Ibid.*, pp. 186–93.

44 For the Strozzi in the fifteenth century, and particularly their operations in Naples, see Richard Goldthwaite, *Private Wealth in Renaissance Florence* (Princeton, N.J., 1968), pp. 31–73, especially pp. 53–7.

45 De Roover, *Rise and Decline*, p. 193.

46 *Ibid.*, p. 47.

47 R. S. Lopez and H. Miskimin, 'The Economic Depression of the Renaissance', *Economic History Review*, 2nd ser., 14 (1962), pp. 408–26; the most successful case-study to challenge the depression argument is that of S. R. Epstein, *An Island for Itself. Economic Development and Social Change in Late Medieval Sicily* (Cambridge, 1992).

48 J. Day, 'The Great Bullion Famine of the Fifteenth Century', *Past and Present*, 79 (1978), pp. 3–54, repr. in Day, *Market Economy*.

49 De Roover, *Rise and Decline*, pp. 346–57.

50 *Ibid.*, pp. 279–311.

51 *Ibid.*, pp. 254–61.

52 For the political setting, see David Abulafia (ed.), *The French Descent into Renaissance Italy, 1494–95* (Aldershot, 1995).

53 P. Dollinger, *The German Hansa* (London, 1970).

3 The great German banking houses and international merchants, sixteenth to nineteenth century

Michael North

Banking in the Holy Roman Empire and later in the German states took place in the form of merchant banking. Merchant bankers combined long-distance trade with foreign exchange and offered a variety of credits. The development of merchant banking followed the patterns of trade, and only in the nineteenth century merchant bankers began to concentrate themselves on private banking, giving up their merchant activities, or organizing those as separate business. In the development of German merchant banking we may distinguish four major stages:

1. south German merchant houses in the sixteenth century
2. immigration and innovation in the seventeenth century
3. Jewish *Hoffaktoren* and the finance of the absolutist states in the seventeenth and eighteenth centuries
4. private banking in the late eighteenth and nineteenth centuries.

South German merchant houses

The south German merchant houses of the early modern period were family companies. They drew partnership capital from family members, relatives and sometimes – like the Welsers – from third parties. Their enterprise had three pillars: international commodity trade, investment in mining, foreign exchange and loans for the princes. They profited from the expansion of European overseas trade, the central European silver and copper mining boom and the ever-growing financial demands of the Renaissance states. Examples of the south German merchant houses were those of Fugger, Welser, Höchstetter or Imhof. The merchant house of Fugger gave the south German epoch of the sixteenth century the name Zeitalter der Fugger.[1]

The Fuggers date back to fourteenth-century Augsburg, where they worked in the fustian business. In the following century they founded the merchant house (*Handlung*) and entered with investments into silver and copper mining. They became famous in 1488, when they received the use of the silver mine at Schwaz in exchange for a loan of 150,000 florins to Archduke Sigismund the *Münzreiche* (the inventor of the Taler) of Tirol.[2] They acquired a silver and later a copper monopoly in Tirol and Hungary (Slovakia), as neither Sigismund nor his successor Maximilian paid the growing debt back. This encouraged further lending activities of the Fuggers, led by Jacob Fugger the *Reiche* (1459–1525) in favour of Habsburg rulers. In 1519 Jacob Fugger raised 543,585 florins of the bribes necessary for the royal election of the young King Charles (the later Emperor Charles V). The Welsers and Italian banking houses supplied the rest of it, altogether 308,333 florins. By this the Fuggers hoped to gain imperial support against the anti-monopoly and anti-usury campaign directed by the German Reichstag to the south German merchant houses.[3]

The imperial military expeditions against the Turks, France and the Schmalkaldic League required new financial means. As the emperor had no regular income in Germany, he had to transfer his liquid and credit resources from the south via Antwerp to the place required. The Fuggers lent the emperor money at Antwerp or supplied him with money via an exchange market elsewhere. The money was to be redeemed on the Castilian fairs (Medina del Campo) or in Seville by assignments to Spanish fiscal income or from the expected silver fleets. Moreover, the Fuggers received by way of redemption the farm of the *Maestrazgos*, the lands belonging to the Military Orders in Spain, including the mercury mines of Almadén.[4]

With the savagery of the military conflicts in the 1540s and 1550s the growing credit demands exceeded by far the amounts redeemed and the profits from the *Maestrazgos*. In this situation Charles V pressed the Fuggers to provide another loan, the Villach *asiento* of 1552. Anton Fugger promised 100,000 ducats and guaranteed to raise another 300,000 scudi in Italy, the interest being 12%. As security, the Fuggers received assignments to income of the Spanish crown, to a certain amount of American precious metals and to state annuities (juros). Moreover, they obtained permission to export tax free 400,000 ducats in coin or gold out of Spain. However, the money was wasted by the emperor in the fruitless siege of Metz.[5] New *asientos* and extensions of loans followed. In 1557 Philip II issued the first state bankruptcy decree. All payments of assignments to fiscal income were suspended, the precious metals of the incoming fleets confiscated. Although the Fuggers entered into an arrangement with the crown three years later, south German merchant houses never recovered from this blow. They had only two choices: to withdraw from the Spanish scene, writing the Spanish claims off; or to remain in contact with the Spanish crown, trying to realize at least some of the claims. That is why the Fuggers witnessed more losses in the following Spanish state bankruptcies of 1575 and 1607. However, they avoided the fate of the Welsers, who went bankrupt in 1614, due to the suspension of payments by France and Spain. Altogether the Fuggers's losses with the Habsburg rulers are estimated to be 8 million florins, and that was a considerable part of their gains as a merchant house.[6]

There was neither specialization nor any innovation in the business of the house of Fugger. The Fuggers represented, above all, the most developed form of the late medieval family companies, differing from their predecessors only with respect to their world-wide activities and the concentration on Habsburg rulers. With regard to their exchange business, they resembled the Italian merchant bankers of the Middle Ages. They maintained a widespread network of branches and factors in the major markets and exchange places of Europe, with the primary objective of advancing funds by bills of exchange, making big profits by exploiting the fluctuations of the money markets. They handled the money remittances of papal collectors and church dignitaries on behalf of the Roman Curia, and they had a foot in the international spice and precious metals trades. They enlarged their working capital, by acquiring money from numerous depositors, ranging from the Cardinal Melchior von Meckau of Brixen to small Augsburg savers.[7]

When the Welsers finally failed and the Fuggers retired on their landed estates, they were replaced by other Augsburg merchant bankers such as the Paler, who tried to combine foreign trade with (deposit) banking and industrial development, avoiding the risks of credits to a sole powerful debtor. However, loans to princes remained important with respect to metal production and metal trade. This shows the example of Nuremberg merchants, whose investments into Thüringen's

Seigerhütten required licences by the dukes of Saxony and the counts of Mansfeld, but strengthened their leading position on the European copper market.[8]

Immigration and innovation

Structural change occurred as a result of immigration in the late sixteenth and especially in the seventeenth centuries. Italian and Dutch merchant bankers, immigrating into the Holy Roman Empire, carried not only their trade and exchange nets to Nuremberg, Frankfurt, Cologne or Hamburg but made also the local merchant communities acquainted with the financial innovations of southern and western Europe. Moreover, the immigrants acquired fairly soon a leading position with respect to trade and banking in those places. In a recent study Lambert Peters has analysed the twenty most important Nuremberg merchant houses according to their transactions at the public exchange bank, the Banco Publico, 1621–4. Among those twenty houses were five Italian, four Dutch, while among the Nuremberg firms only two 'old' patrician merchant houses survived, like the Imhof and the Tucher, the latter on number fifteen, whilst the Italian Lumagos ranked on top of the list.[9] In Hamburg the situation was even more striking. Among the twenty houses with the highest transaction accounts in 1619 were sixteen Dutchmen (three Dutch firms ranking on top), one firm of southern Germany (the Jenischs) and only three merchants of Hamburg. Of the forty most important houses, thirty-two were of Dutch origin.[10]

Other places, which owed their growth as banking places to Dutch and Italian immigration, were Cologne and Frankfurt. Cologne inherited for some years a considerable part of Antwerp's trade and exchange. But when several Antwerpeners returned and others moved to Frankfurt, Frankfurt became for nearly a century the leading banking place of central Europe. Crucial for this was the integration of the Frankfurt fairs into the international clearing system of the Lyon fairs and the Genoese fairs at Besançon and Piacenca, where the Tuscan and later the Genoese merchant bankers had established a setting-off system for international credits and debits.[11] By the mid-sixteenth century this system was extended to Frankfurt, and from 1585 onwards Frankfurt merchants created a setting-off system *sui generis*, which became little by little independent from the *Frankfurter Fastenmesse* and the *Herbstmesse*, when it was centralized at the Frankfurt exchange in the periods between the fairs at weekly pay-days. However, according to the account books of Johann von Bodeck, credits on *deposito* from one fair to the next fair for merchants and princes played an important role during the first third of the seventeenth century.[12]

More innovative than the introduction of the setting-off system via financial fairs was the foundation of exchange banks in Hamburg and Nuremberg. In Hamburg, where Dutch immigrants had contributed to the diffusion of the bill of exchange in the north (*Wechselordnung* of 1601), the public exchange bank was founded – on their initiative – in 1619 after the model of the Amsterdamsche Wisselbank. The bank created two moneys of account, a stable bank money (Mark Banco) and a current money (Mark Courant). Merchants held accounts at the bank and transferred money by assignment from one account to another. The obligation to settle all bills over the value of 400 Mark lübisch through the Hamburger Bank led many merchants to open an account there. That is why the Hamburger Bank became a successful clearing institution for northern and eastern Germany up to 1875, when the Reichsbank overtook its clearing business.[13] Less successful in the long run was the Nuremberg Banco Publico, founded in 1621. Due to the heavy financial requirements, exacted by the warfaring powers during the Thirty Years War, the Nuremberg *Rat* had to resort to the precious metals reserve of the bank, thus risking monetary stability.[14]

In the course of the seventeenth century changes took place within the communities of merchant bankers, old merchant houses being replaced by new firms, and above all Dutch and Italian immigrants. Besides, there were shifts within the structure of the trading and financial centres, reflected in the flows of trade and of bills of exchange. In the beginning of the seventeenth century commodity trade and payments shifted from a south-west route, Venice–Nuremberg–Frankfurt–Antwerp, to a south–north-west route, Venice–Nuremberg–Amsterdam and Venice–Nuremberg–Hamburg–Amsterdam, and to an east–north-west route, Leipzig–Hamburg–Amsterdam, by the end of the seventeenth century, thus integrating Leipzig as the major fair and financial centre for central and eastern Europe in the following century.[15]

Jewish **Hoffaktoren** *and the finance of the absolutist states*

The growing power of the German territorial states after the Thirty Years War, and at the same time their notorious inability to substantiate this power financially, led the states to multiple efforts to raise money, giving way to the rise of a new type of banker, the Jewish *Hoffaktor* or *Hofjude*. Whilst the majority of merchant bankers in the Reichsstädte (like Nuremberg) had suffered financial losses during the war and were, due to bad experiences, no longer willing to risk loans to the princes, Jewish moneylenders – confined in a hostile environment – had no other choice but to harness the fortune of their enterprises to princes' finances. Thus the fiscal demands of the German territorial states opened big opportunities for economic and social advancement. Moreover, the rise of the *Hoffaktoren* was closely connected with the formation of the absolutist state and the struggle between the absolutist ruler and the estates about the finances of the state, especially the finances of the standing army. By securing the necessary financial means, the *Hoffaktoren* contributed to the ruler's independence from the estates' approval in financial matters, thus limiting the political participation of the estates. As a result the *Hoffaktoren* often became a target of accusations by the estates, protected only by a special personal relationship to the ruler. The *Hoffaktor* purveyed the court with food, clothing and luxuries, and provided the financial means. He supplied the mints with silver and gold, often leasing the mints for a fixed sum of money, advanced in cash. To raise the capital, the *Hoffaktoren* made use of their manifold family relations, but accepted also the money of Christian depositors.[16]

Samuel Oppenheimer and his nephew Samson Wertheimer were important *Hoffaktoren* who came from the Jewish community in Worms and became the financiers of the Habsburg Empire. Oppenheimer purveyed as *Kriegsfaktor* the imperial armies in the conflicts with France and the Turks, especially financing the relieving army during the siege of Vienna in 1683. When Oppenheimer died in 1703, the *Hofkammer* was indebted to him with 6 million florins. The *Hofkammer*'s refusal to pay the money back meant the firm's bankruptcy. His nephew Samson Wertheimer was more successful in getting his loans of the War of the Spanish Succession redeemed, and died in 1724 as one of the richest and most distinguished Jews of his time.[17]

Feidel David worked for the *Landgraf* of Hessen-Kassel in the mid-eighteenth century and he negotiated the English subsidies during the Seven Years War. He was superseded by Meyer Amschel Rothschild, a Frankfurt moneychanger, who invested with profit Hessen-Kassel's gains from the mercenaries during the American War of Independence, thus laying the fundament for the rise of the Rothschilds in the following century.[18] In Frankfurt numerous Jewish merchants served as *Hoffaktoren* for different courts, several entering into princely or ducal service. The most prominent became Joseph Süß Oppenheimer (1689–1738), a Frankfurt dealer in commodities and bills of exchange, who gained the leading position during the reign of Duke Karl Alexander of Württemberg. Financing the ducal household and Württemberg's standing army, Oppenheimer helped to strengthen ducal absolutism and to eliminate the political participation of the Württemberg estates. That is why, after the duke's death Oppenheimer was prosecuted, sentenced to death and executed.[19] However, this did not prevent the dukes of Württemberg at the end of the eighteenth century from making use of the services of the Kaullas of Hechingen, who purveyed the army and founded together with the duke the Württembergische Hofbank in 1802. The path to nineteenth-century private banking was prepared.[20]

Private banking

Private banking in the German states had three sources: traditional merchant banking in the north, wholesale trade and carrier business in the west and the centre, and the *Hoffaktor* service especially in the German south. Nineteenth-century private banking meant a long-term process of emancipation from the merchant and carrier activities and concentration upon banking services, a process that came to its end only in the twentieth century. The leading German places of private banking were Frankfurt, Cologne and Hamburg, with other places such as Stuttgart or Berlin ranking far behind.[21] Frankfurt had regained its importance as a centre of banking in central Europe, favoured by its geographically and politically advantageous site (as *Reichsstadt* and later as one of the four *Freie Städte* in the *Deutsche Bund*), and due to the decline of Amsterdam as financial centre in the last decade of the eighteenth century.[22] The leading Frankfurt banking house – before the rise of the Rothschilds – was that of Gebrüder Bethmann. This enterprise succeeded that of the brothers Bethmann's uncle Jakob Adami's trading business in dyestuffs and other colonial commodities and his carrier business. The brothers Johann Philipp und Simon Moritz continued this branch, when the French occupation of Frankfurt during the Seven Years War gave them the opportunity to advance the pay of the French forces and to supply the army.[23] In 1788 Gebrüder Bethmann placed the first loan for the house of Habsburg, splitting the 20,000 florins into bonds of 1,000 florins each (so called *partial-obligationen*), thus mobilizing private savings to a considerable extent. More loans on behalf of Austria followed, altogether 17.2 million florins (1768–93) and 31.5 million florins (1768–96).[24] The Bethmanns charged a commission of 5 to 5.5%, as well as a further commission when the interest was due or the bonds were redeemed.[25] New loans for Austria and for Denmark and Sweden (1783, 1801, 1802) followed; however, it became more and more difficult to find enough subscribers. The political instability, the restrictions on trade, the growing fear of war limited the investment in bonds and the profits of the private bankers. That is why the Bethmanns withdrew from the business in international loans and concentrated on their traditional business as clearing house for the entrepreneurs of the early industry, and expanded their commission trade. Early industrialized regions and innovative entre-preneurs belonged to the Bethmanns's net of clients: the woollen manufacturers in Monschau, the silk fabrication in Krefeld, the brass works in Stolberg and Nuremberg, the wire production in Altena and Iserlohn, etc.[26] How successful this strategy was shows the development of net profits, which rose to an annual 170,000 Taler (1806–16) compared with 136,000 Taler (1778–90) during the Habsburg loans.[27]

Gebrüder Bethmann's interests in industrial innovation led in the 1830s to the promotion of the railway. Bethmanns and Rothschilds received a licence to build the *Taunusbahn* (Frankfurt–Wiesbaden) and issued together a railway loan of 20 million florins. Another licence for the Frankfurt-Hanauer Eisenbahn followed in 1844, and later the Bethmanns participated in several new railway projects in Germany and abroad.[28]

With respect to their volume of transactions and the international dimension of their business, the Bethmanns were superseded in the nineteenth century by a competing Frankfurt banking house, the Rothschilds. In 1810 the former *Hoffaktor* Meyer Amschel Rothschild took his five sons as partners in his firm, changing its name into M. A. Rothschild & Söhne. His sons founded Rothschild banks in London and Paris and branches in Vienna and Naples which belonged to the Frankfurt bank, the principal house. The specialities of the Rothschilds were big international loans and money transfers, such as the transfer of the French war indemnity after the Napoleonic Wars. Among the loans, we may mention the Prussian loans of 5 million pounds (1819) and 3.5 million pounds (1822), placed by Nathan Rothschild in London, the loans for Naples (1821/2), Greece (1833) and Brazil (1824ff). Besides the international loans in the 1840s, the Rothschild banks were engaged in railway finance, especially in France, Belgium and Austria. In the mid-nineteenth century the house of Rothschild became the leading financial power in the world, by far exceeding the role of a Frankfurt private banker house, although the Frankfurt bank participated together with other private bankers in the foundation of railway companies in Hessen and Thüringen.[29] Other houses, such as B. Metzler seel. Sohn & Co., shifted their activities from the participation in state finance to current account relations and commercial credits, which was already the major business of Gebhard & Hauck and other Frankfurt private bankers.[30]

Cologne was an important financial centre, especially for the early industry of the Rhineland and Westfalen. It belonged to Revolutionary and Napoleonic France from 1794 to 1815, when it became Prussian. French legislation abolished the business restrictions by the Catholic *Reichsstadt*, and enabled Protestants and Jews to enter into the carrier business and the commission trade. This formed the basis for the expansion of the great private banking houses I. D. Herstatt, Abraham Schaaffhausen, J. H. Stein, and Salomon Oppenheim jun. & Cie, the last descending from Salomon Herz Oppenheim, *Hoffaktor* at the court of the elector of Kurköln at Bonn. I. D. Herstatt had been founded in 1727 by Isaak Herstatt as a silk weaving mill, and soon acquired a position in the commission trade and the carrier business which it maintained until the 1830s. Together with the commission trade Herstatt developed the trade in bills of exchange. In the 1820s and 1830s the banking activities were expanded with respect to the clearing business and credits on current accounts. Especially the textile industries of the Niederrhein and the Bergische Land maintained current account relations with Herstatt. Moreover, entrepreneurs of the steel and the metal industries (Friedrich Krupp and Friedrich Harkort), and Felten & Guilleaume were among Herstatt's clients.[31] Similarly structured was the banking house J. H. Stein, founded in 1790 by the Mannheim merchant Johann Heinrich Stein. He opened exchange and credit relations with the Stolberg brass works, the iron and metal industries in Wuppertal, Remscheid and Solingen, and the textile industry in Wuppertal and Bielefeld.[32]

Abraham Schaaffhausen was founded in 1791 as a multi branch enterprise. Its specialities were overseas trade on own account, commission trade, carrier, real estate and clearing business. In the early nineteenth century Schaaffhausen maintained clearing and current account relations with the textile industries in Neuß, Rheydt, Viersen, Düren, Aachen, Monschau and Elberfeld, and extended its activities in the 1820s to iron industries, such as Stumm at the Saar, Hoesch at the Eifel, the Gutehoffnungshütte near Sterkrade and Stinnes at Mülheim. Abraham Schaaffhausen became thus in the 1840s one of the most important financiers of the heavy industries of the Rhein and Ruhr area. However, Schaaffhausen seems to have exhausted its resources due to long-term credits. When many of its clients went bankrupt in the economic and political crisis of 1848/9, and Schaaffhausen was not able to realize its claims, due to the limited rediscount opportunities, offered by the Cologne branch of the Preußische Bank, Schaaffhausen had to suspend payments. Schaaffhausen was rescued by the transformation into the first German joint-stock bank, the A. Schaaffhausen'scher Bankverein, and its creditors became shareholders.[33]

The most daring and innovative banking house was Salomon Oppenheim jun. & Cie, which was transferred from Bonn to Cologne in 1801. As a merchant house, in the beginning Oppenheim was trading in grain and wine and gave credits to other merchant houses. From the 1830s, however, the firm concentrated on industrial finance, especially on mining and metallurgical industries in Stolberg, Düren and Eschweiler, and later to the iron industries and the coal mines at the Ruhr. Oppenheim was innovative with respect to the promotional and issuing business. Long-term industrial finance by bonds and shares started around 1840. Even more important was the engagement in railway projects, such as the Rheinische Eisenbahngesellschaft of 1837. From the share capital of 3 million Taler Oppenheim underwrote 325,000 Taler (11%) and participated in the following increases of capital. In 1843 Oppenheim underwrote 1.5 million Taler of the 13 million Taler of the Köln-Mindener Eisenbahngesellschaft. Other promotional activities by Cologne banking houses, led by Oppenheim, in the booming railway business followed.[34]

Summing up the private banking activities of the Cologne houses: up to the 1830s their domain was the trade in bills of exchange and the clearing on behalf of merchants and industry. At the same time current account relations with the industry, offering short-term overdraft credits for 5–6% interest per year were extended. The spread of international commercial credit as acceptance credit, however, was hampered mainly for two reasons. First, Cologne was not included in the international net of exchange places, and Cologne exchange rates therefore were not registered at the major exchange places. Secondly, discounting and rediscounting facilities were lacking.[35] That is why acceptance credit gained in importance only from the 1840s. In the long run perhaps the most important operations were the promotional and issuing activities, first in the case of railway companies, later of industrial joint-stock companies, whereby Cologne houses underwrote and placed considerable proportions of the share capital, thus transforming short-term credits into long-term credits by issuing shares and bonds. On account of this industrial joint-stock companies came into existence, supported by Cologne banking houses: Kölner Bergwerksverein (1849), Hörder Bergwerks- und Hüttenverein (1852), Phönix (1852), Aktien-Gesellschaft für Bergbau-, Blei- und Zinkfabrikation zu Stolberg (1852), Bochumer Verein (1855), Kölnische Maschinenbau Aktien-Gesellschaft (1856).[36]

Hamburg's private banking shows quite a different picture.[37] By the end of the nineteenth century it was dominated by merchant bankers, who were only slightly changing their enterprise compared with previous centuries, some of them dating back to the first (as the Berenbergs) or to the second generation (as the Jenischs) of sixteenth- and seventeenth-century Hamburg immigrants. Those houses – together with other houses, which settled in Hamburg during the eighteenth century – continued their trade, ran ships, and supplied the credit facilities necessary for trade. Offering acceptance credits, in the eighteenth century Hamburg merchant bankers became accepting and discount houses for the merchants of north-western and central Europe, since importers and exporters made frequent use of this form of credit.

At the turn of the eighteenth century the most important Hamburg merchant bank was the Haus Parish. Its founder, the Welshman, John Parish, wrote his memoirs in 1797, thus supplying a valuable source for the study of merchant banking in Hamburg. According to John Parish's calculations of his huge profits in 1795 and 1796 his activities were concentrated upon trade and commission trade on the one hand and to the exchange and accepting business on the other. Parish expanded and stimulated Hamburg's exchange with London and Amsterdam, giving acceptances for bills of exchange, drawn on Parish, and later selling those accepted bills at the Hamburg exchange, the Börse. Moreover, Parish speculated together with Hope & Co. and others in French Assignates, and negotiated and transferred English subsidies to Prussia in 1794.[38] His sons mediated English subsidies to Austria, and underwrote and placed the Austrian loan in 1818, thus contributing to the restoration of confidence in Austria's public debt. In addition, they opened the way for the participation of the Rothschilds in the finance of the Austrian debt. Rewarded for his merits, John Parish jr became a Freiherr von Senftenberg (in Bohemia), and the Hamburg banking house died out.[39] In the long run more successful, but not as exciting as the Parishes, was the house of Conrad Heinrich Donner, which exists still today. Donner, founded in Altona in 1798, was a typical merchant banking house, concentrating upon trade, acceptance credit and shipping. In 1818/19 Donner underwrote and placed the first loan for Denmark of about 4 million Mark Banco, other loans followed. By the end of the nineteenth century Donner gave up the ships, and acquired industrial partnerships, for example in the rubber production and the Hamburgische Electricitätswerke, a foundation the Donners actively promoted.[40]

A similar development shows Hamburg's eldest existing private banking house, the house of the sixteenth-century immigrant family Berenberg, which became in 1791, due to the reception of partners, Joh. Berenberg, Gossler & Co. In the nineteenth century the house was active – as the Parishes before – in the North American trade and its finance. In 1847 Berenberg–Gossler belonged, together with the merchant house H. J. Merck & Co. and Hamburg merchants, to the founders of the Hapag shipping line, and participated later as well in the foundation of the Norddeutsche Lloyd (1857). Moreover, the houses of Joh. Berenberg, Gossler & Co., H. J. Merck & Co., Salomon Heine and several merchant houses founded in 1856 the Norddeutsche Bank, the first joint-stock bank in northern Germany.[41] As regards the Jewish houses, Salomon Heine saw a swift rise by the mid-nineteenth century, whilst M. M. Warburg & Co., which was founded in 1798 by the Warburg brothers, deriving from a moneychanger family, gained international importance only in the late nineteenth and especially in the twentieth centuries.[42] In general Hamburg private banking witnessed only very few changes in the nineteenth century. Hamburg private banking remained above all connected with commerce and trade finance, and it was not until the twentieth century that banking houses gave up their trade. Promotional and issuing activities played a minor role, and were concentrated upon services (shipping, insurance, banking), but not upon manufacturing industry.

Berlin gained significance as a banking place only after the foundation of the Deutsche Kaiserreich in 1871, which exceeds the scope of this chapter. Instead, we have to mention Stuttgart private bankers as regional example of southern Germany. The most important Stuttgart private bank was the Württembergische Hofbank (later Königlich Württembergische Hofbank), founded in 1802 by the duke and the *Hoffaktoren* Karoline and Jakob Kaulla, each partly raising 150,000 florins of the capital. The Hofbank was refinanced by the Württemberg treasury (Staatskasse) with loans at low interest rates. That enabled the Hofbank to support the early industry as the Cannstätter Baumwollfabrik or the Esslinger Maschinenfabrik, with favourable credits. Other banking houses, which also received credits by the Staatskasse, underwrote as well considerable parts of the share capital of the Esslinger Maschinenfabrik in 1846.[43]

Conclusion

Summarizing 350 years of merchant banking, we may state that, unrivalled by other banking institutions, merchant or private banking houses were throughout the whole period the dominant financial institutions in the Holy Roman Empire and the German states. They created credit for public, commercial and industrial demand, thus contributing to the foundation of public debt, the expansion of overseas trade and the progress of industrialization. In providing credit German merchant bankers were not very innovative, creating new credit instruments or institutions. However, they were successful in adapting and spreading instrumental and institutional innovations, such as the bill of exchange, acceptance credit, the public exchange bank, the joint-stock company, or even the joint-stock bank, originally promoted by immigrants or stimulated by models in the south and the west.

In general merchant banking houses were not run as specialized enterprises. With the rise of private banking from the late eighteenth century, however, we witness a sort of regional specialization, whereby different banking places and financial centres emerged, offering special banking services. Whilst Frankfurt became the centre for public finance, Cologne concentrated upon industrial finance, leaving the finance of trade and other services to Hamburg. This division of labour was only to be challenged in the later periods of German industrialization by the universal banks with their branches all over Germany.

Notes

1 Richard Ehrenberg, *Das Zeitalter der Fugger*, 2 vols. (Jena, 1922).
2 Götz Freiherr von Pölnitz, *Jakob Fugger*, vol. I (Tübingen, 1949), p. 39.

3 *Ibid.*, pp. 418ff.

4 Hermann Kellenbenz, *Die Fuggersche Maestrazgopacht (1525–1542)* (Tübingen, 1967); *idem*, *Die Fugger in Spanien und Portugal bis 1560*, vol. I (Munich, 1990), pp. 245ff.

5 Götz Freiherr von Pölnitz, 'Der Asiento Kaiser Karls V. vom 28. Mai 1552', *Historisches Jahrbuch*, 74 (1954), pp. 213–33; Kellenbenz, *Fugger*, pp. 98ff.

6 Ehrenberg, *Zeitalter*, vol. I, pp. 185–6.

7 Götz Freiherr von Pölnitz, 'Jakob Fugger und der Streit um den Nachlaß des Kardinals Melchor von Brixen', *Quellen und Forschungen aus italienischen Archiven*, 30 (1940), pp. 223–94.

8 Reinhard Hildebrandt, 'Augsburger und Nürnberger Kupferhandel 1500–1619. Produktion, Marktanteile und Finanzierung im Vergleich zweier Städte und ihrer wirtschaftlichen Führungsschicht', in H. Kellenbenz (ed.), *Schwerpunkte der Kupferproduktion und des Kupferhandels in Europa 1500–1650* (Cologne and Vienna, 1977), pp. 190–224.

9 Lambert F. Peters, *Der Handel Nürnbergs am Anfang des Dreißigjährigen Krieges: Strukturkomponenten, Unternehmen und Unternehmer* (Stuttgart, 1994), Part II.

10 Hermann Kellenbenz, *Unternehmerkräfte im Hamburger Portugal- und Spanienhandel 1590–1625* (Hamburg, 1954), p. 239.

11 For an overview, see Herman Van der Wee, 'Monetary, Credit, and Banking Systems', in E. E. Rich and C. Wilson (eds.), *The Cambridge Economic History of Europe*, vol. V: *The Economic Organization of Early Modern Europe* (Cambridge, 1977), pp. 315–22.

12 Ehrenberg, *Zeitalter*, vol. II, pp. 248–55. For the Frankfurt fairs in general, see the Bamberg dissertation of Nils Brübach, 'Die Reichsmessen von Frankfurt am Main, Leipzig und Braunschweig (14.–18. Jahrhundert)' (Stuttgart, 1994).

13 Heinrich Sieveking, 'Die Hamburger Bank', in J. G. van Dillen (ed.), *History of the Principal Public Banks* (The Hague, 1934), pp. 125–63; Michael North, *Das Geld und seine Geschichte vom Mittelalter bis zur Gegenwart* (Munich, 1994), pp. 116f.

14 Carl Ludwig Sachs, 'Die Nürnberger Girobank (1621–1827) im Rahmen der kontinentalen Bankengeschichte', in *Beiträge zur Wirtschafts- und Sozialgeschichte (Festschrift Eheberg)* (Leipzig and Erlangen, 1925), pp. 139–61; Peters, *Handel Nürnbergs*, Part I.

15 Markus A. Denzel, *'La Practica della Cambiatura'. Europäischer Zahlungsverkehr vom 14. bis zum 17. Jahrhundert* (Stuttgart, 1994), pp. 481ff; Jürgen Rainer Wolf, 'Hoffaktoren', in M. North (ed.), *Von Aktie bis Zoll. Ein historisches Lexikon des Geldes* (Munich, 1995), pp. 158ff.

16 Heinrich Schnee, *Die Hoffinanz und der moderne Staat*, 5 vols. (Berlin, 1953–65).

17 Max Grunwald, *Samuel Oppenheimer und sein Kreis* (Vienna and Leipzig, 1913); Selma Stern, *The Court Jew: A Contribution to the History of Absolutism in Central Europe* (Philadelphia, 1950), pp. 86ff.

18 See below, p. 42.

19 Schnee, *Hoffinanz*, vol. IV, pp. 109–48; Barbara Gerber, *Jud Süß. Aufstieg und Fall im frühen 18. Jahrhundert* (Hamburg, 1990).

20 Schnee, *Hoffinanz*, vol. IV, pp. 148–78. See also below, pp. 41–3.

21 An overview of nineteenth-century private banking in Germany is presented by Hans Pohl, 'Das deutsche Bankwesen (1806–1848)', in *Deutsche Bankengeschichte*, vol. II (Frankfurt, 1982), pp. 18–42.

22 Hans-Peter Ullmann, 'Der Frankfurter Kapitalmarkt um 1800. Entstehung, Struktur und Wirken einer modernen Finanzierungsinstitution', *Vierteljahrschrift für Sozial- und Wirtschaftsgeschichte*, 77 (1990), pp. 75–92.

23 A. Dietz, *Frankfurter Handelsgeschichte*, vol. IV (Frankfurt, 1925), pp. 622ff.

24 Wilfried Forstmann, *Simon Moritz von Bethmann 1768–1826. Bankier, Diplomat und politischer Beobachter* (Frankfurt, 1973), p. 19.

25 Friedrich Zellfelder, *Das Kundennetz das Bankhauses Gebrüder Bethmann (1738–1816), Frankfurt am Main, im Spiegel der Hauptbücher* (Stuttgart, 1994), pp. 2ff.

26 *Ibid.*, pp. 7ff, 138ff.

27 *Ibid.*, pp. 5–6, 9–10.

28 Johann Philipp Freiherr von Bethmann (ed.), *Bankiers sind auch Menschen. 225 Jahre Bankhaus Gebrüder Bethmann* (Frankfurt, 1973), pp. 186f.

29 The literature on the Rothschilds is numerous. See Bertrand Gille, *Histoire de la maison de Rothschild*, 2 vols. (Geneva, 1965–6); for the German activities, see Karl Erich Born, *Geld und Banken im 19. und 20. Jahrhundert* (Stuttgart, 1977), pp. 84ff, 103ff.

30 Erich Achterberg, *Frankfurter Bankherren* (Frankfurt, 1971), pp. 73–91, 93–112.

31 Alfred Krüger, *Das Kölner Bankiergewerbe vom Ende des 18. Jahrhunderts bis 1875* (Essen, 1925), pp. 44–9.

32 *Ibid.*, pp. 57–64.

33 *Ibid.*, pp. 49–57. Peter Coym, 'Unternehmensfinanzierung im frühen 19. Jahrhundert – dargestellt am Beispiel der Rheinprovinz und Westfalens' (Diss., Hamburg, 1971), pp. 94ff.

34 Krüger, *Bankiergewerbe*, pp. 64–72, 138–46.

35 Dieter Ziegler, 'Zentralbankpolitische "Steinzeit"? Preußische Bank und Bank of England im Vergleich', *Geschichte und Gesellschaft*, 19 (1993), p. 469.

36 Krüger, *Bankiergewerbe*, ch. 3; R. Tilly, *Financial Institutions and Industrialization in the Rhineland, 1815–1870* (Madison, 1966), ch. 7; idem, *Kapital, Staat und sozialer Protest in der deutschen Industrialisierung* (Göttingen, 1980), pp. 49ff.

37 As an overview of Hamburg private banking, see Manfred Pohl, *Hamburger Bankengeschichte* (Mainz, 1986), ch. 2.

38 Richard Ehrenberg, *Große Vermögen*, vol. II: *Das Haus Parish in Hamburg* (Jena, 1904), pp. 38–90.

39 Richard Ehrenberg, *Große Vermögen*, vol. I: *Die Fugger–Rothschild–Krupp* (Jena, 1902), pp. 75ff.

40 Maria Möring, *175 Jahre Conrad Heinrich Donner* (Hamburg, 1973).

41 Berenberg Bank: *Joh. Berenberg, Gossler & Co. Die Geschichte eines deutschen Privatbankhauses* (Hamburg, 1990); Pohl, *Hamburger Bankengeschichte*, pp. 77ff.

42 Eduard Rosenbaum and A. J. Sherman, *Das Bankhaus M. M. Warburg & Co. 1798–1938* (Hamburg, 1976).

43 Ernst Klein, 'Die Königlich Württembergische Hofbank und ihre Bedeutung für die Industriefinanzierung in der ersten Hälfte des 19. Jahrhunderts', *Jahrbücher für Nationalökonomie und Statistik*, 179 (1966), pp. 324–43; Rolf Walter, 'Die (Re-)Finanzierung privater Banken über die Württembergische Staatskasse (1830–1870)', *Scripta Mercaturae*, 24 (1990), pp. 63–80.

4 Public banks, trade and industry
in southern Italy, seventeenth to
eighteenth century

Paola Avallone

Premise

Braudel stated that whatever type of capitalism was considered, it was,
however, necessary to take into consideration that it is placed between
two terms that contribute to conferring a logical meaning to it: *capital*
and *capitalist*. Capital is a concrete reality, easily identifiable and
quantifiable: the means available to operate. But these means may have
a proper function only if the second term, that is the capitalist, inter-
venes. This is the person who controls or strives to control the flow of
capital in a productive process experienced by all societies.[1]

In the light of these observations and to understand how capitalism
could have been influenced by the Neapolitan banks in southern Italy
between the late sixteenth and seventeenth centuries, the question to
ask is whether those institutions involved in banking in the Kingdom
of Naples can be regarded as financial intermediaries or *tout court*
capitalists.

Based on Braudel's definition and considering the history of
Neapolitan public banks, we can assert that they took on both functions.
First of all they were financial intermediaries, for they provided various
services to the public: opening savings accounts, issuing documents of
credit that circulated instead of metallic currency and lending money
against collateral at reasonable rates. We can also define them as
capitalists because, descending from charitable institutions with

consolidated assets,[2] they accumulated wealth by various forms of investment, which was used not only to cover the operating costs of the bank and of the charitable institutions, but to implement further profitable investments as well.

Luigi De Rosa stresses that the Neapolitan public banks were the only banking institutions able to finance the not very vast range of economic operations in the Kingdom of Naples and were certainly the main lenders to the governments of the Kingdom and of the City of Naples.[3] Two fundamental operations carried out by the Neapolitan banks can be identified: the financing of trade (short-term loans = loans upon pledge at interest; long-term loans = loans at interest), and the financing of the government (short-term loans = interest-free loans; purchase of shares of public debt) (see Figure 4.1).

Origins and success of Neapolitan public banks

The Neapolitan public banks were founded in the late sixteenth century in the wake of the bankruptcies of the private bankers. Present since the previous century in southern Italy, and in particular in Naples, private bankers were originally merchants who had merged their main operations in trade and speculative investments with banking. These bankers, mainly Genoese, Venetian and Florentine but also Catalan and Neapolitan, fulfilled the function of collecting savings, which were then mainly invested in productive enterprises and in loans to the government, whenever it was necessary. Shares of public debt were sometimes used as collateral for these loans. During the second half of the sixteenth century, the deterioration of the economic situation along with the viceregal decisions on economic and monetary policies[4] caused many of the private bankers to go bankrupt and escape abroad. In 1598, for instance, the private banks Mari, Olgiati and others went bankrupt. That year they had invested big amounts of money in the purchase of wheat in the hope of achieving a profit on the selling price. Unfortunately, the harvest was abundant, and moreover the government had huge quantities of wheat brought from Sicily for the food board of the city. Therefore the price of wheat fell and the bankers who had speculated were forced to sell it below the purchasing price with big losses.[5]

Many people, to avoid dealing with private bankers, started depositing their money in charitable institutions that at the time had started their credit activity. Anyone who deposited money could personally withdraw it at any moment by exhibiting a document (*fede di credito*) certifying the initial deposit, or drawing a bill (*polizza*) on their account: thus, the *fede di credito* became a *madrefede*, an *ante litteram* checking account.

In the early seventeenth century there were seven banks: the Banco e Monte della Pietà (1570) and the Banco e Monte dei Poveri (1600) originated by gemmation respectively from the Monte di Pietà (1539) and from the Congregazione di Santa Maria del Monte dei Poveri (1563), institutions that engaged in charity granting interest-free loans upon pledge; the other banks, Banco di Ave Gratia Plena (1587), Banco di Santa Maria del Popolo (1589), Banco dello Spirito Santo (1590), Banco di S. Eligio (1592), Banco dei SS. Giacomo e Vittoria (1597), were founded by the governors who managed the hospitals and charitable institutions of the capital. In the mid-seventeenth century the Banco del SS. Salvatore (1640) was the only bank founded by several speculators, collectors of the flour excise, who desired to invest the profits of their activity (see Figure 4.2).[6]

The eight banks were accredited not only by the private investors who showed deep trust in the original institutions, but above all by the Court, which considered these banks as their financial intermediaries. Through viceregal licences and the transferral of income from direct and indirect taxes, the Court designated those banks as public; that is, they could collect deposits without any restrictions issuing *fedi di credito*, which could be used to pay taxes.

Paper money vs. specie: *the* fede di credito

Public banks had a fundamental role in southern Italy's economy, finding a solution to the constant scarcity of metallic currency by issuing paper money. This scarcity was the consequence of the continuous flow of financial assets towards Madrid or other places indicated by it, Genoa for the revenues that the Genoese had accumulated in the Kingdom of Naples and Rome for the money that was sent for various reasons to the Vatican State. This outflow, which resulted in the consequential scarcity of money in the Kingdom, was connected to the counterfeit and shearing phenomena. Shearing was the filing of the edges of the silver coins.[7] Initially, to avoid the depositors running the same risks as in the past, the metallic currency deposited in the banks had to be of the same amount as the *fedi* and *polizze* in circulation. But the practical experience was different. The *fedi* issued by the banks were distinguished in *fedi libere*, when the possessor

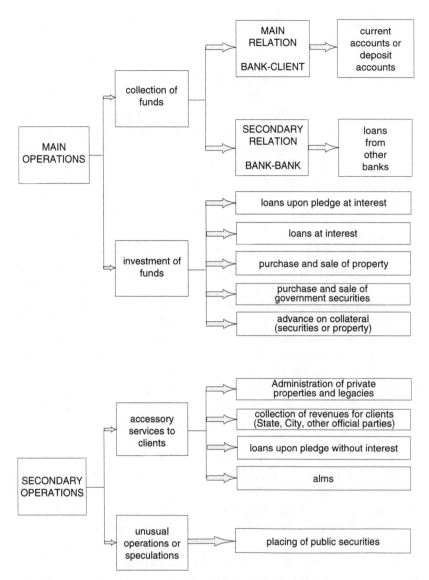

Figure 4.1 Operations carried out by Neapolitan public banks (seventeenth to eighteenth centuries)

could present the deposit receipt and withdraw the whole amount or part of it at any time; *fedi condizionate*, which could be redeemed only at the occurrence of certain conditions; and *fedi vincolate*, which were judicial deposits. Therefore, since the deposit of money was considered juridically irregular, the banks, once the average duration of circulation of the *fedi* and the average deposit of the corresponding amount in metallic currency were calculated, could safely use these sums of money. However, the use of those funds was regulated by the Spanish viceroys to avoid any possibility of repeating the problems incurred with the private bankers, restricting investments only to shares of public debt (loans to the Court and the City of Naples). The Banco dei Poveri, for instance, based on its first statute of 1612, could not lend more than 200 ducats unless there was a good reason and a just cause.[8] In the first statutes of the Banco del Popolo, presented to the viceroy for approval in 1589, it was established that the money of the depositors (*apodissari*)[9] could be loaned only to individuals who had deposited money in the bank (for a loan not exceeding the amount deposited), and to the bank itself to buy shares of public debt of the Court and the City of Naples, using the dividends of those investments to cover the operating costs of the bank and the charitable institution. After twenty months, in 1590, the viceroy count of Miranda agreed on extending the number of people with whom the bank could invest, on condition that the money was not withdrawn from individual accounts, but was part of the dividends earned on public debt, once all the ordinary and extraordinary operating costs were covered.[10] With these measures, besides protecting the depositors, the viceregal government wanted to extend a monopoly on the banks so as to be able to use its deposits when necessary.

However, this strict regulation was never really applied. The governors who managed the banks, and also the charities from which the banks originated, understood that only through greater investments could they collect the sums necessary to cover the increasing expenses of their charitable activities. These expenses increased because of a sharp increase in the birth rate (on the eve of the plague of 1656 the population of Naples was over 300,000) and a continuous rise in prices.

The clients of the banks and the increase of medium- and long-term loans: loans at interest

In their first thirty years of existence, the banks were involved in a difficult search for capital on behalf of the market, which was more and

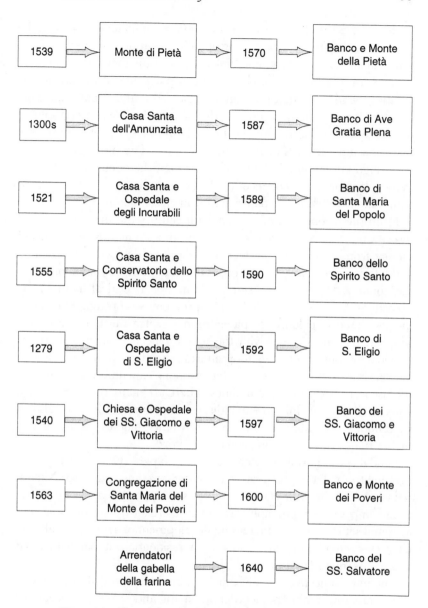

Figure 4.2   The origins of Neapolitan public banks

more depauperized by the effects of the careless financial policy of the government.[11] From the beginning of their operations, as Luigi De Rosa states, in an attempt at consolidating their position, they did not hesitate 'to increase the number of clients and in particular of merchants, by creating *partite morte*, that is accounts indicated in the books as actually registered, recording unsecured credits of considerable sums, in spite of the decrees of the viceroy that prohibited this practice'.[12] As a result, the banks became arbiters of the money market. The monetary mass of the Kingdom increased almost 50% through the circulation of paper money, leaving in the coffers of the banks a specie reserve that covered with difficulty 20% of the paper money in circulation.[13]

From the second half of the sixteenth century the sharp increase of direct and indirect taxation to satisfy the numerous demands of money from Spain and the increase of public debt were both cause and effect of the change in the economic and monetary equilibrium of the country. However, the situation was not as critical as the years preceding the riots of the 1640s. The problem was postponed through the increased circulation of paper money, since the banks not only supplied the government with the funds it needed against shares of public debt, but, through loans at interest, they helped individuals who needed immediate funds to pay for ordinary expenditures because of the rise in the prices of commodities. There are many references in the bank registers not only to expenditures for commodities, but also to superfluous expenditures that show how the standard of living was higher than what each individual could afford.

Feudal power was concentrated in Naples. Consequently, the revenue from all the provinces of the Kingdom flowed towards Naples. If in the mid-fifteenth century Naples still appeared as a city whose urban and social topography was characterized by commercial and artisanal settlements, the increasing development of aristocratic abodes characterized it more and more as a residential city in which the aristocrats squandered their wealth.[14]

The main objective of the Neapolitan banks was to collect money in ever-increasing amounts in order to invest and make the necessary profits to finance their charitable institutions. For this reason, just as banks today offer special deals to individuals who open chequing accounts or take advantage of some of their services, Neapolitan public banks strived in the same way to expand their clientele granting loans to private investors, thus violating the law. The banks, in order to loan money at interest, evaded the ecclesiastical and civil laws, which considered interest as usury, through the formula *compra di annue entrate*. In practice, loan contracts were granted with a buyback clause and the interest became temporary cession of revenue. If it was a loan granted, it was called *compra di annue entrate* (purchase of annual revenues); if it was a loan received, *vendita di annue entrate* (sale of annual revenues).[15]

The borrowers belonged mostly to the highest social class, the aristocracy, residing in great numbers in Naples. Resorting to debt was the only solution for the Neapolitan aristocracy when expenses beyond the ordinary occurred. The loans were mostly aimed at refinancing prior debts,[16] setting aside marriage or monastic dowries,[17] purchasing shares of public debt[18] and only in smaller percentage at productive investments as the purchase of real estate, improvement of property[19] and, in rather rare cases, commercial activities.[20] According to Aurelio Lepre, the investment of capital in farms by aristocrats was not to obtain a capitalistic profit, but was done for the same reasons they purchased shares of excises and houses to rent: to obtain a certain amount of liquid assets to maintain a high standard of living. Even if some aristocrats had what we would call an entrepreneurial spirit, the profit was not always reinvested, but could be used to pay a legate for a member of the family who entered the clergy or to silence a creditor; sometimes also to buy other land, because in financially favourable moments they tended to expand their possessions rather than invest capital in the ones already owned.[21]

The aristocracy had always been the richest social class of the country, living on the income from property in the province.[22] But in addition to this class, another which accumulated wealth was represented by foreign currency operators, merchants, tax collectors, magistrates, lawyers, doctors, officers, etc., who held the reins of the Kingdom's economy. The members of this class, even though they felt socially closer to the so-called 'people', from a strictly economic point of view were in no way inferior to the aristocrats. Sometimes their accounts were much more active, especially the accounts held by merchants. For some of the banks, the members of this class represented their fortune since they were the most important depositors.[23] Therefore, the banks granted them loans at interest, since these deposits could be used as collateral shares of public debt purchased prior to the loan or the property. As a matter of fact, this class mostly preferred investing in land not only because it was a safe investment along with investing in public debt, but also because land gave considerable social status.[24] The return to the land of those who devoted themselves to commercial activities stresses once more the concept of *feudal capitalism*, Sombart's expression taken and extended to the Italian seventeenth century. With regard to southern Italy it has sparked a debate on the phenomenon of *refeudalization*. The debate was between Rosario Villari and Giuseppe Galasso: refeudalization confirmed by the former and denied by the latter, who considered the phenomenon as internal changes of the feudal class itself, since no *defeudalization* had occurred.[25]

A preference for the money market: loans upon pledge at interest

The *compra di annue entrate* (purchase of annual revenues = loans at interest) was an operation that decreased noticeably in the second half of the seventeenth century. After the damage to the banks caused by the crisis of 1622/3, the public banks adopted a policy based on maximum caution, exposing their liquid assets only when they had more than sufficient guarantees and always preferring investments in public debt.[26] The decrease of investments in loans at interest both in number and in amount was due to two concurrent causes. First, all the banks had received viceregal approval to make advance loans upon pledge applying a reasonable interest rate (7%). Secondly, before the Masaniello revolt, the economic and financial policies of the viceregal government, aimed at collecting ever-increasing revenues, were based on the issuing of shares of public debt. What motivated investors in buying them were both the interest rate and the spread between the nominal value and the issuing price, then called *alaggio*. This spread widened proportionately to the increase of the needs of the government and to the scarcity of capital on the market. Worried about keeping an adequate level of liquid assets, it suited the banks to increase the share of money invested in loans upon pledge at interest which, as a short-term investment, could easily be disinvested,[27] and also to invest in shares of public debt, a safe source of income and easily liquidated. The significant discontinuity in the debt register of loans at interest shows the greater interest of the Neapolitan banks in the money rather than the financial market, that is, in short-term rather than long-term loans.[28]

The operation of loan upon pledge at interest was introduced because of the need to find alternative sources to cover the operating costs of the activities carried out by the Neapolitan banks, costs that were previously covered by the liquid assets. The amount to be invested in loans upon pledge at interest was withdrawn from the bank's deposits, and the guarantee for its depositors, if they all decided to withdraw their deposits simultaneously, was represented by the objects pawned. This was a concrete guarantee compared to the higher volatility of loans at interest. The objects that could be pawned ranged from the most precious to the poorest, allowing all social classes access to this type of loan. From a detailed study of the pawn certificates it is inferred that whoever brought precious objects to pawn could be an aristocrat or a well-off person who needed immediate cash for ordinary or extraordinary expenses (consumer credit and commercial credit). Therefore it is certain that a part of the money borrowed was often invested in productive activities.[29] Loans upon pledge could therefore be considered as an index of the economic development of southern Italy, since an increase of the sums loaned upon pledge at interest did not indicate a period of necessity and calamity, but a reawakening of economic activity, as was the case in the period of reforms during the reign of Charles of Bourbon.[30]

In addition to loans upon pledge at interest, only the Banco della Pietà and the Banco dei Poveri granted interest-free loans as well. They loaned small sums not exceeding 10 ducats, receiving in pledge objects of limited value in order to help the poor people who often had nothing to eat. Besides a number of abuses carried out not only by the lower-level employees but also by the directors,[31] it is interesting to point out, as some documents establish, how this type of loan was channelled towards productive activities as well. In 1662, for example, the management of the Banco della Pietà increased the amount to be invested in loans upon pledge without interest in order to increase the number of loans to needy farmers to buy seeds and to help during harvest.[32]

The recovery of loans at interest

If after the crisis during the 1620s the banks reduced the concession of loans at interest to the minimum, it was, however, continued by private investors, as is proven by the accounts in the journals *copiapolizze* of the banks.[33] Some examples of loans at interest granted by individuals or ecclesiastical institutions which had accumulated immense wealth can be drawn from the accounting books of the Neapolitan banks.[34] The subject deserves more attention by scholars, since through a systematic study of the accounts of some of these entities a particularly interesting

economic reality could be outlined. And the notarial source at the State
Archive of Naples could be of great help.

The resumption of the concession of loans at interest by the
Neapolitan banks in the second half of the eighteenth century[35] is
explained by the fact that other more profitable investments did not
exist, compared to the situation in the previous century, since the
buy-back policy of the government, through the establishment of
the Giunta delle Ricompre in 1751, centred on the reacquisition by the
state of those shares of public debt with the highest interest rate and
generally on the conversion of yields on the public debt from 7% to 4%.
If with the founding of the Giunta delle Ricompre under Carlo di
Borbone the yield on government bonds decreased to 4% annually, in
the late eighteenth century it further decreased to 3%.[36] But the
measures taken by the Court applied a policy adopted also in other
countries of northern Europe: in 1749 the British government issued a
law that invited all creditors of the state either to accept a reduction of
the interest to 4% until 1750, to 3.5% until 1755 and finally to 3% from
1755 onwards or to redeem their capital based on the old interest
rates.[37]

Thus, once the preferred instrument of investment disappeared, the
only possible option was to increase loans upon pledge at interest, whose
yield in the meanwhile had decreased only 1% (to 6%), or to grant more
loans at interest to the aristocrats who were able to offer substantive
collateral, even though upon royal assent when feudal property was
involved. But this credit policy, coupled with a faulty economic policy of
the government in the late eighteenth century, caused many problems
to the banks.

Another way to assist their clientele was in borrowing money from
them. This operation expanded to all the banks after the crisis of 1622/3
in the form of *vendite di annue entrate*, and this occurred not because there
was a precise need to collect money by the banks, but to allow private
investors (mostly members or relatives of the management or of
influential people) to invest their funds with the banks. This can be
explained by the fact that in that period the financial market did not
offer safe and more profitable investments than those in public debt.
Therefore private investors found it convenient to entrust their savings
to banks, which had investors' complete confidence, securing an income
between 4% and 5%. The banks, in turn, putting those funds in more
profitable investments, as government bonds or loans upon pledge,
which yielded 7% at the time, profited on the difference.[38] In the

mid-eighteenth century the government invited the banks to avoid borrowing money. The reason for this decision was that when the government borrowed interest-free loans from the Neapolitan public banks, the banks refused stating that there was not enough money because of the interest burden paid to their creditors. But this was only an excuse to avoid lending without interest.[39] Thus the banks reimbursed the funds that private investors had invested with the banks.[40]

Clearing operations

The acceptance on behalf of each bank of the *fedi di credito* issued by other banks gave a major contribution to the development of transactions. Periodically, through the officer called *Riscontratore*, the banks settled the accounts through what today is commonly called clearance. This clearing operation, on the one hand, facilitated payments and was very useful to commerce, but, on the other hand, became an operation through which the so-called *introiti vacui* (the issue of an uncovered note) could be covered. From the documents available it is known that the cashiers, upon orders from the governors and also in agreement with who wrote out the *fedi di credito*,[41] made advance payments on accounts mostly to other banks issuing *fedi di credito* without any cash deposit.[42] The issue of an overdrawn *fede di credito* was allowed by the governors of the banks when they tried to help their privileged clientele who, at the moment, did not have sufficient funds in their accounts. For instance, when some rich client wanted to deposit a big amount of money but lacked a certain amount to reach the sum he wanted to deposit, the banks granted him a line of credit, opening an account in his name and recording a higher sum than that which he really deposited, or they advanced him the sum, which was always higher than usual, upon pledge.[43] For these reasons the clearing operations were many times prohibited by the government, for instance, with the Royal Pragmatic Sanctions dated 22 June 1635 and 17 May 1728. However, it was seldom observed.[44]

The relations with the state

The opinions of contemporary scholars on the Neapolitan banks have not always been positive. After the crisis of the 1620s, Lunetti wrote that the public banks had to be dismantled since they had not been adroit in their management, having employed private investors' funds to pay for operating costs. Thus these banks, founded to help the charitable institutions, had only damaged them, bringing discredit upon themselves. It was instead important to create a single bank, the Tavola di Corte, which had to be connected to an Ufficio dell'Abbondanza with the precise task of borrowing money at a 5% interest rate from the *Tavola*, and in its turn loan the money to the administrators of farms at a 6% interest rate, avoiding the usury of the *contratti voce* (verbal contracts).[45]

A century later, Broggia regretted that private bankers did not operate in the Kingdom any longer, while they would have been vital for the economic development of the country, since they used the money for big enterprises: they loaned money at reasonable rates; promoted industry; avoided usury, while the state enjoyed the advantages. In Broggia's opinion, when these bankers were present in Naples, the city was the centre of a very florid market. On the other hand, he strongly criticized the public banks and considered them detrimental to the economy. To make his opinion clearer he used the similitude of the animal's blood circulation. As the blood circulates in all the animal's body pumped by the heart until it returns to the heart itself, if it does not pump it back into circulation, the body will become ill and die. This is what had to happen with regard to monetary circulation. The money was not to remain idle in the coffers of the banks, but it had to be channelled back into the system. This could give new impulse to the commercial and industrial capitalism of a country. Unfortunately, money remained idle in the coffers of the banks, according to Broggia, leaving the economy of the Kingdom without the means to nourish itself.[46]

These opinions were dictated by the fact that the banks from the 1630s had increased their investments in shares of public debt; a policy imposed by the government that, propelled by pressing demands, knocked at their doors time and again requesting advance on funds which it often did not give back, issuing instead shares of public debt. These advances were defined as *forced* investments. In a report dated 1654 the governors of the Banco dei Poveri stated that they were aware of this serious situation, but that they were not very worried given the high revenue of the forced investments,[47] and considers the fact that the financial market did not offer equally remunerative safe investments.[48] This type of credit-granting on behalf of the Neapolitan banks could have been considered, even though in indirect terms, a profitable investment if the Court had invested the money in productive activities, acting thus as an accelerator for the economic system as a whole. However, if it is taken into account that military expenditures represented a considerable percentage of the budget of the state both during the Spanish and the Austrian viceroyalty and when the Kingdom of Naples became independent, consequently at least a part of the productive capacity of southern Italy was stimulated in order to equip the soldiers where they were fighting (Flanders, Milan or elsewhere) or to provide all the necessary goods to the foreign troops stationed in the Kingdom. Obviously, in the latter case, it is necessary to underline that the money spent by the army in the Kingdom helped to create an additional demand.[49] However, especially since the late eighteenth century, a part of the expenditures were sometimes directed at general public projects. In 1786, for instance, a loan of 7,000 ducats to the tribunal of fortification, brick-building and water systems for the construction of the road of Poggioreale was granted by the banks; between 1787 and 1788 two loans were granted to the Court by all the banks for a total of 300,000 ducats to sustain the drainage expenses of some lands in Calabria Ulteriore; in 1789 another loan of 40,000 ducats was granted to build a nine-mile road in Puglia between Bisceglie and Giovinazzo.[50] Hence Galanti, writing towards the end of the century, manifested that he had a different opinion from Broggia on the public banks. He invited the banks to open branches in the provinces in order to set up manufacturing mills in which to invest their deposits.[51]

Conclusions

In conclusion, even though they did not have the same role as the private banks in Italy and in Europe, the public banks, although founded with different purposes, did not refuse to take the responsibilities of the function. Most of Naples' and southern Italy's savings were deposited in their coffers, and, very often, they had the indirect function of supplying commercial and manufacturing capital. The public banks facilitated commerce, even though without direct financing, by issuing *fedi di credito* accepted by everyone, overcoming a shortage of metal money. Their credit policy adapted itself to the economic policy of the government, helping the state in coping with its increasing exigencies without having to increase or apply new taxes, often not easy to enforce. It was a policy, on the other hand, that had never placed any emphasis on economic development, at least until the mid-eighteenth century. And, furthermore, in an economy characterized by underdevelopment, they assisted in mitigating the misery of the less fortunate classes both with interest-free loans upon pledge and charitable initiatives of the institutions which originated the Neapolitan public banks. In this case they also took on a function of social welfare.

Notes

The following abbreviations are used in the notes: AA = Archivio Apodissario; AP = Archivio Patrimoniale; ASBN = Archivio Storico del Banco di Napoli; ASN = Archivio di Stato di Napoli; BLL = British Library of London; BP = Banco della Pietà; BPOV = Banco dei Poveri; BSAL = Banco del Salvatore; BSS = Banco dello Spirito Santo; d. = ducats; HHStA = Haus, Hof- und Staatsarchiv, Wien; m., mm. = matricola, matricole.

1 Drawn from one of Braudel's interventions in the three conferences held in the United States and published with the title *Afterthoughts on Material Civilization and Capitalism* (Baltimore, 1977).
2 Ludovico Bianchini denounced that the serious damage to southern Italy's industry in this period was caused by the lack of associations of capital. During the viceroy period, charitable institutions multiplied. The result was that public wealth was not invested in productive activities, but was used to ease the spreading poverty, especially in the capital; in so doing, the necessary amount of money and also of work, since many people were confident in being able to obtain some kind of charity, was subtracted from the industry (Ludovico Bianchini, *Storia delle finanze del regno delle due Sicile*, ed. Luigi De Rosa (Naples, 1971), p. 448).
3 Carlo Celano, *Notizie del bello dell'antico e del curioso della città di Napoli divise dall'autore in dieci giornate per la guida e comodo de' viaggiatori*, additions by G. B. Chiarini, ed. A. Mozzillo, A. Profeta and F. P. Macchia (Naples, 1970); in particular see the introduction.
4 Luigi De Rosa, *Il Mezzogiorno spagnolo fra crescita e decadenza* (Milan, 1987), pp. 25–31.
5 Antonio Bulifon, *Giornale di Napoli dal 1547 al 1706*, ed. Nino Cortese, vol. I (Naples, 1932), p. 68.
6 The bibliography on Neapolitan public banks has become substantial. Only some of the most important books are listed below: Michele Rocco, *De' Banchi di Napoli e della loro ragione*, vols. I–III (Naples, 1785); Aniello Somma, *Trattato dei banchi nazionali del Regno delle due Sicile* (Naples, 1844); Giulio Petroni, *De' Banchi di Napoli* (Naples, 1871); Eugenio Tortora, *Il Banco di Napoli. Raccolta di documenti storici e statistici* (Naples, 1883); Eugenio Tortora, *Nuovi documenti per la storia del Banco di Napoli* (Naples, 1882); Riccardo Filangieri, *Storia del Banco di Napoli. I Banchi di Napoli dalle origini alla costituzione del Banco delle due Sicile (1539–1808)* (Naples, 1940).
7 On the topic see De Rosa, *Il Mezzogiorno spagnolo*, p. 95.
8 Luigi De Rosa, 'Le origini curialesche del Banco dei Poveri (1563–1608)', *Bancaria – Review of the Italian Banking Association* (Rome, 1958), pp. 5–29.
9 This is how depositors were called. The term comes from the Greek word αποδεικτικοσ, which means demonstrative since the accounting was held in an analytic form (Tortora, *Nuovi documenti per la storia del Banco di Napoli*, p. 111).
10 Tortora, *Il Banco di Napoli*, pp. lxxvii–lxxxi. The rule was obviously valid for all the banks (HHStA, Neapel/Collectanea, fascio 46).

11 De Rosa, *Il Mezzogiorno spagnolo*, pp. 31–2.
12 Luigi De Rosa, Introduction to *Il Mezzogiorno agli inizi del seicento* (Rome and Bari, 1994), pp. xxiv–v.
13 De Rosa, *Il Mezzogiorno spagnolo*, pp. 89–105.
14 Fausto Nicolini, 'Notizie storiche tratte dai giornali copiapolizza dell'antico Banco della Pietà', *Bollettino* of the Historic Archive of the Banco di Napoli 1-2-3-4 (Naples, 1954); ASBN, *Banco di S. Eligio*, filza m. 58, Naples, 1983, and filza m. 64, Naples, 1984; *Banco di SS. Giacomo e Vittoria*, filza m. 2, 1982.
15 Tortora, *Il Banco di Napoli*, p. lxxvii, note a.
16 Pasquale Villani states that the big feudal families had almost an institutional debt burden (Pasquale Villani, 'Note sullo sviluppo economico-sociale del Regno di Napoli nel '700', *Rassegna Economica* of the Banco di Napoli 1 (Naples, 1972), p. 51). Examples of the destination of the loans for debt refinancing are in ASBN/BP/AP, *Libro maggiore di terze*, years 1613–16, m. 14, ff. 24–5.
17 ASBN/BP/AP, *Libro maggiore di terze*, years 1613–16, m. 14, 23.
18 ASBN/BPOV/AP, *Libro maggiore di terze*, years 1668–70, m. 19, ff. 78, 183. The capital invested in public revenue represented a part of a vaster feudal patrimony. This kind of investment was highly appreciated not only by the aristocrats, but also by whoever had capital to invest, as government bonds represented a safe and higher income than any other on the market. Many people between the seventeenth and eighteenth centuries lived on that income, forming what Luigi De Rosa calls the social class of the *rentiers*, who dominated politically and economically southern Italy (De Rosa, *Il Mezzogiorno spagnolo*, p. 64).
19 ASBN/BP/AP, *Libro maggiore di terze*, years 1668–72, m. 92, ff. 60, 75; ASN, *Cassa di ammortizzazione. Debitori strumentari*, vol. II, years 1640–1717, vol. 648, ff. 361–94.
20 In the first half of the eighteenth century, for instance, the Marquis Bartolomeo di Colletorto and the Duke Ignazio Barretta were involved in commercial activities (ASBN/BSS/AA, *Giornali di cassa*, year 1727, m. 1175, *polizze* of 11/8, 14/10, 29/10 and 18/12; m. 1176, *polizze* of 12/8, 27/8 and 8/11; year 1738, m. 1341, *polizze* of 7/1, 27/1 and 28/5; etc.).
21 Aurelio Lepre, *Storia del Mezzogiorno d'Italia*, vol. I (Naples, 1986), p. 77.
22 Real estate property represented a real guarantee for the banks that granted loans. To evade the law that prohibited loans at interest, the aristocrats sold shares of revenue on their possessions *cum pacto de retrovendendo quadocumque* to the banks (ASBN/BP/AP, *Libro maggiore di patrimonio*, years 1660–93, m. 37, ff. 14–41). In some cases those shares were assigned to the banks by debtors for the payment of interests *pro faciliore exactione* (ASN, *Cassa di ammortizzazione. Debitori strumentari*, vol. II, years 1640–1717, ff. 76–83). Other examples are in ASN, *Cassa di ammortizzazione. Volumi di cautele e diversi dei Banchi napoletani*, Banco della Pietà from m. 647 to m. 633, Banco del Popolo from m. 664 to m. 675, Banco di S. Eligio from m. 676 to m. 680, Banco del Salvatore from m. 681 to m. 690, Banco dei Poveri from m. 691 to m. 715 bis, Banco dello Spirito Santo m. 716.)
23 When in the second half of the eighteenth century the Banco di S. Eligio was closed, the governors presented a memorandum to the king begging him to intervene in favour of its reopening, since the closing had caused a lot of damage to the merchants in the Piazza Mercato area: 'fornai, vaccinai, conciarioti, orefici, giudichieri, pannazzari e altri non pochi venditori di commestibili, che formavano la gente ricca della capitale' (ASN, *Ministero delle Finanze*, fascio 2733). And in the previous century the administrators of the Banco del Salvatore underlined that 'nel Banco negoziava

la maggior parte dei mercanti di questa Fedelissima Città, i quali erano gelosissimi che si sapesse quali denari piglino a cambio o diano ad altri per negozio e traffico' (ASBN/BSAL/AP, *Libro di appuntamenti*, years 1661–1756, m. 24, f. 81).

24 For examples of loans granted by the banks for investments in land, see ASBN/BP/AP, *Libro maggiore di terze*, years 1668–72, m. 92, ff. 60–75; ASBN/BPOV/AP, *Libro maggiore di terze*, years 1668–70, ff. 78, 183.

25 Rosario Villari, *La rivolta antispagnola a Napoli 1585–1647. Le origini* (Bari, 1967); Giuseppe Galasso, *Dal Comune medievale all'Unità. Linee di storia meridionale* (Bari, 1969); Giuseppe Galasso, 'Ceti e classi alla fine del secolo XVII', *Il Mezzogiorno d'Italia* (Florence, 1977).

26 Also the ratio between reserve and money in circulation was rather high (an average of 60/70%) up to the crisis that hit the banks in the last thirty years of the eighteenth century.

27 If the debtors did not give back the money in a year, the banks could sell the objects at auction.

28 On the increase of the amounts invested in government bonds and in loans upon pledge at interest and on the decrease of loans at interest see the data in Luigi De Rosa, 'Il Banco dei Poveri e la crisi del 1622', *Rassegna Economica* of the Banco di Napoli (Naples, 1958), pp. 49–78; Luigi De Rosa, 'Una struttura bancaria napoletana alla vigilia dell'insurrezione di Masaniello: il Banco dei Poveri dal 1641 al 1646', *Bollettino* of the Historic Archive of the Banco di Napoli IX–XII (Naples, 1955); Carlo Di Somma, 'Il Banco dello Spirito Santo dalle origini al 1664', *Annali of the Istituto di Storia Economica e Sociale di Napoli* 1 (Naples, 1960). It can be seen from these studies that the total value of the amounts invested in loans at interest is third after the total value of the amounts invested in government bonds and in loans upon pledge at interest. This investment policy was not modified with the 1648–9 reform. And the causes are found in the fact that the banks were at the government's service (Antonio Di Vittorio, 'L'Austria e il problema monetario e bancario del Viceregno di Napoli 1707–1734', *Rivista Storica Italiana* fascicolo IV (1969)). The Banco della Pietà between 1734 and 1759 granted few loans (thirteen in all) to private investors and only to aristocrats. With regard to the Banco dei Poveri no loans were granted in that period (Ennio De Simone, *Il Banco della Pietà di Napoli 1734–1806* (Naples, 1974); ASBN/BPOV/AP, *Libri maggiori di terze*, years 1729–1760, mm. 45, 46, 48, 50, 52, 54, in particular the *compre e ricompre* account).

29 This is confirmed also in BLL, *Notizie de' Banchi della Città di Napoli*, MS 8679.

30 From 1735 to 1759 the amounts invested in loans upon pledge at interest increased, even though the banks continued to prefer investing in government bonds (ASBN/BPOV/AP, *Volume contenente lo stato dei creditori apodissari con alcune note dei debitori*, years 1691–1776, m. 356; De Simone, *Il Banco della Pietà di Napoli*).

31 Paola Avallone, *Stato e Banchi Pubblici a Napoli a metà del '700. Il Banco dei Poveri: una svolta* (Naples, 1995).

32 ASBN/BP/AP, *Libro di conclusioni*, years 1634–64, m. 239, the conclusion of 2/18/1662, f. 209. The farmers were subject to the oppressive system of the *contratto alla voce*, a widespread usury system in the Kingdom of Naples to the advantage of the merchants that loaned capital.

33 Nicolini, 'Notizie storiche tratte dai giornali copiapolizze', ASBN, *Banco di S. Eligio; Banco di SS. Giacomo e Vittoria*.

34 From an account opened to a high aristocrat, Camillo Caracciolo, in the first half of the seventeenth century, it is revealed that he received a loan from his wife at an

interest between 8% and 10%, and to evade the ecclesiastical and civil laws he stipulated a contract in which he sold annual revenue on a part of his estate for a value equal to the amount borrowed (Fausto Nicolini, 'Le spese di un gran signore napoletano del Seicento', *Bollettino* of Archivo Storico del Banco di Napoli, vol. II (Naples, 1954), pp. 85–97).

35 On the topic, see Carmine Majello, *L'indebitamento bancario della nobilità napoletana nel primo periodo borbonico 1734–1806* (Naples, 1986).

36 Luigi De Rosa, *Studi sugli arrendamenti del Regno di Napoli* (Naples, 1958); Ilaria Zilli, *Carlo di Borbone e la rinascita del Regno di Napoli. Le finanze pubbliche 1734–1742* (Naples, 1990), pp. 110–15, 231–43; Ilaria Zilli, *Imposta diretta e debito pubblico nel Regno di Napoli 1669–1737* (Naples, 1990).

37 Bianchini, *Storia della finanze del regno delle due Sicilie*, p. 377.

38 This policy is confirmed in a report forwarded to Vienna in 1728 under Austrian domination. In this report the right which His Majesty had on the uninvested assets in the Neapolitan banks was underlined (HHStA, Neapel/Collectanea, fascio 46).

39 Avallone, *Stato e banchi pubblici a Napoli a metà del '700*, p. 85.

40 De Simone, *Il Banco della Pietà di Napoli*, pp. 91, 245, 289–91; Avallone, *Stato e Banchi pubblici a Napoli a metà del '700*, pp. 74–85.

41 ASBN/BPOV/AP, *Libro di conclusioni*, years 1622–6, m. 109, conclusions of 1/22/1623, 6/15/1625; *Libro di conclusioni*, years 1637–8, m. 113, conclusion of 2/25/1640; *Libro di conclusioni*, year 1659, m. 127, conclusion of 2/8/1659.

42 Unfortunately, except for some limited facts drawn from archival documents on the recurrence of the operation, it is not possible to quantify the amount of *fedi di credito* and *polizze* that circulated without preventive coverage.

43 There were overdrawn issues also when the advances to individuals or the Court were not tied to guarantees (Luigi De Rosa, 'Banchi pubblici, banchi privati e Monti di Pietà a Napoli nei secoli XVI–XVIII', *Banchi pubblici, banchi privati e Monti di Pietà nell' Europa preindustriale* (Genoa, 1991), p. 508).

44 Alessio De Sariis, *Codice delle leggi del Regno di Napoli* libro VIII (Naples, 1795), pp. 183–6; Rocco, *De' Banchi di Napoli e della loro ragione*, vol. I, p. 77; ASBN/BPOV/AP, *Atti diversi. Riflessioni per sostenere l'uso di prendere i riscontri dalli banchi di questa Capitale (anno 1762)*, years 1621–1774 m. 1046.

45 Victor Lunetti, *Politica mercantile* (Naples, 1630), pp. 36–40, 51–4.

46 Carlo Antonio Broggia. *De' tributi delle monete e del governo politico della sanità* (Naples, 1743). In this case we have consulted a reprint published in Milan in 1804 in the series *Scrittori classici italiani di economia politica*, parte antica, tomo V, pp. 264–306.

47 ASBN/BPOV/AP, *Stati del Banco e della Casa del Sacro Monte e Banco dei Poveri. Breve ma vera relazione dello stato del Banco e Monte dei Poveri nel Nome di Dio per tutto l'anno 1654*, m. 330.

48 Until 1594 these investments yielded up to 15%. But that year, with the Belmosto operation, the interest rates decreased to 7% and 6% (De Rosa, *Il Mezzogiorno spagnolo*, pp. 29, 71–88).

49 This is what happened during the Austrian domination (see Antonio Di Vittorio, *Gli Austriaci e il Regno di Napoli, 1707–1734. Le finanze publiche* (Naples, 1969)).

50 ASN, *Cassa di ammortizzazione. Copia di istrumenti per impieghi di capitali in prestiti del Banco del Salvatore*, years 1776–85, m. 689, ff. 30–7, 309–15; *Cassa di ammortizzazione. Volume di cautele diverse del Banco di S. Eligio*, years 1640–1803, m. 676, ff. 83–91; ASBN/BP/AP, *Libro di conclusioni*, years 1786–8, m. 275, conclusion of 11/24/1786, f. 9; conclusion of 3/30/1787, ff. 81–2; conclusion of 8/29/1788, ff. 352, 356; *Libro di*

conclusioni, years 1788–90, m. 276, conclusion of 8/5/1789, f. 134; ASBN/BPOV/ AP, *Libro di conclusioni*, years 1786–90, m. 151, conclusion of 4/23/1786, f. 64, conclusion of 12/7/1786, f. 131, conclusion of 3/23/1787, ff. 227–8.

51 Giuseppe Maria Galanti, *Della descrizione geografica e politica delle Due Sicilie* (Naples, 1788). In this case we have consulted a reprint edited by Franca Assante and Domenico Demarco (Naples, 1969), vol. II, p. 191.

5   Financial circuits in Spain: merchants and bankers, 1700–1914

Montserrat Gárate Ojanguren

Introduction

The two long centuries covered in this study see some fundamental changes in the workings of the Spanish banking system. Regarding the protagonists of the system, our period was to see the figure of the merchant who also attended to the financial needs of his immediate environment replaced by the great banking firms, constituted as limited companies. In the realm of capital, change was also substantial: family merchant houses and, exceptionally, joint-stock companies benefited from Spain's possession of colonies in America, from which they derived colonial goods and silver. Thus the merchants, the most dynamic economic agents of the time, either had monetary liquidity at their disposal or were to 'create', particularly during the eighteenth century, adequate means of payment – in spite of the absence of a national bank in Spain until 1782. Over the course of the nineteenth century, however, Spain was to see the consolidation of a banking system in which the capital of the new financial institutions, represented in the large number of shares and shareholders, could achieve levels far higher than during previous decades.

During the period under consideration, there were also important developments in the area of banking operations. Thus the banking houses inclined (and during the eighteenth century almost exclusively inclined) toward the financing of commerce would in the nineteenth century become interested in operations relating, for instance, to the financing of public debt, the railways and the purchase of real estate. With the appearance of new financial firms at the end of the nineteenth century, however, and above all during the first fifteen years of the twentieth, greater interest was to be shown by banking in the industrial sector.

Spain's relation to its colonies played an influential part in these changes. Because of the interest shown by many merchants in trans-atlantic trade, and because of the resources which were obtained from Spain's colonial possessions in America, the loss of the greater part of these colonies in the early years of the nineteenth century would give rise to serious problems in the financial sector in general and, more particularly, in the mobility of capital. But despite changes in the international economy and in the political situation in America, transfers of capital between America and Spain would continue throughout the nineteenth century. This is not to claim, however, that the forms of capital transfer remained unaffected. Some of the most active merchants who had been operating in America transferred capital and business to Europe, where some of them became bankers. And via these bankers, more familiar as they were with the mechanisms of capital transfer than any, it was possible to effect further flows of capital across the Atlantic. In the majority of cases, however, the economic destination of this capital indicates the general lack of interest in the process of industrialization of the metropolis (with capital leaving Cuba) or former metropolis (in the case of Mexico, Chile, Peru, etc.).

The transformation of merchants into 'merchant bankers', the expansion and decline of the banking houses, the appearance of issuing banks and the Bank of Spain's monopoly as a producer of bank notes during the last quarter of the nineteenth century are facts which make manifest the general changes undergone in the sector.

We should also note that the relationship between industrialization and the development of banking institutions, a theme which has been given attention by Rondo Cameron *et al.*,[1] can be understood in part by the nature of capital transfers from America to Europe and by the actions of those who from the various different financial centres of Europe were to influence the investment of those assets in different areas of the economy.

These are some of the issues which will be explored in the following paragraphs.

The banking situation in eighteenth-century Spain

The comparatively late appearance of a national bank in Spain had its consequences. The Banco Nacional de San Carlos, founded in Madrid in 1782,[2] was born a hundred years later than its counterpart in London, and even later if compared with that in Amsterdam. Lacking a banking entity providing an adequate means and system of payment, the merchants looked for and made use of whichever means they could in order to sustain the economy of the moment.

Interest in colonial trade during the eighteenth century is observable in the important increase in exchanges between metropolis and colonies. And whilst specie and colonial goods helped sustain the financial system of the metropolis, there was also a proliferation of other means which became necessary for the continuing development of economic relations between Spain and its colonies. Prominent among these means, beyond colonial goods and specie consignments, were bills of exchange and *libranzas* (orders of payment).

And in exchanges with the rest of Europe, it was the silver consignments and goods from the colonies, along with the bills of exchange, *libranzas* and promissory notes, which provided liquidity enough to cover Spain's chronic deficit in the balance of trade with – in the main – the countries of the Atlantic zone. In all of this, the merchants who were the protagonists of the financial system of the period had a fundamental role.

Means of payment and the protagonists of the eighteenth-century Hispanic financial system

Beyond cash, then, among the means of payment prominent for their utilization within the network of exchanges were bills of exchange, which were followed in importance by the *libranzas*. And at the end of the eighteenth century *vales reales* would also attain prominence, given their character of both public debt and means of payment, via the provision of greater liquidity to the system.

The bill of exchange was regularly used in eighteenth-century Hispanic commerce. Bills greatly facilitated compensations and the mobility of resources, whether the case was one of European exchange, exchange with America or exchange within the metropolis itself. The possibility of endorsement offered by this document meant that in practice it could be used as a habitual means of payment until its reaching maturity, the due date by which it must be cashed. During the second half of the eighteenth century it would have been normal for a bill to have been endorsed several times before reaching maturity.

The possibility of turning to bills payable in the European financial centres was of vital importance to those economic agents who had to negotiate the acquisition of goods and services in Europe. The regular purchase of European manufactured goods to be subsequently transported to the Spanish possessions in America gave rise to the need to make payments in Europe. The merchants involved in these transactions therefore looked for opportunities to obtain bills drawn on European financial centres as a useful means of settling debt abroad. What is more, maritime insurance for Hispanic transatlantic crossings was habitually contracted, throughout the eighteenth century, whether for the vessel or for the merchandise being transported, in France, Holland or England. Therefore, to make effective the payment of the premium the use of bills payable in Bordeaux, Paris, Amsterdam or London, for example, depending on the case, would facilitate the operation.

The economy of various Spanish port cities was stimulated by their enablement in 1765 and by the liberalization of direct mercantile commerce with America in 1778. This also accounts for the geographic polarization of certain operations conducted via bills which would be transacted through some of these ports. Thus the 1765 incorporation of Santander, for instance, as a port for direct trade with America, meant that given its geographical location with respect to Europe, this particular centre was the ideal place for the arrival of European merchandise: from here this merchandise would be incorporated into transatlantic traffic. Because it was usual, particularly during the last third of the eighteenth century, to turn to English insurance houses in order to insure voyages such as these, the merchant houses based in the port of Santander requested, in Spain, bills payable in European financial centres, principally London.

Furthermore, there were a large number of bills of exchange in the funds of the eighteenth-century joint-stock companies, such as we might consider the Compañía de Caracas or the Compañía de La Habana. During the 1770s and 80s, for example, bills accounted for over 90% of ready funds. In other words, the bill of exchange, because of the lack of other means of a liberatory character, had acquired the status of habitual means of payment in mercantile transactions.

In 1779, due to the war with England, the financial requirements of the *Hacienda Hispánica* made it necessary to issue public debt in the form of *vales reales*. Their bivalent character (titles bearing interest, and a means of payment with full liberatory power – although use here would be restricted to certain operations) brought about a great demand for these *vales reales* from diverse sections of society. And it was in part in order to realize payment of interest and the redemption of these titles that the National Bank of San Carlos was established in 1782. However, the appearance of the Bank of San Carlos, which also issued bank notes, did not force the disappearance of those who until then had been drawing bills and providing liquidity via diverse means of payment and compensation: that is, the merchant bankers or, simply, the 'bankers' of the time.

These agents were to be found at the nodes of mercantile exchange, that is, on the periphery. But by the mid-eighteenth century the presence of merchant bankers in Madrid had become common, for the Kingdom's capital, despite the undeniable importance of the ports enabled for commerce with America, was fast becoming the centre from which commerce was being directed. The establishment in Madrid, in 1752, of the main offices of the two most important joint-stock companies of the moment, the Guipuzcoana de Caracas and the Guipuzcoana de La Habana, which up until then were to be found in San Sebastián and Cuba respectively, attests to the Villa y Corte's hegemony in the economic world of the metropolis. And the establishment of the Bank of San Carlos in the capital would confirm Madrid's position as economic centre.

The redemption of *vales reales* by the Bank of San Carlos led to a flow of *vales reales* toward the banking houses installed in Madrid. The reasons were plain: when the merchants situated in Madrid or in the ports most active in exchange found themselves in debt to third parties they would *accept* – among other things – bills payable in Madrid by one of the 'bankers' there. In order to compensate the bankers of Madrid for the costs entailed in honouring the bills, they sent them *vales reales*, because these titles were easily disposed of in the city.

This role played by the *vales reales* due to their character as a means of payment attests to the importance of the Spanish economy's being able to count on liquidity for its development. This situation is best expressed in the fact that the *vales reales* attained much higher values than hard cash in the 'liquid' assets of the merchant companies. To a degree, the proliferation of the *vales reales* was to displace the bills of exchange

which up until then had been a significant presence in the funds
of merchant companies. In the 1790s, in the joint-stock companies
such as La Habana, *vales reales* accounted for over 70% of liquid
funds.

Another means which served as a support to Hispanic economic
operations during the eighteenth century was the *libranza*. Although
the *libranza* was not as important as the bill of exchange, their use
throughout the eighteenth century was common among merchants of a
certain type, who used them to settle payments as much within Spain
as between Spain, Europe and its colonies. Because their use was
straightforward and inexpensive, then, *libranzas* were to serve as a means
of payment, of shifting balances from one side of the Atlantic to the
other – in other words, to effect transfers and, moreover, to obtain
financial profit.

The first of the *libranza*'s functions (serving as a means of payment)
appears to have been the most usual. Purchases of colonial goods made
in America were settled with *libranzas* payable in Spain, this also being
common practice between Spain and Europe. And as with bills of
exchange, the possibility of endorsing *libranzas* gave this means
of payment an added advantage. The *libranza* was also used as a means
for providing loans, however. In this case differences in equivalencies
between simple pesos and strong pesos in America and the metropolis
constituted part of the gain: it was common for the advancement of
money in simple pesos in America or the metropolis, for instance, to be
later offset via the cancellation of a *libranza* in strong pesos.

Hard cash, of course, but above all it was bills, *libranzas*, *vales reales*
and bank notes – the latter limited to the Bank of San Carlos and
its environs – that constituted the means of payment for a growing
economy. The movement of these means between America, Spain and
Europe made possible capital flows and compensations. Although the
protagonists of these operations were above all people dedicated to
trade, some of these merchants were gradually beginning to specialize
in these tasks, becoming merchant bankers, facilitating giros and
the payment of bills for third parties. The foundation of the National
Bank of San Carlos before the end of the century did not diminish
the importance of these private 'bankers'. On the contrary, these
bankers were to serve as intermediaries between the Bank and the
merchants.

With the Bank of San Carlos itself relying on correspondents abroad,
then, the survival of the merchant bankers was assured. And these

foreign correspondents easily met the definition of 'bankers': that is, men interested in mercantile business who were able, through their connections, to obtain bills abroad or to honour their payments – such as was the case of the director of the 'Fermín de Tastet' house, the Bank of San Carlos's London correspondent at the end of the eighteenth century – and who relied on other merchant houses run by relations in financial centres strategically situated for exchange, such as San Sebastián, Bayonne, Bordeaux, and London.

The nineteenth century: colonial emancipation and the transfer of capital from Spanish America to Europe

The Hispanic colonial economy would in the nineteenth century see the colonies break away from the metropolis, the process which began at the turn of the century culminating with the loss of Cuba at the century's end. This lag between the movement for independence in the continental colonies and the independence of the Greater Antilles would also affect the forms in which capital leaving the Spanish colonies in America reached Europe, just as it would influence the way in which this capital would be invested.

In general terms, it is possible to distinguish two models of capital transfer between the Hispanic colonies and Europe: (a) sudden transfers of capital resulting from the rapidity of the independence process (this was the case with Mexican, Chilean and Peruvian capital, which leaves the colonies at critical moments in the process of emancipation, and which would continue to leave the colonies even after independence); (b) a slow, steady flow of capital resulting from the process of economic growth within the colony itself (such as was the case with Cuban capital which, prior to the arrival of independence, was during the course of the nineteenth century gradually diverted to several European financial centres). We might consider the protagonists involved in these transfers under the following two variants: (a) those who, possessing capital in America, decided to transfer that capital for reasons of security and profitability; (b) those who served to facilitate such operations. Yet another relevant aspect of these operations which requires consideration is the ultimate destination of this capital. That is, the ways in which this capital was invested.

Those protagonists facilitating the transfer and investment of capital can be understood as a surface manifestation of part of the network of

private banks or banking houses joining America, Europe and Spain –
even if, and without wishing to detract from the importance of this
figure of the private banker, the nineteenth century would see the
decline of their importance alongside the definitive establishment of a
new, modern banking system. For the transformations undergone in the
banking sector, especially in the second half of the nineteenth century,
were considerable. In 1856 legislation gave the legal go-ahead to issuing
banks; and from this point on, together with the merchant banks, new
banking firms with an issuing capacity would emerge. In 1874
new legislation determined that only the Bank of Spain was entitled to
issue bank notes. Before the close of the century, there would be
several novel banking initiatives, but, above all, it was a new era that
was commencing, and the Spanish banking sector would begin to
recognize the importance of investment in industry for the country's
development.

The transfer of Hispanic colonial capital to Europe during the nineteenth century

The emancipatory process in the Spanish colonies at the beginning of
the nineteenth century led to a drastic decline in business between
colony and former metropolis. In the face of a perceived threat to their
business on the part of those who until then had relied on trade with
Spain, it became necessary either to adapt whenever possible, or to seek
more secure forms of investment in Europe. This brought about an
important flow of capital from America to Europe. In those Spanish
colonies where the process of independence originated toward the
beginning of the nineteenth century, there were two basic stages of
capital outflow: (a) during the independence process itself; (b) following
the complete emancipation of the colony from Spain.

Bearing in mind the political upheavals the colonies were experiencing and, indeed, the political situation in Spain,[3] capital leaving the
colonies during the critical years of independence was forced to search
out suitable financial circuits. We can thus understand why capital
leaving Mexico during the first third of the nineteenth century was
directed toward French and British ports rather than to Spanish ones.
The most common ports of arrival during this first stage were
Bordeaux in France, and Liverpool and London in England; and from
these ports, the destinations of these assets were various: some consignments would continue their journey on to Paris or London, places where

there were profit-generating opportunities, whilst others would await transfer to Spain. Following this initial stage, approaching the 1840s, there was another, second flow of capital out of the old Spanish colonies. In this instance the capital originated mainly in the liquidation of patrimony by the owners of real estate in America who had moved to, or secured residence in, Europe.

The flows of Cuban capital to Europe, on the other hand, behaved differently. Because Cuba's emancipation from Spain did not arrive until the end of the century, Cuban capital was able gradually to seep into Europe throughout the nineteenth century. In the case of Cuba it was not the political situation which led to the search for 'refuge' for this capital: rather, these flows of capital were the product of Cuban business. By the forms and intensity with which Cuban capital was shifted to Europe during the nineteenth century, it is possible to distinguish three separate stages: (1) capital transfers between the end of the eighteenth century and the end of the first third of the nineteenth century; (2) the period 1839 to 1863; (3) from 1868 until the last years of the century.[4]

The first of these stages corresponds to the years in which the metropolis found itself immersed in problems of war and political instability. These circumstances meant that those involved in the sugar trade, whether owners of the sugar mills or merchants, were to direct their surplus produce to other European or to North American destinations, where the sale of the product led to surpluses which were reinvested in the growth of the business – the purchase of ships, machinery, and so on – or in real estate outside Cuba.

The second stage (1839–68) corresponds to the expansion of the sugar market. According to Bahamonde,[5] Great Britain became the main recipient of Cuban capital because at the time it was an important centre in the sugar trade. And again, just as with the old Spanish colonies on the American continent, part of the capital flowing from Cuba into Europe was linked to the liquidation of patrimony. During this second stage, then, capital flows were directed by a variety of means to Great Britain, France and on a smaller scale to Spain.[6]

The final stage, the years between 1868 and Cuban independence, saw a high flow of Cuban capital to the most important European cities. In London, Paris or Madrid, this capital encountered many different types of investment opportunity, among them mercantile commerce and industry, investment in real estate, investment in banks and investment in public debt.

*From transatlantic merchants in the Spanish colonies in America to
bankers in Europe*

There are certain paradigmatic cases among the protagonists of these
operations of capital transfer. Some of those who had been effective
in the development of mercantile business in the Spanish colonies in
America chose to transfer their capital to Europe. But once in Europe
they became merchant bankers or – later – simply 'bankers'. From their
establishment as private bankers in Paris, Bordeaux or London, they
were able to facilitate new capital transfers and to function as intermediaries in investment in different areas of the economy. And these
bankers formed part of the banking network joining Spain to other
European financial centres.

   The most representative examples of these bankers were
'Aguirrebengoa and Uribarren' in France, and 'Mildred and Goyenche'
and 'Murrieta and Company' in London. In each of these cases we find
common characteristics: (a) their 'primitive accumulation' of capital
originates in merchant business related to the Spanish colonies in
America; (b) with the processes of independence they each transfer their
business to Paris or London and recentre their operations in banking
activity; (c) they were all, at some point during the nineteenth century,
correspondents of the Bank of Spain; (d) they were barely able to see out
the nineteenth century as bankers, for they were eventually forced to
yield in the face of the appearance of the great banking firms constituted
as limited companies.

   The history of the Aguirrebengoa bank clearly responds to these
characteristics. For the first years of the nineteenth century, the founder
of what would become the Aguirrebengoa banking house had already
accumulated a significant quantity of capital in Mexico through transatlantic exchange. His mercantile activity, begun in viceroyal Mexico
toward the end of the eighteenth century, had accustomed him to the
modes of payment, of monetary transference and of compensation
of the time. As well as making use of bills of exchange, *libranzas* and
promissory notes, the Aguirrebengoa house transferred capital to the
metropolis via the straightforward shipping of colonial goods whose sale
in the metropolis would guarantee there a certain amount of hard cash.

   Already in Mexico in 1819 the Aguirrebengoa merchant house began
to suffer the negative effects of political upheaval in the metropolis and
of the turmoil to come in Mexico. As a result, they decided to transfer
their assets and business to France, choosing the port of Bordeaux as

the place to continue their economic activity in Europe during the 1830s. But having established a merchant house in this French city, they wisely established their head office in Paris, where they directed their business toward the banking sector (alongside the Parisian banking house and under the trade name 'Aguirrebengoa fils et Uribarren'[7] they do, nevertheless, set up a banking house devoted exclusively to mercantile business). Their establishment in the financial centre of Bordeaux meant that they could realize transatlantic capital transfers with greater ease; whilst from their banking house in Paris they were able to invest their clients' capital in diverse sectors.

The Aguirrebengoa bank maintained regular relations with banking houses in Spain. Prominent among these banking houses for the sheer volume of operations carried out was the 'Miqueletorena hermanos' banking house established in Madrid.[8] The Aguirrebengoas were also connected to various parallel firms established in London. The importance of London as a financial centre, not only within Great Britain but from an international perspective,[9] must not be forgotten. The correspondence between the Aguirrebengoas and London bankers, particularly with the Murrieta banking house, was frequent; and these and other connections helped the Aguirrebengoas provide their clients with a more complete banking service. As Paris bankers, throughout their history they were the correspondents in the French capital of the Bank of San Fernando, successor to the Bank of San Carlos, and later the Bank of Spain. During the second half of the nineteenth century they shared this position with the Rothschild bank. Both banks supplied the Bank of Spain with consignments of specie of mainly Mexican origin, whilst they also served to support other operations with French financing firms, such as the harnessing of resources to finance the Spanish public debt, investment in Spanish railway business, and, on a lesser scale, investment in other forms of industrial activity being initiated in Spain around the middle of the nineteenth century.

If, however, we attempt an outline of the operations and investments which were carried out by the Aguirrebengoa banking house with respect to capital originating in the colonies, we find the following: (a) more than 75% of the capital invested on behalf of third parties was invested in the Spanish public debt; (b) this was followed, in terms of volume, by investment in the French public debt; (c) the majority of the bank's clients and its clients' capital came from Mexico and Cuba; (d) those who invested in public debt through the Aguirrebengoa bank were rentiers resident in Paris – the majority of them women – which only confirms the interest in a 'refuge' investment at a low but relatively risk-free profit.

Furthermore, if we look at the agents – bankers too – with whom the Aguirrebengoas maintained relations, whether in Cuba, Great Britain or Spain, we observe that they tended in the main, to be correspondents of the Bank of Spain – just as, as we have seen, were the Aguirrebengoas themselves. In London the best protectors of the Aguirrebengoa business were the Murrietas, whilst in Havana it was Francisco de Goyri (also a Bank of Spain correspondent) who would help manage Aguirrebengoa affairs. This was a pattern which was repeated when the Aguirrebengoas were granted proxy in San Sebastián, Bilbao and other Spanish provincial capitals.

The operations carried out by this bank on its own behalf are also illustrative. The Aguirrebengoa banking house and its successors had an interest in the Banco de Fomento y Ultramar, in which they were stockholders; they provided many loans in Cuba, whose repayment was guaranteed with sugar mills; they also lent to the governments of Spain and the Dominican Republic; they were founding members of the Crédito Mobilario Español; and they were involved in the Spanish railway construction enterprise, specifically lending a large sum for the Tudela–Bilbao stretch of line. However, in all these operations an interest in industrial investment is barely perceptible. There appears to have been some investment only in the emerging industry of Biscay toward the end of the 1840s.[10] Countering this lack of interest, then, we find them securing their fortune with the possession of real estate in their country of origin.

In the second half of the nineteenth century mercantile activity – which had characterized and had been the origin of their fortune – was terminated because it had become an entirely secondary interest. Involvement in the ownership of certain trading vessels was reduced in favour of other investments of a 'financial' type. It is perhaps because of these types of investment that the original Aguirrebengoa bank, at the end of the century called 'Abaroa and Goguel', was unable to survive beyond 1903. There was also the fact that the changes that had come about in the international and the Spanish banking systems made the dynamics of the private banker somewhat anachronistic. In 1903 a bankrupt Abaroa and Goguel bank was forced to close its doors.

Turning our attention back to London, like Paris a financial centre of the highest order during the nineteenth century, and ever-increasing in importance over time, we find two other banking houses with a deal in common with the Parisian Aguirrebengoas: 'Cristóbal de Murrieta and Company' and 'Mildred & Goyenche'.

The Murrieta house was already established in London during the first third of the nineteenth century. Of Basque origin, Murrieta business had developed around American commerce. The expansion of this bank follows the model of the merchant who establishes a network of factors and commissioners at different strategic locations, Bilbao, Cádiz, Buenos Aires, Havana and London being some of the commercial centres where the Murrietas kept family members to make their operations effective. With a fairly solid capital base, and from their house in London, the Murrietas began to move around the world of merchant banking, serving, like the Aguirrebengoas, as intermediaries in processes of capital shipment and in operations related to America. At moments of difficulty for colonial capital – particularly at the height of the independence conflict – the Murrietas continued receiving capital (if not actual goods), going on to invest this capital according to the wishes of its respective owners. They also offered their clients financial services in the realization of payments, transferences and compensations in the various European financial centres. For their operations in Europe, they could rely on Aguirrebengoa and Uribarren of Paris, or on the 'Miqueletorena hermanos' of Madrid. Their knowledge of opportunities for investment in Great Britain, France or Spain, whether direct or through their business correspondents, placed them in an advantageous position regarding services to their clients.

The Murrietas do not stray significantly from the model outlined for the Aguirrebengoa bank. Like the Aguirrebengoas the Murrieta banking house was a London correspondent of the Bank of Spain, sharing this position with the Rothschild bank and with the Mildred & Goyenche house. But with the development of the great banking firms in Great Britain, particularly during the last quarter of the nineteenth century, the Murrieta bank was no longer able to compete. Dragged down by the crash of the Barings bank, the Murrieta house went bankrupt during the first years of the 1890s.

Merchant bankers and issuing banks in nineteenth-century Spain

The changes, from the perspective of the international economy, which came about during the last quarter of the nineteenth century also had repercussions in the Spanish banking sector. The Bank of San Carlos, founded in the eighteenth century, was succeeded in 1829 by the Bank of San Fernando. Mobilized for reasons of public finance, the Bank of San Fernando was not exactly the best ally for the country's mercantile operations, and even less so for the country's industrialization. With the particular prosperity of the Spanish economy in 1855, it was the most active economic groups situated on the periphery that were to demand a banking law enabling the creation of financial institutions capable of meeting the needs that had arisen. Thus, under the protection of the 1856 law, the green light was given to the creation of issuing banks, along with the regularization of the creation of credit societies.

The response to the new legislation was swift. That same year steps were taken toward starting up various provincial issuing banks. Within a few years banks were established in cities such as Málaga, Seville, Bilbao, Valladolid and San Sebastián. And where credit societies are concerned, a mere ten years saw the foundation of no less than thirty-five. Those who held stock in the new banks came, not surprisingly, from the merchant sector. However, some of those who became involved in the newly founded banking firms had maintained their own banking houses, and their ascription to these new 'modern' banking firms did not lead them to abandon their banking business in the form that they had been developing until then. Also, the Bank of San Fernando itself, having become the Bank of Spain in 1856, maintained its foreign correspondents in just the same way as before, relying, that is, on merchant bankers.

But the changes in the nineteenth-century Spanish banking system would go still further. Banking legislation, of necessity preceding its effects, took an important step following the Decree of 1874 (Law of 17 July 1876).[11] From this point onwards the Bank of Spain was granted sole issuing privilege, which meant that the different banks which had appeared under the normative of 1856 lost their issuing capacity. These new legislative changes were not, however, followed by the creation of new financial firms. On the contrary, only the Banco Hispano Colonial was created in 1876, and was at first tied more to financing the Cuban war than to financing Spain's business. In addition, the banks' general lack of interest in the industrial sector continued unabated in the last decades of the nineteenth century. Nor had the banking houses situated in Europe which were of 'Hispanic-American' origin shown any signs of increasing interest in Spanish industrial development. Investments made on their own behalf or on behalf of their clients, as far as one can tell, were mainly directed toward the financing of public debt, and to a lesser degree toward rail-related business. The very concentration around Madrid – where the development of the industrial sector was very weak – of capital tied to the banking and credit institutions, as Gabriel Tortella has argued,[12] makes manifest the lack of significant relationship between industry and the financial sector.

Qualitative changes on the eve of the First World War

Nevertheless, the beginning of the twentieth century was going to see an increase in the appearance of new financial firms, along with a widening of their economic interests. The year 1899 saw the creation of the Banco Guipuzcoano, which developed significantly during the early years of the twentieth century; in 1900 the Banco Hispano-Americano was set up in Madrid; 1901 also saw the creation of the Banco de Vizcaya and the Crédito de la Unión Minera; the following year the Banco Español de Crédito was founded; and these were followed by (among others) the Banco Mercantil, the Banco de Oviedo, and the Banco de San Sebastián.

Moreover, alongside the appearance of these financial firms, with capital much greater than that of the family banking houses which had coexisted with banks in the nineteenth century, Spain witnessed the penetration of foreign financial firms. The growth of the industrial sector began to run parallel to that of the banking sector, banks demonstrating a much greater interest in industry. The Spanish economy experienced a phase of growth on a much more solid footing than during previous years. Merchant banking houses of the family type had to yield in the face of these developments, but not before having played their part in the development of the Spanish economy, whose modernization took a long time.

Conclusion

Economic growth during the eighteenth century was favoured in Spain by the increase in exchanges with America. While the colonies provided the metropolis with specie and goods, the metropolis had to purchase European products and services for the provision of the colonies. These processes necessitated an adequate system of means of payment, on the one hand, and on the other, economic agents to facilitate compensations, debt cancellation and transferences. Lacking an issuing bank and adequate liquidity, the merchants made use of whichever means of payment were available to them, getting the most out of bills of exchange, *libranzas*, and the *vales reales*. With these means they were able to transfer payments between Europe and America, to provide loans and to settle balances.

The creation of the Bank of San Carlos in 1782 did not diminish the importance of those who from Santander, Cádiz, or, particularly, Madrid, devoted themselves to both mercantile negotiations and financial operations. Before the eighteenth century was over, it is possible to observe in Madrid a healthy number of merchant bankers who facilitated the extinguishment of bills, the provision of loans and so on.

The loss of the major part of Spanish possessions in America during the nineteenth century led to flows of capital from America to Europe larger than those of previous periods. Some of those who had made their fortunes in mercantile operations in the colonies not only transferred their capital to Europe, but once themselves in Europe and relocated in one of the important financial centres (such as Paris, Bordeaux or London) founded banking houses in order to collaborate in the further flows of capital across the Atlantic. As 'bankers' in Europe they offered various services to their clients, among them the investment of capital.

Relations between these 'bankers', knowledgeable about mercantile business between America and Europe, and other bankers situated in the different financial centres of Europe and America, facilitated their operations and effectiveness. They were thus able to realize financial transactions such as compensations, payments and investments. Their position as correspondents of the Bank of Spain (in some cases) seems to have narrowed the relationship between investment and the needs of public finance. It is perhaps for this reason that the investments recommended to their clients by these banks or, indeed, which were requested by these clients, tended to be related mainly to the financing of the Spanish public debt rather than to the promotion of industry.

At the same time as these family banking houses were developing their operations, both in and beyond Spain, Spanish banking legislation underwent important transformations. Most significantly, the law of 1856 made possible the creation of issuing banks, whilst in 1874 the Bank of Spain was constituted as the sole issuing bank. However, the attitude of the banking sector toward the industrial development of the country did not change. It was only at the beginning of the twentieth century that the consolidation in Spain of a strong and dynamic banking system led to an increased interest in industrial development. Inevitably, in the face of this new situation, the bankers or banks of the family type virtually disappeared. Some of them were unable to compete with the new banks; others joined their wealth to the assets of the modern banks to become stockholders among others; and if some banking houses were in fact able to survive beyond 1900, their business activities were certainly no longer comparable to those of earlier times – for the new-look modern bank required greater, and more stable, capital.

Notes

This paper is part of the research project 'Historia de la banca (I). Formación de entidades financieras en el País Vasco: de las casas banca a los banco emisores', supported by the University of the Basque Country. UPV 230.251–HA 067/92.

1 R. Cameron *et al.*, *La Banca en las primeras etapas de la industrialización* (Madrid, 1974).

2 See the important work by Pedro Tedde, *El Banco de San Carlos* (Madrid, 1988).

3 The Mexican independence movement almost coincides with a change in the political system in Spain. In 1820 there was a shift from absolutism to a constitutional system which lasted barely three years. Such changes were not at all beneficial to the economic process. In addition, in 1833 another period of political conflict began with the Carlist war.

4 In the recent work by Angel Bahamonde and José Cayuela, *Hacer las Américas. Las élites coloniales españolas en el siglo XIX* (Madrid, 1992), the authors distinguish, in the nineteenth century, two periods: from 1836 to 1868, and from 1868 on. They also explain the links between outflows of Cuban capital and the type of investment for which this capital was destined.

5 *Ibid.*, pp. 60–2.

6 Germany, Belgium and Holland also received Cuban capital, as Bahamonde and Cayuela state: *ibid.*, p. 64. Nevertheless, residence of 'proprietors of independent means' – as they were to describe themselves – coming from Cuba was far greater in London and in Paris than in other European capitals.

7 The early Aguirrebengoa and Uribarren banking house changed its name, for obvious reasons, to J. J. Uribarren and then to Uribarren and Abaroa. And at the end of the twentieth century, a new partner in the person of the banker Goguel joined the house, which then came to be called Abaroa and Goguel.

8 The origin of this banking house, also in overseas mercantile business, dates to the eighteenth century. The bank's involvement in companies such as the Real Compañía de Caracas only confirms their interest in transatlantic trade.

9 G. Tortella *et al.*, *Una Historia de los Bancos Central e Hispanoamericano, 1901–1991. Noventa años de gran banca en España* (Madrid, 1994), pp. 6–7.

10 Such as involvement in the blast furnaces of Santa Ana in Bolueta (Biscay).

11 Tortella *et al.*, *Una Historia de los Bancos Central e Hispanoamericano*, pp. 14–15.

12 G. Tortella, *Los orígenes del capitalismo en España*, 1st edn (Madrid, 1973).

PART TWO

The banks' influence in leading industrial economies

6 Banking and the evolution of the British economy, 1694–1878

H. V. Bowen and P. L. Cottrell

Historians concerned with Britain's economic development during the eighteenth and early nineteenth centuries have predominantly placed the emergence of the banking system within a broad context constituted by the various processes associated with industrialization. Such an approach is hardly surprising since it addresses some of the major questions which stem from Britain's transformation as the 'first industrial nation'. The arising investigations have largely taken as their premises the approach to, and chronology of, the *classic* 'Industrial Revolution' – a 'spurt' or 'take-off' between *c.* 1760/80 and 1830/40. This periodization coincides precisely with the decades when various formal financial institutions, particularly 'country' banks, began to be established in some numbers. Furthermore, during these very decades the financial 'system' in general began to facilitate the more widespread deployment and diffusion of resources throughout the economy. With such a seemingly clear-cut chronological correlation between the two developments – real and financial – it was only natural that there should have been scholarly attempts to establish connections between the emergence of 'modern' banking on the one hand and the initial stages of industrialization on the other.

Such studies have tried to identify where, and precisely how, the nascent financial sector acted as an agent of change for an economy that was undergoing a structural transformation. These scholarly endeavours achieved notable successes, as in the 1950s when firm links were demonstrated, above all by Pressnell, between the rise of country banking and the growth (involving the further structural development) of mining, metallurgy and textiles between 1770 and 1820. His work found that many late eighteenth-century bankers had industrial origins and that many industrial entrepreneurs borrowed from banks in which they were partners.[1] Yet even Pressnell, who titled his magnificent, seminal work *Country Banking in the Industrial Revolution*, was forced to concede that the available evidence failed to provide firm links between the manufacturing and extractive sectors of industry and *non-industrial* banks. So much was this the case that generally 'the picture between banking and industry is inevitably impressionistic'.[2]

Pressnell's prudent caution has been reflected, to varying degrees, in the subsequent work of other financial historians. In the 1960s, for example, Cameron, who was seeking to revise the generally received view that capital accumulation had 'little to do with banking',[3] saw the pattern of financial intermediation mirroring that of the process of industrialization. He pointed to the burgeoning number of banks coinciding with the classic 'take-off' period of 1780 to 1800/30. This linked chronology, he argued, was a significant marker 'bearing on the relationship between banking and industrialisation'. However, and like Pressnell, he found that an important qualification had to be made – that this parallelism was, ultimately, only powerful 'circumstantial evidence' relating to any connection between the two.[4] In time, further case-studies of *non-industrial* banking firms may well transform this into a solid foundation, but now, some thirty years later, consideration of the role of banking in the process of industrial development before *c.* 1820/30 remains largely where Pressnell and Cameron left it.

Few first generation 'modern' bankers seem, from the surviving documentary evidence, to have been prepared to invest in any industrial activity, other than their own.[5] Moreover, the English legal code prevented the establishment of banks with more than six partners and this meant that, substantially, the initial importance of 'modern' banking to industry did not arise from the facilitation of fixed capital investment. Of greater significance was the extension of (renewable) credit in the form of working capital or other short-term finance, which was used to supplement the reinvestment of profits by successful entrepreneurs.[6] Although there are indications that banks were willing formally to 'lend long' to established manufacturing and extractive enterprises, they seldom provided the initial capital of new industrial projects.[7]

The work of historians such as Pressnell and Cameron was set firmly within chronological and methodological parameters defined by what they, as economic historians, saw as the prevailing industrial spirit of the age with which they were concerned. In common with many others, these scholars freely used the words 'industry', 'industrial revolution', and 'industrialization' in the titles of books and chapters relating to economic activity in Britain between 1750 and 1850. Although they have undoubtedly been successful in establishing important connections between banking and industry, their scholarly writings are often notable for the amount of consideration devoted to banking in *non-industrial* contexts. Of course, this is a reflection of the fact that British industrialization was a multi-faceted and interactive process, encompassing much more than just manufacturing and mining, activities which have often received a disproportionate amount of attention from scholars. However, it also serves as a useful reminder that the development of banking in Britain ought not to be examined in chronological contexts that arise, somewhat teleologically, solely with the emergence of the first industrial nation in mind. This is particularly important, as in recent years historians have been busy redrawing the temporal and quantitative contours of British economic development between 1700 and 1850.

Revised figures for the growth of national product and productivity suggest that industrialization was not the rapid and dramatic process which the past use of the word 'revolution' implied. Rather, in overall terms, growth was slower than once thought – to the extent that it is now argued that industrial production per head began to accelerate only from the 1810s/20s.[8] Indeed, some historians have seized upon the quantitative research of Crafts, Harley and others in attempts to dispatch even the *concept* of the 'industrial revolution' to the historical dustbin.[9] This iconoclastic interpretation has, not surprisingly, provoked a fierce controversy in which the 'industrial revolution' has been vigorously defended. Such counter-revisionists have maintained that, regardless of 'national' growth rates based upon tentative estimates and often incomplete data,[10] all-round change was dramatic enough to transform the economy and society of Britain in numerous and markedly different ways.[11]

This is not the place to debate the merits of various interpretations of the process of British industrialization, but it should be stressed that, rightly or wrongly, the 'Industrial Revolution' is far from being the immovable landmark in British history that it was two or three decades ago. This prompts the need for a reassessment of where banking stands in relation to a process which many now characterize as historical development and change based upon evolution, diversity and regionalism. If industrialization is seen as having few 'national' features, then, inevitably, questions arise over the extent to which banks possessing different various functional forms belonged to any 'system' which might similarly be considered to have been countrywide. For, as Mathias has pointed out, there was no national capital market in Britain, and the market(s) that emerged contained many institutional imperfections and weaknesses.[12] Yet, historians often refer to a 'banking system', as if an ordered and well-established institution with fully interacting components had come into existence over the second half of the eighteenth century.

British banking activities during the eighteenth century almost defy placement in any 'system', even after 1750 when the market growth of formal country banking occurred. There are a number of reasons for this. First, throughout the eighteenth century many of those individuals who performed recognizable banking functions neither called themselves bankers nor restricted themselves to specialist financial activities. Instead they operated generally as agents, attorneys, brokers and correspondents within the broad and rapidly growing financial service sector. Equally, they moved freely and easily between quite different types of financial and commercial activity.[13] Second, in some spatial regions of the economy the emergence of formal banking institutions was retarded by the existence of an enterprise culture in which influential groups of wealthy individuals performed quasi-banking functions. This was particularly the case in the north-west, where, until the 1790s, many merchants engaged in banking activities.[14] Not only did this limit the scope for the formal development of banks in that region, but it also meant that this area generally did not develop strong ties with London and, hence, it was not formally integrated into the emerging national credit structure.[15] Third, even banks grouped by historians under descriptive titles which imply the existence of broad generic types were often quite different from one another. For example, the institutions known collectively as the London 'private' banks individually experienced quite different lines of development during the eighteenth century. The 'West End banks', despite some links with commerce, dealt increasingly with the requirements of the landed elite, whereas the banks of Lombard Street in the City concentrated on servicing the needs of the capital's mercantile community.[16] Similarly, those grouped under the broad heading of 'country banks' often had little in common with one another, apart from the fact that they were located at some distance from the metropolis. Their customers, and the functions that each bank performed, were quite different, depending largely on the form of economic activity engaged in by the local community. Williams, Davies & Co. of Aberystwyth were located firmly within a Welsh-speaking rural community and can not be readily placed alongside the likes of Gurney & Co. of Norwich, a bank which developed a wide range of regional business interests together with close links to the London money market.[17] This may be an extreme contrast, but, nonetheless, it points up the problem of aggregation, which may, in turn, imply a shared experience of 'country banking'. Such examples draw attention to extraordinary diversity within domestic banking even before consideration is given to the various types of Scottish banking institutions, both public and private, which operated in a socio-legal context that was quite different from that prevailing to the south of the border.[18]

In short, now that there is no longer any need to force the study of banking into the temporal and conceptual strait-jacket imposed by the 'classic Industrial Revolution', the position of banks, bankers and quasi-bankers within the coalescing 'national' economy can perhaps be more comfortably accommodated within a different context. This would recognize the existence of broad forms of industrial and non-industrial financial enterprise and different local or regional settings. Of course, the emphasis must not be shifted too far in favour of diversity as some unity of purpose and function existed between various types of banks, if only because in practice many of them proved in the last resort to be heavily dependent upon connections with the metropolitan economy and its society. The outbreak of crisis often pointed up the implicit financial relations within the economy.[19] It was particularly during times of panic that the 'country banks' had little choice other than to try and make use of the disproportionately sizeable resources, established institutions and well-developed skills of England's capital. It was this, at least in hindsight, which served increasingly to give at least some sense of form, order and coherence to *British* banking.

If the issues outlined above are not sufficient to prompt a reconsideration of the relationship between banks and economic change in

Britain, then it should be recognized that the whole question of the historical context in which banking should be located during the eighteenth century has equally been a matter for debate in recent years. This has arisen from the way in which historians have reassessed the overall position of industry within both broad economic development and the various processes which contributed to British state and empire building. In particular the debate about the timing and form of industrialization has made it difficult for straightforward connections to be made between the growth of industry and the building of an empire. As a result, the emphasis has increasingly shifted away from analysis of, and thereby a stress upon, industrialization as an engine for expansion overseas towards interpretations which grant a central role to finance and the development of the service sector.

Cain and Hopkins, in particular, have drawn attention to the way in which the City acted as a channel for investments into the wider world. They have defined a 'gentlemanly capitalist' form of enterprise which drew landowners, merchants and monied men together in a powerful political and socio-economic alliance of mutual benefit.[20] This amalgam not only left its imprint on the British presence overseas, but also it helped to create the economic environment shaping domestic banking developments. Their approach, *pace* the protests it has drawn from imperial historians who argue that metropolitan factors have been granted far too much importance, does serve as a reminder that the growth of banking was prompted not simply by the needs of an industrializing nation, but also by the rising volume of *various* transactions within all sectors of economic activity. The individuals concerned, who often held very broad portfolios of assets, were drawn from right across the middling and elite sections of society. Moreover, gentlemanly capitalists were not only passive customers of banks but also the promoters of banks, and this enabled them to facilitate transactions, develop credit mechanisms and establish investment links with both the metropolis and overseas commercial ventures.

Although, unlike most developments elsewhere in Europe, English-style formal banking during its nascent phases was tied to the world of domestic rather than foreign trade,[21] by the eighteenth century many British overseas merchants were nonetheless diversifying into a wide range of banking activities. In England, merchants, in some numbers, moved comfortably between the closely related worlds of trade and finance[22] and there was a similar relationship within Scottish commerce. For example, the Glasgow business elite developed a broad range of economic interests, including private banking, as demonstrated during the mid-eighteenth century when the Ship, Arms and Thistle banks were established by members of this city's tobacco merchant community.[23] Moreover, the landed interest was not above, or aloof from, such activities and there are many examples of country gentlemen moving with enthusiasm and vigour, if not expertise and success, into banking and related activities. In sum, formal banking grew as a cornerstone of the gentlemanly order which by no means excluded industrial activity but which regarded it as only a part of a broad inter-related series of economic activities.

While the growth of empire was the outward manifestation of British success in mobilizing and deploying financial resources on an increasingly global scale during the eighteenth century, the empire was, of course, built upon a state which had secure administrative and institutional foundations. Here, too, in this process of state building, banking played a central role. In recent years historians have devoted considerable attention to the financial arrangements which attended the creation of what has been called the 'fiscal-military' state. They have drawn attention to the importance of the national debt and the taxation system in allowing Britain to come to terms with a century punctuated by wars and crises.[24] At the heart of the financial 'revolution' stood the Bank of England which emerged as the central institution in the management of state finance.

The Bank of England acted as the key mechanism through which loan finance was made available to hard-pressed governments and it increasingly acted in practical and administrative terms as the supervisor of the national debt. This role was in itself of the greatest importance, but, equally, the nature of the relationship between the state and the Bank was such that the Bank became much more than simply the banker to the state. The general framework of its operations, developed by trial and error after 1694, allowed it to become a powerful private commercial organization through business activities encompassing bullion purchases, note issuing, and discounting strategies.[25] By the mid-eighteenth century the resources, credit and stability of the Bank were such that it had also become the institutional heart of the City and it was soon to be able to start acting as lender of last resort.[26] The Bank's position was protected by statute, which prevented the establishment of rivals with more than six partners. Yet, despite this effective monopoly and its commercial strength and 'mercantile credit', the Bank of England played a limited direct role shaping economic activity in the nation at large. There were a number of broad reasons for this.

First, because of the way in which financial institutions developed within a constitutional and statutory context, English banking was, in effect, state-driven. The needs of the state were of paramount importance; hence, the Bank of England was developed and protected by a state which had become financially dependent upon it. This meant that, provided the state's interests were not threatened in any way, private banks were, by and large, able to go their own way and develop commercial activities as they wished. This meant that the 'commercial revolution' that occurred after 1650 was accompanied by, and dependent upon, a growth of banking institutions of all sorts. Second, as is well known, within its own commercial context of private business operations, the Bank remained to all intents and purposes the Bank of London. The strength and diversity of the metropolitan economy was such that the Bank (and, it should be said, many private London bankers) had ready, uncomplicated access to all business demands that could be met without having to deal with unfamiliar people in far-away places. There was no market pressure for the Bank to look elsewhere to support its profit-making activities and this circumstance goes a long way to explain why the Bank refused, implicitly or explicitly, to move into the realm of branch banking. Finally, the Bank stuck rigidly with the type of business and the type of businessmen its directors and officials knew best. Forays into new areas of activity were rare and the Bank remained an institution devoted to servicing the credit needs of the capital's close-knit elite merchant community. Mortgages, individual loans and assistance for industrial activity were rare and became increasingly so as the century unfolded.

With the boundaries of the Bank's operations and private business so tightly drawn, it is not surprising that the number of banks in the provinces and Scotland grew significantly after 1750. Equally, their numbers increased sharply after 1797 when cash payments were suspended by the Bank and new note issuing institutions arose to assist with the circulation of paper currency as gold became increasingly scarce. In this context, it might be argued that the growth of provincial banks was not so much stimulated simply by the need to meet local commercial and industrial requirements, but rather it was also to fill the gap that the Bank of England, or the Mint, could not, or resolutely would not, fill.[27]

In seeking an approach that frees the study of British banking from undue concentration upon the financial servicing of manufacturing's structural transformation, it may seem incongruous to narrow the focus of this discussion and review. However, banking history during the three-quarters of a century after Waterloo has often been analysed in terms of reaction to instability, a characteristic made plain by the frequency of crisis. The pattern of crises experienced by the economy and its financial sector is so clearly marked that it cannot be ignored. Sayers has rightly called that challenging sequence – the panics of 1825/6,[28] 1836, 1839,[29] 1847,[30] 1857, 1866[31] and 1878 – the punctuation of the nineteenth century. Contemporaries wrestled with analysing the causes of these maelstroms which greatly disturbed the economy's material progress, ultimately leading to the formulation of theories of the 'trade cycle',[32] while the state was confronted with an all-too evident problem of financial instability, which it attempted to meet by legislative cures.

The crisis of 1825/6 has frequently been taken as a convenient historical divide in British banking development. The state's reaction consisted of legislation, which both permitted the development of what has come to be called commercial joint-stock banking and facilitated the establishment of the Bank of England's provincial branches. A major feature of the crisis was a collapse of private banking, *both* metropolitan and provincial. Readily available data sources only present an indication of the extent of the apparent fragility of country banking since 'Commissions of Bankrupt' exclude London banks. In the provinces at least eighty banks closed their doors during 1825 and 1826. Yet, for many of these institutions this proved to be only a temporary embarrassment and, subsequently, they met their liabilities in full and resumed business.[33] However, it was the apparent prostration of country private banking which finally persuaded the Commons to lift the legal prohibition on the number of partners constituting an English banking company and tempered, albeit temporarily, the opposition of the Bank of England to the wider development of joint-stock banking.

A broader chronological perspective – from 1740 to 1840 – reveals a somewhat different pattern of banking development. Provincial banking before 1826 can, in many respects, be regarded as a child of the *classic* Industrial Revolution *and* the Napoleonic Wars. It was a lineage in which one overriding factor was reinforced – the poor state of the circulation. The further rise of a market economy from the 1740s called for money – bank notes – and the particular inflationary environment after 1793, but especially between 1808 and 1814, only augmented this demand. The extent of the problem of circulating media is further pointed up by industrialists' issues of trade tokens, the wartime acceptance of overstamped Spanish silver dollars (following an earlier circulation of Iberian coin in the West Country), and the import of French coin during the mid-1810s. These difficulties with the circulation are mirrored in the very number of provincial banking companies formed. Quantitatively, as measured by licences issued from 1808, when this series becomes available (but not unfortunately by balance sheet data), private country banking peaked in 1814 and then secularly declined as prices fell and the foreign exchanges improved. The first phase of the postwar reconstruction period, 1814 to 1816, was marked by more country bank failures (eighty-nine) than the mid-1820s crisis. After 1814 the number of country banks declined from an inflationary wartime mushroom peak. This secular decline of private country banking also contains a rhythm of the 'trade cycle' – as with a recovery in licences issued from 769 in 1820 to 809 in 1826 and a fall over the late 1820s, down to 671 by 1830. Yet, the crisis of 1825/6 also marked a structural, spatial change, as the country banks which closed their doors for good during these two difficult years were largely located in the market towns and cities of the rural shires. This was one sign of change in the complexion of the British economy.

The crisis of 1825/6 probably acted as a once and for all winnowing of rural private banking. Those country banks in predominantly agricultural regions that stood the test of 1825/6 subsequently proved largely able to stand their ground until the 1880s. In this they were assisted by shelter arising from the Bank of England's post-1826 metropolitan note issuing monopoly which encompassed much of the agrarian south-east. Yet, even with the rise of fully fledged deposit banking over the second quarter of the nineteenth century, the Home Counties were not substantially affected and so remained largely the preserve of private bankers until the 1860s.[34] Indeed, by the late 1870s private country banking was *only* of some importance in the agricultural districts of England and Wales. These areas then had some 159 private banks with 400 branches, which were now competing for business against the 380 branches of some 43 joint-stock banks.[35]

For many good reasons the 1825/6 crisis, and more particularly contemporary reactions to it, are often largely viewed within the perspective of the great British monetary debate. This had begun in 1802, with Thornton's examination of the relationship between monetary expansion and the fall of the exchange, and then thundered on until Peel's Bank Charter Act of 1844. During the 1820s the monetary culprit was found in the 'small note' of the country banks.[36] As a result, in 1826 the legal minimum denomination of bank notes was increased to five pounds, a measure which Scottish bankers were able successfully to oppose. Initially note issuing remained important south of the border to the extent that one of the major reasons which motivated Horsley Palmer to develop the Bank of England's branches after 1826 was to block a scheme which could have transformed the Mint into a rival national bank.[37] Nonetheless, many of the so-called joint-stock banks formed in England and Wales between 1827 and 1833 did not issue notes. One possible reason for this reluctance to take full advantage of the 1826 legislation was that the Act prohibited the new banks' notes being payable in London, but possibly another was that Scottish banking experience had revealed the small profits attributable to issuing notes.[38] However, almost within a decade of the passage of the 1826 Act and prior to Peel's 1844 Bank Charter Act, the private note was in secular decline north and south of Hadrian's Wall. Only 15% of joint-stock banks formed in England and Wales between 1837 and 1844 sought a note issuing licence. In 1825 notes only made up 13% of Scottish banking liabilities and thereafter were only of significance for Scottish provincial banks as opposed to the Scottish public banks and the new joint-stock banks being established in Edinburgh and Aberdeen. Between the mid-1820s and the mid-1830s English and Scottish banks increasingly concentrated upon amassing deposits, possibly a reflection of the new market opportunities given by the rise of middle-class incomes that came with industrialization.

London banking, especially its further development after 1815, calls out for a historian.[39] In 1871 the aggregate deposits of all London banks, private and joint-stock, were still on a par with those of the English and Welsh provincial joint-stock banks, with estimates of their respective share of total banking deposits being 33.4% and 30.2%.[40]

During the 1825/6 crisis London private banks had proved to be as weak in the face of financial stringency as their provincial peers. The eruption of crisis in December 1825 came with the failures of two leading 'City' banks – Pole, Thornton & Co. and Williams, Burgess & Co. – which led to a general run in Lombard Street and in turn caused further metropolitan banking failures. The 1825/6 crisis both revealed the dependency of 'City' banks upon the Bank of England and led to the inception of a general policy amongst London banks of keeping their reserves with the Bank, thus laying the foundation of a 'central' reserve system. Nonetheless, this organic development in interbank relationships was to be reconsidered at least twice – during the mid-century and again over the fin-de-siècle period.[41] The course of the events of the 1825/6 crisis also pointed up the existence of a nascent 'national' banking system.

One result of the Bank's decision in mid-1825 to restrict discounts was increased pressure upon London banks from their country correspondents. However, not every country bank, and especially the smallest, had London accounts,[42] while few country bankers cast even a draft balance sheet in which 'London reserves' and local holdings of cash were offset against short liabilities. Currently available evidence for Glyn, Mills, which by the mid-nineteenth century was a major London agent for country banks, points to a slow yet relentless growth from the late eighteenth century until the mid-nineteenth century of formal financial links between the metropolis, in particular Lombard Street, and the rest of the Kingdom including Scotland. In 1790 Glyns, largely through the personal and marital connections of its partners, held four country agency accounts; by 1810 this private 'City' bank had thirty-eight such accounts and in 1849 it had sixty.[43] The increase of Glyns' country business ran in parallel with the institutionalization of the London money market and which was initially promoted by agrarian profits obtained during the Napoleonic wars.

London bill broking developed formally from the 1800s, whilst the increase in the price of wheat, especially between 1795 and 1820, both increased nominal rent receipts placed with 'West End' banks by estate stewards and augmented the nominal deposits of country banks in south and eastern agricultural districts. In 1841 Moon James gave evidence, so often quoted, demonstrating how the further growth of the London money market had reached the point where the nation's regional surplus and deficit balances of credit were offset by metropolitan intermediation in a 'normal' year. During the decade and a half following the 1825/6 crisis, Lombard Street had been further transformed through the emergence of discount houses, led by Overend, Gurney, as the principals in the money market. These new intermediaries capitalized upon the opportunities that came with the market structure of interest rates during the late 1820s and then the partial repeal of the Usury laws in 1833. They were specialised houses, which were to remain unique to London, and which augmented directly the growing network of institutional connections between the metropolis and the provinces. Such was the insight of King's *History of the London Discount Market* that this very particular segment of the metropolis's financial services industry has subsequently received little by way of major reconsiderations.[44]

The banking legislation, which followed immediately in the wake of the events of 1825/6, is often regarded in generalized accounts as a crisis-induced reaction by the state. Closer consideration has always revealed that the crisis provided a catalyst enabling the state to legislate, while the sequence of legislation, running through the mid-1820s, allowed the transfer of already accumulated financial expertise and practice between the provinces of the United Kingdom.[45] By 1822 the government had come to the conclusion, driven by Ricardo's powerful speeches in the Commons, that the Bank of England's monopoly of joint-stock banking constituted a financial constraint to economic development. Discussions began with directors in April 1822 and centred on a renewal of the Bank's charter to 1843 in return for limiting the Bank's monopoly until August 1844 to a metropolitan area, formed by a sixty-five-mile radius from central London. Furthermore, parliamentary opposition to any extension of the charter spurred the Bank's Court to make a compact. These discussions between Whitehall and the Bank took place while Joplin published his polemical analysis. In its first version this maintained that the Bank's monopoly only applied to note issuing and went as far as calling for an approach to the government to enable the foundation of a joint-stock bank in the coal-mining districts of Northumberland and Durham. Two years later Joplin published a prospectus for a London joint-stock bank with a capital of £3m.

In his campaign for the introduction of joint-stock banking, Joplin made great play of the apparent stability of the Scottish financial system. However, his contrasts of the character of the financial climate north and south of the border were overdrawn. When Joplin was writing, there was only one Scottish joint-stock bank undertaking business – the Commercial Bank of Scotland, formed in 1810 – and no further comparable institutions were established until 1825. The Scottish public banks, such as the Bank of Scotland and the Royal Bank of Scotland, were more comparable with the Bank of England and consequently can not be compared with English and Welsh country banks. However, the more numerous Scottish provincial banks, either private partnerships or moderately sized co-partneries, were similar in character to English and Welsh private banks and almost as liable to fail. One in five of this generic group of Scottish banks closed their doors during the period up to 1830, almost approaching the level of bank failure in England and Wales – one in three.[46]

The interest of Lord Liverpool's ministry in commercial banking reform initially focused upon Ireland. This was first expressed in legislation in 1821, designed to address a financial crisis in southern and western Ireland by permitting the formation of note issuing banks with more than six partners beyond fifty miles of Dublin – a restriction of the monopoly of the Bank of Ireland. However, the 1821 Act was flawed since it failed to repeal relevant sections of a statute of 1756. These required all banking partners to be formally engaged in any business transaction undertaken and which therefore involved the listing of all their names on any notes and receipts. The 1756 Act also prevented any person conducting foreign trade from being a partner in a bank. The 1821 legislation indicated that Parliament would in due course enable banks, constituted under its provisions, to sue and be sued in the name of a public officer. However, the necessary Act was not passed until 1824 – in response to pressure from Belfast merchants and private bankers arising from their attempts to constitute a financial institution to service the growing demands of their city's linen industry.

Despite the remedies of the 1824 Act, the promoters of the Provincial Bank of Ireland still detected three continuing uncertainties in the newly liberalized Irish banking code. First, the fresh legislation appeared to imply that only Irish residents could become co-partners in new Irish banks, so preventing the introduction of English capital. The other two impediments arose from the continuing corporate powers of the Bank of Ireland and Joplin was employed to seek a remedy. However, this publicist for joint-stock banking could not enable the nascent Provincial Bank either to issue notes within the Dublin area or to become a full corporation. As a result, the bank's promotional group, largely comprising Irish MPs, introduced a private bill which, following its first reading, was superseded by a government measure. This Act, which received Royal Assent on 10 June 1825, clarified the provisions of the 1824 statute, in particular by specifically encouraging the introduction of British capital into Ireland. The Provincial Bank of Ireland was legally constituted in August 1825 and about two-thirds of its capital came from shareholders in London, the seat of its board. However, this bank replicated Scottish management practice with the conduct of its fourteen branches being overseen by local directors, and followed Scottish approaches to banking by paying interest on deposits – to be mobilized through cash credits. J. W. Gilbart managed the Provincial Bank's Kilkenny and Waterford branches, an experience which helped to shape his *Practical Treatise on Banking* (1828), for decades a leading textbook. In the mid-1820s Gilbart was appointed the general manager of the newly formed London & Westminster Bank and subsequently became one of the leading joint-stock bankers.[47]

The further banking legislation that followed the crisis of 1825/6 was not immediately put to use to promote provincial joint-stock banks in England and Wales. Only fifteen large banking co-partneries, for that is what they legally were, were constituted between 1826 and 1830. The first to begin business was a development of interests of the renowned private banker, Vincent Stuckey. He took advantage of the 1826 legislation to consolidate his investment in five West Country banks into one institution. The outcome was a bank of thirty-nine shareholders who contributed a nominal capital of £65,000 to a business which had nineteen branches. It was to prove to be typical, and untypical, of the second phase of country banking which ran from 1826 until the 1878 crisis. Few country private bankers followed Stuckey's lead, yet in many respects their new joint-stock competitors – subsequent products of the booms in bank formation that occurred during the mid-1830s, the mid-1860s and the early 1870s – were generally not substantially different from the pre-1826 country banks that they came to displace, especially in industrial areas. Most were unit banks having few branches – unlike Stuckey's bank – and generally they had relatively small capitals and relatively few 'shareholders'. On average the fifty 'new style' banks formed by the end of 1833 had 200 shareholders. However, it is difficult to speak of an average bank following the 1826 legislation. At one end of the spectrum was Stuckey's Bank, at the other were the likes of the Bank of Manchester, with a nominal capital of £2m and 600 'shareholders', and the Manchester & Liverpool District Bank in which 1,054 'shareholders' subscribed for a nominal capital of £3m through initially putting up £1 for every £100 share.[48]

By the early 1840s there were about 100 joint-stock banks in the provinces of England and Wales. Most had been established during the mid-1830s speculative bank formation boom and were survivors of the crises of 1836 and 1839.[49] Geographically their offices were largely located in a broad swathe of the country, running from north-east to south-west, bounded on one side by the high Pennine block and on the other by the Bank's metropolitan region. Only the National Provincial's branches were scattered throughout this belt – from Durham in the north to Devon in the south. Otherwise, branch, or agency, banking, the growing feature of concurrent Irish and Scottish developments, was largely a Welsh feature. In the Principality, there were not only offices of the National Provincial, but also of the North & South Wales Bank and, in the south, of both the Glamorganshire Banking Co. and the Monmouthshire & Glamorganshire Banking Co.[50] It has been argued that the contrasting local, or regional, nature of English joint-stock banking was due to poor communications. However, the coming of the railway made little difference and even in 1871 an English joint-stock bank had on average only 6.4 offices.

Over the mid-century period the organizational structure of banking was in part frozen by the onerous conditions of Peel's 1844 Joint-Stock Bank Act.[51] This had been an attempt to remedy by legislation the problems of speculative bank promotion made evident by the experience of the mid-1830s. However, it failed to deal with, or rather could not address, one basic continuing weakness – poor management. As a result of the 1844 Act's effective bar upon further bank creations which continued until 1857, existing joint-stock banks were given an effective monopoly, augmented by the continual waning of private country banking in industrial districts. Yet, joint-stock banks, especially in new major industrial conurbations, did not enjoy, outwardly, local monopolies. Most cities and towns of any size had more than one joint-stock bank, which often pursued their businesses in a local financial market also comprising, at least initially, private institutions. For example, during the third quarter of the nineteenth century four joint-stock banks had their head offices in Sheffield, while other extra-local joint-stock banks opened branches there.[52] Furthermore, when Peel's banking code was repealed between 1857 and 1862, further joint-stock banks were established over the following two decades – to meet the complaint of the early 1860s that banking in England was 'underdone'.[53]

Banks are increasingly regarded as important nodes in information networks to the extent that intermediation in information is coming to be regarded as even more important than intermediation in financial resources. The continued persistence of largely parochial banking in England before the 1880s may have been due to the local monopolies of information enjoyed by the unit banks which predominantly characterized the financial sector of the economy. Many of these banks were established by local commercial and industrial communities specifically to meet their own needs, which in turn gave great diversity in the functions that they performed. Like private country banking, the services of the post-1826 joint-stock banks were predominantly personal. Local bankers knew their customers, or relations of their customers, and consequently personal security was frequently the most important form of collateral. A growing literature provides increasing support for this generalization. Lescent has demonstrated the links between bankers and industrialists of the secondary metals and engineering trades of the West Midlands.[54] Newton has found that, in the case of Sheffield banks, their directors were frequently local industrialists and that personal security was the most common form of collateral proffered by prospective borrowers. With the increasing pace of economic and technological change, personal networks of information were ultimately inadequate. Yet, some local unit banks attempted to straddle this hurdle by turning to specialists and, for example, in 1872 the Sheffield Union Bank appointed Denis Davy, of a local engineering and steel manufacturing concern, to process 'more fuller information respecting the premises, plant and stock, and also the modes of doing business' of this bank's customers.[55] Lastly, there was a balance between client and bank in these particular local, or regional, information networks, as the unitary nature of English banking was mirrored in the largely atomistic organizational structure of manufacturing and commerce. The size of firms, albeit measured by their labour forces, points to a prevalence of small-scale enterprise continuing until at least the 1880s.[56]

Such a business strategy had a price and especially for banks in industrial areas. Locally, they could only meet the demands for credit placed upon them, and which exceeded their deposit bases, by rediscounting in London. They were 'overlent' and many remained so until the 1880s.[57] Their growing businesses in which assets, such as bills, advances and loans, accumulated faster than liabilities, could only be balanced by an increasing reliance upon the resources of the London money market obtainable through a correspondent. However, although such correspondent and agency relationships were expensive, they remained a marked feature of English banking until almost the end of the nineteenth century. English banks were prepared to pay the price for remaining locally or regionally based, unlike their Scottish peers, which opened London offices, beginning with the National Bank of Scotland in 1864.

The predominantly unitary character of provincial banking, a continuity from the mid-eighteenth century, was given some semblance of a system by the expensive interacting correspondence network that placed the London money market at its centre. Remittances to London were also facilitated by the service provided by the post-1826 provincial branches of the Bank of England. The prime aim of these new branches[58] was to improve the quality of the national circulation but provincial note issuing by the Bank necessitated provincial discounting. Provincial note issuing also led to compacts with provincial private and joint-stock banks, whereby the latter gave up their circulations in return for credit lines, which frequently in practice led to the Bank of England acting as their London agent. The extent of these arrangements varied substantially, region by region, but in general they generated a regionally based financial system. This was congruent with the spatial dimensions of the greater importance of manufacturing and commerce over the mid-century as the Bank's most important branches were in the new industrial and merchanting centres, with Manchester, Liverpool and Birmingham heading the list. An equal pointer to this congruency was the early closure of the Bank's Exeter branch and the transfer of its business to Plymouth, a branch sustained by state transactions arising from the town's naval dockyard.

A fuller emergence of a banking system, albeit one largely restricted to England and Wales, and 'policed' to a degree by the branch agents of the Bank of England in a role somewhat comparable to that performed by Scotland's three public banks, nonetheless did not ensure general financial stability before the 1880s. The new banking after 1826 had been inaugurated in an atmosphere of animosity which pervaded the relationships between the 'old' country private banks and the branches of the Bank of England and was further soured by the competition posed by the rise of joint-stock country banks during the mid-1830s. Such distrust, bred by an understandable fear of new competitors, also characterized the transformation of metropolitan banking from the early 1830s. The Bank of England and the London private banks placed every obstacle possible in the way of the London & Westminster and subsequent metropolitan joint-stock institutions. As a result, for instance, the metropolitan joint-stock deposit banks did not gain entrance to the all-important Clearing House until the 1850s. Furthermore, unease was to characterize the relationship between the Bank of England and the major commercial clearing banks until the 1910s.

Institutional friction arising from competitive jealousies was but one ingredient of financial instability. International factors played an increasing role, particularly with the greater growth of overseas dealings – goods, services and financial resources – over the mid-century. Collins's new research has only pointed up the dilemma over the extent to which the domestic commercial banks were the initiator of cyclical change. The balance sheet data that he has managed to collect displays short-term movements which mirror the fluctuations of the trade cycle in the timepath of nominal GNP. However, this data set also implies that bankers reacted to banking crises, as shown by both a long-term rise in the cash ratio, and the upward ratchet movements in cash ratios following the crises of 1866 and 1878.[59] Above all, his further research has revealed that previously historians had not given due credence to the wider effects of the City of Glasgow Bank crash of 1878.[60] He has highlighted the role that banking contraction following 1878 may have played as the mechanism for the transmission of monetary deflation to the economy. This was a further effect of the crisis, joining its already well-known results of causing the general adoption of limited liability by banks and spurring bank amalgamations.[61] For a whole range of reasons, the 1878 crisis marked a greater turning point in the development of domestic banking than previous panics – from 1825/6 to 1866.

Banking in Britain before the 1880s was somewhat like Adam Smith's famed pin factory, being characterized by a substantial division of labour, both functionally and regionally (in a spatial dimension). The nature of this contribution has meant a necessary concentration upon only a few aspects of this 'parallel' system of finance. However, specialization pervaded the gamut of the evolving financial services industry. Corporate overseas banking remained a separate component – and one that was equally marked by diversity, both regionally and functionally.[62] The provision of international trade credits developed until the mid-1860s as a distinct service – met by what would now be termed acceptance houses. Equally, the flotation of overseas securities was largely undertaken by another group of institutions, although with some overlap with the general body of acceptors.[63] Such a high degree of specialization challenges the crystallization of generalizations and, similarly, with its regional diversity, makes interregional, let alone intereconomy, comparisons hazardous.

This review of some aspects of the relationship between the emergence of modern banking and the transformation of industry and commerce in Britain has had the simple intents of both pointing to areas of neglect, despite the great richness of the existing scholarly literature, and indicating the possibility of a wider perspective. Much of banking history has been written to attempt to respond to two major questions: 'how was industry financed during the industrial revolution' and 'what part, if any, did the financial sector play in Britain's debatable economic eclipse during the decades before 1914'. This contribution has not sought to denigrate the importance of those questions and the answers that they might elicit. Rather, it has tried to show, if only partially, that the emergence of modern British banking contains other equally important historical problems: some have been plumbed by recent scholarly research, while others should be part of the historian's agenda.

Notes

We are extremely grateful for the assistance provided by the British Academy and the Royal Historical Society which enabled our participation in the Montreal Congress.

1 L. S. Pressnell, *Country Banking in the Industrial Revolution* (Oxford, 1956), pp. 14–36, 322–43.

2 *Ibid.*, p. 322.

3 R. Cameron, 'England 1750–1844', in R. Cameron *et al.*, *Banking in the Early Stages of Industrialization* (New York, 1967), p. 18.

4 *Ibid.*, p. 23.

5 Pressnell, *Country Banking*, p. 337.

6 Cameron, 'England', pp. 36–9. For a recent review of the literature, see P. Mathias, 'Financing the Industrial Revolution', in P. Mathias and J. A. Davis (eds.), *The First Industrial Revolution* (Oxford, 1990).

7 P. L. Cottrell, *Industrial Finance 1830–1914. The Finance and Organisation of English Manufacturing Industry* (London, 1980, repr. 1993), p. 15.

8 N. F. R. Crafts, S. J. Leybourne and T. C. Mills, 'Trends and Cycles in British Industrial Production', *Journal of the Royal Statistical Society*, 152 (1989); and C. K. Harley, 'British Industrialization before 1841: Evidence of Slower Growth during the Industrial Revolution', *Journal of Economic History*, 42 (1982). For a recent review which stresses the transition to faster growth in the late eighteenth century, see R. V. Jackson, 'Rates of Industrial Growth during the Industrial Revolution', *Economic History Review*, 2nd ser., 45 (1992).

9 For examples of this, see J. Hoppit, 'Counting the Industrial Revolution', *Economic History Review*, 2nd ser., 42 (1990), p. 174, n. 9.

10 For a discussion of the methodological problems surrounding the creation of national accounts framework, and a plea for the use of qualitative evidence in conjunction with quantitative data in assessments of economic change, see Hoppit, 'Counting'.

11 M. Berg and P. Hudson, 'Rehabilitating the Industrial Revolution', *Economic History Review*, end ser., 45 (1992).

12 P. Mathias, 'Capital, Credit and Entrepreneurs in the Industrial Revolution', *Journal of European Economic History*, 2 (1973); but see M. Buchinsky and B. Polak, 'The Emergence of a National Capital Market in England, 1710–1800', *Journal of Economic History*, 53 (1993).

13 This range of financial intermediation is explored in P. Hudson, *The Genesis of Industrial Capital: A Study of the West Riding Wool Textile Industry, c. 1750–1850* (Cambridge, 1986).

14 Cottrell, *Industrial Finance*, p. 15; F. J. T. Acaster, 'Benjamin Heywood, Manchester 1788–95', *Three Banks Review*, 119 (1978); idem, 'Partners in Peril: The Genesis of Banking in Manchester', *Three Banks Review*, 138 (1986).

15 B. L. Anderson, 'Provincial Aspects of the Financial Revolution of the Eighteenth Century', *Business History*, 11 (1969). For a similar example, see M. Miles, 'The Money Market in the Early Industrial Revolution: The Evidence from the West Riding Attornies, c. 1750–1800', *Business History*, 23 (1981).

16 D. M. Joslin, 'London Private Bankers, 1720–1785', *Economic History Review*, 2nd ser., 7 (1954); see also F. T. Melton, 'Deposit Banking in London 1700–90', *Business History*, 28 (1986).

17 For banking in Wales during the eighteenth century, see R. O. Roberts, 'Financial Developments in Early Modern Wales and the Emergence of the First Banks', *Welsh History Review*, 16 (1993). On regional diversity, see also D. J. Moss, 'The Private Banks of Birmingham, 1800–27', *Business History*, 24 (1982); and P. Ollerenshaw, 'The Development of Banking in the Bristol Region, 1750–1915', in C. Harvey and J. Press (eds.), *Studies in the Business History of Bristol* (Bristol, 1988).

18 S. G. Checkland, *Scottish Banking: A History* (Glasgow, 1975).

19 For one example, see F. E. Hyde, C. N. Parkinson and S. Mariner, 'The Port of Liverpool and the Crisis of 1793', *Economica*, n.s., 18 (1951); and C. K. Gonner, 'Municipal Bank Notes in Liverpool, 1793–5', *Economic Journal* (1896).

20 P. J. Cain and A. G. Hopkins, *British Imperialism: Innovation and Expansion 1688–1914* (London, 1993), especially pp. 1–104.

21 E. Kerridge, *Trade and Banking in Early Modern England* (Manchester, 1988).

22 H. V. Bowen, *Elites, Enterprise and the Making of the British Overseas Empire, 1688–1775* (London, 1996), ch. 3.

23 Checkland, *Scottish Banking*, pp. 112, 124–5, 131–3.

24 For the 'fiscal-military state', see J. Brewer, *Sinews of Power: War, Money and the English State 1688–1783* (London, 1989); for a detailed study of the funding of the state, see P. J. M. Dickson, *The Financial Revolution in England. A Study in the Development of Public Credit 1688–1756* (Oxford, 1967).

25 The classic study of the Bank remains Sir J. H. Clapham, *The Bank of England. A History*, 2 vols. (Cambridge, 1944). For a recent survey of the early development of the Bank, see H. V. Bowen, 'The Bank of England during the Long Eighteenth Century', in R. Roberts and D. Kynaston (eds.), *The Bank of England. Money, Power and Influence 1694–1994* (Oxford, 1995).

26 M. C. Lovell, 'The Role of the Bank of England as a Lender of Last Resort in the Crises of the Eighteenth Century', *Explorations in Entrepreneurial History*, 10 (1957).

27 For a relatively recent contribution to this particular area, see F. S. Jones, 'Government, Currency and Country Banks in England, 1770–9', *South African Journal of Economics*, 44 (1976).

28 B. Hilton, *Corn, Cash, Commerce. The Economic Policies of the Tory Governments 1815–1830* (Oxford, 1977), pp. 202–4, 207–10, 215–17.
29 M. Lévy-Leboyer, 'Central Banking and Foreign Trade: The Anglo-American Cycle in the 1830s', and R. C. O. Matthews, 'Comment', both in C. P. Kindleberger and J.-P. Laffargue (eds.), *Financial Crises. Theory, History and Policy* (Cambridge and Paris, 1982).
30 H. M. Boot, *The Commercial Crisis of 1847* (Hull, 1984); and R. Dornbusch and J. A. Frankel, 'The Gold Standard and the Bank of England in the Crisis of 1847', in M. D. Bordo and A. J. Schwarz (eds.), *A Retrospective on the Classical Gold Standard 1821–1931* (Chicago, 1984).
31 P. L. Cottrell, 'Railway Finance and the Crisis of 1866: Contractors' Bills of Exchange and the Finance Companies', *Journal of Transport History*, n.s., 3 (1975); and R. A. Batchelor, 'The Avoidance of Catastrophe: Two Nineteenth-Century Banking Crises', in F. Capie and G. E. Woods (eds.), *Financial Crises and the World Banking System* (London, 1986).
32 P. L. Cottrell, 'Credit, Morals and Sunspots: The Financial Boom of the 1860s and Trade Cycle Theory', in P. L. Cottrell and D. E. Moggridge (eds.), *Money and Power. Essays in Honour of L. S. Pressnell* (London, 1988).
33 S. E. Thomas, *The Rise and Growth of Joint Stock Banking*, vol. I: *Britain to 1860* (London, 1934), p. 55, n. 5.
34 The irony was twisted upon itself; Crick and Wadsworth long ago pointed out – in a footnote – that, when the London & County began opening London suburban and provincial offices, this spatial expansion of the bank's 'area' was restricted to the region marked out by the Bank's sixty-five-mile metropolitan radius. W. F. Crick and J. E. Wadsworth, *A Hundred Years of Joint Stock Banking* (London, 1936; 3rd edn, 1958), pp. 36–7, p. 37, n. (i).
35 W. Newmarch, 'The Increase in the Number of Banks and Branches . . . 1858–1878', *The Bankers' Magazine* (1879), pp. 849–61.
36 I. Bowen, 'Country Banking, the Note Issue and Banking Controversies of 1825', *Economic History*, supplement to *Economic Journal* (1938–40).
37 F. W. Fetter, *Development of British Monetary Orthodoxy 1797–1875* (Cambridge, Mass., 1965), pp. 124–6; Hilton, *Corn, Cash, Commerce*, pp. 232–8.
38 Thomas, *Joint Stock Banking*, pp. 89–90.
39 The only recent contribution dealing with the post-1815 period is E. Healy, *Coutts & Co. 1692–1992* (London, 1992).
40 P. L. Cottrell, 'The Domestic Commercial Banks and the City of London, 1870–1939', in Y. Cassis (ed.), *Finance and Financiers in European History, 1880–1960* (Cambridge, 1992), p. 46, table 3.5, drawing from F. Capie and A. Webber, *A Monetary History of the United Kingdom, 1870–1982* (London, 1985).
41 L. S. Pressnell, 'Gold Reserves, Banking Reserves and the Baring Crisis of 1890', in C. R. Whittlesey and J. S. G. Wilson (eds.), *Essays in Money and Banking in Honour of R. S. Sayers* (Oxford, 1968).
42 The importance of local financial flows, and of inter-regional flows, as against periphery-metropolis movements, has been shown by I. Black, 'Geography, Political Economy and the Circulation of Capital in Early Industrial England', *Journal of Historical Geography*, 15 (1989).
43 The only history of Glyns, that remarkable London private 'City' bank, is R. Fulford, *Glyn's 1753–1953* (London, 1953).
44 W. T. C. King, *History of the London Discount Market* (London, 1936).

45 See C. W. Munn, 'The Coming of Joint-Stock Banking in Scotland and Ireland 1820–25', in T. M. Devine and D. Dickson (eds.), *Scotland and Ireland* (Edinburgh, 1983); and *idem*, 'The Emergence of Joint Stock Banking in the British Isles: A Comparative Approach', *Business History*, 30 (1988).
46 C. W. Munn, *The Scottish Provincial Banking Companies 1747–1864* (Edinburgh, 1981).
47 G. L. Barrow, *The Emergence of the Irish Banking System, 1820–1845* (Dublin, 1975); P. L. Cottrell, 'The Businessman and Financier', in Sonia and V. D. Lipman (eds.), *The Century of Moses Montefiore* (Oxford, 1985), pp. 34–7; P. Ollerenshaw, *Banking in Nineteenth Century Ireland* (Manchester, 1987).
48 The foundations of the post-1826 joint-stock banks and their subsequent relationships with their customers are currently being investigated by P. L. Cottrell and L. A. Newton with the support of the Leverhulme Trust.
49 For one local example, see F. S. Jones, 'Instant Banking in the 1830s: the Founding of the Northern and Central Bank of England', *Bankers' Magazine*, 211 (1971); *idem*, 'The Manchester Cotton Magnates' Move into Banking, 1826–50', *Textile History*, 9 (1978); and *idem*, 'The Cotton Industry and Joint Stock Banking in Manchester 1825–1850', *Business History Review*, 20 (1978). Another is provided by anon., 'The Yorkshire District Bank, William Deacon's and 1836', *Three Banks Review*, 89 (1971).
50 See P. L. Cottrell, 'Banking and Finance', in J. Langton and R. J. Morris (eds.), *Atlas of Industrializing Britain* (London, 1986), Map 19.8.
51 K. S. Toft, 'A Mid-Nineteenth Century Attempt at Banking Control', *Revue Internationale d'Histoire de la Banque*, 14 (1972).
52 See anon., 'Ironmakers and Duke's Agent: The Sheffield and Rotherham Bank – the Early Days', *Three Banks Review*, 73 (1967); and L. A. Newton, 'The Finance of Manufacturing Industry in the Sheffield Area c. 1850–c. 1885' (unpublished PhD thesis, University of Leicester, 1993), especially ch. 3.
53 B. L. Anderson and P. L. Cottrell, 'Another Victorian Capital Market: A Study of Banking and Bank Investors on Merseyside', *Economic History Review*, 2nd ser., 28 (1975).
54 I. Lescent, 'Financing the XIXth Century Iron Industry: A Re-Evaluation of the Role of British Banks between 1850 and 1880', paper presented at N. W. Posthumus centre, European post-graduate training programme in social and economic history: seminar on the history of banking and finance, Sandjberg Manor, Denmark (November 1991). See also M. Collins and P. Hudson, 'Provincial Bank Lending: Yorkshire and Lancashire, 1826–1860', *Bulletin of Economic Research*, 31 (1979); and P. Hudson, 'The Role of Banks in the Finance of the West Riding Wool Textile Industry, c. 1780–1850', *Business History Review*, 60 (1981).
55 Newton, 'Finance of Manufacturing', p. 59.
56 V. Gatrell, 'Labour, Power and the Size of the Firms in Lancashire Cotton in the Second Quarter of the Nineteenth Century', *Economic History Review*, 2nd ser., 30 (1977); R. Lloyd-Jones and A. A. Le Roux, 'The Size of Firms in the Cotton Industry: Manchester, 1814–1841', *Economic History Review*, 2nd ser., 33 (1980); M. J. Lewis, 'The Growth and Development of Sheffield's Industrial Structure, 1880–1930' (unpublished PhD thesis, Sheffield City Polytechnic, 1989); Newton, 'Finance of Manufacturing', especially chs. 2 and 6.
57 S. Nishimura, *The Decline of Inland Bills of Exchange in the London Money Market 1855–1913* (Cambridge, 1971).
58 One area where ignorance has been recently rolled further back is the examination of the activities of the Bank's branches. See M. Collins, 'The Bank of England at

Liverpool, 1827–1844', *Business History*, 14 (1972); F. S. Jones, 'The Bank of England in Manchester, 1826–1850', *Bankhistorisches Archiv*, 11 (1985); D. J. Moss, 'The Bank of England and the Country Banks: Birmingham 1827–33', *Economic History Review*, 34 (1981); *idem*, 'The Bank of England and the Establishment of a Branch System, 1826–9', *Canadian Journal of History*, 27 (1992); D. Ziegler, transl. E. Martin, *Central Bank, Peripheral Industry. The Bank of England in the Provinces, 1826–1913* (Leicester, 1990).

59 M. Collins, 'English Banks and Business Cycles, 1848–80', in Cottrell and Moggridge, *Money*.

60 M. Collins, 'The Banking Crisis of 1878', *Economic History Review*, 2nd ser., 42 (1989). See also, D. Ziegler, 'The Banking Crisis of 1878: Some Remarks', *Economic History Review*, 2nd ser., 45 (1992). An even wider significance is detected by W. P. Kennedy, *Industrial Structure, Capital Markets and the Origins of British Economic Decline* (Cambridge, 1987).

61 F. Capie and G. Rodrick-Bali, 'Concentration in British Banking, 1870–1920', *Business History*, 24 (1982).

62 P. L. Cottrell, 'The Coalescence of a Cluster of Corporate International Banks, 1855–1875', *Business History*, 33 (1991); *idem*, 'Great Britain', in R. Cameron and V. I. Bovykin (eds.), *International Banking 1870–1914* (New York and Oxford, 1991); and G. Jones, *British Multinational Banking 1830–1990* (Oxford, 1993).

63 Recent general treatments are provided by S. Chapman in *The Rise of Merchant Banking* (London, 1984) and *Merchant Enterprise in Britain. From the Industrial Revolution to World War I* (Cambridge, 1992). There has also been a welcome and much-needed flurry of histories of particular merchant banks: J. Orbell, *Baring Brothers & Co., Limited. A History to 1939* (London, 1985); K. Burk, *Morgan Grenfell 1838–1988. The Biography of a Merchant Bank* (Oxford, 1989); R. Roberts, *Schroeders, Merchants and Bankers* (London, 1992).

7 Banks, economic development and capitalism in France

Eric Bussière

Since at least the early nineteenth century, the part played by banks in France has been a widely debated and indeed often polemical topic. Such criticism has mostly been concerned with either the general lack of finance the economy was a prey to, or with shortages more specific to certain sectors of activity or social groups.

It has also been largely based on comparisons with other nations. The idea sometimes put forward that France was lagging behind the British or more generally the Anglo-Saxon model existed alongside that of the allegedly greater efficiency of the 'Rhineland' model based on the German-style universal bank.

French banking historians long ago moved beyond analyses of this type, trying to relate the way the economy and capitalism were structured and the development of banking. In most cases their conclusions have been that in several periods the existing system was in a position to meet needs and hence, implicitly, to develop.

That is the view that will be adopted in the following pages, with an emphasis on the factors shaping such transformations. In particular, special attention will be paid to the part played by the state, outside influences and the circumstances bringing them into play. Once the developments of the modern era have been put into a suitable perspective, we shall concentrate particularly on changes in the last two centuries which have very largely shaped present-day structures.

From the fairs of the Champagne region to the beginning of the centralization of banks in Paris

The modern era saw the gradual growth of a network of banks in France covering the main markets and centred on Paris. Two factors influenced this development: the early existence of a centralized state and the important part played by foreign bankers.

The growth of banking activities in France was, classically, linked to that of trading centres. The vital centres of banking activity therefore fitted into the flow of goods, shaping a 'moving' geographical field of banking until centralization in Paris became dominant in the eighteenth century. This explains the emergence of an important pole of activity in northern France initially centred on the fairs of the Champagne region. At first it was temporary, but by the twelfth and thirteenth centuries it was tending to become more stable as the fairs became more permanent, and to shift to Paris when Champagne was annexed and became part of the royal possessions. The south of France, however, with its links with Italy, Spain and the East, was also an essential pole of activity. Avignon enjoyed a certain importance when the popes were in residence there, but Lyons soon emerged as a competitor, complementing Geneva. The growing importance, due to royal influence, of the fairs held there determined its pre-eminence in the fifteenth and sixteenth centuries, and despite periodical crises the market only became second to Paris as a result of the payments crisis of 1709. The banking network in France was thus structured around the capital and major interregional markets such as Lyons, the major trading ports for colonial foodstuffs on the Atlantic coast and a certain number of centres of activity in the Midi-Languedoc closely connected to the Mediterranean basin. The growth of banking was thus closely linked to that of trade, often with no clear distinction between the two within a single firm, a state of affairs which was to persist in France until well into the nineteenth century. The fairs gave rise to considerable clearing operations by means of transfers, which were quite naturally linked to exchange operations, themselves sometimes linked to loans, either on a single market or between markets. Italian merchants standardized such operations, giving the Lyons fairs their edge in the sixteenth century, and the quality of the banking services on offer partly explains their prosperity.[1] The growing irregularity of payments as a result of unfortunate transactions with the royal treasury also accounts for their decline. The fairs, then, made the spread of modern banking techniques possible in France. The consolidation of the network of banking market places from the seventeenth century onwards meant that techniques could both spread and become the norm, and the use of letters of exchange, which was at first restricted to large transactions between major financial centres, became more widespread by the fifteenth century. In the seventeenth they became simple negotiable bills quite separate from exchange agreements. In the eighteenth, following the streamlining of the economy after the abolition of the Law system, the advent of monetary stability regularized activities and practices, and discounts became an increasingly common way of financing trade and one of the essential activities of banking as a profession.[2] Although their role was not an exclusive one if we take into account that of the Templars in the twelfth and thirteenth centuries, the presence of foreigners was one of the major characteristics of the growth of the banking system in France. From the twelfth to the sixteenth century, the Italians were dominant at the Champagne fairs, and in Paris and Lyons, a position they subsequently lost to the Protestant diaspora operating from the Swiss banking centres, including Geneva. From Paris, where they were established by the beginning of the eighteenth century, they moved out towards the Atlantic ports, financing for example a section of the cotton cycle. Even though a large Catholic bank emerged in that century, foreign bankers appear to have played a major part in spreading banking techniques throughout the economic and social fabric of France in modern times. The way in which they were integrated, in successive waves of which the last, with the Mallets and the Hottinguers, made up the 'senior Protestant' bank, suggests that religious restrictions offer less of an explanation of their role than the fact that, as a result of the networks they were able to establish, they were more favourably placed in the major flows of transactions in Europe.[3]

The state played an important part in the development of trading activities by supporting those of the fairs, and in doing so it encouraged banking. However, its own requirements also determined the structuring of the banking system. Its need for sources of finance, which had always played an essential part in the financial affairs of the realm, grew from the end of the seventeenth century as a result of the increasingly urgent shortfalls arising from the military operations of the monarchy. Historiographers have drawn a distinction between financiers, the wealthy holders of royal offices, responsible for collecting direct and indirect taxes and making loans to kings, and bankers, whose activities were directly linked to those of the economy.[4] The line between the two types of activity should not, however, be too firmly drawn. The major bankers had always also been bankers to princes. Jacques Cúur, for instance, was simultaneously a trader, a banker and the financial support of the monarchy,[5] and the Crozets and subsequently the Paris brothers combined banking and financing the treasury. The fact of the matter is that in the eighteenth century public and private finances were to a large degree interlinked as a consequence of the spread of paper bonds in private portfolios through the intermediary of bankers, a trend which became more marked in the closing years of the ancien regime. Thus the state encouraged the centralization of banking activities in Paris. However, it did earmark some of the advantages of such a situation for itself, perhaps encouraging a tendency in private investors to opt for income to the detriment of high-yield investment.

The closing years of the ancien regime therefore bequeathed to the country a banking system developing hierarchically around Paris, which made it possible for trading to grow and the country to take its place in a certain number of international flows and which, overall, was able to meet the needs of the economy.[6] It did not, however, benefit as much as it might have done from all the possible advantages of the centralization of power in Paris. This was due in particular to the fact that as a result of the failure of Law's efforts the creation of an issuing institution for banks and trading was delayed, despite several attempts to set one up and the significant progress represented by the founding of the Caisse d'Escompte in 1776. It was not until 1800 that the creation of the Bank of France really got the process under way.

Introducing a 'French-type' system

The mid-nineteenth century certainly saw the major break in the history of French banking in that it brought about the introduction of a national system with its own hierarchy. It originated in the change from a relatively scattered to a massive and centralized demand for finance linked to the construction of the railway network, and was also marked for the first time by a real debate on the relationship between economic development and the banking system. In Saint-Simonian thought, financing was seen in universal and rationalizing terms, and this influenced both the Crédit Mobilier experiment and the creation of the major banking establishments at the turn of the 1850s. The end result, around 1880, was not, however, completely in line with that particular way of thinking.

After the Revolution, the banking profession was still characterized by the practices of the preceding century, and based on trading commercial papers and on discounting drafts. For a long time such short-term operations remained well outside a standardized and hierarchical organization. In Paris a certain number of 'senior banks', founded for the most part under the ancien regime, dominated the market by virtue of a rigorously selected clientele and a rejection of all but first-order bills and drafts. The majority of paper transactions, however, were carried out, both in the provinces and in Paris, by discount houses or local banks with fairly lowly financial standing and fairly stringent terms. Despite the gradual creation of networks of correspondents in a position to send papers back to Paris or the main provincial centres, the money market was still an expensive place. There were considerable differences in rates between one centre and another, and they varied considerably over the year, as periods of high monetary tension were often associated with seasonal flows in the economy.[7]

The founding of the Bank of France in 1800 marked the first step in the creation of a national organization of the short-term money market, but the scope of its operations was not quite as wide as had been hoped and its governors slowed down efforts to broaden its bases of activity. These deficiencies were to a certain extent compensated for by the creation of departmental issuing banks or discount banks, often short-lived, during the 1830s.

Longer-term financing was for a considerable time arranged by means of extended cash credits for faithful and reliable customers. It might seem that such solutions would be capable of providing finance for the first period of industrialization, which did not require huge amounts of capital, but very often when bank holdings were inadequate bank credit had to be supplemented with loans from notaries or lenders' syndicates on what were sometimes very burdensome terms. Though regional banks often began to enter into partnerships with industrial concerns in the 1830s, it was still usually hard for collieries or metallurgical industries to find the capital they needed, given the insufficient holdings of the banks willing to help them.[8]

There was thus a basis for the Saint-Simonian position in the negative aspects of the situation. Indeed, the main architects of the 'banking revolution' in mid-nineteenth-century France moved in such circles and drew their ideas and arguments from them. The most

active of them played a decisive part in the debate shaping the modernization of the credit system. All of them, however (Laffitte, Pereire and
Arlès-Dufour, the co-founder of the Crédit Lyonnais), were also
engaged in the practice of banking and anxious to set up structures
capable of financing the growth of business, in which they were actively
involved.[9]

Any of his followers could have observed the deficiencies noted by
Laffitte in 1837:

> Industry can only obtain capital at high interest; its products are
> expensive, consumption is limited to the home market and selling
> abroad is difficult. For its part, the export trade lacks the capital for
> long-term undertakings . . . We therefore need fairly powerful
> associations and rather intelligent organization if we are to support
> trade and industry in times of prosperity and come to their assistance
> when times are hard.[10]

These views are echoed in the aims declared by the Pereires when the
Crédit Mobilier was founded in 1852, namely, 'to make it easier to
amass the capital needed to complete the railway programme and
develop all of the associated industries, to bring down interest rates and
thus have an effect on the improvement of public credit and the growth
of the work of the nation'.[11]

Although the aims were defined at a fairly early stage, it took some
time to set up the structures to be adopted. All the founders, and in
particular Laffitte and the Pereires, saw the question in its totality
as involving the extension of discounts and short-term credit and
providing firms with the funds and long-term resources they needed.
The plan for a central mutual credit bank drawn up by the Pereires in
1853 and aimed at increasing the bases of short-term financing was
in line with the creation of the Caisse Générale pour le Commerce et
l'Industrie, launched by Laffitte in 1837, which broadened the credit
base considerably by attracting deposits. The major job, however, was
to set up powerful establishments capable of financing long-term investment. Laffitte's 1825 dream of society as a partner in industry was very
close to the vision behind the Crédit Mobilier, set up in 1852.

Such schemes were based not on the idea that there was insufficient
capital available, but on the view that there was a reluctance to invest it
in new undertakings. The establishment to be created would therefore
have a promotional role to play, thus offering its shareholders the
guarantee of its own shares. The description given in June 1825 by

Thiers, a close associate of Laffitte ('the aim of this association is to supply capital to every new undertaking needing it . . . It will acquire shares in every limited company . . . As it will be involved in all existing undertakings and will hold all the different stocks for all possible ones; profits from one will compensate for losses in another'[12] is not so far from I. Pereire's words at the shareholders' general meeting of the Crédit Mobilier in 1859, when he defined the omnium as 'the single security made up of various mutually guaranteeing shares'. The aim of the omnium was to increase operations, which would help to reduce costs and limit risk but it tended to create monopoly situations as a result of a would-be rational and all-encompassing project for economic development: 'we wish above all to see each branch of industry that we have an effect on develop through associations and mergers rather than competition, through a more economic use of their strengths than mutual opposition and destruction.[13]

In fact the Crédit Mobilier project was soon outmoded. We can account for its difficulties and irremediable decline after 1867 in terms of its over-ambitious nature, but it was based on a concept which underestimated the current opportunities offered by the growth of savings and markets. The desire of competing groups and, no doubt, the public authorities to avoid the emergence of a situation of dominance, the growing influence of free-market thought and the emergence of many new needs brought about a new generation of establishments set up in the wake of the 1860 free-trade treaty and under the provisions of the 1863 law on limited liability companies.

The Crédit Industriel et Commercial, the Crédit Lyonnais and the Société Générale, created in 1859, 1863 and 1864 respectively, belonged very clearly to a 'new generation' of banks. These, which were soon joined by a number of other banks, were to make up the group of credit establishments forming the infrastructure of the French banking system until the present day. The system was completed by the appearance of the 'business banks', namely the Banque de Paris et des Pays-Bas in 1872 and the Banque de l'Union Parisienne in 1904. At the beginning of the present century, then, the French banking system could be seen as consolidated.[14]

Traditionally, it has been described in terms of an internal duality, with on the one hand deposit banks specializing in short-term operations and on the other business banks orientated towards the longer-term financing of firms. This picture needs to be adjusted from several points of view.

Those institutions created at the turn of the 1860s still belonged in the Saint-Simonian tradition by virtue of their universal nature. The new banks set up enormous networks in order to capture deposits, putting into practice on quite a different scale a policy initiated by Laffitte between 1830 and 1840. But these establishments also engaged in partnerships with firms. Talabot of the Société Générale did so in a particularly consistent way, participating in financing collieries, iron mines, steelworks and railways, and his overall plan was no different from that publicized by the Pereires in 1852. Similarly, the early years of the Crédit Lyonnais were marked by large investments in firms.[15] Thus the model of the mixed bank adopted by the major French banks combined all the Saint-Simonian aims by putting into operation the types of financing hitherto lacking.

This clearly could not be the final answer. Scarcely had the system been consolidated than it found itself faced with the throes of the Great Depression. After the first scare in 1867 the Crédit Lyonnais was severely shaken by the 1882 crisis, which caused a run on its deposits, and other establishments paid the price of over-bold investments in their turn. From that point onwards, the major credit houses were fairly quickly forced to give priority to short-term operations with severe liquidity norms.

The business banks cannot be compared to establishments which, unlike the deposit banks, still adhered to the practices of mixed banking. The model for these was the Banque de Paris et des Pays-Bas (Paribas), with which the Banque de l'Union Parisienne largely aligned itself.

It had been created as a result of the desire of the senior banking houses to pool their resources in order to acquire the necessary standing for participating in large-scale financial operations rather than Saint-Simonian-type projects. It consequently limited its network to one or two branches abroad and spent little time seeking deposits. It did not, of course, abstain from those industrial partnership operations which were a feature of the mixed banks, but the events of the early years of its existence helped to discourage it from them. Thus, as had happened in 1882 in the case of the Crédit Lyonnais, the 1873 crisis and subsequent difficulties in the wake of the Comptoir d'Escompte affair called for prudence where industrial investment was concerned. The favourable economic circumstances of the 1890s may have produced a new series of initiatives, but a number of unfortunate experiences explain the return to a relatively inactive role in the early years of the present century. Consequently, the business banks consolidated their activities in the field of promoting firms, usually in the public services area, chiefly in the hope of stimulating growth in their financial operations. From the beginning of the century, they also sought to create and then develop a series of banking operations. In the France of the 'belle époque' the refusal to lock up capital in long-term risky partnership operations and a preference for financial engineering and banking operations became the norm in business banks.[16]

The growth of a major financial market during the nineteenth century was probably one of the reasons why the French banking system took the form it did around 1900. The 'omnium' system the Saint-Simonians had dreamed of towards the middle of the nineteenth century can be largely accounted for by its shortcomings and above all by the fact that 'industrial' stocks were still rather foreign to the French mentality. The growth of the government stock market and then railway and public service shares during the Second Empire no longer justified Crédit Mobilier-type formulas. Although the business banks took to keeping bundles of company shares in their portfolios, it was with a view to off-loading them on the market later. In addition, the piecemeal growth of a division of labour between credit institutions and business banks was gradually to shape the function of the major French establishments, enabling some to invest with their customers and providing others with financial expertise.

The assessment we can make of the French banking system at the beginning of the twentieth century does not justify the recurrent criticisms made of it. The system of major credit banks was inevitable, and siphoned off an increasing share of the liquid funds in the economy. The combined deposits of the three main credit houses increased sixfold between 1880 and 1914, rising four times as fast as the national income. Discounting and short-term credit were, of course, the norm for the biggest establishments, but their rise made the money market much more homogeneous. Their inevitable competition with the private houses and the Bank of France brought the cost of credit down considerably and, given the high liquidity of those years, credit establishments were increasing their portfolios and offering credit rates often below the Bank of France's discount rate.[17]

Nor were the major firms short of long-term resources. Over the whole system, they were largely able to call on an abundant capital market. The charges that the banks were largely responsible for long-term capital exports have long since been refuted. Even though foreign stock issues became very important on the Paris market and did not always directly determine the flow of exports, there was a high degree of correlation between them and waves of exports.[18]

However, the question of financing medium-sized firms remains unanswered. Even if it is granted that in most cases there was a high level of self-financing, the question of long-term resources was indeed a problem for firms finding access to the capital market difficult during their period of growth, and the part the major Parisian business banks were able to play here should not be overestimated, given the path they took during the 'belle époque'. Nevertheless, historiographers stress the long-term help such firms obtained from regionally-orientated banking establishments heavily involved in the industrial scene. The spotlight has rightly been turned on banks such as the Charpenay, in the Isère, or those in Nancy, but establishments of that kind were rather unstable and some of them, like the Société Marseillaise de Crédit, had to give up certain types of partnership and move towards the model of the credit bank on the eve of the First World War.[19]

State intervention and the loss of a specific identity

The two world wars and the subsequent periods of reconstruction and crisis both saw the appearance of new financing requirements and showed up the inadequacies of the old system. They also led to ever-increasing state involvement, firstly in the setting-up of public credit organizations to fill the gaps in that system and later in a desire to assume overall, rationalizing responsibility harking back to the Saint-Simonian view. These changes, however, were not irreversible, and the last decade, in the context of a French economy ever more linked to the international economy, has seen new directions highlighting certain continuities with nineteenth-century structures.

The chief effect of both wars was to reduce the relative importance of the establishments forming the basis of the structure of banking in France. Here, inflation played a fundamental part by reducing the value of their assets. Thus, after a long period of collapse, those of the six main counter banks did not reach their 1913 level again until 1928. Although deposits were swollen by the influx of floating capital and were a good way above that level by 1928, their own funds did not manage to keep up with inflation in spite of the substantial increases in capital achieved or planned at the end of the 1920s. This state of affairs affected the business banks in particular, since their ability to invest, which was linked to their own funds, was reduced for a long time.[20]

The economic and monetary instability of the 1930s jeopardized the relative consolidation achieved in the late 1920s. The withdrawal of floating capital from 1934 and particularly 1936, capital accumulation and the crisis of confidence in banks, all further reduced their ability to intervene. The business and regional banks were worst hit by these phenomena.

Banks did not meet the situation passively, and during the 1920s in particular the deposit banks sought to compensate for the effects of inflation by developing their network of branches, whilst the business banks increased their clientele, their networks of correspondents and their subsidiaries. As has been said, such efforts were fruitful to some degree, but not until the late 1920s.

However, the system seems to have been marked by greater rigidity in the field of activities. Reconstruction, marked industrial growth after the First World War, new patterns of consumption and the financing of rearmament in the second half of the 1930s created both new needs and new opportunities.

Clearly, financing firms means that the business banks had to move more unambiguously in that direction. By the end of the war, both the Banque de l'Union Parisienne and Paribas had developed group strategies. Similarly, the regional banks had moved further in the direction we have already noted, and the Banque National de Crédit had adopted a strategy close to that of the mixed banks.[21] However, such initiatives were not to be long-lasting. Although it did not actually pull back, Paribas adopted a much more cautious approach after the 1921 crisis, and the Banque de l'Union Parisienne distanced itself from the Schneider group. By the end of the 1920s they were tending to leave wide-ranging industrial strategies to the industrial groups, going back to their job of financing engineering and market operations as a result of the healthy state of the stock market at the end of the 1920s.[22] By the end of the 1930s those banks still engaged in this type of operation, and especially the regional institutions, were experiencing serious difficulties.

The banks also tried to meet industry's increasing need for medium-term credit. The large deposit banks created several specialized establishments in the late 1920s, certain of which were associated with the setting-up of hire-purchase companies founded at the initiative of motor-car manufacturers.

Overall, however, banks were reluctant to make any significant changes to their own practices or question the *de facto* codification that

had taken place at the beginning of the century. The main areas
of innovation at the time involved the setting-up of specialized establishments and thus were not directly the work of the major credit
banks. In particular, the state was induced either to undertake or to
encourage the creation of the establishments required if new needs were
to be met.

Thus in 1919 the period of reconstruction brought about the creation
of the Crédit National, which subsequently emerged as the permanent
source of medium- and long-term credit for firms. In other fields the
Banque Française du Commerce Extérieur, des Chèques Postaux was
set up, and in 1936 the Caisse Nationale des Marchés was made
responsible for granting advances on state orders. The Caisse des
Dépots et Consignations gradually changed the structure of its functions
and acquired a portfolio of stocks and shares in firms. Finally, the state
also encouraged the growth of both the Crédit Agricole and the
Banques Populaires in an attempt to fill the gaps that were visible by
the early years of the century.[23]

The changes in banking occurring as a result of the Second World
War were from several points of view a continuation of those arising
in the interwar years. In many ways, however, they had to do with
complex and even contradictory concerns and their effects did not
always coincide with the desired aims, often necessitating further
adjustments by the mid-1960s.

This range of reforms, involving a combination of the nationalization
of the four major credit establishments plus the issuing institution and
the strict regulations introduced in 1941 (and merely amended in 1945)
was aimed primarily at the existing system.[24] They harked back to the
voluntarist and rationalizing motifs of Saint-Simonian thought and their
aim was, in General de Gaulle's words, 'to direct the savings of the
nation towards huge investments' needed for the modernization of
the economy.[25] The effect combining all these rules and regulations with
a major development of state-aided credit organizations was in fact not
the creation of a type of capitalism based on the state banks, which
might have taken the form of a participation by the big nationalized
banks in industry, but a more segmented and specialized banking
activity. State participation in this area was in fact organized independently of its participation in banking.

The regulations emerging from the war laid down strict norms for
establishments with regard to functions and resources, and their effect
was to harden the division between deposit and business banks by

artificially stressing the features of each kind, which restricted the former to resources and short-term loans and the latter to long-term investment and financing. The system was complemented by a number of regulations embodying purely administrative safeguards, to such an extent that a virtual cartel was established by law and competition was non-existent.

During the same years the state encouraged the growth of specialized bodies directly dependent on it or the special considerations it gave them in order to meet specific financing needs. This meant that the Caisse des Dépots siphoned off an increasing proportion of savings and used it to finance local authorities. It also encouraged the growth of the Banques Populaires or Banques du Crédit Mutuel aimed at the middle classes or small and medium-sized firms, and in particular that of the Crédit Agricole. The latter's share of deposits increased considerably between 1950 and 1970, thus reducing markedly, and much more than in the inter-war years, the market of those banks that had grown out of the banking revolution in the middle years of the nineteenth century.

However, the fact that the whole system was becoming more rigid did not rule out every kind of development or adaptation. The business banks were revitalized as a result of their greater participation in industrial investment, and on the edges of the system there were new, highly specialized credit establishments for financing housing, consumption and certain types of industrial plant, and for meeting needs the major establishments could not cater for.

And yet it was not so much the renewal of the structures of the banking system itself as the new ways and means of providing finance that made it possible to cope with the enormous increase in investments during the years of reconstruction and prosperity. The major innovation in this field was the rapid growth in medium-term credit, which meant that what had been a gap in the interwar credit system in France could now be filled, and also that banks could mobilize part of such debts in the issuing institution to provide some of the funds for monetary financing. In 1961 medium- and long-term credits accounted for almost 60% of the sources of finance in the economy. Although the banks played an important part in distributing such credits, they themselves provided only a small proportion of them, given the importance of short-term resources in their total turnover. With the necessary guarantees from state organizations they were in a position to extricate themselves from some of the financing and the risks attendant upon such types of credit.[26]

The reforms initiated from 1966–7 and relaunched in the early 1980s after a break were aimed at encouraging banks to take risks again and at moving the system into what was now a global and market-regulated world. There was in fact a measure of continuity between 1966–7 and the 1984 reforms. The objective of the former was to begin to make the banks less specialized by abolishing in practice the rigid division between deposit and business banks. The 1984 law took the process further by granting all banks the uniform status of credit establishments. In the same way the gradual disappearance of government-subsidized credits removed the special status of institutions like the Crédit Foncier or the Crédit National, and the privileges establishments like the Crédit Agricole still enjoyed were once again called into question. The privatization of the major establishments from 1986 completed the trend.[27]

Such reforms went hand in hand with that of the money market, which was aimed at both reducing the monetary financing of the economy and reducing the cost of credit. It was begun in the second half of the 1960s, was temporarily interrupted by a return to a planned economy, and was in place from 1985. The result was an enormous international market offering a huge spectrum of types of borrowing and open to a wider range of participants.

The effects of the 1966–7 reforms were not, however, exactly what had initially been anticipated. They had produced a wave of mergers in which a large number of banks of secondary importance were absorbed into more powerful groupings, thus reinforcing the oligopolistic nature of the French system. The movement towards the model of the universal bank proposed by Jean Bouvier in his 1972 analyses did not occur, however.[28] From that point of view, the case of the business banks is very informative. Although at first they struggled to approach that model by surrounding themselves with a huge range of establishments covering every sector of the market, the development was never brought to a proper conclusion. During the 1980s they moved away from the heavy industrial commitments they could not take on, opting for a clear return to financial engineering and forms of organization in terms of function. In the same way, the obvious drift of certain deposit banks such as the Crédit Lyonnais towards investment banking stopped short in the early 1990s. It was as if the freedom that had been given back to banks, within a framework of new boundaries between establishments and activities, was tending to lead to a new kind of specialization in terms of each one's basic functions, but without the legal constraints introduced during the post-war years and in an extremely competitive environment. That development is still under way.

It can be explained by the accelerated international opening-up of the French economy in the 1980s. By fitting firms into a new world-wide framework, it was setting up market structures offering them even greater opportunities for financing than those they had enjoyed during the 'belle époque'. Given the same sequence of cause and effect, the new way of seeing things was not very conducive to a return to the model of the universal bank.

The continuity between the turn of the century and the present day has not, however, been absolutely complete. The contemporary period has also seen a more rapid world-wide growth of markets for industrial products and services, and the general internationalization of banks. The latters' ability to fit into a world capital market has, to a far greater extent than at the end of the nineteenth century, made it easier for French firms to do the same. From this point of view the very marked difference at the beginning of the century between international banking activity and the activity of firms is becoming less evident. The trend in recent years thus seems to some extent to be to bring to an end the period of retreat and central planning initiated by the First World War. As the French banking system is now figuring more on the market than it did in the early years of the century, certain of its unique characteristics are disappearing.

Conclusion

The French banking system as it existed at the beginning of the modern period (and from many points of view at the end of the nineteenth century) adapted to meet the needs of an economy that was still largely rural, with flows siphoning off its production and linking it to the outside world. Gradually, a network of increasingly polarized private houses capable of stimulating a wide circulation of commercial papers along-side a widespread use of discount emerged in the capital and on one or two major axes. The investments necessitated by the first period of industrialization were largely covered by the extension of existing credit methods between firms or periodically renewed bank credits. In its existing form the system could not cope with the enormous demands made by the railway building programme. The system of universal banks suggested in the middle of that century was adapted to a rapid rise in demand and a still rather unstructured money market, and the slowing down of growth by the end of the Second Empire, combined with certain excesses, explains why it was almost universally abandoned by the late 1880s. The 'French-style' banking system thus achieved a satisfactory balance, adapted as it was to a country with fairly slow growth and a relatively restricted internal market characterized by the existence of a large, high-return financial market combined with a plentiful circulation of commercial papers and the use of discount. In that kind of context it is difficult to imagine the banks imposing forms of domination on firms, something which was never the case in the France of the time. The medium- to long-term financing of firms had no access to the financial market, which was no doubt a deficiency in the system, as the crises of the 1930s and the requirements in both periods of reconstruction indicated.

A certain new rigidity in the system during the 1920s and 1930s, a fall in the resources of banks and a reduced power of absorption in the financial market led, after one or two tentative efforts, to a widening of the range of banking operations with the massive and permanent introduction of long-term credit. This meant that the investment needs of the years of reconstruction and growth could be met. As the markets regained their power in the 1980s, the range of possible forms of borrowing and ways of providing capital simply increased.

The combination of the role of the state and outside influences brought to bear via the markets was certainly one of the major factors accounting for changes in the French banking system, in ways of financing the economy and hence in the structures of French capitalism. The early existence of a centralized state in France had probably produced a concentration of major banking activities in Paris by the eighteenth century without, however, making it possible for a modern banking system to appear as early as it did in England. In the same way, the combination of the centralism emerging in the modern period and of Saint-Simonian-type theories claiming to rationalize investment led to the setting-up of the hybrid and rigidified system that France had after 1945.

Such ideas never came to full fruition, however. French banks have always maintained full relations with the international market, and the forms of the domination of industry by banks as pictured by Hilferding via the model of the universal bank have never existed in France.

The international opening-up of the economy is the second key to an understanding of the ways in which the French banking system has evolved. The insertion of the economy into the flows of goods and capital led to periods of apprenticeship, with Italian bankers in the past and more recently through contacts with Anglo-Saxon finance. The part played by the senior banks, which was extended by that of the business banks, is an essential ingredient in an explanation of an ongoing process. That opening-up, which has been accentuated over the last ten years or so, currently seems to be leading French banking and industrial capitalism towards something fairly close to the Anglo-Saxon model.

Notes

1 H. Van der Wee, R. Bogaert and G. Kurgan-van Hentenryck, *La banque en Occident* (Antwerp, 1991), pp. 143–8.
2 J. Bouvier, 'Vers le capitalisme bancaire: l'expansion du crédit après Law', in F. Braudel and E. Labrousse (eds.), *Histoire économique et sociale de la France*, T2 (Paris, 1970), p. 304.
3 On this topic, see H. Lüthy, *La banque protestante en France de la Révocation de l'Edit de Nantes à la Révolution*, 2 vols. (Paris, 1959–61).
4 It is the case of Bouvier, 'Vers le capitalisme bancaire', pp. 306 and 320.
5 On this topic, see M. Mollat, *Jacques Coeur ou l'esprit d'entreprise* (Paris, 1988).
6 Bouvier, 'Vers le capitalisme bancaire', p. 302.
7 One can find a precise description of this system in B. Gille, *La banque et le crédit en France de 1815 à 1848* (Paris, 1980), and in M. Lévy-Leboyer, *Les banques européennes et l'industrialisation internationale dans la première moitié du XIXième siècle* (Paris, 1964).
8 Gille, *La banque et le crédit en France*, pp. 154–5.
9 See, for instance, J. Bouvier's analysis in *Naissance d'une banque: le Crédit Lyonnais* (Paris, 1968), pp. 15–25.
10 Quoted by Gille, *Le banque et le crédit en France*, p. 114.
11 Quoted by J. Autin, *Les frères Pereire* (Paris, 1984), p. 112.
12 Quoted by Gille, *Le banque et le crédit en France*, p. 112.
13 Quoted by Autin, *Les frères Pereire*, pp. 118 and 128.
14 M. Lévy-Leboyer gives a synthesis of this evolution in Braudel and Labrousse (eds.), *Histoire économique et sociale de la France*, T3 (Paris, 1970), pp. 347–67.
15 See Société Générale, 1864–1964 (published in Paris by the Société Générale, 1964) or Bouvier, *Le Crédit Lyonnais*.
16 E. Bussière, *Paribas, Europe and the World, 1872–1992* (Antwerp, 1992).
17 A. Plessis, 'Les banques, le crédit et l'économie', in M. Lévy-Leboyer and J.-C. Casanova (eds.), *Entre l'Etat et le marché. L'économie française de 1880 à nos jours* (Paris, 1991), pp. 335–44.
18 See M. Lévy-Leboyer, in *La Position Internationale de la France* (Paris, 1973).
19 M. Lescure, *Banques, régionales et croissance économique. L'exemple de la Société marseillaise de crédit*, Chambre de commerce de Marseille (Marseilles, 1983), pp. 103–30.
20 J. Bouvier and A. Plessis's analysis in Plessis, 'Les banques, le crédit et l'économie', pp. 344–64.
21 Bussière, *Paribas, Europe and the World*, and H. Bonin, 'Les banques françaises de la seconde industrialisation', *Revue Historique*, 268 (1982), p. 215.
22 E. Bussière, 'Les banques d'affaires françaises au XIXième siècle: des établissements

en quête d'identité?', in *Les banques en Europe de l'ouest de 1920 à nos jours. Comité pour l'histoire économique et financière de la France* (Paris, 1995), pp. 223–35.

23 J. Bouvier, 'L'interventionnisme bancaire et l'Etat', in F. Braudel and E. Labrousse (eds.), *Histoire économique et sociale de la France*, T4, vol. II (Paris, 1980), pp. 697–704.

24 See C. Andrieu, *La banque sous l'occupation* (Paris, 1990).

25 Quoted by Plessis, 'Les banques, le crédit et l'économie', p. 322.

26 J. Bouvier, 'Les entreprises financières', in F. Braudel and E. Labrousse (eds.), *Histoire économique et sociale de la France*, T4, vol. III (Paris, 1982), pp. 1177–221.

27 H. Bonin, *L'argent en France depuis 1880* (Paris, 1989), pp. 54–6.

28 J. Bouvier, *Un siècle de banque française* (Paris, 1973).

8 The influence of banking on the rise and expansion of industrial capitalism in Germany

Dieter Ziegler

Any attempt to assess the influence of banking on the rise of industrial capitalism in Germany ought to begin with Alexander Gerschenkron's model of a successful path to industrialization of 'moderately backward countries'. Contrary to contemporary thought, for Gerschenkron it was not the pattern of industrialization of the more developed country that was to be imitated by a successful 'latecomer'. As the 'latecomer' lacked certain prerequisites of the 'pioneer', it was the necessity to substitute for these prerequisites that forced the 'latecomer' to divert from the 'pioneer's' model. In addition, different degrees of backwardness demanded different institutional substitutes for the lacking prerequisites, so that the industrialization patterns among national industrializers finally became substantially different. In his tripartite typology of backwardness (least backward, moderately backward and extremely backward) most continental European countries were classified as 'moderately backward', for which, in the first instance, bank finance of industry was crucial to successful industrialization:

> In a relatively backward country capital is scarce and diffused, the distrust of industrial activities is considerable, and, finally, there is greater pressure for bigness because of the scope of the industrialization movement, the larger average size of plant, and the concentration of industrialization processes on branches of relatively high ratios of capital to output. To these should be added the scarcity of entrepreneurial talent in the backward country. It is the pressure of

these circumstances which essentially gave rise to the divergent development in banking over large portions of the continent as against England. The continental practices in the field of industrial investment banking must be conceived as specific instruments of industrialization in a backward country.[1]

Among continental European countries Germany was seen as the prototype of a successful 'latecomer' that solved the problem of directing finance to the capital intensive 'new industries' of the mid-nineteenth century by developing an institutional substitute for the missing prerequisite of 'original accumulation':[2] the universal bank.

The 'mixed' or 'universal' banking practices of the German banks were seen as a compromise between the English note issuing (and later deposit) banks and vulnerable Crédit Mobilier-style investment banks:

> The difference between banks of the Crédit Mobilier type and the commercial banks in the advanced industrial country of the time (England) was absolute. Between the English bank essentially designed to serve as a source of short-term capital and a bank designed to finance the long-term investment needs of the economy there was a complete gulf. The German banks, which may be taken as a paragon of the type of the universal bank, successfully combined the basic idea of the Crédit Mobilier with the short-term activities of commercial banks.[3]

As the universal bank extended its investment banking activities by cultivating short-term business, it gained flexibility in order not to find itself locked in by frozen (long-term) loans or unsaleable stock when the capital market tightened. Contrary to the Crédit Mobilier and to the English finance companies which had been modelled after the French investment bank, both the German universal joint-stock banks (Disconto-Gesellschaft, Berliner Handelgesellschaft and Darmstädter Bank für Handel und Industrie) and the 'universal' private banks survived the crises of 1857, 1866 and 1873. Also in contrast to an English commercial bank which served more or less passively the needs of industry and commerce by the provision of means of payment or bill discounting, the universal bank, because of its much closer involvement in the fate of its industrial customers, had to supervise closely the latters' activities. Bank control was facilitated by the legal division between executive and supervision within corporate organizations, since the bank in return for a larger current account credit margin often demanded a seat on the supervisory board. By such 'institutional bridgehead' the bank could at times extend supervision far beyond financial control into that of entrepreneurial and managerial decisions. Finally, the cumulation of supervisory board seats enabled the banks to perceive quickly profitable opportunities of cartelization and amalgamation of industrial enterprises and thus became not only important agents for the direction of funds, but also agents of market integration and regulation.[4]

Despite the numerous criticism of Gerschenkron's model, both as regards the general framework and certain individual cases (Austria in particular), the emphasis on the importance of banking to German industrialization has stood the test of time quite well. Yet, some modifications have become necessary. First, Gerschenkron was fixed on the universal, that is, the joint-stock branch. Apart from a converted private bank in 1848, joint-stock banks were founded only when German industry was already 'spurting'. Gerschenkron unnecessarily weakens his own argument of bank importance by not paying attention to the pioneers of the mixed banking practices and fixing on the Crédit Mobilier model, that was in fact imitated and adapted to the German environment by the joint-stock banks founded in succession to the Crédit Mobilier, but which fell back also on elder German mixed banking traditions.

The second critical point also concerns Gerschenkron's exclusive concentration on the universal joint-stock bank. 'Banking' consists of more than one specific institution, even if it is called 'universal bank'. The term 'universal' must not be understood as if the bundling of various functions 'under one roof' meant that all financial services were covered by this institution. The German banking system before the First World War was much more diversified than is recognized even by informed historians.

Finally, Gerschenkron's relatively strict association of the degree of backwardness with certain institutional innovations[5] led to an underestimation of the role of the state in the German industrialization process. This was true not only for economic policy ('Gewerbeförderung', customs union) and the building up of an efficient infrastructure (railways, education), but also for the development of the banking systems. In Prussia in particular the central note issuing bank was indispensable for the industrialization process, both directly as provider of means of payment and indirectly as the backbone of the emerging universal banking system.

The banks and the 'big spurt'

In the recent past the notion of a 'big spurt', a discontinuity in industrial growth,[6] that had been central in Gerschenkron's approach to industrialization, and particularly its linking with the degree of backwardness,[7] has been strongly criticized. Even in the case of the German 'Industrial Revolution' which was for a long time regarded as a prototype of an industrial 'take-off', modern empirical and econometric research has shown that there was neither 'a "kink" in the curve of industrial output' nor is Germany confirmed as a country whose labour force was significantly rapidly – in comparison with Britain – redeployed out of agriculture into industry.[8] However, those who tentatively support Gerschenkron's view, while concentrating on the mid-nineteenth-century 'new industries', have argued that it was the so-called leading sector complex (railways, coal, iron and mechanical engineering) that experienced extraordinarily high growth rates. These sectors were not only linked with each other, but also, and the railways in particular, with the rest of the economy, and therefore the development of this leading sector complex was crucial for the industrialization of other sectors including agriculture.[9]

In the 1840s railways and heavy industry, however, were much more capital intensive sectors than the textile industry had been in the case of the industrial pioneer in the eighteenth century. Since Germany did not suffer from a capital shortage in the early stages of industrialization, the problem of finding capital for industrial purposes lay neither in the aggregate size of savings nor in their liquidity but in their availability. Owners of funds were not yet used to invest in industry and commerce, and parts of the Prussian bureaucracy and the majority of the Junkers were for political reasons opposed to any transfer of capital from agriculture into industry. The missing prerequisite of available capital in connection with the comparatively high capital requirements of railways and heavy industry demanded financial intermediaries, either by the modernization of existing banks or by the creation of a new type of financial institution, which would be able to mobilize the society's productive capital by channelling funds into the new and more profitable sectors. However, the traditional financial centres, the Free Cities of Frankfurt and Hamburg, were hardly interested in these new developments. After 1830 their traditional markets, the financing of the Anglo-German trade in Hamburg[10] and exchange dealings and the financing of the various German states in Frankfurt,[11] reached their zenith, and neither the Hamburg merchant bankers nor the Frankfurt private bankers were prepared significantly to diversify their activities into such unknown and seemingly risky territory as the financing of railways; and even when they did, as in the case of the Taunus Railway (Frankfurt–Wiesbaden), they burnt their fingers. With the exception of Gebrüder Bethmann no major Frankfurt banking house was engaged in railway financing over the crucial decades of the 'big spurt', not even M. A. Rothschild & Söhne, the Parisian and Viennese houses which had been among the most active railway promoters in Europe.[12] In consequence, in 1851 the Frankfurt Stock Exchange listed only five railways, three banks and three other stocks, but altogether fifty-five German and foreign state loans.[13]

Industrialization in Germany resulted not only in a displacement of formerly advanced manufacturing regions by the new industrial centres, but also in a shift in the relative importance of the country's financial centres. After the loss of Frankfurt's independence in 1866, when it was annexed by Prussia, and by the unification of German currencies it lost its traditional markets. Although Frankfurt remained the most important German market for foreign stocks, the Frankfurt Stock Exchange and the great Frankfurt private banks had lost their premier position to the Berlin Stock Exchange and to Berlin and Cologne private banks. In addition, the new joint-stock credit banks were either founded in Berlin (Berliner Handelsgesellschaft, Disconto-Gesellschaft and later Deutsche Bank and Nationalbank für Deutschland) or they had to shift their head office to Berlin, if they were keen to extend their regional market to the national scale (Darmstädter Bank, Dresdner Bank and to a lesser extent Schaaffhausenscher Bankverein, which remained a 'provincial great bank' despite its Berlin branch established in 1892;[14] after the turn of the century the Commerz- und Discontobank, originating from Hamburg, and the Mitteldeutsche Creditbank (Meiningen and Frankfurt) became also Berlin great banks).

The importance of Cologne and later Berlin as financial centres grew rapidly in step with the industrialization of Rhineland-Westphalia and the Berlin area. In Prussia, many railways which, unlike those in most other German states, had been built by private enterprise, owed their existence to the newcomers in private banking such as Oppenheim, Stein and Schaaffhausen in Cologne, von der Heydt-Kersten in Elberfeld, Schickler, Mendelssohn (only in the initial stages of railway development) and later also Bleichröder in Berlin, Ruffer and Heimann in Breslau. These bankers did not only grant (*de facto* long-term) current account credits to the railway companies, organized the issuing of stock and even held shares of substantial quantity in case of need, but many bankers themselves (Oppenheim, von der Heydt, Ruffer) engaged as railway promoters.

However, investment banking was a dangerous business, and very soon, long before the Crédit Mobilier had been founded, the enterprising Rhenish private bankers had to develop techniques that protected them from collapse when the financial market tightened. The early history of the Rhenish Railway (connecting Cologne with Antwerp via Aachen and the Belgian State Railway) illustrates the particular problems of investment banking in the beginnings of German industrialization, when the financial infrastructure was still totally underdeveloped. Despite a very promising beginning in 1835 the company faced enormous difficulties when the cost estimate proved to be insufficient. Unfavourable circumstances in the late 1830s (including seemingly hostile legislation) made it from the outset a forlorn hope to raise additional finance through the market. Since the Prussian state was also very reluctant to support the company, it relied heavily on its bankers. In 1838 a consortium consisting of three Cologne banking houses agreed to take up the total new stock issue of 1.5 million Taler. However, downward price movements of stock rendered the shares held by the banks unsaleable, and the 'lock up' of the bankers' resources posed a serious threat to the latters' solvency. At first both sides agreed to bridge the problems by a secret repurchase of stock by the railway company, but as market conditions did not improve and the construction of the track was in danger of being suspended, both the railway company and its bankers were only saved by the Belgian government, which finally agreed to pay for the stock.[15]

A few years later, Abraham Schaaffhausen, who had not only been engaged in two railway companies, the Rhenish textile industry, real estates and house building, shipping and insurance but also in mining and mechanical engineering, was less fortunate. In 1846 the real estate market collapsed and in 1848, as a result of the Parisian revolution, stock prices also fell into an abyss at the stock exchanges of Paris, Amsterdam and Frankfurt. In March 1848 even gilt-edged investments that were meant as a liquidity reserve[16] were 'locked in' and as the Prussian Bank was only prepared to rediscount bill parcels worth 2,000 Taler per day and customer, the Schaaffhausen bank had to close its doors.[17] Although Schaaffhausen was finally saved by the conversion into a joint-stock bank and a state guarantee, the fact that a basically sound investment bank might experience a temporary lock up of its portfolio ought to have induced the Rhenish bankers to develop the short end of their lending business in order to balance the whole portfolio structure. A retreat from their industrial customers, however, was impossible, because there was no alternative to the fast-growing Rhenish industry, and in 1857 Schaaffhausen was even more heavily engaged in heavy industry and railways than before.[18] In addition, the banking house Seydlitz & Merkens which shied away from this business after 1848 lost ground to its rivals and was finally liquidated and taken over in 1870 – ironically – by Schaaffhausen.[19] Contrary to the fate of Seydlitz & Merkens new and enterprising private banks, which were closely tied to fast-growing heavy industry concerns, expanded as quickly as their customers. This was particularly true for the banking house Deichmann & Co. which had been founded in 1858 by the former senior partner (and later director) of Schaaffhausen, Wilhelm Ludwig Deichmann. As the 'house bank' of Krupp Deichmann had already by the late 1860s become a premier Rhenish banking house.[20]

The expertise gained by these bankers was directly transferred into the nascent universal banks, because almost all successful universal banks were founded by experienced private bankers:

> Darmstädter Bank (by the Cologne banker Oppenheim and the Schaaffhausen director Mevissen),[21]
> Berliner Handelsgesellschaft (by the most important Berlin bankers including Bleichröder, Mendelssohn, Gelpcke, Warschauer, but also by Oppenheim and Mevissen again),
> Deutsche Bank (by almost all important Berlin bankers led by Delbrück and many other bankers from Bremen, Cologne, Frankfurt and other places),
> Commerz- und Discontobank (by many Hamburg bankers including Warburg, but also by the Berlin banker Mendelssohn and the Frankfurt banker Goldschmidt),
> Dresdner Bank (by conversion of the Dresden private banking house Michael Kaskel).

These founding activities can be interpreted as an attempt to institutionalize some form of cartel for those transactions which had become too large for a single private banking house. Consequently, the relationship between the bankers and 'their' joint-stock banks was more or less cordial and the bankers still kept both an influential position and adequate quotas in all syndicate agreements.

The banks and the state

In all German states the development of banking was very closely linked
with government interference. Apart from the distrust of any 'paper
money' resulting from the French 'assignat' inflation on the part of
the public, it was the state's exclusive right of coining ('Münzregal') in
particular and the fear that the provision of means of payment by a
privately owned bank might impair the states' power that prohibited
the creation of private banks of issue not only in Prussia, but even in
the Free Cities of Hamburg and Frankfurt. As the public was barely
prepared to accept paper money of larger quantities, even those (state-
owned) banks which had been founded as note issuing banks, such as the
Royal Bank of Prussia (Königliche Giro- und Lehn-Bank), were unable
to circulate their notes.[22]

However, in the early nineteenth century there was obviously no
shortage of means of payment. The problem was the currency chaos of
the German states. Although almost all German states had adopted
a silver standard, in the Prussian Rhineland alone at least seventy
coins from Holland, France, Belgium and the various German states
were reportedly in local circulation after the annexation of 1815.[23] In
addition, the comparability of different coins of even the same
denomination, like the Taler, was difficult, because in practice their
respective metal value was different.[24] It was of particular importance,
therefore, to unify the coinage system. The creation of a unified
'national' currency was first attempted by the new Kingdom of Hanover
in 1817 and secondly by Prussia in 1821. Although it took several years
until the official currency had replaced the foreign coins in circulation,
in 1838 the Zollverein states agreed to a coinage convention with fixed
exchange rates between the two coinage systems (Taler and Gulden)
with common metal-content specifications. Each member state had to
opt either for the Taler or for the Gulden. In practice north Germany
became the Taler area while the south German states adopted the
Gulden as the basic monetary unit.[25] The relative success of the German
states' efforts to organize the coinage system extended the period when
the traditional purely metallic currency proved to be sufficient and
lessened the necessity to convert the existing state banks into note
issuing banks. Instead, from the late 1820s the Prussian government
developed its government bank, the Prussian Sea Trading Corporation
(Seehandlung) into a sort of 'educational bank' for Prussian industrialists. Already in 1794 its charter had stated that the Corporation was

'permitted to undertake every sort of commercial business without exception'.[26] After having overcome the disastrous effects of the Napoleonic War on the Prussian state finances the bank began to act accordingly: it granted credits (short-term and long-term), took part in the management of those enterprises which relied on the bank's injection of finance and finally it founded some new factories and took over others, many of which were nearly bankrupt. Although the intention of this policy lay in the direction of the Prussian eighteenth-century mercantilistic tradition, the outcome was a strong modernizing effort. The bank was anxious to install the most modern machinery so that the factories could become models which could be inspected and copied by private industrialists.[27] Although historians are still divided on the question of the long-term efficiency of such modernization 'à la Prusse', the history of the Seehandlung in the 1830s fully supports David Good's assertion, who maintained, following Gerschenkron, that moderately backward countries relied more heavily on qualitative support from the banking system (which lay somewhere in the 'entre-preneurial sphere') rather than on quantitative assistance (measured by an asset/GNP ratio).[28] However, the activities of the Seehandlung were concentrated on depressed areas such as Lower Silesia aiming at the stabilization of the explosive social and political situation of unemployed pre- and proto-industrial labour. The more advanced regions, the whole western part of the Kingdom, did not receive any assistance from the Seehandlung, and the Rhenish (mostly liberal) industrialists and private bankers heavily criticized the anti-liberal economic policy of the state, which prohibited the provision of credit to industry and commerce by the Royal Bank and its inability to act as an efficient rediscounting agency on the one hand,[29] whereas the Seehandlung, on the other hand, pumped its means into a few, partly inefficiently managed, enter-prises.

In the mid-1840s, when railway construction in Prussia experienced its first upswing, the demand for more flexibility of the monetary system and the scarcity of credit for industry and commerce became more pressing. When in 1844 the capital market collapsed and not only state-supported railway companies got into trouble, but even the state itself could not get credit, the Prussian government finally realized that it had either to reform its two state banks or to permit the establishment of joint-stock banks of issue. As the second solution was still out of question, the king ordered first that no new industrial establishments should be set up or taken over by the Seehandlung in order to make room for the provision of credits to the state, and, secondly, one year later, in 1846, the Royal Bank was reorganized as the central bank of issue.[30]

The regulations for the issue of bank notes, however, were so restrictive that there was almost no room to manoeuvre and – as it has been shown above in the case of the Schaaffhausen insolvency – in the political crisis in March 1848 the new Prussian Bank (Preußische Bank) was unable to back the finance markets. Similar to the 1844 regulations for the English country banks the Prussian Bank was not allowed to extend its issue beyond a legally fixed maximum amount, irrespective of the silver holdings in its vault. In addition, at least one third of the notes in circulation had to be covered by metal. In the 1850s the maximum limit proved to be so low that the silver cover of the notes in circulation was on average 100% or even more. As the Prussian government was still most restrictive as regards the establishment of private banks of issue,[31] the Rhenish bankers began to establish private note issuing banks in the neighbouring states of the Taler area. These banks, the issue of which was almost entirely meant to circulate in Prussia, posed a serious threat to the Prussian 'Münzregal'.[32] Finally, in order to keep this 'foreign' money out of the country, the Prussian Parliament lifted the maximum limit and the Prussian Bank was allowed to circulate as many bank notes as required by the public provided that at least one third of its circulation was covered by silver.[33]

By the early 1860s note issue had virtually become a government monopoly, which was not seriously in question during the ensuing decades. Contrary to its rediscounting practices in the crisis of 1848 and contrary to the restrictive lending policy of the private banks of issue, the Prussian Bank rediscounted freely during the weeks of the international monetary crisis of 1866, which was in the Prussian case aggravated by the outbreak of the Austro-Prussian War. As the political and economic crises of 1870 and 1873 respectively were also satisfactorily handled by the Bank, it proved to be a reliable 'lender of last resort', and a large majority of contemporary economists supported the transformation of the Prussian Bank into the Reichsbank in 1875. However, the regulations for the issue of Reichsbank notes differed from the 1856 legal code as a maximum limit of the fiduciary issue was (re)introduced. Contrary to the regulation of 1846 this maximum was not meant as a strict limit, but the Reichsbank was allowed to extend its issue beyond this limit subject only to a 5% tax. This provision did not seriously impair the flexibility of rediscounting even in times of liquidity pressure, which had distinguished the Prussian Bank with its unlimited issuing right. In consequence, the universal banks could hold more risky portfolios than would have otherwise been the case.[34] In addition to its (re)discounting facilities, the Reichsbank with its more than 200 branches dominated the country's payment business, which was extensively used by the (largely unit) credit banks. Though not intended, the historical result of the almost autonomous development of universal banking and of the state-controlled central banking was an efficient division of labour between Reichsbank and credit banks with the provision of means of payment and short-term trade credits on the one hand and industrial credit and security loans on the other hand.[35]

The universal banking system and the mature economy

Following Riesser and other contemporary observers[36] it has been regarded as an established wisdom that although even in Germany retained profits were by far the most important source for fixed capital investment,[37] the provision of long-term finance was the strong point of the German banking system. Contrary to the English deposit banks, the universal banks were not only involved in industrial finance by current account credits, but if demand of industrial corporations became too large or too long term for an overdraft (and if market conditions seemed to be favourable), they were also prepared to undertake the issue of stock on behalf of the customer, and the banks were also prepared to purchase stock, if necessary. This mechanism ensured that the issuing bank was not only interested in the success of the issue, but also in the success of the issuing industrial corporation.

It has been argued, however, that the universal banks only granted 'development assistance for the strong', that is, for big industry, while small- and medium-sized industry was left without any assistance from the universal banks. To these critics, the net effect of this misallocation of funds on the economy's growth was negative.[38] True, it cannot be denied that the great banks from their very beginnings have confined their business to railway companies, heavy industry and later also to the 'new industries' of the so-called Second Industrial Revolution. Other sectors were only occasionally assisted, if, as the Darmstädter Bank management was instructed in 1853, the respective customer promised to generate a business volume of at least 50,000 Gulden per year.[39]

By the late nineteenth century, the great banks were still Berlin banks with hardly any branch in the provinces, and their business was Berlin business,[40] that is, the great banks' provincial connections were confined to large industrial concerns which were looking for access to the formal capital market. In regard to this particular clientele the comparative advantage of offering direct access to the Berlin Stock Exchange[41] – in addition to the larger credit margins that the great banks were able to grant for individual customers – compensated for the disadvantage of having no branch in the place.

However, it would be a serious misunderstanding of the functioning of the German banking system to believe that, first, the 'universal bank' was equated with the 'great bank', and, secondly, that the banking system was narrowed to the credit banks. The sheer quantitative weight of the great banks (and even of all credit banks) in the German banking system does not at all justify the commonly held disregard of the other financial institutions. Table 8.1 clearly proves that the great banks left an important part of the economy's financial business to other institutions; and, indeed, taking the whole banking sector into account, there was no bias towards heavy industry and against light industry before the First World War, but a clear division of labour between different financial institutions: great banks, internationally operating private bankers, 'provincial great banks', small provincial joint-stock banks, local private bankers, mortgage banks, savings banks, co-operative banks and banks of issue (including the Reichsbank).[42]

Division of labour between these institutions substantially differed from the English division of function financial system. In England different financial institutions were specialized in specific services in financial intermediation: bill acceptance or bill discount, dealing in stocks or issuing of stock and underwriting, and so on. True, special services, such as the issue of stock, were only demanded by a small group of customers, but in England it was the specific service that structured the customers, whereas in Germany it was the other way round. The financial institutions were specialized on a specific group of customers and provided for all financial services demanded by this group. Big industrial concerns demanded a wide range of services from bill discounting to the issuing of stock, and therefore the great banks' business was the most universal banking business (in terms of function).

The same range of services, with the exception of the issuing of stock, was also provided by the 'provincial great banks' for their clientele, the medium-sized industry of their respective region. As the industrial customers of the provincial banks were only occasionally incorporated as joint-stock companies, the appropriate assessment of the credit

Table 8.1. *Assets of German financial institutions 1880–1938 (in billions of marks)*

	1880	1900	1913	1925	1929	1932	1938
Bank of issue	1.57	2.57	4.03	4.82	6.93	5.79	10.84
Great banks	0.90	3.30	8.40	6.14	13.77	8.80	9.01
Other credit banks	0.45	3.66	13.64	4.47	7.20	5.15	9.88
Private banks[a]	2.50	3.50	4.00	2.00	3.60[b]	2.10	1.25
Savings banks[a]	2.78	9.45	23.56	4.60	18.56	20.47	31.14
Co-operative banks	0.59	1.68	6.17	3.64	6.10	5.60	8.08
Mortgage banks	1.85	7.90	14.00	1.48	7.44	8.05	8.19
Other	1.45	2.85	1.00	2.78	4.45	5.74	6.98
Total	12.10	35.00	74.80	30.00	68.00	61.70	85.10

[a] Including Girozentralen and Zentralsparkassen respectively.
[b] 1930.
Source: H. Wixforth and D. Ziegler, 'The Niche in the Universal Banking System. The Role and Significance of Private Bankers within German Industry', *Financial History Review*, 1 (1994), table 2.

margin of a partnership's current account required bank monitoring on a local or regional level. If the fixed capital investment needs outran the resources of the provincial 'house bank', industrial enterprises turned to the great banks; and as this held for heavy industry and electrical industry in particular, the 'provincial great banks' specialized in light industry. While the Rheinisch-Westfälische Discontogesellschaft (Aachen) had already been founded as a 'textile bank', the Allgemeine Deutsche Credit-Anstalt (Leipzig) became the Saxon 'textile bank' when it was cut off from its Saxon heavy industry links by the Dresdner Bank, which originated from Saxony and by the newly amalgamated Commerz- und Privatbank, one component of which originated from Magdeburg in Prussian Saxony. In addition, even those provincial banks which were situated in the core of heavy industrial centres, such as the Essener Credit-Anstalt which had nursed many iron and steel enterprises in the last quarter of the nineteenth century, diversified into potash and brown coal mining, electric power generation, brewing and building industry by the turn of the century.[43]

While the 'provincial great banks' had built up regional branch networks, the majority of the provincial banks (including local private bankers) kept to their local markets and served locally operating small-sized industry, wholesaling and similar businesses. Finally, the credit needs of smaller businessmen, retailers, craftsmen and farmers were served by personal (mostly short-term) credits ('Mittelstandskredit') that were granted by co-operative banks.[44] Before the First World War the savings banks which had been founded for philanthropic reasons as well as for fiscal reasons of local authorities were as yet not directly involved either in industrial finance or in 'Mittelstandskredit'.[45] However, the importance of the local savings banks for the industrialization process has often been substantially underestimated. By mortgages and communal credit the savings banks mobilized the savings of domestic servants, industrial workers and parts of the 'Mittelstand' for the urbanization process that accompanied industrialization. By financing both housing and the infrastructure of the so-called 'municipal socialism' (gas and water, sewage, electricity, tramways) the savings banks were thus, too, indispensable for the development of industrial capitalism.[46]

The smaller the average individual business transaction of a particular clientele became, the more restricted became the range of financial services demanded, and before the First World War neither the savings banks nor the co-operative banks had to develop universal banking practices. The same was also true, of course, for the only financial institution in the German banking mechanism that was functionally specialized, the mortgage bank.[47] Finally, the old-established private bankers, who had first developed the mixed banking practices in Germany, diverted from the credit business since the competitive pressures, particularly arising from the growth of provincial joint-stock banks after 1880 (cf. Table 8.1), became too strong. The private bankers' specialization on few, although large, customers enabled them to devote more time to the cultivation of each customer. This became a particular competitive advantage which enabled a number of private bankers to overcome the disadvantage of their relatively limited resources by specialization in the provision of advice and complementary services, particularly if they had close business (and sometimes even family) connections to foreign finance markets.[48]

War and inflation disrupted the division of labour between the different financial institutions in Germany. Although the reasons for the mess in the financial sector were manifold, the lack of efficiency of the German banking system in the Weimar Republic has been analysed as a German 'Macmillan Gap' for mainly two reasons: the destruction of bank capital and the concentration process which strengthened the relative weight of the great banks within the German banking system at the expense of the provincial banks.

War and inflation had not only destroyed the open and hidden reserves of the banks; even the aggregate paid-up capital was seriously diminished. In the Goldmark opening balances of January 1924 the paid-up capital of all commercial banks was valued at only about 30% of their pre-war level and total assets were even reduced to 21%.[49] The situation for the provincial banks had been even more dramatic than on average. Although aggregate data presented a distorted picture of the situation because of the closing of a large number of provincial banks, two of the largest provincial banks which had survived war and inflation, Allgemeine Deutsche Credit-Anstalt and Barmer Bankverein, were left with only about 20% of their pre-war capital and (open) reserves despite several takeovers of smaller provincial banks.[50]

Under these conditions many provincial banks were unable to survive and agreed to takeovers by stronger banks. The great banks, on the other hand, took advantage of the smaller banks' weakness and bought them up 'for a song', as a contemporary observer stated in 1928.[51] Between 1914 and 1925 the Deutsche Bank took over twenty-one banks, Dresdner Bank sixteen banks, Disconto-Gesellschaft twenty-nine banks, Darmstädter Bank (from 1922 Danat Bank) thirty-six banks, and Commerz- und Discontobank (from 1920 Commerz- und Privatbank) as many as forty-two banks.[52]

Before the war the 'provincial great banks' had already begun to buy up smaller provincial joint-stock banks and provincial private bankers.[53] But this concentration process did not affect the group of customers on which the particular financial institutions had been specialized. On the contrary, the average size of the individual industrial customer and consequently the credit demand grew, so that the 'house bank' had to enlarge its resources in order to keep the customer. Merger was thus an adequate strategy satisfactorily to serve the credit demand of the particular provincial banks' customers. In addition, in their pre-war takeovers the provincial banks did not go outside the regional boundaries, and therefore the 'provincial great banks' had been able to continue the business relations of the affiliated bank without major changes.

A second cornerstone of the pre-war division of labour was the so-called 'Interessengemeinschaft'. These bank alliances are normally understood as the beginning of the concentration process in the banking sector which finally ended with the formation of the 'Big Three' (Deutsche Bank, Dresdner Bank and Commerzbank) after the banking crisis of 1931. The view that the 'Interessengemeinschaften' might lead to an English-style amalgamation movement was already held by contemporary observers[54] and it was reinforced by the fact that a large number of provincial banks were taken over by 'their' Berlin bank in the 1920s. Yet, a closer look at the arrangements of these alliances shows that it was rather the institutionalization of the division of labour in the banking system than the beginning of a subordination of the provincial banks under the Berlin banks which led directly or indirectly to the conversion of the provincial banks into great bank branches.

By the 'Interessengemeinschaft' the provincial banks almost completely preserved their independence, while simultaneously being able to offer a direct link to the Berlin capital market and – by the backing of the alliance partner – they could also extend the credit margins for fast-growing customers beyond the limit that had otherwise to be kept to. The Berlin great banks, on the other hand, were interested in building up new business relations with provincial customers, but before the war they were not prepared to establish an extensive branch network and they were thus not interested in buying up banks in the provinces which were difficult to supervise from the head office.[55]

After the war and particularly from the stabilization of the mark in 1924 onward, when the whole extent of the destruction of bank capital became obvious, the remaining banks were facing a much too large and expensive banking apparatus, partly resulting from the amalgamated banks and partly resulting from high employment during the inflation. As a consequence staff was reduced and some minor branches were closed.[56] A further attempt to reduce administrative costs was the concentration of the great banks' lending on big industry even in those places where a formerly independent provincial bank had served a much wider range of customers. In the face of the 'capital shortage' after the inflation a small number of large credits was much easier to handle and to supervise by head office than a larger number of smaller credits.

Consequently, the managers of the new branches had little flexibility. The Deutsche Bank, for example, prohibited its branches from granting credits in excess of 100,000 marks without head office's consent, which was only rarely granted, because large *de facto* long-term loans for medium-sized industry (even for limited companies in the form of a GmbH) could not be converted into stock and unloaded at the stock exchange. In addition, as branch managers were not compensated in line with the profitability of their branch, they had little inducement to utilize even the scope they had.[57] Although all branches of industry complained about the 'capital shortage', big industry after 1924 was not only able to utilize foreign (largely US) capital markets,[58] but profited from the concentration of the bank capital at the great banks. As the relative weight of the financial institutions which had been specialized on medium-sized industry had overwhelmingly suffered, it was this particular clientele which suffered most from the disruption of the division of labour between the different financial institutions. The result was, as already stated by Alfred Lansburgh in 1931, 'a gap in the German banking system'[59] to the detriment of smaller- and medium-sized industries which had lost much of their former (*de facto* long-term) overdraft facilities by the conversion of many provincial banks into great bank branches which were too small for an issue of stock overseas.

The great banks which had taken over resources of the provincial banks, but only part of the traditional clientele, were not the only financial institutions which shied away from taking on this task. The credit co-operatives which had been founded for the 'Mittelstand' were only able to grant short-term credits because of the structure of their liabilities which consisted largely of short-term deposits. After the demise of the provincial banks only the savings banks had been able – theoretically – to fill the 'gap' in the banking mechanism; and, indeed, during the inflation, when their traditional long-term credit business had become less calculable, the savings banks began to enter the traditional domain of the co-operative banks. The share of personal credits on a strictly short-term basis, which had been of almost no significance in the savings banks' portfolios before the war, substantially grew until the stabilization of the mark.[60] Unlike the co-operative banks, the savings banks were neither legally restricted (from 1921) nor restricted by their liabilities structure to extend their services. First, after the inflation when confidence was quickly restored, short-term giro balances were quickly superseded by savings again, so that the liabilities structure did not prohibit long-term lending any longer. Secondly, the deregulation of the savings banks laid the basis for the development of universal banking practices which had been usual for the provincial banks.[61]

However, the savings banks did not exploit the opportunities that had been given to them, but concentrated on their traditional clientele and restricted themselves to the financial services, which had been demanded for decades. They were not prepared to serve the more sophisticated financial needs, on which, for example, medium-sized industry relied on for mainly two reasons. First, the local authorities which had taken on new social services after the revolution of 1918 were unable to fund their social programmes by taxes but relied on credits from their savings banks. Secondly, the savings banks were as yet only prepared to lend long term against real estates. Small- and medium-sized industry, however, was largely unable to offer the securities demanded, as machinery and other mobile assets were not yet accepted as collateral by the savings banks.

Contemporaries were well aware of this problem, but even the attempt to solve the problem of long-term credit to small- and medium-sized industry by particular mortgage banks for industrial purposes ('Industrieschaften') failed,[62] so that until the end of the Weimar Republic the gap in the banking mechanism left by the demise of the provincial banks was not filled. Financial assistance of small- and medium-sized industry was possible only if the financial institution which was specialized on this particular clientele was independent enough to grant the local manager discretion as to the loan conditions for individual customers. Formal rules concerning the quality of securities in connection with the term and the size of the loan prohibited an adequate provision of finance for this particular clientele. Therefore it was only when during the 'Wirtschaftswunder' the traditional clientele of the savings banks, local craftsmen in particular, became industrialists that the savings banks specialized on this neglected group of customers; and it was only in the early 1960s that the antiquated regulations concerning the collateral for long-term loans were finally lifted.[63]

Conclusion

On balance, this overview of the development of banking in Germany from the early stages of industrialization into the twentieth century supports the Gerschenkronian assumption that in the case of Germany banking was crucial for the successful catching-up process of industrialization. Before the First World War Germany did not only have an industrial economy of the first rank, but also a highly developed and efficient financial system. In addition, the final result was completely different from the model of the 'pioneer' and even served as a model for other 'latecomer' economies.

In contrast to the early stages of English industrialization, by the mid-nineteenth century, when industrialization in Germany began, the world economy had reached a new stage in its industrial development, which means that newcomers had to supply financial services unknown to the pioneer. However, it was not only a 'natural' development of challenge and response and it was not only the market that called forth the banking it needed. Instead, institutional factors had also been important in shaping the banking system. The state in particular had various objectives and motives for intervention (or non-intervention) which were inconsistent with a policy of letting the market adjust banking to industrialization.

Moreover, even if it intended to be helpful to that aim, the outcome was not necessarily so. For example, the early development of 'mixed banking' was not least due to state intervention designed specifically to achieve macro-economic stability, by most restrictive regulations for the issue of central bank notes accompanied by the suppression of private note issuing banks. However, the suppressed bank note circulation did not result in greater stability, but contributed to the worst economic and political crisis of the nineteenth century. At the same time, the suppression of note issuing business forced many bankers to break new ground. Instead of adjusting their assets into the kind of structure of liabilities which prevented extensive long-term lending in England, they had to adjust their liabilities to fit the necessary asset structure, that is, they needed a larger portion of proprietors' capital and reliable current account balances in order to engage in the remaining promising business of financing industry both by short-term and long-term credits. The development of the 'mixed banking' structure was thus neither the result of design by a far-sighted government nor simply created by auction markets. Rather, it was the result of a mixture of chance, of unwitting government intervention and of the pressing demands of an expanding industrializing economy.

Secondly, the development of German banking also shows that not only pure investment banking but also the 'mixed banking' was inherently unstable. Although we lack detailed case-studies, it seems most likely that the *de facto* liquidity guarantee of the Reichsbank for fundamentally sound banking houses, the assets of which had been temporarily rendered unavailable, had been a necessary precondition for survival. As the banking crisis of 1931, when the Reichsbank had refused to act as a 'lender of last resort', has also shown, the micro-economic function of the central bank as the bankers' bank must not be subordinated to its macro-economic functions such as stable monetary conditions.

Thirdly, even the universal banking system was in no way universal in the sense that one financial institution provided for all financial services of all possible customers. On the contrary, division of labour between several financial institutions, each specialized on a particular clientele, was crucial to prevent serious allocative inefficiencies. By the 'house bank' principle the respective financial institution was better able to reduce informational deficiencies by monitoring its customers than those financial institutions which were specialized in a particular service. Monitoring was also advantageous for the respective customer, since informed intermediaries were willing to extend their services for their supervised customer to a level which had to be regarded as too risky by division of function financial institutions which lack the monitoring possibilities of universal banks. In addition, by building up a network of information the bank also acted as a source of information and advice on financial and business organization.

In theory, corporate finance in a mature economy has to be seen as a continuum of financial services defined according to the elasticity of their cost with respect to the degree of information. A newly established firm is normally forced to rely exclusively on the proprietors' wealth and retained profits. After a successful beginning, however, the firm can approach its bank for an overdraft (or other forms of bank loans). By monopolizing the current account transactions the bank can monitor the actions of the firm and reduce informational asymmetries accordingly. As the firm matures and the credit margin constantly increases, the bank has to unload part of the credit on to the public by the issue of stock. As the house bank is normally unable to keep its monopoly as provider of financial services for the firm, it has to develop new and additional forms of supervision. In this case German corporate legislation permits a bank to take equity of the firm and to send a bank nominee on to the firm's supervisory board. By its direct involvement in the firm's fortunes the bank provides a positive signal to outside investors. Investors' confidence in the firm's future does not only cheapen the costs in the case of bond issues, but also reduces the firm's exposure to financial distress generally.

True, one cannot expect that any single financial institution was in a position to follow this whole 'pecking order' of corporate finance 'from the cradle to the grave'. In particular, before 1914 the German great banks were normally not prepared to start business relations 'at the cradle' of a firm, whereas the provincial banks had no access to the Berlin Stock Exchange. Even in Germany the functioning of the model thus relied on a smooth transition between the financial institutions involved. In this respect the close collaboration of the provincial banks with one particular Berlin great bank was a major advantage for the banking mechanism, as the provincial bank could pass on those customers, whose credit demands had become too large, to its allied Berlin bank without losing the business. On the other hand, contrary to contemporary opinion, the customer was not facing a cartelized banking sector, as different provincial banks in the region were allied with different great banks, so that competition among banks was still alive. Industry was thus able to reap the fruits of the banking system's economies of scope and the individual firms prevented monopoly prices for financial services by playing off competing banks which even sat on their supervisory boards.

Notes

1 A. Gerschenkron, *Economic Backwardness in Historical Perspective. A Book of Essays* (Cambridge, Mass., 1965), p. 14.

2 Gerschenkron adopted the Marxian concept of original accumulation, but confined the possibility directly to convert previously accumulated wealth 'into claims against current national income, so that entrepreneurs can get the means to compete labour and materials away from consumption and old firms' to the English (that is, 'pioneer') pattern. In addition, the profits of the successful pioneers of British industry were sufficient in relation to capital needs even to sustain extension after the initial phases of industrial development. See A. Gerschenkron, *Europe in the Russian Mirror* (Cambridge, Mass., 1970), p. 101; also R. Sylla, 'The Role of Banks', in *idem* and G. Toniolo (eds.), *Patterns of European Industrialization. The Nineteenth Century* (London, 1991), pp. 47–9.

3 Gerschenkron, *Backwardness*, p. 13.

4 See *ibid.*, pp. 14–16. See also V. Wellhöner, *Großbanken und Großindustrie im Kaiserreich.* (Göttingen, 1989); *idem* and H. Wixforth, 'Unternehmensfinanzierung durch Banken – ein Hebel zur Etablierung der Bankenherrschaft?', in D. Petzina (ed.), *Zur Geschichte der Unternehmensfinanzierung* (Berlin, 1990), pp. 11–33; R. Tilly, 'Zur Entwicklung der deutschen Universalbanken im 19. und 20. Jahrhundert. Wachstumsmotor oder Machtkartell?', in S. Pollard and D. Ziegler (eds.), *Markt, Staat, Planung* (St Katharinen, 1992), pp. 128–56; H. Wixforth and D. Ziegler, '"Bankenmacht". Universal Banking and German Industry in Historical Perspective', in Y. Cassis, G. Feldman and U. Olsson (eds.), *The Evolution of Financial Institutions and Markets in Twentieth Century Europe* (Aldershot and Brookfield, 1995).

5 While the banks were seen as the agents of industrialization in moderately backward countries, the state as agent of industrialization was confined to extremely backward countries. The scarcity of capital in extremely backward countries 'was such that no banking system could conceivably succeed in attracting sufficient funds to finance a large-scale industrialization . . . Supply of capital for the needs of industrialization required the compulsory machinery of the government, which, through its taxation policies, succeeded in directing incomes from consumption to investment.' Gerschenkron, *Backwardness*, pp. 19–20.

6 'After a lengthy period of fairly low rates of growth came a moment of more or less

sudden increases in the rates, which then remained at the accelerated level for a considerable period. That was the period of the great spurt.' A. Gerschenkron, *Continuity in History and Other Essays* (Cambridge, Mass., 1968), p. 33.

7 'The more delayed the industrial development of a country, the more explosive was the great spurt of its industrialisation, if and when it came.' Gerschenkron, *Backwardness*, p. 44.

8 H. Kaelble, 'Der Mythos von der rapiden Industrialisierung in Deutschland', *Geschichte und Gesellschaft*, 9 (1983), pp. 106–18. This view is confirmed by Eckhard Schremmer's recent reworking and extension of Hoffmann's series on industrial investment, see *idem*, 'Die Badische Gewerbesteuer und die Kapitalbildung in gewerblichen Anlagan und Vorräten in Baden und in Deutschland 1815 bis 1913', *Vierteljahrschrift für Sozial- und Wirtschaftsgeschichte*, 74 (1987), pp. 18–61.

9 This view, based on Reinhard Spree's quantitative evidence (*idem*, *Die Wachstumszyklen der deutschen Wirtschaft von 1840 bis 1880* (Berlin, 1977)), was particularly stressed by Richard Tilly. See *idem*, 'Germany', in Sylla and Toniolo, *Patterns*, pp. 176–8, and literature cited there.

10 An overview of the development of merchant banking in Hamburg in M. Pohl, *Hamburger Bankengeschichte* (Mainz, 1986), pp. 57–8; see also Michael North's contribution to this volume.

11 U. Heyn, *Private Banking and Industrialization. The Case of Frankfurt am Main, 1825–1875* (New York, 1981), pp. 376–7; H.-P. Ullmann, 'Der Frankfurter Kapitalmarkt um 1800: Entstehung, Struktur und Wirken einer modernen Finanzierungsinstitution', *Vierteljahrschrift für Sozial- und Wirtschaftsgeschichte*, 77 (1990), p. 92; see also Michael North's contribution to this volume.

12 See Heyn, *Private Banking*, pp. 381–2; K. Grunwald, 'Europe's Railways and Jewish Enterprise. German Jews as Pioneers of Railway Promotion', *Yearbook of the Leo Baeck Institute*, 12 (1967), pp. 163–209; H. Jäger, 'Jüdische Unternehmer und die deutschen Eisenbahnen (1835–1933)', in W. Mosse and H. Pohl (eds.), *Jüdische Unternehmer in Deutschland im 19. und 20. Jahrhundert* (Stuttgart, 1992), pp. 119–21; E. C. Conte Corti, *Das Haus Rothschild in der Zeit seiner Blüte 1830–1871* (Leipzig, 1928).

13 K. Häuser, 'Kreditinstitute und Wertpapiermärkte in Deutschland – Perioden ihrer Entwicklung', in *Kreditinstitute und Wertpapiermärkte*, Bankhistorisches Archiv Beiheft 14 (1989), p. 17. It has to be noted, however, that the south German states, the traditional market of the Frankfurt banks, built state-owned railways, so that part of the state loans issued from the early 1840s were meant to finance the respective state's railway network.

14 See R. Tilly, 'Kapital und Capitalisten des Schaaffhausenschen Bankvereins 1895–1899', in J. Schneider (ed.), *Wirtschaftskräfte und Wirtschaftswege. Fs. Kellenbenz*, vol. III (Stuttgart, 1978), pp. 501–20.

15 See K. Kumpmann, *Die Entstehung der Rheinischen Eisenbahngesellschaft 1830–1844* (Essen, 1910); M. Stürmer *et al.*, *Wägen und Wagen. Sal. Oppenheim & Cie.* (Munich, 1989), pp. 84–5.

16 From the mid-1840s on bankers began to call for repayment of advances in order to build up a securities portfolio consisting of foreign and domestic state loans. See R. Tilly, *Financial Institutions and Industrialization in the Rhineland, 1815–1870* (Madison, 1966), p. 93.

17 See E. Koenigs, *Erinnerungsschrift zum 50 jährigen Bestehen des A. Schaaffhausenschen Bankvereins* (Cologne, 1898), pp. 10–16.

18 See the list of industrial customers in *ibid.*, p. 32.

19 A. Krüger, *Das Kölner Bankiergewerbe vom Ende des 18. Jahrhunderts bis 1875* (Essen, 1925), p. 75.

20 *Ibid.*, pp. 79–83.

21 Mevissen himself described the Schaaffhausen Bank as a 'private bank of a higher order', contrasting it with the real joint-stock banks such as Darmstädter Bank or Berliner Handelsgesellschaft. See R. Tilly, 'German Banking 1850–1914: Development Assistance for the Strong', *Journal of European Economic History*, 15 (1986), p. 120.

22 The Royal Bank was founded in 1765 following the example of both the Bank of England and the Hamburg Giro Bank. Yet, the financial services of the models, that is, simplification of payment transactions and bill discounting, were hardly demanded by the Prussian mercantile community, so that the Bank became a *de facto* mortgage bank. See M. von Niebuhr, *Geschichte der Königlichen Bank in Berlin* (Berlin, 1854; repr. Glashütten, 1971).

23 Tilly, *Financial Institutions*, p. 20.

24 See C.-L. Holtfrerich, 'The Monetary Unification Process in 19th-Century Germany: Relevance and Lessons for Europe Today', in M. deCecco and A. Giovannini (eds.), *A European Central Bank* (Cambridge, 1989), p. 218.

25 H. Rittmann, *Deutsche Geldgeschichte 1484–1914* (Munich, 1972), pp. 538–41; B. Sprenger, *Währungswesen und Währungspolitik in Deutschland von 1834 bis 1875* (Cologne, 1981), pp. 46–50.

26 Quotation from H. Pohl, 'Das deutsche Bankwesen (1806–1848)', *Deutsche Bankengeschichte*, vol. II (Frankfurt/Main, 1982), p. 49.

27 See W. O. Henderson, *The State and the Industrial Revolution in Prussia, 1740–1870* (London, 1967), pp. 131–8; W. Radtke, *Die Preußische Seehandlung zwischen Staat und Wirtschaft in der Frühphase der Industrialisierung* (Berlin, 1981), pp. 129–244.

28 D. Good, 'Backwardness and the Role of Banking in Nineteenth Century European Industrialization', *Journal of Economic History*, 33 (1973), p. 850.

29 For the role and importance of the Cologne branch of the Royal Bank in the local money market see Tilly, *Financial Institutions*, p. 67.

30 H. von Poschinger, *Bankwesen und Bankpolitik in Preußen*, vol. I (Berlin, 1878), pp. 227–33.

31 Although five private banks of issue had been founded in the Prussian provinces in the 1850s, these banks were only drops in the ocean as their issuing rights were also strictly limited. See N. Hocker, *Sammlung der Statuten aller Aktien-Banken Deutschlands* (Cologne, 1858); Sprenger, *Währungswesen*, table 9, p. 68.

32 Between 1850 and 1856 in the neighbouring states of Prussia fifteen banks of issue were established (Sprenger, *Währungswesen*, table 9, p. 68). The bank note circulation of all banks in north and central Germany outside Prussia was of about the same magnitude as the Prussian Bank limit of 21 million Taler (F. Thorwart, 'Die Entwicklung des Banknotenumlaufs in Deutschland von 1851 bis 1880', in *Jahrbuch für Nationalökonomie und Statistik*, 41 (1883), p. 202).

33 See D. Ziegler, 'Zentralbankpolitische "Steinzeit"? Preußische Bank und Bank of England im Vergleich', *Geschichte und Gesellschaft*, 19 (1993), pp. 494–5.

34 On this point see W. P. Kennedy and R. Britton, 'Portfolioverhalten und wirtschaftliche Entwicklung im späten 19. Jahrhundert. Ein Vergleich zwischen Großbritannien und Deutschland', in R. Tilly (ed.), *Beiträge zur quantitativen und vergleichenden Unternehmensgeschichte* (Stuttgart, 1985); R. Tilly, 'Zur Finanzierung der Wirtschaftswachstums in Deutschland und Großbritannien 1880–1913', in

E. Helmstädter (ed.), *Die Bedingungen des Wirtschaftswachstums in Vergangheit und Zukunft* (Tübingen, 1984), pp. 263–86; *idem*, 'German Banking', pp. 128–39.

35 Tilly, 'German Banking', pp. 122–3; *idem*, 'Germany', in Sylla and Toniolo, *Patterns*, pp. 132–3.

36 J. Riesser, *Die deutschen Großbanken und ihre Konzentration im Zusammenhang mit der Entwicklung der Gesamtwirtschaft in Deutschland* (Jena, 1912), pp. 443–59; A. Weber, *Depositenbanken und Spekulationsbanken*, 3rd edn (Munich, 1922), pp. 352–60; G. von Schulze-Gaevernitz, *Die deutsche Kreditbank* (Tübingen, 1922), p. 153.

37 See R. Rettig, 'Das Investitions- und Investierungsverhalten deutscher Großunternehmen 1880–1911' (PhD thesis, University of Münster, 1978).

38 See H. Neuburger, *German Banks and German Economic Growth. From Unification to World War I* (New York, 1977), pp. 123–4; *idem* and H. Stokes, 'German Banks and German Growth: An Empirical View', *Journal of Economic History*, 34 (1974), pp. 710–31.

39 A few years later this minimum was even raised to 150,000 Gulden. Tilly, 'German Banking', p. 121.

40 This was true even for those great banks which had provincial origins. Schaaffhausenscher Bankverein, Darmstädter Bank and Dresdner Bank were only well established in Berlin and those localities where they came from. See Riesser, *Großbanken*, appendix VII, pp. 718–44.

41 Joint-stock companies whose policy was shaped by the great banks were seen as less risky by the investor who was consequently prepared to pay a higher premium. Rettig, 'Das Investitions- und Investierungsverhalten', p. 274.

42 On this point see also Tilly, 'German Banking', pp. 146–8.

43 German banking historians have largely failed to notice the importance of the 'provincial great banks'. For an assessment of the provincial banks' role in the German banking mechanism see most recently D. Ziegler, 'The Origins of the "Macmillan Gap": Comparing Britain and Germany in the Early Twentieth Century', in P. L. Cottrell *et al.* (eds.), *Finance and Industry in the Age of the Corporate Economy: Britain and Japan* (Leicester, forthcoming).

44 For the co-operative banks see most recently A. Kluge, *Geschichte der deutschen Bankgenossenschaften* (Frankfurt/Main, 1991).

45 In Prussia the share of personal credits ('Kredite auf Schuldscheine' and 'Kredite gegen Faustpfand und Wechsel') even declined from 17.5% of aggregate savings banks' assets in 1860 to 3.4% in 1910. Deutsche Bundesbank (ed.), *Deutsches Geld- und Bankwesen in Zahlen 1876–1975* (Frankfurt/Main, 1976), table D1 2.04, p. 68; see also H. Pohl, 'Die mittelständische Wirtschaft und ihre Finanzierungsprobleme bis zum Zweiten Weltkrieg', *Sparkasse*, 100/8 (1983), p. 303; *dem*, 'Von der Spar-Kasse zum Kreditinstitut (Anfänge bis 1908)', in J. Mura (ed.), *Die Entwicklung der Sparkassen zu Universalkreditinstituten*, Sparkassenhistorisches Symposium 1986 (Stuttgart, 1986), pp. 18–19.

46 J. Wysocki, *Untersuchungen zur Wirtschafts- und Sozialgeschichte der deutschen Sparkassen im 19. Jahrhundert* (Stuttgart, 1980).

47 F. Schulte, *Die Hypothekenbanken* (Munich, 1918).

48 H. Wixforth and D. Ziegler, 'The Niche in the Universal Banking System: The Role and Significance of Private Bankers within German Industry', *Financial History Review*, 1 (1994), pp. 99–119.

49 W. M. von Bissing. 'Die Schrumpfung des Kapitals und seine Surrogate', Untersuchungsausschuß für das Bankwesen 1933, *Untersuchungen des Bankwesens*, part 1

(Berlin, 1933), table 1e, p. 86; M. Pohl, *Die Konzentration im deutschen Bankgewerbe (1848–1980)* (Frankfurt/Main, 1982), pp. 298–9; *idem*, 'Die Situation der Banken in der Inflationszeit', in O. Büsch *et al.* (eds.), *Historische Prozesse der deutschen Inflation* (Berlin, 1978), p. 89; C.-L. Holtfrerich, 'Die Eigenkapitalausstattung deutscher Kreditinstitute 1871–1945', *Bankhistorisches Archiv Beiheft*, 5 (Frankfurt/Main, 1983), p. 83.

50 Ziegler, 'Origins'.

51 S. Strauß, *Die Konzentrationsbewegung im deutschen Bankgewerbe* (Berlin, 1928), p. 66; see also G. Feldman, 'Banks and Banking in Germany after the First World War: Strategies of Defence', in Y. Cassis (ed.), *Finance and Financiers in European History, 1880–1960* (Cambridge, 1992), pp. 248–9.

52 For a detailed account of the concentration process, see Pohl, *Konzentration*, pp. 307–25.

53 In 1911 the ten largest provincial joint-stock banks in the Prussian provinces Rhineland and Westphalia had altogether 105 branches, whereas the four great banks originating from Berlin (Berliner Handelsgesellschaft, Disconto-Gesellschaft, Deutsche Bank, Nationalbank für Deutschland) had only 18 inland branches, but 137 deposit agencies concentrating on Berlin and its suburbs (see Riesser, *Großbanken*, appendix VII, pp. 718–44). Contrary to the branches the deposit agencies did not need close supervision, because their autonomy was much more restricted than the independence of a branch manager in the provinces who had to compete successfully with the provincial banks.

54 Riesser, *Großbanken*, p. 571.

55 For the relationship of the alliance partners, see Ziegler, 'Origins'.

56 Untersuchungsausschuß für das Bankwesen 1933, *Untersuchung des Bankwesens*, part 2 (Berlin, 1933), p. 179.

57 G. D. Feldman, 'Banks and the Problem of Capital Shortage in Germany, 1918–1923', in H. James *et al.* (eds.), *The Role of Banks in the Interwar Economy* (Cambridge, 1991), p. 60; H. James, 'Banks and Bankers in the German Interwar Depression', in Cassis, *Finance*, pp. 272–3.

58 Several examples from the Ruhr area are given in H. Wixforth, *Banken und Schwerindustrie in der Weimarer Republik* (Cologne, Weimar and Vienna, 1995).

59 A. Lansburgh, 'Die Finanzierung des Kapitalbedarfs der Mittel- und Klein-industrie', in B. Harms (ed.), *Kapital und Kapitalismus* (Berlin, 1931), p. 134.

60 E. Walb, 'Übersetzung und Konkurrenz im deutschen Kreditapparat', in Untersuchungsausschuß für das Bankwesen 1933', *Untersuchung des Bankwesens*, part 1, p. 152.

61 The legal basis for the cultivation of short-term credits had been a reform of 1908 which had allowed cheque drawing rights. In addition, in 1900 safe custody of securities was permitted and during the war the savings banks acted as paying agency for the German War Loans. In 1920 the savings banks were permitted dealings in gilt-edged securities on their customers' account and in 1921 the securities permitted were even extended to all stocks listed at the German stock exchanges. See Untersuchungsausschuß für das Bankwesen 1933, *Untersuchung des Bankwesens*, part 1, p. 338; K. Borchardt, '"Das hat historische Gründe" – Zu Determinanten der Struktur des deutschen Kreditwesen unter besonderer Berücksichtigung der Rolle der Sparkassen', in H. Henning *et al.* (eds.), *Wirtschafts- und sozialgeschichtliche Forschungen und Probleme. Fs. K. E. Born* (St Katharinen, 1987), pp. 270–87.

62 Pohl, 'Mittelständische Wirtschaft', p. 304.
63 See U. Beyenburg-Weidenfeld, *Wettbewerbstheorie, Wirtschaftspolitik und Mittelstands-förderung 1948–1963* (Stuttgart, 1992); J. Mura, 'Das gewerbliche Kreditgeschäft seit 1908', in Sparkassenhistorisches Symposium 1988, *Entwicklungslinien im Personalkreditgeschäft* (Stuttgart, 1989).

9 Banks and the rise of capitalism in Switzerland, fifteenth to twentieth century

Youssef Cassis

Swiss banks have been closely connected with most debates surrounding the rise and nature of capitalism, ranging from highly intellectual controversies, such as those aroused by Max Weber's thesis on 'The Protestant ethic and the spirit of capitalism', to more mundane concerns about the 'less acceptable face of capitalism', especially, in this case, the laundering of dirty money. This chapter will discuss the long-term relationships between banking and capitalism in Switzerland, from the fifteenth to the twentieth century.

Such a long view appears particularly well suited to the Swiss case. Since the end of the Second World War, Switzerland has ranked among the major international financial centres: until the recent rise of Tokyo, it was usually considered as occupying third place behind London and New York. Five centuries earlier, in particular in the years 1425 to 1465, Geneva might well have been the premier European financial centre. Of course there is little in common between the worlds in which a fifteenth-century merchant banker and a twentieth-century international banker operated, and one should beware of too easy historical parallels. It is also true that continuities can be observed in the banking development of several Western European countries: Frankfurt, Amsterdam and of course London are among the most conspicuous examples.

Nevertheless, the Swiss banking experience does exhibit some long-term trends and specific characteristics, which this chapter will try and

identify. Two areas will be investigated. The first concerns the basis of
Switzerland's position in the world of international finance and will
make up the bulk of the following pages. This position constitutes the
more original aspect of the Swiss case and is particularly propitious to
long-term analysis as, until the eighteenth century, the 'capitalist' part of
the world economy was mostly made up of international commercial
and financial activities.[1] The second area of investigation is concerned
with the contribution of Swiss banks to domestic industrial development.

A number of recurrent, sometimes permanent, factors have affected
the long-term development of Swiss banking, both at the international
and domestic levels. They will be briefly outlined in an introductory
part, while the remainder of the text will evaluate the extent of their
impact, which has varied over time and according to regions, and may
or may not have differentiated Switzerland from the other, or some
of the other, European countries. Given the space available for this
chapter, its chronological span and the state of research on the subject
such an evaluation cannot hope to be more than tentative.

A first, obvious factor is the small size of the country. In absolute
terms, the impact of Switzerland on international finance has necessarily been limited, in particular when compared to that of her larger
neighbours, although in no way insignificant. The Swiss peculiarities are
twofold. First, in relative terms, Switzerland has always played a role
disproportionate to her size. And secondly, there have been periods in
history when this role reached a truly global dimension. The second
factor is the decentralized structure of the country, which has persisted
to this day; before the foundation of the federal state in 1848, the
Confederation was no more than a loose collection of cantons. This is
reflected in the absence of a single financial centre, this role being
shared, in turn or simultaneously, by three cities: Geneva, Basle and
Zurich. Even today, Zurich's overwhelming predominance has not
entirely superseded the international role of Geneva and Basle.[2]

A third factor is the beneficial effects which international wars have
generally had, since the fifteenth century, on the Swiss economy and
in particular on Swiss finance. This was mainly the result of two
quintessentially Swiss institutions: the mercenary service and neutrality.
A fourth factor is the early integration of Switzerland in the world
economy, both as a capital exporter and as a home for foreign capital
and financial institutions and a strategic base for their world-wide
operations. The fifth factor is the role of the state in financial activities

not at the federal level, where non-interventionism has been the rule,[3] but at the cantonal level where public banks have been a regular feature of the institutional setting.

One possible factor, however, must be ruled out from the outset: the influence of religion, namely of Calvinism. Recent scholarship, in particular the conclusions of Herbert Lüthy's monumental work,[4] has clearly put Calvin's position on usury and its effects on banking practices in perspective. This cannot be developed within the context of this chapter. Three points, however, can be briefly stressed. First, the specific context of Geneva: since 1387 the city had enjoyed the unique privilege of being permitted to practise usury, although at reasonable rates; this economic context undoubtedly influenced Calvin's doctrine. Secondly, the major innovations in banking practices, in particular the introduction of bills of exchange by Italian bankers in the fourteenth century, preceded the Reformation. Thirdly, the practices of Protestant bankers were not different from those of their Catholic counterparts and until the end of the eighteenth century, their use of interest remained largely confined to what used to be permitted by the canon law.

Swiss banks and international capitalism

Switzerland's prominent position in the world of international finance has enjoyed exceptional longevity. Few countries have been able to retain, with hardly any interruption, a financial centre of international significance from the fifteenth century to the present. However, no financial centre situated within the Swiss borders has ever reached a truly world status, such as that enjoyed by Genoa, Venice, Antwerp, Amsterdam, London and New York, or even Paris, Frankfurt or Berlin, even in an age when the financial pre-eminence of a city did not require the backing of a large national economy. In other words, Swiss cities have always enjoyed top position, but within the second tier of inter-national financial centres. The only possible exceptions are Geneva in the mid-fifteenth century and Zurich in the mid- to late twentieth century. Furthermore, financial centres located in Switzerland have prospered by using not only their own resources, but also, directly or indirectly, those of foreign individuals, foreign firms or foreign states, and by serving as a financial entrepot.

From the fifteenth to the eighteenth century, international financial operations were closely linked to commercial fairs. These expanded in the fifteenth century. Frankfurt played a crucial role in linking central

Europe to the Brabantine fairs of Antwerp and Berg-op-Zoom, and Geneva's four fairs were a major centre for Italian exports and re-exports beyond the Alps. By the early fifteenth century, Geneva had in fact become the very heart of the large commercial transactions taking place in continental Europe and, by way of consequence, a financial centre of the first order.[5]

However, these international transactions, both commercial and financial (the latter including multilateral clearing of debts, buying and selling bills of exchange and arbitrage on foreign exchanges), were entirely dominated by the big Italian houses, above all the Florentines, which had all opened a branch in Geneva. The most important one was the Medici Bank. Its Geneva branch was opened in 1425, and was successively managed by two prominent fifteenth-century financiers, who both left Geneva to manage the entire 'holding company' from its head office in Florence. Although we have no details about the Geneva business of the Medici bank, balance sheets for the years 1441 and 1451 show that in the former year, the Geneva branch came first among all the Medici companies, ahead of Venice and Florence, whereas in the latter year it ranked second, immediately behind Florence.[6]

Geneva's role as an international financial centre ended abruptly between 1464 and 1466, when the Italians, including the Medicis, decided to move their representatives to neighbouring Lyons. This was mainly the result of the competition from the Lyons's commercial fairs, strongly supported by King Louis XI. The departure of the Italian merchants and bankers left a gap which neither the Genevese nor the Swiss were able to fill, as they had hardly taken any active part in the commercial and financial activities generated by the fairs, although they had undoubtedly benefited from them. From then on, and for about five centuries, Swiss cities were only to play a secondary, although not insignificant, role in international finance.

From the sixteenth to the eighteenth century, Switzerland's specific contribution to international capitalism has been shaped by two major factors: the first one is its relative wealth, the second one the integration of some of its economic elites to international capitalist networks, namely those formed by the Huguenot diaspora. Swiss financial fortunes have always been strongly connected with wars. If neutrality in two world wars facilitated the emergence of Swiss capital markets in the twentieth century, the mercenary service greatly contributed to the wealth of the cantons before the French Revolution. The Swiss were already selling their military power in the fifteenth century, becoming famous for their prowess and very much in demand by the neighbouring powers, keen to use their military force for their own benefit. This had led, by the early sixteenth century, to the conclusion of several peace and alliance treaties, all linked to lucrative financial allowances. The signature, in 1516 and 1521, of a perpetual peace with the king of France was to prove particularly profitable. First, as a source of cash income: between 1517 and 1612, the French paid between 3,600,000 and 4,700,000 golden ecus to the Swiss cantons in order to ensure an exclusive peace treaty and to levy troops in the country. This levy, however, was done through Swiss captains and incurred further expenses, not included in the figures quoted above.[7] Secondly, and more importantly, these treaties stimulated Swiss trade. In return for its right to levy troops in Switzerland, the French crown guaranteed that Swiss products had a privileged access to French export markets, thus further integrating the Swiss economy to international trade and finance.

These military pensions enriched a number of wealthy ruling families as well as the treasuries of the major Swiss cities. As a result, most Swiss cities, with the notable exception of Geneva, were able to build substantial fortunes in the course of the sixteenth century. To the mercenary service, however, must be added the benefits of the 'peace factor'. The ordinary tax and duty receipts of the major Swiss cities increased 2.76 times in the course of the sixteenth century. Thus pensions were not the only source of wealth. In the case of the richest city, Basle, they made up only 15.7% of ordinary receipts, whereas they reached 66.5% in the case of Fribourg.[8]

Significantly, it is in the cities least involved in the mercenary service that this accumulation of wealth led to the development of new financial institutions. This was done through public rather than private banks. The most significant event was the foundation of the Stadtwechsel (Municipal Exchange) of Basle in 1504. Public banks had developed in Europe in the course of the fifteenth century, especially in Italy, with the foundation of the Casa di Sangiorgio, in Genoa, in 1407, but also in Spain and in the Low Countries, mainly as a result of the difficulties encountered by private bankers in an uncertain political and economic climate. Public banks remained in favour in the following century and beyond, despite the marked recovery of the private banks. Italy was once again in the forefront, with the foundation of several such banks in the second half of the sixteenth century, the most famous being the Banco della Piazza di Rialto, in Venice, established in 1567.[9]

Although its main function consisted of foreign exchanges, the Municipal Bank of Basle offered a broad range of services. It took deposits, from Basle and other neighbouring cities, Berne and Strasburg being among the largest depositors; granted credits to merchants, artisans, the nobility, churches, convents as well as Swiss and German cities; cleared multilateral debts of public bodies, merchants and artisans; issued loans on behalf of cities, both Swiss and foreign, the nobility, the dukes of Savoy, the kings of France, the emperor. From the late sixteenth century, it undertook portfolio management and from the early seventeenth century dealt with bankruptcies. In other words, it was a modern bank, offering all banking services known in the sixteenth century, with the exception of stock exchange operations.[10]

As a banking instrument dominating the world of Swiss finance, and the only one of its kind in Switzerland, the Municipal Bank of Basle greatly contributed to Basle overtaking Geneva as the undisputed premier financial centre of the country. According to a recent estimation, nearly two-thirds of the private capital invested in loans issued in Switzerland between 1500 and 1600 originated from Basle. However, as an international financial centre, Basle never reached the global status of its predecessor. The Municipal Bank firmly controlled the region's capital market, leaving no room for speculators seeking a quick buck on financial transactions, and who preferred to turn to Lyons, Antwerp, Frankfurt and Augsburg. As a counterpart, the Municipal Bank offered the stability of a state bank and, already in those days, banking secrecy. State control, however, became too tight in the course of the seventeenth and eighteenth centuries, with adverse effects on the city merchants who established their own private banking services. After a period of decline, it was liquidated in 1744.[11]

Capital exports continued in the seventeenth and eighteenth centuries and were indeed encouraged by the authorities in order to prevent a collapse of interest rates. In Zurich, a public bank, Leu & Cie (it was named after the then canton's Finance Minister) was established to that effect in 1755. This was, however, small scale. The Swiss banks which played a role of some significance at the international level in the eighteenth century were those established by the Huguenot refugees, who had immigrated to Switzerland. They had remained part of an international capitalist network, where Swiss cities, above all Geneva, but also Basle and, to a lesser extent, a few others, were essential links. As in earlier and later periods, the international conjuncture and close connection with foreign capital contributed to the formation of international financial centres in Switzerland. This was clearly the case with eighteenth-century Geneva.

By the early eighteenth century, the financial role of Geneva had grown out of proportion to the size of this tiny Republic. Geneva had been able to take advantage of its neutrality and of its position at the very heart of the 'Huguenot International' to become a major link in the process of collecting foreign funds to finance the European wars of Louis XIV. Geneva's cosmopolitanism was already apparent, not only in the composition of its business class, described by Herbert Lüthy as 'a society devoided of a clearly defined nationality',[12] but also in the diversity, perhaps unique in Europe, of its investment portfolio: a roughly equal amount of French and British bonds, to which were later added Dutch, Italian, Scandinavian and Imperial ones.[13] So, despite being a small provincial city with a thrifty puritan middle class, Geneva possessed an unusually strong expertise in foreign investments.[14]

From the mid-eighteenth century, Geneva also became a centre for the issue of foreign loans. Between 1742 and 1752, eight loans were issued on behalf of the Kingdom of Sardinia; a Danish loan was issued in 1760 and an Austrian one in 1765. Geneva could call on the resources of its rich Swiss neighbours, in particular Berne and Zurich, which were looking for opportunities of outward investment; their massive subscriptions compensated for Geneva's limited resources.[15] However, Geneva did not develop into a truly international financial centre. From 1770, the Geneva bankers' attention increasingly turned towards the French debt, in the financing of which they were to play a pivotal role. The links between Geneva and Paris had anyway remained very close, even during the prolonged period, between 1720 and 1770, when French financial markets were at their most flat, with no loan issue on the French side and no foreign securities quoted on the Paris Stock Exchange. Geneva, however, had kept a substantial portfolio of – often depreciated – French securities, which required the presence in Paris of a number of bankers to sort out the various claims of their clients. They also acted on behalf of foreign holders as they had become, by the mid-eighteenth century, the only representatives of international banking left in Paris.[16]

The situation changed when Necker was appointed Comptroller of French finances in 1776. Born in Geneva, Necker had made his banking career in Paris, his bank Thellusson, Necker & Co., having become by 1770 one of the three largest houses in Paris, and possibly in continental Europe.[17] In his five years in office, Necker borrowed £530 million, £386 million of which were in the form of annuities, which were particularly popular with the public, as they were calculated on an outdated life expectancy of twenty years and could be based on lives other than one's own. The Geneva private bankers turned these old-fashioned government annuities into highly marketable, and highly speculative, investments. They did so by rationally selecting lives (women from the Geneva bourgeois families had a particularly long life expectancy), devising reinsurance schemes guaranteeing the annuity payment even in case of death, and offering the possibility of purchasing annuities by instalments. Demand for French annuities became a mania in late eighteenth-century Geneva, with investments reaching some £100 million; it spread to other cities through the international networks of the Huguenot bank, and turned into a speculative fever before collapsing in the financial turmoil brought about by the Revolution.[18]

If Geneva's financial role in the eighteenth century was disproportionate to its size, it remained of secondary importance world-wide and way behind such centres as Amsterdam or London. This was even more true of its position, and that of the other Swiss centres, namely Basle and later Zurich, in the nineteenth, and early twentieth, centuries. This does not mean that a group of private bankers did not prosper during that period, in particular in the first half of the nineteenth century. In fact, the main dynasties of private bankers were established in the late eighteenth and early nineteenth centuries, with such names as Pictet, Lombard, Odier, Hentsch or Mirabaud in Geneva, Ehinger, La Roche, Dreyfus or Burckhardt in Basle. Some of them, in particular in Geneva, have survived to this day. Little is known about the history of these private banks. But they were members of the European *Haute banque*, the main functions of which consisted in accepting bills of exchange and granting other facilities such as advances and foreign exchange; they also issued foreign loans and managed their clients' portfolios.[19] One of the main strengths of the Swiss private banks, especially as far as international financial operations were concerned, derived from their close links with the Parisian *Haute banque*.[20] The Genevan private bankers enjoyed a privileged position as the major component of the Parisian *Haute banque*; the latter was formed during the first half of the nineteenth century by several waves of immigration, coming from both neighbouring foreign countries (in the first place Germany and Switzerland) and provincial France.[21]

The foundation of the large commercial banks from the mid-nineteenth century did not enhance the international position of the Swiss financial markets. Their international impact was relatively weak: they hardly expanded abroad before 1914, whether in the major financial centres (the London branch of the Swiss Bank Corporation, opened in 1898, was the only exception) or in the developing economies (the Crédit Suisse's two subsidiaries in Argentina being the only recorded cases).[22] This absence of multinational banks, in particular in developing countries, could well have been a consequence of the absence of Switzerland's formal, or direct, imperialism,[23] in contrast even to small countries such as Belgium or Holland. Few international loans were issued in Switzerland, and only a handful of foreign banks had opened a branch there, the most notable exceptions being the Geneva branches of the Crédit Lyonnais and the Banque de Paris et des Pays-Bas. Switzerland's international financial role in the nineteenth century was in fact commensurate to the country's size and level of economic development, i.e. it was no more than that of a small industrialized country, comparable to, although carrying probably less weight than, Belgium or Holland, despite the fact that Switzerland was a huge capital exporter, possibly the largest per head in 1913.[24]

However, Swiss banks were far from being left out of the big capitalist ventures of the day. But they were not in the lead, working instead in association with foreign banks, or taking advantage of the opportunities offered by the initiative of larger capitalist players, in particular French and German. Swiss banks, for example, preferred a representative to a formal branch in a foreign country: the Crédit Suisse had had such a presence in Paris since 1890. An interest in a foreign bank constituted another alternative: the Swiss Bank Corporation had participated in the foundation of the Banque Internationale de Bruxelles in 1898, followed by the acquisition in 1906 of a significant interest in the Banque Suisse et Française (Paris).[25]

Rather than being a centre for the flotation of new issues, Switzerland played an important role as a base from which direct investments were made, in conjunction with foreign capital, in various parts of the world. (It is significant in that respect that direct investments formed a large proportion of Swiss capital exports.)[26] This was especially the case in the electrical industry, where powerful finance companies were established in partnership with the large German banks and electrical concerns, in order to promote new companies for the production and supply of electricity. Thus the Elektrobank was founded in 1895 with the

Algemeine Electrizitäts-Gesellschaft (AEG), the Deutsche Bank, the Berliner Handelsgesellschaft and the Crédit Suisse as the largest shareholders. Siemens initiated the foundation of Indelec in 1896 with, among others, the Commercial Bank of Basle and a group of German and Swiss private bankers; while in 1898 Schneider & Cie and the Banque de Paris et des Pays-Bas took part in the foundation of the Société Franco-Suisse pour l'Industrie Electrique, together with the Union Financière de Genève, the Swiss Bank Corporation and the Crédit Suisse. Swiss capital was therefore in a minority in these companies. However, Switzerland was chosen as head office because of the country's banking facilities, and also because of the advantages offered by the Swiss company legislation.[27]

Switzerland's international financial position was augmented in the course of the twentieth century. This happened in two stages, each following a world war. During the First World War, Switzerland was approached by both the Central Powers and the Entente for credits. In the climate of monetary disorders which followed the hostilities, especially the Austrian and German hyperinflations, the post-war strength of the Swiss franc, like the Dutch guilder, attracted inflows of foreign funds. Such inflows continued in the 1920s, possibly exceeding 1 billion Swiss francs by 1929, and were part of the 'hot money' of the 1920s.[28] As a financial centre, Switzerland gained new international roles, particularly through floating new overseas issues, and a number of foreign banks opened for business there, especially Lloyds Bank and Barclays Bank in Geneva, American Express Bank in Zurich, and the Bank for International Settlements, though mainly for reasons of geographical convenience, in Basle.

However, Switzerland's international financial influence remained limited, whether measured in global terms or through the overseas expansion of its banks which continued to rely on mere representation in overseas centres, or on acquiring interests in foreign banks. In addition, the big Swiss banks were hit by the 'Great Slump' and the Austrian and German banking crises of 1931. The 'big' banks were most affected because of the magnitude of their foreign transactions, their total assets falling from 8.6 billion francs in 1930 to 4.1 billion in 1935. Only the two largest banks (Swiss Bank Corporation and Crédit Suisse) were able to avoid large reductions of capital. The Banque d'Escompte Suisse, Geneva, collapsed in 1934 and the Swiss Volksbank, Berne, was only saved by the intervention of the Federal government.[29]

The decisive step towards a global international status was taken during the Second World War. Yet Switzerland's role during the hostilities, especially with regard to its relationship with Germany, has generated considerable controversy.[30] Since Switzerland was, from 1941, the location of virtually the only free market for gold and foreign exchange, approaches came from all the belligerents. This led to the Swiss franc gaining a double function – as a 'refugee' currency and as an international medium of payments. There are no precise data available regarding the amount of funds deposited in Switzerland during the war, but it is evident that their volume exceeded 3 billion francs.[31]

The period from the 1950s to the 1980s has come to be regarded as the 'golden age' of Switzerland as an international financial centre. By the 1960s, Swiss financial markets, with Zurich firmly in the lead, ranked third behind London and New York. In 1965, Switzerland's share of international banking activity, as indicated by banks' foreign assets, was 8.3%, only surpassed by the United States with 23.7% and the United Kingdom with 17.1%. A decade later, the respective positions were Switzerland 8.4%, the United Kingdom 22.2% and the United States 9.7%.[32] Swiss markets have never attempted to compete with major international financial centres with regard to the overall volume of transactions. Rather its competitive advantage has lain in the specialist development of a certain number of 'niche markets' such as those for the international bonds, foreign exchange, private portfolio management and trade in bullion, all of which experienced considerable growth during the 'long boom' of the third quarter of the twentieth century.

The 'big' banks became increasingly involved in international business, on both sides of their balance sheet: their foreign assets reaching 41.3% of the total in 1971 and their foreign liabilities 59.4%.[33] They opened branches in all major financial centres: from a mere 11 foreign branches of Swiss banks in 1965, the figure rose to 41 in 1975 and 79 in 1985, and would be 179 in that year if representative offices were to be added. The international importance of Swiss financial markets during the third quarter of the twentieth century was also reflected in the growing importance of foreign banks operating within Switzerland, their total number rising from 88 in 1970 to 120 in 1985, by when they accounted for 11.9% of total Swiss banking assets.

Swiss banks and industrial capitalism

The role played by the banks in the rise of industrial capitalism in Switzerland does not really start before the nineteenth century, making it impossible to take as long a historical view as in the previous section on Swiss banks and international capitalism. Nevertheless, a Swiss pattern can be outlined and traced back to Switzerland's early traditions in financial organization.

Banks played a negligible role in Switzerland's early industrialization, which was limited to cotton spinning. Investments required little capital and consisted of ploughed back profits. Moreover, the Swiss banking system, as it existed in the late eighteenth and early nineteenth centuries, was almost entirely orientated towards foreign business. However, banking cannot be separated from trade during that period and few bankers were then engaged in purely financial activities. The 'Huguenot International', the importance of which has already been stressed, was as much a commercial as a financial network, as can be seen, for example, in the export of printed calicos to France, or in the financing of shipping companies.[34] Merchants and merchant bankers, as is well known, indirectly paved the way towards industrialization by securing both a supply of raw material – Geneva had started to import and re-export cotton from the late seventeenth century – and export markets. But they also played a direct role by financially supporting the nascent modern cotton mills.

This was particularly the case in Zurich which, by the late eighteenth century, had caught up with Geneva and Basle and become a major commercial and financial centre in its own right. Its big merchant houses had become increasingly powerful; they had established their own network of correspondents in the main European financial centres and were acting directly on the international money market, thus adding to their commercial profits those deriving from financial operations, in particular foreign exchange and investments. However, contrary to Geneva and Basle which continued to finance foreign, and in particular French, commercial and industrial activities, Zurich used its surplus of capital for domestic industrial purposes, thus laying the foundations of its future economic dominance. The big merchant houses specialized in the import of raw cotton, financed their industrial customers, some of them, such as Escher Wyss, turning themselves into cotton spinners. In the poorer areas of eastern Switzerland, by contrast, merchants were unable to play such a role, thus delaying the modernization process.[35]

The role of the banks in the second stage of Switzerland's industrialization is less clear and undoubtedly requires further historical investigation. New financial institutions emerged in the first half of the nineteenth century, alongside the old-established private banking dynasties. The first to appear were the savings banks: the movement swept the whole of Western Europe, and in Switzerland 100 such banks were founded between the Congress of Vienna in 1815 and the revolution of July 1830. The second were the cantonal banks, the foundation of which started in the 1830s, during the transitional period from the restoration to the era of political regeneration; they were publicly owned by the various Swiss cantons and were created with the aim of encouraging economic development while providing the cantons with a strong political instrument against the federal government.[36]

From the 1850s, this combination of international and regional banking proved inadequate to finance large investment projects. The gap was filled by the large commercial banks which could mobilize deposits to that effect. The Crédit Suisse was founded in 1856, partly as a nationalist reaction to prevent the control of the country's railway network by foreign groups, and controlled from the start the North-Eastern Railway Company. Other banks were soon to follow: the Bank in Winterthur[37] and the Commercial Bank of Basle in 1862, the Federal Bank in 1863, the Popular Bank in 1869, the Swiss Bank Corporation in 1872.

However, in the present state of research, their contribution to industrial development cannot be properly assessed.[38] The large Swiss banks were universal banks, and in this capacity offered a wide range of services to their industrial customers. It is usually admitted that the *Kontokorrent* credit was particularly well suited for the needs of trade and industry, but it is more difficult to establish to what extent these bank accounts, designed for running expenditures and incomes, were used by industrial companies to finance investment. Recent research on German industrial finance suggests that the role of the large credit banks has been overestimated.[39] This could well apply to Switzerland where, as in other countries, self-finance played a decisive part in the financing of industrial growth. Swiss commercial banks issued securities on behalf of their industrial customers and the links between large banks and large industrial companies also took the form of overlapping directorships: representatives of large corporations formed a third of the board members of the Crédit Suisse and the Swiss Bank Corporation in the interwar years, and two-thirds in the 1960s.

In the absence of definite answers based on empirical evidence, a few hypotheses on the relationships between banks and industry can be formulated, on the basis of Switzerland's specific banking organization.

Whether Switzerland was closer to the German model of universal banking than to the British model of deposit banking might in the end not matter very much, as bankers are likely to have been close to their industrial customers, including the small- and medium-sized enterprises, and thus in a favourable position to reduce information asymmetries. Close links could have derived from the decentralized character of the Swiss banking system, in particular the persistence of the local and regional banks well into the twentieth century, and the strength of the cantonal banks, which apart from a short period in the 1920s, remained the largest group of banks within the Swiss banking system until the 1960s; political motives could also force the cantonal banks, which were public institutions, to intervene in industrial matters for the better or for the worse. Close links could also have derived from the fact that the 'big' banks remained, at least until the Second World War, in the hands of cantonal elite groups, strongly connected to the other elite groups of their cantons: until 1960 the members of the board of the Crédit Suisse were in a majority from the canton of Zurich, and this proportion was as high as 70% before 1914. In the Swiss Bank Corporation, the natives of Basle lost their absolute majority after the First World War, but continued to form a significant, and by far the largest, minority – between 35 and 40%.[40] The Swiss large commercial banks thus successfully brought together the often conflicting traditions of regional industrial finance and international banking operations.

Notes

I should like to thank Béatrice Veyrassat for her helpful comments on an earlier draft of this chapter.

1 This is the view developed in particular by Fernand Braudel in *Civilisation materielle, Economie et Capitalisme XVe–XVIIIe siècle*, vol. II: *Les jeux de l'échange* (Paris, 1979).

2 On this point, see the interesting remarks of Charles Kindleberger, 'The Formation of Financial Centres', *Princeton Studies in International Finance*, 36 (1974), pp. 1–78.

3 The Banking Act of 1934, which introduced state supervision of the banking system, was the first direct intervention of the federal state.

4 H. Lüthy, *La banque protestante en France de la Révocation de l'Edit de Nantes à la Révolution*, 2 vols. (Paris, 1959–61), vol. I, p. 424.

5 H. Van der Wee, R. Bogaert and G. Kurgan-van Hentenryck, *La banque en Occident* (Antwerp, 1991), pp. 134–5.

6 See J. F. Bergier, *Genève et l'économie internationale de la Renaissance* (Paris, 1963); M. Cassandro, 'Banco et commercio fiorentini alle fiere di Ginevra nel secolo XV', *Revue suisse d'histoire*, 26 (1976).

7 M. Körner, *Solidarités financières suisses au XVIe siècle* (Lausanne, 1980), pp. 111, 414.

8 *Ibid.*, pp. 112–14.
9 Van der Wee, Bogaert and Hentenryck, *Banque en occident*, pp. 87–94, 131.
10 Körner, *Solidarités financières*, pp. 333–6.
11 *Ibid.*, pp. 336, 440–4.
12 Lüthy, *Banque protestante*, vol. II, p. 80.
13 *Ibid.*, vol. I, p. 427.
14 *Ibid.*, vol. II, p. 69.
15 *Ibid.*, vol. II, pp. 69–75.
16 *Ibid.*, vol. I, pp. 424–7.
17 *Ibid.*, vol. II, p. 142.
18 *Ibid.*, vol. II, pp. 369–748; B. Veyrassat, 'Genève et l'internationale du capitalisme. Un capitalisme genevois?', in A.-M. Puiz and L. Mottu-Weber (eds.), *L'économie genevoise de la Réforme à la fin de l'Ancien Régime XVIe–XVIIIe siècles* (Geneva, 1990), pp. 603–11.
19 On the general activities of the *Haute banque* see D. Landes, *Bankers and Pashas* (Cambridge, Mass., 1958), pp. 1–40.
20 On the functions of the Parisian *Haute banque* in the early nineteenth century, and the role of the Genevan private bankers, see M. Lévy-Leboyer, *Les banques européennes et l'industrialisation internationale dans la première moitié du XIXième siècle* (Paris, 1964), pp. 418–44.
21 L. Bergeron, *Les Rothschild et les autres. Le gloire des banquiers* (Paris, 1991).
22 Y. Cassis, 'Swiss International Banking, 1890–1950', in G. Jones (ed.), *Banks as Multinationals* (London, 1990), pp. 164–5.
23 This, however, should not mask the fact Swiss businessmen and financiers were involved in multiple overseas activities through companies in foreign hands or registered in other European countries. This phenomenon has been described as a 'colonialisme oblique' (Roland Ruffieux, 'La Suisse des radicaux 1848–1914', in *Nouvelle Histoire de la Suisse et des Suisses*, 3 vols. (Lausanne, 1982–3), vol. III, p. 74), while Switzerland's world-wide business expansion has been characterized as a 'hidden empire' (L. Stucki, *Das heimliche Imperium* (Berne and Munich, 1968), French edition, *L'empire occulte* (Paris, 1970)).
24 According to the estimates of Paul Bairoch, 'L'économie suisse dans le contexte européen', *Revue suisse d'histoire*, 34 (1984), p. 480. On the limitations of Switzerland's international financial role before 1914, especially its dependence on the French capital markets, see also the recent thesis of S. Guex, *La politique monétaire et financière de la Confédération suisse 1900–1920* (Lausanne, 1993).
25 Cassis, 'Swiss International Banking', p. 169.
26 Bairoch, 'Economie suisse', pp. 480–1. Any precise estimate of the respective part of direct and portfolio investments is impossible in the present state of research.
27 See P. Hertner, 'Les sociétés financières suisses et le développement de l'industrie électrique jusqu'à la première guerre mondiale', in F. Cardot (ed.), *1880–1890. Un siècle d'électricité dans le monde* (Paris, 1987), pp. 341–55; S. Paquier, 'Banques, sociétés financières, industrie électrique', in Y. Cassis and J. Tanner (eds.), *Banques et crédit en suisse, 1850–1930* (Zurich, 1993), pp. 241–66.
28 B. Worner, *La Suisse, centre financier européen* (Argenton, 1931), pp. 101–11.
29 See P. Ehrsam, 'Die Bankenkrise der 30er Jahre in der Schweiz', in Eidgenössische Bankenkommission, *50 Jahre eidgenossische Bankenaufsicht* (Zurich, 1985), pp. 83–118.
30 See in particular W. Rings, *L'or des Nazis* (Lausanne, 1985); P. Marguerat, *La Suisse face au IIIe Reich* (Lausanne, 1991).

31 M. Perrenoud, 'Banque et diplomatie suisse à la fin de la deuxième guerre mondiale: Politique de neutralité et relations financières internationales', *Etudes et Sources*, 13–14 (1987–8), p. 51.
32 International Monetary Fund, *International Financial Statistics Yearbook* (1981).
33 K. Speck, *Strukturwandlungen und Entwicklungstendenzen im Auslandgeschäft der Schweizerbanken* (Zurich, 1974), pp. 35, 42.
34 See Veyrassat, 'Genève et l'internationale du capitalisme'.
35 See B. Veyrassat, *Négociants et fabricants dans l'industrie cotonnière suisse 1760–1840. Aux origines financières de l'industrialisation* (Lausanne, 1982).
36 See F. Ritzmann, *Die Schweizer Banken. Geschichte Theorie-Statistik* (Berne, 1973).
37 The Bank in Winterthur merged in 1912 with the Toggerburger Bank under the name of Union Bank of Switzerland.
38 See a discussion of the current state of research in P. Marguerat, 'Banque et industrie en Suisse, fin 19e–1945: considérations préliminaires', in Cassis and Tanner, *Banques et crédit en Suisse*, pp. 201–8.
39 See V. Wellhöner, *Grossbanken und Grossindustrie im Kaiserreich* (Göttingen, 1989).
40 Y. Cassis and F. Debrunner, 'Les élites bancaires suisses, 1880–1960', *Revue suisse d'histoire*, 40 (1990), pp. 259–73.

10 The influence of banking on the rise of capitalism in north-west Europe, fourteenth to nineteenth century

Herman Van der Wee

Introduction

Traditional historiography distinguishes two main turning-points in the long-term growth of European banking from the Middle Ages until the Industrial Revolution: first, the successful revival of banking in Italy during the late Middle Ages; second, the decisive progress in financial techniques in England about 1700, including the rise of the modern banking system. Attractive as this hypothesis may appear, however, it disregards, in my view, a vital link in the history of European banking, i.e. that which the Low Countries were able to create during the transition from the late Middle Ages to the Early Modern Period.[1]

The first turning-point, occasioned by the revival of banking in Italy from the twelfth century onwards, is well known in the historiography of banking, and is rightly emphasized, it seems to me. During the twelfth and thirteenth centuries, clearing and deposit banks and pawnbroking banks arose throughout Italy; even merchant banks emerged, specializing in buying or selling bills of exchange, a specialist banking activity that implies a complete network of money markets spreading the innovation of bills of exchange and arbitrage all over Europe, including the Low Countries.

Between the Italian banking revival of the twelfth and thirteenth centuries and the English financial revolution of the eighteenth century, a number of important improvements in banking techniques took

place in the Low Countries, where successively Bruges, Antwerp and
Amsterdam were the main financial centres and therefore the cities in
which one would expect to find the improvements in place. Bruges,
undoubtedly the most important *piazza di cambio* of north-western
Europe in the fourteenth and fifteenth centuries, fully assimilated the
Italian financial innovations, adopting in particular the Italian deposit
banking system and integrating it into the local moneychangers'
business. Antwerp, the commercial and financial metropolis of the West
in the sixteenth century, was breaking new ground by a more creative
combination of the Italian innovations with the more primitive
techniques in use at the time in northern Europe. In achieving the
transition from transferability to negotiability in the circulation of
commercial paper, Antwerp created an original, autonomous banking
and credit system, a more modern and flexible system that in fact
proved to be a helpful element in shifting the economic centre of
gravity from the Mediterranean to the North Sea around the end of the
sixteenth century and the beginning of the seventeenth, and cleared
the way for the English financial revolution of the eighteenth century.

By contrast, Amsterdam, Europe's most dynamic trade centre and
most powerful money and capital market of the seventeenth century,
re-established features of the traditional Italian banking system, trying
further to refine the old deposit and clearing techniques again in fashion
since the revival of the public deposit and clearing banks in Italy during
the second half of the sixteenth century.

My analysis will start with an initial short section on deposit and
clearing banking as it developed in the Low Countries during the late
Middle Ages and the Early Modern Times. Medieval Bruges was the
first centre in the Low Countries to take over from Italy and to develop
the technique of deposit and clearing banking. The technique fell into
discredit in the Low Countries at the very end of the Middle Ages, but
it was most successfully reintroduced in Amsterdam at the beginning of
the seventeenth century, once again under Italian influence, as public
deposit and clearing banking had reappeared in Italy on a large scale in
the course of the sixteenth century. Hence my decision not to follow a
strict chronology, but to study Bruges and Amsterdam in one and the
same section.

A second section will focus on the specific Antwerp innovations of the
sixteenth century and their direct links with the development of
financial techniques in England during the seventeenth and eighteenth

centuries. A third will briefly analyse the progress made in banking techniques in the course of the nineteenth century.

The Italian deposit and clearing bank system as a model for the rest of Europe

Bruges and the Italian connection[2]

The wide diversity of coins in circulation made moneychangers indispensable in medieval Italy, as indeed it did in all other European cities of consequence, particularly in the Low Countries, a great centre of international trade, where merchants from all over Europe were bringing in foreign coins. The moneychangers' original function consisted of such monetary activities as the manual exchange, for the payment of a small fee, of foreign coins for coins of their own region, or of coins which were banned from circulation by the sovereign for coins which were not. By virtue of this monetary function, the money-changers were held responsible by the king, duke or count for the supply of bullion to the royal, ducal or county mints, and in this way played a crucial role in underpinning monetary policy and in stabilizing monetary circulation.

Having safes to protect their own stocks of coins and bullion, the moneychangers were soon prepared to take charge of the money of the public. The custody function gradually became a banking function, first in Italy, later, by way of imitation, north of the Alps, and specially in the Low Countries and southern Germany, which last was linked with Italy through a special commercial relationship from the eleventh and twelfth centuries onwards. Furthermore, merchants increasingly asked the moneychangers to take on the function of book deposit bankers, i.e. to make or receive payments by transferring assets from their own to their creditors' accounts and vice versa. When the transfer from one account to another had become an ordinary procedure, the various moneychangers of Bruges, in their capacity as deposit bankers, gradually introduced a mutual clearing system. Lastly, not only merchants, but soon also private persons, used the financial services of deposit and clearing offered by the moneychangers in their capacity as deposit bankers.

The moneychangers invested part of the deposited money in personal ventures, knowing from experience that it would never all be withdrawn at the same time: they participated in trade or in the farming of tax collection and advanced loans to kings, towns and private persons; in a word, they became bankers.

For the Low Countries, the question remains, however, whether the moneychangers in their capacity as deposit bankers were as numerous during the fourteenth and fifteenth centuries as the late Raymond de Roover, the well-known Belgian financial history specialist, suggests. Apart from Bruges, few traces of deposit and clearing banks have been discovered in Flanders, Brabant, Holland, or Zeeland. Furthermore, those that were discovered elsewhere than Bruges seem to indicate clearing practices that were still at a primitive level.

The decline of the late medieval deposit and clearing bank system in the Burgundian Low Countries

In the course of the fifteenth century, the moneychanging business and the private deposit and clearing bank system declined in both Flanders and Brabant, as indeed it did in Italy and in southern Germany, too. Both the private moneychanging business and the related private deposit and clearing bank system in Flanders and Brabant went through a serious crisis, the private bank system even vanishing completely. The causes for the crisis are not yet very well understood. De Roover stresses the hostile attitude of the Burgundian dukes towards the money-changers, and their prohibition of private deposit and clearing banking because it conflicted with the centralization policy in the fifteenth century, aimed at controlling financial activity even at local level.[3]

Ducal *monetary* policy, too, should be given special attention. From 1389 onwards, a ducal policy of monetary stability was pursued more or less successfully and was soon to be reinforced by the unification of the monetary system in the Burgundian Low Countries in 1433–5. In conditions of monetary stability and of a unified, silver monetary system, with, over and above, a limited range of golden coins being used, the moneychangers saw their opportunities for changing money and for earning commission diminishing. They could no longer be so active in profitable monetary speculation or manipulation. As a result, their business and the related bank activity went through a period of structural crisis.

Other factors, financial as well as industrial and commercial, played a part. The moneychangers had always been closely connected with the export trade in cloth, having their banks in the cloth-guild halls and engaging in on-the-spot exchanging of the foreign coins which clothmakers received in payment for their products. The money-changers eventually advanced money to the clothmakers if the latter had to pay cash to their suppliers of wool, to their spinners or to those involved in the finishing and dyeing of their cloth, and if they themselves had to accept postponement of payment from their customers who bought the finished cloth. When the traditional cloth export trade declined, particularly in the course of the fifteenth century, the money-changers' business in the textile towns declined likewise.[4]

On the other hand, urban long-term borrowing, by means of systematic sales of annuities, met with particular success as soon as the dukes introduced a policy of stable money from 1389–90 onwards. The selling of annuities by towns developed into a major financial business, attracting buyers from a wide geographical area. In order to organize this booming financial trade, the towns eventually created municipal banks, public institutions that were required to promote the sales of annuities in and outside the town, to collect the money of the buyers of these annuities and to secure the yearly payment of the annuities. Because of their public character, the municipal banks inspired confidence. Moreover, because of their dealings with buyers from other towns and regions, they were regularly involved in moneychanging, whereby they became successful competitors of the private money-changers in not only the changing of coins, but even the sphere of deposit and clearing banking. The municipal banks indeed started to keep current accounts for their customers, who had to receive their yearly annuities, but who were very often buying new ones at the same time. Out of this deposit and clearing banking emerged credit operations.[5]

The municipal deposit and clearing banks did not survive. During the last third of the fifteenth century, the expansionary policy of the Burgundian dukes and the Flemish War which followed served to increase the burden of urban taxation enormously. The pressure was met by the sale of huge amounts of annuities, but the overselling led to a disastrous financial crisis in the towns, to the collapse of the municipal banks and to the disappearance of public deposit and clearing banking altogether.

During the same period, the private moneychangers at the fairs of Antwerp and Bergen-op-Zoom continued to flourish, as a result of the successful integration of these fairs into the revival of European overland trade via Germany and later via France. However, these moneychangers were not very active in the sphere of deposit and clearing banking, as the seasonal pattern of the fairs ran counter to a banking system based rather on continuous financial activities. As far as is known, private deposit and clearing banking had completely ceased in Antwerp and Bergen-op-Zoom at the end of the fifteenth century, after the ducal prohibitions, as indeed was the case in the rest of the Low Countries. However, the vigorous expansion of Antwerp's world trade was at that very moment generating an urgent need for the extension of payment and credit facilities. As a rapid revival of deposit and clearing banking was prevented by the ducal ban, there was a spate of autonomous financial innovation in the city, which brought about the spectacular rise of the Antwerp money market during the first half of the sixteenth century.

The Amsterdam exchange bank: a continuation of Italian traditionalism

Though deposit and clearing banks thus played no determining part in the process of technical innovation in Antwerp during the first third of the sixteenth century, they nevertheless managed after 1530 to penetrate into Antwerp's financial system. This penetration was favoured by three distinctive circumstances: first, the expansion of public deposit and clearing banking in Italy in the course of the sixteenth century; secondly, the intensification of commercial and financial contacts between Italy and Antwerp during the second third of the sixteenth century, reintroducing the idea of deposit and clearing banking into the Low Countries; thirdly, the democratization of international trade in the Low Countries, enabling a large number of small merchants to take part in world trade by means of participation and commission. Increasingly, cashiers rendered financial services to small merchants from both the northern and southern Low Countries, active in Antwerp, making payments and cashing money on behalf of their customers, and, by doing so, gradually reintroducing private deposit and clearing banking in Antwerp. However, the political and military upheaval during the first phase of the Revolt against Spain (the Eighty Years War, 1568–1648), as well as the crisis following the reconquest of the town by Farnèse in 1585, prevented a general breakthrough of the system. In fact, the transition of the Antwerp deposit banking business into a full and modern private deposit and clearing bank system was to be completed in Amsterdam only in the course of the seventeenth century, and even then after a considerable lapse of time, again due to the Eighty Years War.

After the closure of the Scheldt in 1585, the Antwerp cashier-bankers, together with merchants and craftsmen, fled to the north, where they introduced or improved a variety of Antwerp industrial, commercial and financial techniques – among others, deposit banking and the related clearing banking. At the same time, the chaotic currency situation caused by the war offered the private bankers new opportunities for making extra profits by manipulating the coinage. The Amsterdam authorities first tried to restrict the speculative activities of these bankers, but without success. They then took more drastic measures, founding in 1609 a public deposit and clearing bank, the Amsterdam Exchange Bank (Amsterdamsche Wisselbank); instead of trying to regulate and restrict the speculative activities of the private cashier-bankers, the city simply prohibited them from engaging in any financial activity and replaced them by a municipal deposit and clearing institution. The demonstrative effect was strong. Similar public deposit and clearing banks were founded in Middelburg (1616), Delft (1621), Rotterdam (1635) and even in some other towns of northern Europe, such as Hamburg. The Amsterdam Exchange Bank proved to be an enormous success: its growth was rapid and spectacular, trust in its solvency became unshakeable; its great reputation was even acknowledged by Adam Smith in 1776.[6]

In financial techniques, however, the Amsterdam Exchange Bank was not as innovatory as observers of the seventeenth and eighteenth centuries, and even scholars of the twentieth century, have suggested. In fact, this bank was only a further stage – and then not a crucial one – in the development of a banking system that had already been introduced in the Middle Ages by the Italians. Moreover, the Amsterdam institution was a direct copy of the public deposit and clearing banks that had reappeared in Italy during Italy's economic revival from the second third of the sixteenth century onward, the most famous example of them being the Banco della Piazza di Rialto, founded in Venice in 1587.[7]

The whole Amsterdam banking system set up in 1609 conformed to the Italian-Spanish tradition. It was based on the principle of a stable money of account, the very principle that had secured the success of both the financial fairs of Geneva and Lyons in the fifteenth and sixteenth centuries, and the financial fairs of Besançon and Piacenza in the late sixteenth and early seventeenth centuries, all of which were dominated by the great Italian banking houses. The Amsterdam system also made multilateral clearing possible, in the way it had matured in the sixteenth century at the Castilian fairs under Spanish leadership. The system was simply refined further in this respect, i.e. by concentrating all accounts at a single bank, in contrast to the practice at the Castilian fairs, where multilateral clearing was organized by the assembly of moneychangers present at them.

Initially, the Amsterdam Exchange Bank aimed at fostering the trade of the northern Netherlands with the Baltic, the Levant and the Far East by making coins of excellent quality available at fixed rates, the so called *negotiepenningen*. At a moment of monetary chaos and monetary uncertainty, this exchange function gave a powerful impetus to the trade expansion of Amsterdam, especially to that part of trade that had to be financed in cash.

The second aim of the bank was the establishment of a clearing system based on transfers from one client's account to another's in bank guilders of account representing a constant silver content. These Amsterdam clearing transactions acquired a special dimension because of the city's dominant position in world trade at that time. The obligation imposed by the municipality to clear all bills of exchange of an amount above 600 guilders through the bank induced all-important Amsterdam merchants and in fact all important firms involved in world trade to open an account at the Amsterdam Exchange Bank, which thus grew in the course of the seventeenth century into a bank of world stature – indeed, into *the* great clearing house for international trade, with the stable bank guilder serving as the world's convertible key currency. In principle, the bank was not allowed to lend money to anybody. The statutes of 1609 were very explicit on the matter: in order to maintain confidence, all sums deposited had to be kept in the safes of the bank. Over the years, however, the bank would make two exceptions: it would regularly advance money on a short-term basis to the flourishing United East India Company, and on a long-term basis to the city, the owner of the bank.

By the end of the seventeenth century, the deposit and clearing function of the Amsterdam Exchange Bank had passed its zenith and the bank had lost its leading position in the field of international payments; only in the trade of gold and silver coins did it continue to play a significant role. However, despite the bank's waning importance as a deposit and clearing bank, the Amsterdam money and capital market remained very active throughout the entire eighteenth century. This continuing financial vitality displayed by Amsterdam was due mainly to the dynamism of its *private* bankers, who succeeded in gradually converting the Dutch *commercial* capitalism of the seventeenth century into the Dutch *financial* capitalism of the eighteenth.

After 1650, private bankers had made a spectacular comeback by accepting deposits and performing clearing operations in current guilders of account, which, during the second half of the seventeenth century, also became a stable currency and, for that reason, were again commonly used in international trade. The private bankers, moreover, had an important comparative advantage vis-à-vis the Amsterdam Exchange Bank in that they could grant cash credits, modern discount credits and acceptance credits, all in current guilders. Out of these successful private enterprises a number of great merchant banks emerged, which in the course of the eighteenth century initiated the issue of long-term government bonds on behalf of the European monarchs and even, after 1776, on behalf of the government of the United States.

It remains a mystery why the revival of the private deposit and clearing banks in Amsterdam and the simultaneous expansion of modern discount and acceptance credit during the second half of the seventeenth century did not lead to the emergence of a modern discount and issuing bank system. Let me advance an hypothesis. Wartime psychosis and monetary chaos around 1600 caused the Amsterdam authorities to distrust and finally prohibit private banking. The direct contacts of the Dutch merchants with Italy and with Venice in particular during the same period, thanks to the expansion of the so-called Dutch *Straatvaart* (i.e. Dutch shipping through the straits of Gibraltar), opened the way to the introduction of the system of public deposit and clearing banking, a system which, in the given circumstances of war and monetary confusion, inspired greater confidence.

The effect was twofold. First, the successful introduction of the traditional Italian formula temporarily halted the development of the new Antwerp technique of modern discount banking in Amsterdam. Second, following the Italian tradition, a distrust of hand-to-hand circulation of short-term commercial paper made itself felt, which impeded the transition from clearing to issuing banking.

From Antwerp to London: the birth of the modern discount and issuing banking system

The Antwerp origin of endorsement and of modern discount

The primitive methods of payment still common at the fairs of Brabant at the end of the fifteenth century were inadequate to cope with the

vigorous commercial expansion of Antwerp during the previous
decades and a significant adjustment and modernization of financial
techniques had to be made.[8] The postponement of payment through
private and commercial current accounts, for example, was extended
enormously, thereby enlarging the opportunities for mutual offsetting of
debt. Progress was no less important where writings obligatory were
concerned, whose use also involved postponement of payment. The
simple use of writings obligatory had long been common practice, but
in the course of the fifteenth century, *inter alia* thanks to the recent
general incorporation of a bearer clause into the instrument, their use
increased remarkably in Antwerp. Especially the English Merchant
Adventurers, though also the Hanseatic, German, Dutch and native
merchants, regularly made payments by means of these instruments,
using the dates of the fairs of Brabant as three-monthly expiry dates.
Legal and financial problems, however, prevented widespread *hand-to-
hand* circulation of writings obligatory in Antwerp. In most cases,
writings obligatory, therefore, even those with a bearer clause, stayed
in the creditor's portfolio until the expiry date. The Antwerp authorities, however, soon tried to break through the legal and financial
obstacles. Already in 1507, any holder of a writing obligatory or bill of
exchange with a bearer clause was able to take a defaulting debtor
directly and immediately to court. Previously, this had only been legally
possible in Antwerp after an official transfer of the title by a formal
cessio.[9]

Putting formal and informal transfers on the same footing thus had a
legal advantage for the transferee, but at the same time it entailed an
important *financial* disadvantage for him. As soon as the informal
transfers were considered as formal ones (i.e. *cessios*), the new bearers
could no longer call the creditors to account when the debtor was in
default. By applying the principle of *assignment* to the transfer of writings
obligatory, this financial problem was resolved in turn. In the Low
Countries, assignment was already commonly used in the Middle Ages,
especially for payments in cash: a creditor who demanded payment of a
debt was assigned by his debtor to a third person, who himself was in
debt to the debtor.

Assignment had a substantial *financial* advantage: it was not
considered an effective payment until the creditor was satisfied with it.
Applying the principle to the transfer of writings obligatory or bills
meant that, when assigning to a third person, each assigning debtor
remained responsible for the payment of the debt until the assigned

creditor declared himself satisfied. Transferability could now be transformed into negotiability.

The Antwerp innovation soon spread to the rest of the Low Countries. By the Imperial Edicts of 1537 and 1541, every payment made by transfer of writings obligatory or other commercial bills with a bearer clause was considered as payment by assignment. Book-keeping accounts, manuals of business practices, commercial correspondence, court and municipal archives all bear witness to the fact that payment by transfer of writings obligatory or bills of exchange using the technique of assignment developed into *la usanza entre mercadores* in Antwerp during the second third of the sixteenth century. The assignment technique made it desirable to find an appropriate formula for recognizing the successive assignors, but ways of identifying assignments emerged only very slowly in the Low Countries. The custom of concentrating payments at the Antwerp Exchange four times a year at the expiry dates of the great fairs brought great numbers of creditors and debtors together. Dealings in writings obligatory or bills of exchange with a bearer clause occurred at these times on a very large scale and often lasted until the creditors themselves received their own writings obligatory or bills as means of payment. In this system, written notes proving the assignment were irrelevant.

Endorsement as the central feature of the new system of negotiable commercial paper emerged in Antwerp only shortly after 1600 and was closely linked with the emergence of the endorsement of bills of exchange, which at that time became common practice in Antwerp, though it still reflected the traditional assignment principle. By way of illustration, an endorsement from 1611 in favour of Robert Rug was indicated in the following way: 'received by me, underwritten by Mr. Robert Rug, whom I have assigned to receive it'.

The increasing use of endorsement when making payments by transferring writings obligatory and bills of exchange in Antwerp, and later in Amsterdam, London or elsewhere, greatly stimulated the hand-to-hand circulation of commercial paper, thereby strengthening confidence in the practice of paying debts with paper instruments, without the use of currency, and also opening the way to the intro-duction of bank notes as a means of payment.

In the second quarter of the sixteenth century, the technique of modern discounting also surfaced in Antwerp, a new technique that is to be understood as a sale of a commercial writing obligatory or a bill of exchange to a third party before the date of expiry, for an amount lower than its nominal value. Relevant in this context is a 1540 Imperial Ordinance indicating the rise of a new group of private Antwerp bankers (the cashier-bankers), 'faisant des marchandises d'argent les donnant à gain et frait'. In times of tension on the Antwerp money market, these bankers started to buy up for cash and at a discount, commercial paper which had fallen due, from merchants who had sold on credit and had received writings obligatory or bills of exchange in payment, but were unable to cash them in at the expiry date, because of a momentary liquidity crisis.

It would not be long before commercial paper began regularly to be bought up before its expiry date, not only at moments of financial tension, but also in normal years. Modern discounting of *long-term* writings obligatory with a bearer clause became general practice in Antwerp well before the end of the sixteenth century; an English example dating from the 1530s (in the papers of Thomas Kitson) was then still exceptional. After 1600, discounting of *short-term* bills of exchange became normal practice, too. Thus the foundations of modern discount banking were laid in Antwerp before the end of the sixteenth century, though the decline of Antwerp in the seventeenth century prevented the Antwerp money market from expanding this innovation into a system of modern discount and issuing banking. This would be taken care of by the London goldsmith-bankers.

The English financial revolution: developing Antwerp's sixteenth-century innovations

In the course of the seventeenth century, London adopted Antwerp's financial innovations of the previous century, following the example of the Amsterdam private bankers. The continuity between Antwerp and London as far as financial techniques were concerned was facilitated by the close ties which had existed between the London Merchant Adventurers and the Antwerp market in the sixteenth century; in this context, the strong links between the English crown and the Antwerp money market during the same period also deserves mention, the Royal Exchange, opened in London in 1571, having been modelled entirely on the Antwerp Exchange. The emigration to London of several thousand Protestants from the Low Countries at the end of the sixteenth century, among whom were a fair number of Antwerp merchants and cashier-bankers, was another factor that facilitated the adoption and further development of Antwerp's financial techniques by London's commercial community.

The financial chaos under the early Stuarts and the turmoil of the English Civil War caused some delay in the process of assimilation of Antwerp techniques by the London merchants, which developed fully only during the second half of the seventeenth century, when international trade was expanding so fast in London that new forms of credit for financing it had to be found. The goldsmiths played a big part in this, with tension in the sector of public finance being an important factor, too.

Initially, as was the case in Antwerp and Amsterdam, the London goldsmiths played the role of cashier-banker for English and foreign merchants. By doing so, they developed a successful, though still traditional, deposit and clearing banking system, limiting their banking activities to transfers from one account to another. Gradually, they came to issue interest bearing deposit certificates and later also genuine promissory notes. To these certificates and notes the merchants applied the practice of endorsement, thereby stimulating their success and widening their hand-to-hand circulation. At the same time, the London goldsmiths began systematically to discount short-term government paper with cash and increasingly with promissory notes, the so-called goldsmiths' notes. It was in this combined system of deposit, clearing and discount banking that the modern bank note had its origins.[10]

The decisive step in completing the process was taken by the Bank of England, founded in 1694. In fact, the Bank of Stockholm in Sweden was the first European bank to receive a royal charter for issuing paper money, but it went bankrupt three years after its foundation in 1661. The Bank of England, on the contrary, became a very successful financial institution. In addition to its deposit, clearing and discounting functions, its trade in bullion, bills of exchange and government bills, bonds or annuities, it was also granted parliamentary authority to issue bank notes. On the occasion of its new charter in 1707–8, the right of issue was more clearly defined, and the bank was proclaimed as the only joint-stock bank in England. Owing to its close links with the government and to its growing prestige as a solid financial institution, its bank notes, at first still written by hand, but shortly to be printed and standardized, were soon accepted as a means of payment by the majority of London merchants and by the London public in general. Private bankers increasingly came to deposit their gold reserves at the Bank of England, adopting more and more the use of its bank notes.

English gold reserves now being concentrated in the safes of the Bank of England, a central issuing banking system came into being, the Bank of England increasingly assuming the function of bank of last resort.[11]

European banking in the nineteenth century

The English banking model, characterized by a powerful central issuing bank system and a large number of private bankers extending short-term credit to international trade by discounting commercial paper with the bank notes of the central bank, was imitated by many countries in continental Europe in the course of the nineteenth century. Indeed, the European central banks, through their rediscounting facilities, gained substantial influence over monetary policy and, by manipulating the discount and interest rate, they were able to control the circulation of money and the volume of credit in their respective countries.

The English banking model was entirely oriented towards the extension of short-term credit. In an era of industrial revolution, with a growing demand for long-term investment, this short-term orientation of credit was a serious weakness. Innovations in the banking system on the continent filled the gap, the introduction of the modern system of mixed banks and holding companies, which first took concrete form in Belgium, being crucial in this respect. The Société Générale de Belgique, founded in 1822 as a commercial bank, quickly applied itself to the creation of a modern industrial portfolio, and soon became a very successful 'mixed' bank, combining long-term investment in modern industry with the normal activities of a private commercial bank. The 'mixed' bank became a common financial institution in Belgium, evolving gradually into the more sophisticated formula of the modern holding company.[12] The French Crédit Mobilier and the German investment banks that emerged during the second half of the nineteenth century were modelled on the Belgian system. Even the later Anglo-Saxon investment trusts can basically be traced back to the Belgian formula of 'mixed' banks and holding companies.

Conclusion

The central hypothesis of this chapter can be summarized as follows. The Low Countries took a decisive part in the creation of the modern banking system. Without their own creative contribution, the link

between England and Italy would not have been possible. In the
innovative process, Antwerp was the main creative force. The influence
of the new Antwerp techniques on the development of the transferability, the negotiability and the discounting of commercial paper
was decisive. From Antwerp the innovations managed to penetrate
successfully into Amsterdam and London, except that in London they
were refined further and converted into a new coherent banking system,
the modern deposit, clearing, discount and issuing bank system, the
dominant system of nineteenth-century Europe. During the Industrial
Revolution, however, the need for long-term investment became
urgent, stimulating the emergence of new financial institutions
specialized in long-term credit and long-term investment. In this respect
Belgium once again played a crucial role, the so-called 'mixed' bank
pioneering modern investment banking.

Notes

1 For general overviews, see C. P. Kindleberger, *A Financial History of Western Europe*,
2nd edn (Oxford, 1993); H. Pohl (ed.), *Europäische Bankengeschichte* (Frankfurt, 1993);
R. Bogaert, G. Kurgan-van Hentenryk and H. Van der Wee, *A History of European
Banking* (Antwerp, 1994). For a general overview concerning the late Middle Ages
and Early Modern Times, see H. Van der Wee, 'Monetary, Credit and Banking
Systems', in E. E. Rich and C. Wilson (eds.), *The Cambridge Economic History of Europe*,
vol. V (Cambridge, 1977), pp. 290–392 and 651–99. For general overviews
concerning the Modern Period, see K. E. Born, *International Banking in the 19th and
20th Centuries* (Leamington Spa, 1983); M. Pohl and S. Freitag (eds.), *Handbook on the
History of European Banks* (Aldershot, 1994).
2 The Italian influence on north-west Europe as far as banking during the late
Middle Ages is concerned has been studied in particular by R. de Roover, *Money,
Banking and Credit in Mediaeval Bruges. Italian Merchant-Bankers, Lombards and Money-
Changers. A Study of the Origins of Banking* (Cambridge, Mass., 1943); M. M. Postan,
Medieval Trade and Finance (Cambridge, 1973); R. Goldthwaite, 'Italian Bankers in
Medieval England', *Journal of European Economic History*, 13 (1984), pp. 763–71;
F. Irsigler, 'Juden und Lombarden am Niederrhein im 14. Jahrhundert', in
A. Haverkamp (ed.), *Zur Geschichte der Juden im Deutschland des späten Mittelalters und der
frühen Neuzeit* (Stuttgart, 1981), pp. 122–58.
3 E. Aerts, 'Middeleeuwse bankgeschiedenis volgens Professor Raymond de Roover',
Bijdragen tot de Geschiedenis, 63 (1980), pp. 48–96.
4 E. Vercouteren, 'De geldwisselaars in Brabant (1430–1506); een bijdrage tot de
economische geschiedenis van de Zuidelijke Nederlanden', *Bijdragen en mededelingen
betreffende de Geschiedenis der Nederlanden*, 100 (1985), pp. 3–25.
5 H. Van der Wee and J. Materné, 'Het kredietsysteem in Brabant tijdens de late
middeleeuwen en in het begin van de nieuwe tijd', in H. F. J. M. Van den
Eerenbeemt (ed.), *Het geld dat zoekt zijn weg (Van Lanschot-Lectures over acht eeuwen
geldwezen, bankieren en kapitaalbeweging)* ('s-Hertogenbosch, 1987), pp. 26–7.

6 On the history of the Amsterdam Exchange Bank, see in particular J. G. Van Dillen, 'The Bank of Amsterdam', in J. G. Van Dillen (ed.), *History of the Principal Public Banks* (The Hague, 1934), pp. 79–123. For a more recent analysis, see J. de Vries and A. Van der Woude, *Nederland 1500–1815. De eerste ronde van moderne economische groei* (Amsterdam, 1995), pp. 163–97.

7 For a more detailed analysis of the hypothesis, see my chapter on Amsterdam in Bogaert, Kurgan-van Hentenryk and Van der Wee, *A History of European Banking*, pp. 199–226.

8 For a more detailed analysis, see H. Van der Wee, *The Low Countries in the Early Modern World* (Aldershot, 1993), pp. 145–66.

9 Prof. John Munro discovered that from the fifteenth century onwards English merchants holding a writing obligatory or a bill of exchange with a bearer clause could, on the basis of customary law, sue a defaulting debtor without a previous formal *cessio*. Prof. Pierre Jeannin discovered that similar practices were becoming commonplace in the Hanseatic business world, too, during the second half of the fifteenth century. The author thanks both scholars for the information.

10 W. R. Bisschop, *The Rise of the London Money Market, 1640–1826*, 3rd edn (London, 1968), pp. 39–67; R. D. Richards, *The Early History of Banking in England* (London, 1929), pp. 15–18; R. Ashton, *The Crown and the Money Market 1603–1640* (Oxford, 1960), pp. 12–16.

11 P. G. M. Dickson, *The Financial Revolution in England. A Study in the Development of Public Credit 1688–1756* (London, 1967); see also J. Clapham, *The Band of England. A History*, vol. I (Cambridge, 1967); J. M. Holden, *The History of Negotiable Instruments in English Law* (London, 1955).

12 H. Van der Wee and M. Goossens, 'Belgium', in R. Cameron and V. I. Bovykin (eds.), *International Banking 1870–1914* (Oxford, 1991), pp. 113–29.

PART THREE

*The banks' impact on 'follower'
and 'latecomer' economies*

11 The influence of banking on the development of capitalism in the Scandinavian countries

Håkan Lindgren

Credible commitment by the state to stable property rights both promotes private investments and lowers the transaction costs to the state of raising revenue.

T. Eggertsson, *Economic Behavior and Institutions*
(Cambridge, 1990), p. 348.

Introduction

In the fields of economic history and applied economics, much attention has been paid to the relationship between banking, or banks, and the rise of industrial capitalism. The growth of organized credit and venture capital markets parallels industrialization, and banking constitutes part of capitalism's superstructure. As Fernand Braudel puts it, banking (or finance) *is* the outright core of capitalism.[1] By elaborating my argument along these lines, the problem implicit in the title might be solved by cutting a Gordian knot. That, however, would be too easy. It is just too obvious that capitalistic modes of production require financial instruments carrying various degrees of risk and a system that makes financial intermediation – savings accumulation and credit distribution – feasible.

Historically, the development of capitalism has occurred concurrently with economic growth, at least in the long-run transformation of those economies that today are classified as industrially advanced. A reformulation of my title, focusing on the relationships among banking, industrialization and economic growth, is one way of making my task tractable. This approach, however, gets me out of the frying pan and into the fire, or rather, puts me in the middle of a long-standing and extensive scholarly debate.

Prior to the First World War, long before the concepts 'institutional economics', 'property rights' and 'transaction costs' were incorporated into the scientific vocabulary, economists such as Rudolf Hilferding and Joseph Schumpeter provided theoretical justification to the idea that banking was the engine – the 'driving force' – that explained not only economic growth, but also societal development in general. In the 1950s and 1960s, Alexander Gerschenkron posited a theory of economic development in which both the banking sector and the state were given important roles. In the 'follower' economies, those that arrived on the industrial scene late relative to England, the banks (in, for example, Germany) or the state (Czarist Russia) played a missionary role, initiating and organizing the industrialization process.[2]

Empirical research with the objective of examining or 'testing' various theoretical generalizations has not demonstrated that any particular way of organizing the banking system (or the entire financial sector) is *generally* more favourable to economic growth than any other structure. The most obvious demonstration of this non-result is the still ongoing debate concerning the contribution of universal banking. There is much empirical support for the conclusion that close co-operation between banks and industry, sometimes involving bank dominance over industry, is an effective way to reduce information costs. On the other hand, there are numerous examples of overly close relationships creating lock-in effects. Far-reaching support of their industrial clients by banks produces a growing mutual dependence often resulting in greater risk-taking and, ultimately, following ever greater credit commitments, even in a threat to bank solvency.

The intertwined relationship between the growth of the financial sector and the development of capitalism makes it difficult to determine, with any degree of certainty, whether banking precedes economic growth (production) or whether the causal relationship mainly runs in the opposite direction. This fundamental scientific conundrum was also recognized in the old controversy among economists over the relative importance of monetary versus 'real' forces – technical change, innovations, population growth and the like – in explaining economic fluctuations.

There is an obvious danger of overstating the importance of the new banking institutions – e.g. savings and commercial banks, mortgage institutes, rural credit associations – which came into being during the nineteenth century. One simple reason for this bias is the difficulty of developing quantitative evidence of the size of the pre-existing 'informal' credit market. It is quite clear, however, that viable financial markets had existed long before the establishment of public and private enterprises specializing in monetary and financial transactions. In these informal markets personal relationships dominated. Family and kinship ties helped maintain confidentiality. In addition, wholesale dealers and brokers in the towns, as well as prosperous farmers and foundry owners in the countryside, served as professional moneylenders.

Penetrating studies of Swedish war finance during the seventeenth century have revealed a complex and sophisticated money market revolving around merchants and bankers in Amsterdam. War bills were discounted at rates that were highly sensitive to fluctuating Swedish battle field fortunes.[3] Another field of inquiry that developed quickly in the 1980s is research on 'proto-industrial' ways of organizing production in the countryside. Considering the still unresolved ambiguity of that concept, let me summarize the situation as follows: modern research in 'older' forms of production and distribution has clearly demonstrated the overwhelming importance of credits in the old 'Verlag' system. In Sweden this is obvious, not only for large-scale organized production and exportation such as in the mining and iron industries, but also for products such as iron hardware and textiles to be distributed by pedlars. On the basis of plentiful probate records, the production and marketing system of the Eskilstuna smithies of the early nineteenth century has been characterized as 'a complex network of credit relations', being not only vertical (e.g. merchant–craftsman relations) but to a large extent also horizontal (within identical socio-economic strata).[4]

Nonetheless, the establishment of an 'organized' financial system, consisting of specialized financial firms, was of immense importance. It was a real springboard for the expansion and spread of capitalism. Markets, whose main function was to provide investment outlets for cash balances in the business sector, as well as to promote long-term savings by individuals and households, were created. As mentioned above, it is, of course, quite impossible to imagine modern industrial capitalism without liquid stock markets. They are required for the indispensable mobilization of venture capital *en masse*.

Thus there are many good reasons for concentrating on the development of new banking institutions. The aim of this chapter, however, is rather modest. It is to give an overview of the organized financial sector in Denmark, Finland, Norway and Sweden from the middle of the seventeenth century, when the first attempts were made to establish public credit banks, to the First World War. It will concentrate on the close links existing between politics and banking practices. The main arena for policy formulation and the implementation of 'reasonable and workable rules' (to use the apt terminology of J. R. Commons) constraining the financial sector was the state. For this reason, it is important to remember that Norway did not become a fully independent nation state until 1905, having been united with Denmark and then, after 1814, with Sweden. Finland was a part of the Swedish realm up to 1809, when it was ceded to Russia. Finland then became a, substantially autonomous, grand duchy within the Russian Empire up to 1917.

In the last summary section of this chapter, 'The structure of banking systems', my intention will be to discuss the bases for determining the structure of a 'banking system'. In doing so, I will illustrate how identical financial needs were solved in different institutional environments. The resulting new organizations and institutions were in some ways highly favourable, in other ways less favourable, to economic success.

Banking, the state and the organization of the monetary economy

History contains very few examples of private monetary system. As pointed out by Robert King, those 'free banking' systems usually referred to, such as the New York State regime of 1838–63, were neither 'free' nor 'unregulated'. In fact the New York private money system bore a great resemblance to the Swedish note issuing system of 1830–1903. In the latter, private bank notes were convertible into National Bank of Sweden ('the Riksbank's') notes and thus were effectively denominated in a specific weight of specie.[5] Quite the opposite of free banking, intervention by political bodies – be they a feudal lord, the municipal authorities, a mercantilist sovereign or an elected parliament – to raise revenues, to create confidence and to create reliable financial institutions is the standard historical experience.

With the gradual emergence of the nation states, and the changing political structures that followed, new basic property rights were created. With regard to financial instruments used to facilitate payments, the fundamental role of the state was to generate confidence and trust, a trust which is related to political stability and state power. Monetary and rate of exchange confusion was extremely prevalent in early modern Europe. The simultaneous circulation of several, more or less adulterated, coinages with different origins and varying specie content complicated exchange and increased transaction costs. With the guarantee of the City authorities, the first viable public bank was established in Amsterdam in 1609. Its fundamental objective was to regulate and limit the abuse of money. This was done by replacing coins by bank money: an account holder could deposit all types of coins, and, after deduction of a moderate fee, his account would be credited with the intrinsic value of the coins. Transfers between different deposit accounts could also be ordered.[6]

During the following decades, the successful practices of the Bank of Amsterdam were imitated, and several public deposit banks were established in other provinces of the Dutch Republic, as well as in the important trading city of Hamburg (1619). In Sweden an innovative Dutch merchant, Johan Palmstruch, introduced the new ideas. In 1657 he was appointed general manager of Stockholms Banco, a bank owned by the state. Its business, like that of the Amsterdamsche and Hamburger banks, basically consisted of accepting deposits and making giro transfers. Palmstruch, however, added two important innovations: he combined the deposit business with lending and, in 1661, in response to economic necessity, he introduced the first bank notes in Europe.

From the very beginning, the deposit receipts of Stockholms Banco were popular as a substitute for the heavy, not to say massive, copper coins which constituted the legal tender. When loans were granted, the borrowers were paid in standardized claims on the bank, that is bank notes drawn in even sums. During some years the bank notes of Stockholms Banco were quoted at a premium over coin. Finally, however, after lending had become too generous and had ceased to be constrained by deposit levels, the notes depreciated relative to the copper coinage. The Palmstruch 'bubble' ended with a bank run. The bank could not honour its obligations and closed in 1668. All note holders, however, eventually had their notes redeemed at par after the borrowers had repaid their loans.

A new public bank, owned, administered and run by the Swedish Parliament – Rikets Ständers Bank – was established in 1668, making it the oldest, still operating central bank in the world (the Bank of England was founded a quarter of a century later). To call it a central bank, however, is anachronistic. The Riksbank (as it later was renamed) was a publicly owned commercial bank, mainly offering subsidized loans to trades and industries favoured by the official mercantilistic policy.

Administered by the three upper estates (not until 1800 did the peasantry start to participate) the Riksbank became an instrument of parliamentary economic policy. The king was excluded from formal influence, and the issuing of bank notes originally was forbidden. The experience of the Stockholms Banco also helps explain why a strict demarcation line was drawn between the two units of the bank, the *Växelbanken* for giro business, and the *Lånebanken* for lending. Both units based their activities on deposits, but deposits at the Giro Bank were not to be used by the Lending Bank. An innovation when it was introduced in the 1670s was the payment of interest on deposit accounts with the Lending Bank.[7]

The receipts issued in return for silver and copper money deposited at the Riksbank soon began to circulate as a means of payment, transferable as they were to a third party. In 1726 these so called *transportsedlar* (transferable notes) were accepted as legal tender in public tax collection. The 1740s witnessed a real breakthrough of bank notes in domestic payments; in 1745 convertibility into coin was suspended, and bank notes as small as 6 daler kmt (roughly equivalent to 3 English shillings) were issued.

As in Scotland, the issuing of bank notes for small sums allowed paper money quickly to take the lead as a medium of exchange, dominating the total circulation. A century later, following resumption of the silver standard in 1776, and once again in 1834 following the monetary turbulence of two separate Russian wars, bank notes were so common in Sweden that people generally wore money clips, not purses, for daily use. In the 1840s, bank notes totally dominated the system of exchange. In France, a country all too well known for its preference for specie, less than 10% of all payments were then made in bank notes.[8]

In Denmark–Norway the first bank was not chartered by the king until 1736. Kurantbanken, as it was generally called, was a semi-public bank. It combined deposit, exchange and lending businesses, and it had the privilege of issuing notes redeemable for specie. Originally it was privately owned, although the king appointed a minority of the managers. Like many other eighteenth-century nation states, Denmark suffered chronic fiscal deficits. Naturally, the bank soon became an instrument for providing the funds needed to cover government expenditures, mainly by relying on the printing press. In 1757, the bank notes were declared unredeemable, and in 1773 the Kurantbanken was nationalized.

Political stability and state power are necessary conditions for creating the confidence needed for an exchange system built on token money to function. This old truth was confirmed in 1813 when the Danish monetary system collapsed. As a consequence of Danish participation, as an ally of France, in the Napoleonic Wars, the Danish state suspended all payments and the Kurantbanken was closed. When a currency reform was carried out in 1813, the bank notes were quoted at a mere 6% of their specie par value. A new semi-public bank, the National Bank of Denmark, established in 1818, was endowed with exclusive note issuing rights and given the assignment of restoring paper money convertibility at the old specie rate. To prevent future government abuse of the note printing monopoly, Nationalbanken was organized as a private joint-stock bank. After a long period of deflationary policy, when a successive reduction of notes in circulation was effected, the old par value was restored in 1838. From 1845 onwards, the full convertibility of bank notes into silver was legally maintained.[9]

In contrast to Denmark and to England, the central bank of Sweden did not serve as a fiscal agent of the government. In 1789 a special public agency, the Swedish National Debt Office (Riksgäldskontoret), was created to market the rapidly expanding debt during the war with Russia 1788–90. This Office was controlled by the Parliament. The national budget crises of the Napoleonic Wars were also devastating in Sweden. After the Revolution of 1809, and after joining the alliance against France and Denmark, Sweden quickly took advantage of the new political situation. In 1812 the Swedish Parliament decided not to honour debts to enemy countries. This act of repudiation cancelled two-thirds of the foreign debt. The coexistence of the Debt Office and the Bank of Sweden meant that Sweden had two organizations which, always independently and not infrequently at cross-purposes, were instrumental in designing national monetary and credit policies.[10]

In 1816, following the dissolution of the union with Denmark and the forced establishment of somewhat weaker bonds with Sweden, the Norwegian Parliament, Stortinget, created a bank of its own endowed with a bank note issuing monopoly – the Bank of Norway. Like its Danish counterpart, it was privately owned, and its principal assignments were to manage the money supply and restore the old silver standard. The latter goal was achieved in 1842. As a remarkable fact, it can be noted that there was little public interest in subscribing for the shares of the bank. The equity capital of the Bank of Norway had to be raised by forced subscription, engineered by a special tax levied by the Storting.[11]

In the Russian grand duchy of Finland (1809–1917), Swedish monies were allowed to circulate parallel with Russian kopecks and rubles until 1840. Not until 1860 was Finland granted the right to create a currency of her own. The Bank of Finland was founded in 1812 as a semi-public bank. It was not fully nationalized until 1868 and did not obtain the exclusive right to issue bank notes until 1892. The silver standard was adopted in 1865. When Denmark and Sweden formed a Scandinavian Monetary Union based on a common gold standard in 1873 (joined by Norway two years later), Finland remained outside, although a shift to the gold standard occurred in 1877.

Like the other public or semi-public national banks in Scandinavia, the Bank of Finland combined some activities which today are associated with 'fundamental central bank functions' – primarily the management of the money supply – with normal commercial bank activities, that is, the accepting of deposits and the distributing of credits to trade and industry. Endowed early on with note issuing privileges, in Denmark and Norway from the 1810s, the national banks had a decisive competitive advantage over other banking institutions. These had to rely on very poorly developed deposit markets to finance their lending. The longer bank notes stayed in circulation before they were presented for redemption – and small denomination notes remained in circulation longer than did those of greater value – the lower were the bank's costs of raising external funds.[12]

The new banking organizations of the nineteenth century

Other than the public or semi-public national banks, the first banking institutions to emerge were the savings banks. Denmark, being the richest and most developed of the Scandinavian countries, witnessed the birth of her first *sparekasse* in 1810. In Norway, Sweden and Finland the first savings banks were established in various provincial adminis-trative centres in the 1820s, but their breakthrough in the countryside did not come until later. In Norway the expansion started in the mid 1830s, in Sweden in the 1840s, and in Finland not until the 1870s. Their numbers rapidly increasing, the new financial mutual societies generally remained small everywhere. They were part of a decentralized, regional and mostly unit bank savings bank system. Because of their great numbers, however, they served the important function of creating a market for deposits by introducing the general public to the possibility of institutional saving.

The original motivation of the savings bank movement was a philanthropic one. The objective was to encourage self-help among people of limited means by helping them accumulate assets to be used during old age or in case of sickness. Of course, the other side of the coin was the hope that increased personal savings would reduce the cost of poor relief to local governments. In reality it seems that the growth of deposits was long dominated by the savings of wealthier people. The investment behaviour of the savings banks varied a great deal, depending on the socio-economic structure of their home communities. Generally, however, the savings bank were of much greater importance to business in Norway than in Sweden and Finland.

In Denmark, savings banks up to 1862 were allowed to place their deposits in interest bearing accounts with the Public Treasury. For safety reasons they preferred these investments. Thus the Danish savings banks did not get involved in large-scale lending to the general public until the 1850s, when redepositing with the Treasury was made less profitable. After that point, however, the savings banks quickly became among the most important actors on the Danish credit market. Their lending operations were quite varied, although mortgage lending was given top priority. One important group of clients were tenant farmers wishing to purchase their tenancies.[13]

The profound transformation of agriculture in all the Scandinavian countries during the nineteenth century, to a surprisingly large extent, was financed outside the organized credit markets. Starting at the end of the eighteenth century, the spread of the institution of mortgages – the practice of securing financial claims by encumbrance and registration in court – helped improve the market for long-term rural credits. Mortgage loans were provided by the Swedish savings banks from their very inception in the 1820s. Above all, the reclamation of land, both through large drainage projects and through the lowering of lakes, investments and various lake-lowering projects, was financed via the organized markets. This was also the case with the conversion of tenant farms into peasant freeholds. In Denmark in particular, where feudal property rights had been much more comprehensive than in the rest of Scandinavia, the purchase of tenant holdings was extensive.

The first Scandinavian credit society specializing in the lending of money to rural landed estates was established in 1836 in Scania, the southernmost province of Sweden. Like the German *Landschaften*, it was a mutual mortgage institute, the members/clients being jointly liable for the society's debts. Later, mortgage institutes of this same kind were established in other regions, and in 1861 they formed a central organization, the General Mortgage Bank of Sweden. This bank was provided with a state guarantee in order to facilitate its long-term foreign borrowing. In Denmark, mutually organized credit societies became common after 1850, when a special law regulating their operations and making the floating of mortgage institutions' bonds easier was enacted. In the 1880s, a new wave of mutual credit society creation occurred in response to the growing demand for mortgaging facilities from smallholders. The bonds of these smallholders' mortgage institutes were issued both in Danish crowns and in British pounds. Moreover, they were provided with a government guarantee, and, therefore, were easy to place abroad.

Mortgage institutes and mortgage banks developed more slowly in Norway and Finland than they did in Denmark and Sweden. While they had captured almost one third of the organized credit market in Denmark and Sweden by 1875, they formed only 10–13% of the aggregate volume of credit in the organized markets in Norway and Finland. In Finland only one mutual credit society had been founded by 1861, Finlands Hypoteksförening. This institute depended for its survival on intermittent support from the Bank of Finland. Significantly for the Finnish financial system, it was the large commercial banks which founded mortgage granting branches or subsidiaries when the monetization of the economy accelerated and a real estate market arose in the 1890s.[14]

In Norway the difficulty of raising private capital for banking projects opened the gate for state domination in the financial sector. As late as 1890, almost one third of all credits in the Norwegian loan market were provided by public sector banks. Consistent with this tradition, rural mortgage credits, by and large, were the business of a government bank, Kongeriket Norges Hypotekbank. The establishment of the Hypotekbank in 1851 made it possible for the central bank, the Bank of Norway, to reduce its mortgage business.

In Denmark and Sweden the mortgage institutes dominated the long-term credit markets, granting amortization loans for sixty (Denmark) or forty (Sweden) years mainly within the building and agricultural sectors. To finance their lending, these mortgage institutes were allowed to issue bonds. Being mutual and private associations in both Denmark and

Sweden, the mortgage institutes were of great importance in developing a domestic market for non-governmental bonds. In the late 1840s and early 1850s, the Swedish mortgage institutes financed their long-term lending by issuing short-term bonds callable in (up to) six months. The claim has been that this practice, while increasing the risk exposure of the mortgage institutes, made Swedish investors familiar with new short-term instruments. This, in turn, paved the way for the commercial banks' shift from note issue to deposit financing of their operations.[15]

In addition to the construction and agricultural sectors of the economy, growing domestic and foreign trade was an increasingly important source of credit demand. During the lengthy, incremental process through which capitalism and industrialism evolved, traditional modes of financing commerce and transportation long seem to have been adequate. Sound business practices and mutual trust were the key characteristics of a network of credit relations which formed a surprisingly well-established, international business community. The nodes in the network were merchant houses, bill brokerage firms and private bankers, the ties among them being maintained and strengthened by personal kinship, information streams and durable business relations.

In all the Scandinavian countries, merchant houses were the links between primary production, exports and foreign markets. The merchant exporters were able to draw bills on their foreign customers or to exploit the credit facilities furnished by large banking firms in Hamburg and London, and, in turn, to grant seasonal advances to the domestic producers. With growing production and trade this system of commercial credits became increasingly vulnerable to fluctuations in trade. The complicated chain of endorsements among individuals was no stronger than its weakest link. The post-Napoleonic depression, and the recurrent financial crises of 1847, 1857 and 1866, the depression and banking crisis of the late 1870s and the Baring crisis of 1890–1 all witnessed the liquidation of even very respectable bill brokerage and banking firms.[16]

Consequently, during the nineteenth century, the role of merchants and bankers in financing the ongoing expansion of commerce and industry gradually was assumed by a new group of important financial organizations, the commercial banks. This process started in most of the Scandinavian countries in the 1850s – in Finland, however, not until the 1870s – and was, more or less, completed at the turn of the century.

Integration of national financial markets, 1850–1913

The importance of commercial banking was not merely that it replaced existing forms of financial organization. Along with commercial banking followed several basic innovations, all of which contributed to reduce transaction costs by spurring the development of nationally integrated financial markets.

First of all, transfer accounts were introduced. By uniting the commercial banks into a national clearing and payments system, these accounts greatly facilitated the transfer of capital from surplus to deficit regions. In Sweden the early joint-stock commercial banks, established in provincial towns starting in 1830, financed their lending mainly by issuing bank notes. In contrast to Denmark and Norway, where note issuing was a central bank monopoly, this definitely had a 'monetization' effect on the Swedish economy. The shortage of means of payment was alleviated, and the demand for commercial credits in the country districts was satisfied.

Moreover, note issuing was a relatively cheap way of raising funds when commercial banks had to compete on the deposits market, not only with savings banks but also with moneylenders and merchant firms. Hence, the note issuing privileges extended to the private joint-stock banks by the state were in all probability a vital factor in explaining why commercial banks, compared to mortgage institutes and savings banks, were able to play a much more important role in Sweden than in Denmark or Norway.

Another stimulus towards a closer integration of financial markets was the development of branch banking, which was extensive in Sweden and Finland, 'normal' in Denmark and hardly noticeable in Norway. From an integrative point of view, however, Denmark probably had the most concentrated banking system. Copenhagen was the unchallenged commercial and financial centre of the country, and Danish big business was the exclusive clientele of the three big Copenhagen banks – Privatbanken, established in 1857, Landmandsbanken (1870) and Handelsbanken (1871). 'The big three' totally dominated the Danish commercial banking sector. In addition, there were many small commercial banks in the provinces serving local businesses. Most of the small banks were associated with some of the big Copenhagen banks, the latter serving as clearing centres for the former.[17]

In the Swedish capital, opposition to the creation of new banks was very strong, both from influential private moneylenders and from the national bank of Sweden. As mentioned above, the Riksbank served as the commercial bank of Stockholm, distributing state-subsidized loans to trade and industry. Finally, when Stockholms Enskilda Bank received its royal charter in 1856, the commercial banks in the provinces were allowed to open transfer accounts in the new bank. This mechanism, further developed by Skandinaviska Kredit AB (later Skandinaviska Banken) after its founding in 1864, allowed a national network of commercial banks to be built up. Distant regions were integrated into a national payments and clearing system. The Swedish financial system gradually became extremely commercial bank oriented. At the turn of the century, in 1900, half of the organized credit market was in the hands of the commercial banks.[18]

While Finland was a late starter in commercial banking, she moved swiftly towards financial market integration. The first commercial bank, Föreningsbanken i Finland, was not established until 1862; later followed by Nordiska Handelsbanken in 1873, Wasa Aktiebank in 1879 and the Finnish-national Kansallis-Osake-Pankki in 1889. From their very inception all of them, but especially the Föreningsbanken of 1862, had national ambitions, and they quickly opened a large number of banking offices all over Finland. The transfer of payments was facilitated by the introduction of Swedish-type post bills by Förenings-banken. The commercial banks established later generally accepted these post bills for redemption, and thus an embryonic bank cheque system emerged. As in Sweden, the foundation was laid for a commercial bank hegemony in Finland. As early as in 1900, 47% of all credits in the grand duchy were granted by commercial banks.

Despite having a 41% share of the organized credit market in 1900, the Norwegian commercial banking sector was weak. In fact the entire Norwegian financial system was strikingly non-integrated. Norway was no slower than the other Scandinavian countries when it came to the founding of banks. The first commercial banks, Christiania Kreditkasse, Bergens Privatbank and Den Norske Creditbank, were established fairly early: in 1848, 1855 and 1857 respectively. Because of intense local chauvinism, however, attempts to open branch offices in other regions failed. Commercial banks in Norway remained small, striving to serve their local business community with bill brokerage, short-term discount credits and deposit services. Not surprisingly, interest rates varied widely among regions in Norway. As one observer puts it: 'In fact a real national money or capital market did not exist.'[19]

Characteristically enough, the only bank in Norway to develop a branch-based organization was the Bank of Norway. Endowed with a note issuing monopoly and having built up a system of bank offices in all the main cities, the national bank captured the lead position in the organized credit market. In 1850 the Bank's market share was almost 60% (!), in 1875 about 15%, and still in 1900, 6%. Being the chief competitor of the other banks in the discount market for commercial bills, the Bank of Norway long refrained from developing clearing or lender of last resort functions. This was clearly demonstrated during the Norwegian banking crisis of the 1880s, and not until the crisis in the early 1900s did the Bank of Norway act as a true lender of last resort (LLR), supplying liquidity to the financial system.[20] Of course, this reluctance to accept central bank responsibility in this respect was devastating in a system where individual banks could not balance their liquidity through branch office adjustments.

The introduction of a politically based organization, further responsibility for the short-run elasticity of the money supply added a finishing touch to the development of credible financial market commitments by the state up to the First World War. By the turn of the century, the LLR function clearly had been recognized in all the Scandinavian countries as one of the central bank's essential duties. Even earlier, however, all the central banks (with the signal exception of the Bank of Norway) had, in order to prevent general bank panics, supported illiquid (but solvent) commercial banks and had rediscounted commercial bills.

In Denmark, the experience of the 1857 financial crisis caused the National Bank, under new management, to accept full central bank responsibility by the 1860s. During the two financial crises of 1877–8 and 1885 the National Bank promptly intervened, providing support not only to commercial, but also to savings banks. The Bank of Finland began to co-operate with the existing commercial banks in the late 1870s, but it was not until the 1890s that a system of rediscounting commercial bills was introduced. The system functioned according to central bank principles: tight money market conditions motivated a large, and easy conditions a small, volume of rediscounting.[21]

To some extent the Bank of Sweden had supported the commercial banks with liquidity as early as the crises of 1857, 1866 and 1878–9. Until the middle of the 1870s, however, it was mainly the Swedish National Debt Office which acted in a LLR role vis-à-vis both the commercial banks and, interestingly enough, vis-à-vis some of the more important private banking firms. During the Baring crisis of 1890, the

Bank of Sweden explicitly performed the role of banker of last resort to the commercial banks, allowing the rediscounting of commercial bills. Starting in 1893 this was done on a regular basis, with most commercial banks being allowed to join the rediscounting system.[22]

Bank–industry relations

As noted above, in the Scandinavian countries commercial banking developed in response to the demands of the growing domestic and foreign trade of the nineteenth century. Commercial banking slowly replaced merchants, brokers and private banking firms, the resources of which were inadequate to finance the increasing volume of transactions and too small to resist the strains of recurrent financial crises. The early commercial banks concentrated on bill discounting and short-term lending, financing their operations by issuing bank notes (the situation for all Swedish joint-stock banks before 1864) or by attracting short-term deposits. A lengthy industrial transformation, starting in the 1830s and 1840s and taking off in the period 1895–1913, gradually caused demand to shift from short- to long-term credits. Consequently Scandinavian commercial banking, to varying degrees in each country, also became involved in medium- and long-term industrial finance and even in investment banking.

The idea of combining private capital from many partners into a joint-stock banking organization to promote industrial development was originally imported to Scandinavia from Belgium and France. Those who took part in the political discourse were well acquainted with the Société Générale de Belgique, formed in Brussels in 1822, and the French Caisse Générale de Crédit pour le Commerce et l'Industrie, founded in 1837 by Jacques Laffite. In 1852, with the blessing of the new Emperor Napoleon III, these views found a programmatic expression in the foundation of the Crédit Mobilier de Paris. This bank long served as a prototype for, and gave a generic name to, banks engaged in long-term credit financing and which did not hesitate to take ownership positions in industry and transport.

In 1864, one determined attempt was made to establish a Scandinavian Crédit Mobilier with mixed Danish, Dutch and Swedish ownership. That year Skandinaviska Banken was launched as the first non-issuing joint-stock bank in Sweden. The true motivation was to prevent branches of new British banks from opening in the country. Owing to the sudden international crisis of 1863, however,

Skandinaviska Banken became a purely Swedish enterprise, operating in the same fields as the other commercial banks.

There are two Scandinavian commercial banks that developed close relations with big business, the Swedish Stockholms Enskilda Bank and the Danish Privatbank. One scholar has even characterized Stockholms Enskilda Bank as a Swedish Crédit Mobilier.[23] Neither of those banks, however, was founded as an investment bank. Stockholms Enskilda was long the archetypical note issuing 'Scottish' deposit bank on Swedish soil and it did not develop into an industrial bank until the turn of the century, when the second generation of the Wallenberg family took charge. Privatbanken, under the management of C. F. Tietgen, swiftly evolved into a universal bank of the German type, combining traditional retail or deposit banking with corporate financing and venture capital provisions to industry. A great number of important mergers in Denmark took place in the 1860s, 1870s and 1880s, launched and supported by Tietgen and Privatbanken, e.g. DFDS (United Steamships Co.) in 1866, Burmeister & Wain in 1873, Tuborg in 1873 and De Danske Spritfabrikker (the Danish Distilleries) in 1881.[24]

The direct involvement of the Copenhagen banks in big business was made possible by the, relative to the other Scandinavian countries, early introduction of joint-stock corporations in Denmark and by the existence of a fairly well-developed securities market. When modern rules governing daily trading at the Copenhagen Stock Exchange were introduced in the 1870s, the new ordinance only codified long-standing practice. Quotations had been published daily, officially or unofficially, since the 1840s. In the early 1880s, the Copenhagen Stock Exchange numbered no less than eighty-five brokers dealing in the shares of seventy-eight listed companies. The Stock Exchanges in Stockholm, Oslo and Helsinki did not even approach those numbers until the stock market book of the 1910s.[25]

Danish commercial banks were free to formulate their own business strategies. In contrast to the laws regulating the formation and activities of mortgage institutes (1850, 1861) and savings banks (1880) there was no regulatory legislation, and no public supervision, covering commercial banking in Denmark until 1919. This situation is an important institutional factor helping to explain the quick adoption of universal banking by the Copenhagen commercial banks as soon as share trading and new share issues had become commonplace.

In the field of restrictive commercial bank legislation, both Denmark and Norway stand apart from Sweden and Finland. By charters and by law in 1874 the note issuing Swedish banks were strictly *verboten* to invest in shares and in real property. This prohibition was extended to the joint-stock non-issuing banks when legislation applicable to them was enacted in 1886. Finland was the first Scandinavian country to introduce a general banking law in 1866. As was the case in Sweden, the opportunities for banks to pursue ownership functions were restricted by a section of the Act that prohibited the banks from administering industrial firms or from acquiring real property.

Despite the freedom from formal restrictions enjoyed by Norwegian commercial banks, they barely developed any universal or investment bank activities prior to the First World War. The reason is simple, but still of fundamental importance. The decentralized and non-integrated Norwegian economy, having a relatively weak manufacturing sector and no large industrial firms, had little need for universal banking. Starting in 1895, however, commercial banking expanded rapidly, capturing market shares from the, until then, dominant savings banks. This occurred despite the fact that the commercial banks limited themselves to 'retail' business, preferring self-liquidating discount credits and short-term loans. Industrialization progressed rapidly between 1895 and 1913, but the Norwegian banks took hardly any part in the mobilization of venture capital for the booming industries. Most capital came from abroad, especially for hydro-electricity and for the electrochemical and metallurgical industries. In 1909 foreign investors owned almost 40% of the total equity of Norwegian manufacturing firms.[26]

The influence of real sector demand in shaping the actual performance of a financial system is clearly demonstrated by the Swedish case. By law and by tradition, the commercial banking system was firmly rooted in retail or deposit banking. In fact, however, the principal demand from private railway construction firms and from the emerging industrial sector was for the long-term financing of fixed capital. Thus, in practice, the banks increasingly included corporate finance and investment banking activities in their repertoire. Being the principal creditor in many industrial firm failures, and being concerned to protect their interests, Swedish commercial banks often ended up taking an active ownership responsibility for reconstructing firms, both financially and operationally.[27]

At the turn of the century, the prohibition against Swedish banks owning shares became the subject of public controversy. German economic growth was impressive and many contemporary Swedes saw the successful participation of the German universal banks in the industrialization process as an ideal way of using 'idle' bank funds as venture capital to promote growth and economic transformation. With the enactment of a new banking law in 1912, a certain freedom to purchase shares was granted. Even before that, however, the commercial banks in fact had participated in corporate finance and industrial venture capital mobilization on a large scale. One way had been to organize private consortia or syndicates, while another had been to form investment and share-issuance companies. These firms did the kind of business forbidden to the parent banks. Formally, the Swedish commercial banks were thus deposit banks, but in reality, they clearly behaved like universal banks.

Finland illustrates the case of a centralized financial system, dominated by commercial banks, but without either the legal or the industrial prerequisites needed to develop universal banking. As in Sweden, the prohibition against commercial bank ownership of industrial enterprises made direct involvement in industry, for example through underwriting operations and interlocking directorates, impossible. At the same time, the growing, but still immature, industrial sector was dominated by closely held and family-owned corporations. There was no regular market for private securities until the mid-1910s. Industrial expansion was mainly financed internally, profits being ploughed back into operations, or by share-issues subscribed to by family members. In general, equity–capital ratios in industry were impressively high. Despite the importance of commercial banks in the aggregate credit market, lack of demand for capital meant that investment banking and close bank–industry relations did not emerge in Finland until well after the First World War.[28]

The structure of banking systems

The Scandinavian cases described in this chapter support two main conclusions. First, the analysis emphasizes the immense indirect importance of the political system in the development of monetary, banking and financial regimes, all of which constitute essential parts of capitalism. In all the Scandinavian countries, political bodies, the king, the government or the Parliament, took the initiative and/or assumed the ownership role in early banking organizations. The public or semi-public national banks, even when they had originated from an urgent need to solve chronic budget deficits, had the important long-term effect of creating public confidence in token money as a medium of exchange. Moreover, in all these countries the national bank long positioned itself as the most important commercial bank, distributing loans and short-term credits to trade and industry.

Thus the political system was important in creating general credibility for new financial instruments, bank notes as well as governmental and private bonds, treasury bills, promissory notes, deposit receipts, bank books, etc. When private capital and private incentives were lacking, the state also intervened directly, taking the initiative for founding public credit organizations to handle the financial requirements of the expanding business community. This interventionist policy was the most straightforward in nineteenth-century Norway. Public sector banking dominated the banking system. Even in 1890 the Bank of Norway, the government-run mortgage bank and the various other government agencies constituted almost one third of the total Norwegian credit market.

Thus, in all probability, public banking had a certain 'crowding-out effect' restricting the growth of private commercial banking in Norway. This is not to say, however, that the relatively slow development of a commercial banking sector in Norway was primarily an effect of a powerful public sector. Rather, it seems likely that both variables were dependent on the specific structure of the Norwegian economy, that is, on the 'real' forces mentioned in the introductory section of this chapter.

This leads to the second general conclusion to be drawn from the comparative analysis of the Scandinavian cases. In a global, or even European, context, the Scandinavian countries stand out as institutionally relatively homogeneous. This includes numerous 'rules of the game' that are derived from culture, religion, formal education, literacy and political tradition. Despite that, on the eve of the First World War, the organized financial markets varied considerably among the individual countries, with different types of financial organizations and contrasting degrees of market integration. These divergent developments are basically explained by differences in economic structures, that is by demand from the real sector of the economy.

Thus the relatively great importance of mutual mortgage institutes in the Danish financial system can only be explained by the importance of the agricultural sector, expressed above all in the rise of a peasant proprietor class and widespread purchase of tenant holdings. It is also quite obvious that the Norwegian banking system basically responded to the demands of the Norwegian economy. Even at the turn of the century, Norway had a relatively non-integrated economy. The leading, fast-growing, industries were fishing and shipping. Traditionally, these had been financed by local, sometimes quite complex, partnerships and, accordingly, they did not generate demand for new credit organizations.

Thus, in a sense, a country will always get the financial system it 'deserves'. But this is not the whole story. The fact is that identical needs were solved differently in the four countries in response to varying foreign cultural and ideological influences. When explaining the rapid growth of mutual mortgage institutes in Denmark (and in southern Sweden), the close cultural links to Germany and its *Landschaften* societies must be considered. Similarly, the introduction of universal banking principles in Swedish commercial banking around 1900 was, to a large extent, inspired by ideas imported from Germany and justified with the rapid growth rates achieved by that emerging Great Power.

Last, but not least, it is important to stress the self-reinforcing mechanisms in the development of financial systems. Certainly the savings banks had obtained a comparative advantage over the non-issuing commercial banks by being the first to develop local deposits markets. To a large extent this advantage was retained because of the trust these banks had earned over time. The duration of business relations unquestionably has an important bearing on the strength of a financial contract between bank and customer. Path dependence is thus an important partial explanation for the much more rapid growth of savings, compared to commercial, banks in Norway up to the end of the nineteenth century. When the Swedish commercial banks were provided with an opportunity to raise funds cheaply through the issue of bank notes, a self-reinforcing mechanism that quickly led to the dominance of the commercial over the savings banks was started.

The same path-dependence mechanisms also can be recognized behind the powerful Norwegian public banking sector. Once the government-dominated system had emerged, reinforcement tendencies became operative. In fields such as capital imports, for example, public banking was more effective than private in mobilizing foreign capital at reasonable cost. Being the most influential lending bank in the country, the Bank of Norway, through its note issuing privileges, had a clear competitive advantage over the private commercial banks.

Notes

1 Fernand Braudel distinguishes two levels of economic activity separate from everyday material life: the 'economic life', characterized by routine exchange, and 'capitalism', characterized by sophisticated business activity featuring risk-taking and speculation (F. Braudel, *Les jeux de l'échange* (Paris, 1979), esp. ch. 4).

2 The different approaches, and the different theoretical constructs of Hilferding, Schumpeter and Gerschenkron are concisely discussed in P. L. Cottrell, H. Lindgren and A. Teichova (eds.), *European History and Banking between the Wars. A Review of Bank–Industry Relations* (Leicester, 1992), pp. 1–7. A historiography of the debate of the last twenty years, starting with Cameron's assertions of the late 1960s and early 1970s, is to be found in H. W. Nordvik's 'The Banking System, Industrialization and Economic Growth in Norway, 1850–1914', *Scandinavian Economic History Review*, 41, 1 (1993).

3 H. Landberg, L. Ekholm, R. Nordlund and S. A. Nilsson, *Det kontinentala krigets ekonomi*, Studia Historica Upsaliensia 36 (Uppsala, 1971), particularly the Landberg contribution, 'Krig på kredit', pp. 125ff.

4 L. Magnusson, *Den bråkiga kulturen. Förläggare och smideshantverkare i Eskilstuna 1800–1850* (Stockholm, 1988), p. 235; K.-G. Hildebrand, *Swedish Iron in the 17th and 18th Centuries. Export Industry before the Industrialization*, Jernkontorets Bergshistoriska Skriftserie, 29 (Stockholm, 1992), pp. 97–108.

5 R. G. King, 'On the Economics of Private Money', *Journal of Monetary Economics*, 12, 1 (1983), pp. 127–58.

6 The business practices of the Amsterdamsche Wisselbank are described in detail by Adam Smith in his *Wealth of Nations*, vol. I, book IV (London, 1964), pp. 422–31.

7 I. Nygren, *Från Stockholms Banco till Citibank* (Stockholm, 1985), pp. 13–22.

8 Bank notes as small as 8 skilling banco, one-sixth of a riksdollar, were issued starting in 1834. According to the official rate of exchange, 8 Swedish skilling banco was then equal to less than 4d in London. In England, following the suspension of convertibility of bank notes into coin in 1797, £1 and £2 notes were issued. They were, however, soon withdrawn, starting in 1817 (C. P. Kindleberger, *A Financial History of Western Europe* (London, 1984), pp. 62–3, 77; T. Lindgren, *Riksbankens sedelhistoria 1668–1968* (Stockholm, 1968), pp. 55–7; *Sveriges Riksbank 1668–1924*, vol. V (Stockholm, 1931), pp. 146–53; G. B. Nilsson, *Banker i brytningstid. A O Wallenberg i svensk bankpolitik 1850–1856* (Stockholm, Stockholm School of Economics, 1981), pp. 328–33).

9 E. Hoffmeyer, *Strukturaendringer på penge- och kapitalmarkedet* (Copenhagen, 1960), pp. 14–23; S. A. Hansen and K. E. Svendsen, *Dansk pengehistorie 1 1700–1914* (Copenhagen, 1968), pp. 84–136. In 1936, the private ownership of Nationalbanken was dissolved. Even today, by custom, the Danish central bank holds a relatively independent position vis-à-vis the government. The situation was quite different for the Swedish and Norwegian central banks (for the latter, at least up to 1985).

10 G. Ahlström, 'Riksgäldskontoret och Sveriges statsskund före 1850-talet', in E. Dahmén (ed.), *Upplåning och utveckling. Riksgäldskontoret 1789–1989* (Stockholm, 1989), pp. 95–112.

11 Å. Egge, 'Transformation of Bank Structures in the Industrial Period: The Case of Norway, 1830–1914', *Journal of European Economic History*, 12, 2 (1983); Nordvik, 'The Banking System', pp. 51–72.

12 It has been estimated that Swedish private joint-stock banks, chartered with note issuing privileges could raise funds at an effective cost of 2% in the 1840s and the 1850s. At the same time, the rate of interest on loans was limited, both by charter and by practice, to a maximum of 5.25%. See M. Larsson and H. Lindgren, 'The Political Economy of Banking: Retail Banking and Corporate Finance in Sweden, 1850–1939', in Y. Cassis (ed.), *Finance and Financiers in European History, 1880–1960* (Cambridge, 1992), p. 340.

13 Hoffmeyer, *Strukturaendringer på penge- og kapitalmarkedet*, pp. 23–6; S. A. Hansen, 'The Transformation of Bank Structures in the Industrial Period', *Journal of European Economic History*, 11, 3 (1982), pp. 582–5.

14 E. Pihkala, 'Kredit och kreditformer i Finland 1840–1914', in G. Authén Blom (ed.), *Utviklingen av kreditt og kredittinstitusjoner i de Nordiske land ca. 1850–1914* (Trondheim, 1978); A. Kuusterä, 'Uppkomsten av den nationella kapitalmarknaden i Finland', paper presented at 'Nordiskt seminar i bank- och finanshistorie', Sole Hotell, Norway, 1–2 June 1992.

15 Egge, 'Transformation of Bank Structures in the Industrial Period', pp. 277ff; Nygren, *Från Stockholms Banco till Citibank*, pp. 36ff.

16 See, e.g. E. Lange, 'The Norwegian System of Banking Institutions', in NORAS, *Research on Banking, Capital and Society*, Report no. 58 (Oslo, 1994), pp. 5f; Larsson and Lindgren, 'The Political Economy of Banking', pp. 337ff; and Hansen, 'The Transformation of Bank Structures', pp. 580ff.

17 E. Lange, 'Financial Institutions and Markets in Twentieth-Century Scandinavia', in G. G. Feldman and U. Olsson *et al.* (eds.), *The Evolution of Modern Financial Institutions in the Twentieth Century*, Proceedings of the Eleventh International Economic History Congress, Milan, Università Bocconi, September 1994, p. 52; P. H. Hansen and H. Chr. Johansen, *Det danske finansielle system ca. 1850–1992*, in NORAS, *Research on Banking, Capital and Society*, pp. 8ff.

18 Larsson and Lindgren, 'The Political Economy of Banking', pp. 339–42; Nygren, *Från Stockholms Banco till Citibank*, p. 140.

19 Egge, 'Transformation of Bank Structures in the Industrial Period', p. 280.

20 Lange, 'The Norwegian System of Banking Institutions', pp. 3–8; Nordvik, 'The Banking System, Industrialization and Economic Growth in Norway', pp. 60, 72.

21 P. H. Hansen, 'Banking Crises and Bank Regulation: Denmark in the Interwar Period', in NORAS, *Research on Banking, Capital and Society*, Report no. 60 (Oslo, 1994), pp. 3–6; Kuusterä, 'Uppkomsten av den nationelle kapitalmarknaden i Finland', pp. 16–17.

22 I. Nygren, 'När lång upplåning blev korta krediter 1840–1905', in Dahmén (ed.), *Upplåning och utveckling*, pp. 190–210.

23 B. Gille, 'Banking and Industrialisation in Europe', in *The Fontana Economic History of Europe*, vol. III (London, 1973), p. 274.

24 Hansen, 'The Transformation of Bank Structures in the Industrial Period', pp. 586–7.

25 The Stockholm Stock Exchange was not organized in its modern form – with daily transactions and daily quotations – until 1901. The Helsinki exchange followed suit and reorganized in 1912, but it did not operate on a regular basis until 1915. In Norway the Kristiania boom of the late 1890s produced an initial stock market breakthrough, but the Oslo bourse did not introduce weekly quotations until 1908. Daily quotations for all kinds of securities were not provided until 1922 (I. Gejl, *Indenfor Snorene. Fondborsvekselerernes historie – isaer til 1945* (Århus, 1989), pp. 105–16;

S. Algott, 'Bidrag till Stockholms fondbörs historia', in *Stockholms fondbörs 100 år* (Stockholm, 1963), pp. 32–103; F. Tiderman, *Helsingfors börs 1912–1937* (Helsinki, 1937), pp. 19–45; *Kapitalkilde for naeringslivet. Oslo bors gjennom 175 år* (Oslo, 1994), pp. 48–62).

26 S. Knutsen, 'From Expansion to Panic and Crash. The Norwegian banking system and its customers, 1913–1924', NORAS, *Research on Banking, Capital and Society*, Report no. 59 (Oslo, 1994), pp. 3–6.

27 The acquisition of shares or real property as a result of loan default has always been allowed by Swedish banking law. This was the case notwithstanding the general prohibition against acquiring and trading shares. See Larsson and Lindgren, 'The Political Economy of Banking', pp. 348ff.

28 A. Kuusterä, 'Makten över företaget', preliminary paper presented at the seminar 'Managerial Constraints in Various Business Organizations', 6–8 November 1989, Sigtuna, Sweden.

12 Banking and industry in central Europe, nineteenth to twentieth century

Alice Teichova

For almost a century, the interaction between banks and industry has been the subject of speculation and debate. Scholars have explored the role of banks in industrialization, the nature and causes of concentration in industry and the general impact of banks on business cycles and on long-term economic growth. This discussion gained further momentum among economic historians in the mid-1960s with Alexander Gerschenkron's views on the role of banks under conditions of relative economic backwardness[1] and the rediscovery of Rudolf Hilferding's *Finanzkapital* (published in Vienna in 1910; in English for the first time in 1981), which looked at the nature of the interaction between banking and industrial capital. Only one year after the first appearance of *Finanzkapital* Joseph Schumpeter published his main work *Theorie der wirtschaftlichen Entwicklung* in which he regarded the role of banking and credit, next to that of the entrepreneur, as a crucially important factor in economic growth.[2] In my opinion, it is not accidental that all three authors, who greatly influenced economic thought, came from the Austro-Hungarian Empire where, in Vienna, the intellectual mainstreams of the Vienna School and Austro-Marxism clashed.

I will concentrate here on universal banks – those institutions that combined the short-term business of deposit banking with the long-term activity of investment banking, and, in addition, performed stock-broking functions, managed clients' portfolios, acquired shares and voting rights in joint-stock companies on their own and their clients' account. With the exception of the United Kingdom, and, possibly, also France, universal banks spread throughout Europe during the phase of buoyant expansion in capitalism from the 1880s to 1914. Close relationships between industrial companies and banks developed everywhere, although the pace at which this happened differed somewhat from country to country.

I limit my study to central Europe, where the union of banking and industry was especially marked. Germany is often seen as a 'model' of this trend. There is less agreement among scholars about the rest of central Europe – Austria-Hungary until 1918, and the successor states to the Dual Monarchy thereafter. In this chapter special attention will be focused on the Habsburg Monarchy and its two economically most advanced successor states, Austria and Czechoslovakia. I draw on the results produced by an international research project under my direction, which investigated the financing of industry by banks in Austria, Czechoslovakia, Hungary and Sweden.[3]

I

The geographical diffusion of universal banking across Europe accompanied the rapid, parallel rise of large-scale enterprise, of formal cartels and of other monopolistic and oligopolistic formations. These trends led to concern about the excessive concentration of economic power in banks and their apparent dominance of industry. Awareness of this issue by contemporaries is shown by the early appearance of the first book on cartels, written by Friedrich Kleinwächter and published in Innsbruck in 1883.[4] It may seem strange that this first systematic description of modern concentration in industry, trade and finance should have been produced within the Habsburg Monarchy, which is often viewed by economic historians as a laggard in industrialization. But the backwardness of the Austro-Hungarian economy has often been over-stated in macro-economic assessments. This view of 'sluggishness' has continued largely because of the Monarchy's uneven economic development.[5] Too much attention is often focused on the Monarchy's south-eastern regions – among the most economically backward of Europe – and too little on its western lands (Bohemia, Moravia, Silesia and the Alpine lands), where an industrial revolution comparable to those of Western Europe had taken place. This spatially differentiated capitalist development in Austria-Hungary cannot exclusively be

explained by Gerschenkron's approach to relative economic backwardness.[6]

Contrary to the widespread assumption amongst scholars that
Germany became the home of universal banking *par excellence* after the
failure of the Crédit Mobilier in France, its purest form actually can be
found in Austria-Hungary. Most typically this was expressed by the
foundation in 1855 of the K. k. privilegierte Österreichische Credit-
Anstalt für Handel und Gewerbe (hereafter Credit-Anstalt) as a joint-
stock bank on the pattern of the Paris brothers Pereire's Crédit Mobilier
but adapted to Austrian conditions. At its cradle stood the Minister of
Finance, Carl Freiherr von Bruck, who was aware of the urgent need to
reform the finances of the state and to build a transport and banking
system as well as of the need to alleviate the lack of capital suffered by
the Empire's industry. Among the most active supporters of the
Austrian crédit-mobilier project and the main subscribers to the Credit-
Anstalt's equity was the Viennese House of S. M. von Rothschild
which forestalled the Pereire brothers' intention to open a branch in
Vienna.[7]

Important private banking houses had existed before the foundation
of the Credit-Anstalt but they were mainly concerned with government
finance as well as providing credit for the estates of the high aristocracy,
and only to a lesser degree with promoting companies. Also the
Österreichische Nationalbank founded in 1816 conducted some regular
banking business which, in the long run, was unable to satisfy the rising
demand for credit. In 1853 the Niederösterreichische Escompte-
gesellschaft received imperial permission to provide trade and industry
in Lower Austria with money by discounting bills of exchange. But the
Credit-Anstalt remained the only universal banking institute operating
throughout the whole Habsburg Monarchy until the 1860s. In 1863
the Allgemeine österreichische Boden-Credit-Anstalt (hereafter Boden-
Credit-Anstalt) was founded which combined mortgage business with
commercial banking.[8] It derived its privileged position among the
Viennese banks from acting as the banker of the imperial family and
the Court. As a mediator between the financial centres of London
and Vienna the Anglo-Österreichische Bank started its activities in
1864. Somewhat later, in 1869, the Wiener Bank-Verein was established as an associate of the Boden-Credit-Anstalt, but its business took
off only after 1881. These were to become the most famous of the great
Vienna banks.

Until the late nineteenth century the big commercial banks of Vienna did not fulfil the expectations placed in them as promoters of industry. As 'profit-maximizers and risk-minimizers'[9] they preferred the funding of railway construction and public borrowing to financing of industry. Only after overcoming the Great Depression of the 1870s, after the railway book had run its course, and after profits especially from handling government loans began to decline the Vienna banks began cautiously to turn to industrial lending. From their very beginnings they did not see their role in encouraging entrepreneurial spirit when promoting industrial enterprises, but directed their business to well-established firms.[10] Neither were they in the forefront of founding new industrial ventures but they preferred to convert profitable enterprises into public limited companies.[11]

At least since the last quarter of the nineteenth century contemporaries, even senior officials within the Austrian Ministry of Finance, regarded the relationship between industrial and banking capital as one of power and they assumed that the power in its most expressive form lay with the banks.[12] The first attempt to analyse bank–industry relations also emanated from this part of Europe. Rudolf Hilferding's *Finance Capital*, completed in 1909 and first published in Vienna in 1910, was influenced by conditions in the author's homeland: 'Austria . . . provides the clearest example of the direct and deliberate influence of bank capital upon cartelization.'[13] Of course, Hilferding examined the interlocking of bank and industrial capital not only in Austria, but also in Germany. There the financing of large industrial concerns by and through banks intensified to such a degree before 1914 that he drew the hasty political conclusion from his assumption of the supremacy of banks over industry that capitalism could be replaced by socialism in one stroke: 'Even today, taking possession of six large Berlin banks would mean taking possession of the most important spheres of large-scale industry, and would greatly facilitate the initial phases of socialist policy.'[14] The power of banks over industry was, and largely *is still* widespread. Recently, the assumption of the banks' supremacy over industry was tested with regards to Wilhelmine and Weimar Germany and was found to require revision.[15] Nevertheless, a hypothesis about the *potential* hierarchical relationship between banks and industrial enterprises can be a useful tool in empirical research. Gerschenkron, who like Hilferding had an Austro-Hungarian background,[16] reproduced essentially Hilferding's chain of thought, when he assessed the role of banks in both financial industrial companies and furthering concentration. Moreover, his ideas are not unlike those of Hilferding with respect to how banks assume control over their client industrial enterprises, especially through financial operations and by serving on the boards of their subsidiary companies. However, Gerschenkron drew a fundamentally different conclusion about the implications of this relationship. He did not regard the dependence of industrial enterprises on banks as a necessary result of capitalist development, but as a feature of 'latecomer' industrial economies that marked only a limited phase in their overall development and persisted only until the initial scarcity of capital was overcome.[17] Consequently, Gerschenkron assigned a 'missionary' task to the credit banks (*Kreditbanken*) in relatively backward European countries before 1914. In the light of empirical evidence Alexander Gerschenkron's conviction that the big banks performed a 'missionary' task in furthering industrialization has to be qualified. Yet, in the view of some authors, the banks continued financing industry without any break into the interwar period. To be sure, after 1918 the banks were not so much promoting industrial enterprise as rescuing their own industrial subsidiary enterprises from collapse.[16] Richard Tilly, too, downplays the role of the mixed banks in Germany between 1870 and 1913 by calling their support for industry 'development assistance for the strong'.[19]

The principal findings on the nature of pre-1914 European universal banking provide signposts for the interwar period, especially as the First World War was not a discontinuity for concentration of either industrial or financial capital. Rather, the war accelerated such concentration. Similarly the need for the financing of industry by banks was not diminished – indeed, the turmoil of post-war inflations and financial crises intensified such demand.

II

Before 1914 the level of joint-stock banking assets in the Austrian financial sector compared very favourably with that of other developed European economies. As in Germany, the universal banks of the Habsburg Empire preferred to extend credits to enterprises that were profitable or had a long-standing customer relation.[20]

Legal and fiscal regulations determined the specific nature of the relationship between banks and industry within Austria-Hungary. Industrial joint-stock companies avoided long-term credit and instead chose financing by floating new shares through the banks because tax laws unfavourably affected the growth of joint-stock enterprise. Until its amendment in 1899, company law hindered the development of an adequate capital market;[21] the big credit banks stepped in to fill the void.

According to Alois Mosser's analyses of Austrian company balance sheets for the period 1880 to 1914, the majority of joint-stock companies obtained capital in two main ways: first, through ploughing back their own financial resources; and, second, by taking up frequently prolongable short-term credit from the banks, with the latter being eventually amortized by the issue of shares. In aggregate, credit to joint-stock companies rose fourfold over the period 1880 to 1913, while long-term credit decreased relative to short-term credit.[22] The Austrian banking system performed the usual functions of accumulating and mobilizing capital as in other developed countries, but it played a much greater active role in the allocation of capital.[23] As there were no legal constraints to the ownership of shares by banks, bank credits were secured by shares, preferably those of the largest and soundest industrial enterprises. The banks strengthened their supervision of client companies through interlocking directorships, while they encouraged cartelization and initiated or mediated mergers. The banks frequently performed marketing operations for enterprises within their spheres of interests or, in the case of cartels, acted as the cartel bureau for whole industrial sectors, especially in sugar, coal and wood.

By 1914 the eight great Viennese banks accounted for about two-thirds of the total capital of all the financial institutions of the Empire.[24] These institutions had secured strategic positions in almost all branches of industry and their influence radiated out from Vienna to encompass all the territories of the Dual Monarchy. In the Hungarian portion of the Monarchy, only one bank was on a par with the leading Viennese institutions – the Hungarian General Credit Bank – which itself was linked to the Austrian Credit-Anstalt. Ránki has estimated that in 1913 this bank controlled sixty-three industrial enterprises which, in aggregate, accounted for 16% of the total capital of Hungarian joint-stock companies.[25] While in the Czech Lands the only bank which exceeded with its capital resources and business operations the size of a provincial bank was the Živnostenská banka of Prague.

The League of Nations' examination of the shattered post-war Austrian financial system yielded the famous Layton–Rist Report, which assessed the pre-1918 functions of the Viennese banks:

They served every relatively important operation in all areas: shares issues, formation of syndicates, placing of loans or any larger industrial credit. Relations with international finance are concentrated in Vienna – here foreign credits were taken up and administered for the entire Empire. Viennese banks led the penetration of Eastern and Southeast Europe with Austrian capital.[26]

With the break-up of the Monarchy in 1918, the big Viennese universal banks found themselves suddenly standing at the centre of what were now multinational diversified concerns.[27] During the short period from 1919 to 1923, the leading Viennese banks were penetrated by international capital and two of them – the Österreichische Länderbank and the Anglo-Österreichische Bank[28] – had become fully foreign-owned Paris- and London-based institutes.

Despite these sudden transformations, the evolution of bank–industry relations within the successor states during the interwar period was strongly marked by characteristics carried over from the pre-war system. Accordingly, a parallel development of the bank–industry structure in Austria, Czechoslovakia, Hungary, Italy, Poland and Yugoslavia occurred after the dissolution of the Empire.

The banking system inherited by the successor states had several common features. The tradition of the 'universal' banks serving as the source of finance for industrial enterprises continued unbroken. The banks' assets consisted largely of industrial equities, whose prices fell under crisis conditions and rendered them illiquid. Domestic deposits were mostly insufficient and, towards the end of the 1920s, decreased. Liquidity problems arose perennially, the banks defaulted on their enormous debts in the crisis of the 1930s, and concentration within banking, through mergers, intensified. By 1937, 75% of the equity of commercial banks in Romania and Yugoslavia, and at least 30% in Poland and Bulgaria were in foreign, mainly Western hands. While the share of foreign ownership was relatively high (no precise figures are known as yet) in the case of Austrian universal banks, no more than 15% of the total capital of all joint-stock banks in Czechoslovakia were foreign owned.[29]

In many respects, the development of the Czech banking system both in the Habsburg Monarchy and during the existence of the independent Czechoslovak state between 1918 and 1938 differed from that of the other successor states. As early as the upswing in the business cycle between 1907 and 1912 the Czech banks had achieved a dominating position in the local (Bohemian, Moravian and Silesian) money market.

They had succeeded in ousting the Bohemian-German banks by a tighter concentration of banking capital, and by building up both stronger industrial concerns and centrally controlled networks of branches and affiliates throughout the Austro-Hungarian Empire, and, to a lesser extent, beyond its eastern and south-eastern borders.[30] The Czech universal banks, especially the strongest among them – the Živnostenská banka – constituted a threat to the Viennese financial institutions. In their competitive expansion into the Slav areas of the Austro-Hungarian Empire, they employed the nationalist slogans of 'mutual Slavonic interests' and 'Slav brotherhood' against the established Viennese and Budapest banks. Although by the outbreak of the Second World War the capital of the twenty-two largest Viennese banks still amounted to 71.4% of the total banking capital of the Austrian half of the Dual Monarchy, the number of Czech banks rose from four to thirteen, and their share in total banking capital from 1900 to 1913 rose from 7.9% to 13.3%.[31]

From the turn of the century, the Czech national movement in Bohemia and Moravia built up a financial presence in the credit co-operatives movement and the small savings banks.[32] Through their central organizations, these institutions provided capital for the big Czech banks and their powerful industrial clients in Prague and Brno, where the actual reins of financial and economic power were concentrated in the independent Czechoslovak Republic after 1918.[33]

In post-1918 Austria, the savings banks, due to the impact of inflation and crises on the propensity of the population to save, provided insufficient domestic resources for the commercial banks. They created a centralized organization, the Girovereinigung der Sparkassen, only in December 1937. In contrast, the Czech savings institutes founded the Ústřední banka Českých spořitelen (Sporobanka) (Central Bank of the Czech Savings Institutes) already in June 1903, which became a constant source of funds for the big Czech banks where the concentrated savings were deposited.[34] While the Czech banking system was not immune to the vagaries of crises in the interwar period, it avoided the crashes that characterize the Austrian system. This, as Weber pointed out,[35] was undoubtedly due to the better performance of the Czechoslovak in comparison with the Austrian economy. However, the policies of the Živnostenská banka were, in the historical context, more cautious than the Viennese banks in granting credit to industrial enterprises and in paying out dividends, and were more farsighted in building up reserves.[36]

In the case of Vienna, the former financial centre of the Danube basin, bank–industry relations were dramatically affected by the disintegration of the Empire. The big Viennese commercial banks attempted to carry on 'business as usual', but in very much changed circumstances. Expecting to resume their role as the financial leaders, the Viennese banks retained a hand in financing at least a part of the business in the former imperial lands.[37] This policy was pursued despite their having lost most of their branches; of the 143 branches possessed by the ten biggest Vienna banks outside Austria in 1918, only 9 had remained by 1924.[38] They lost a large part of their subsidiary industrial enterprises through 'nostrification', which involved transferring head offices of companies from Vienna to the new successor states. Above all, the Viennese banks lost control of their most profitable industrial enterprises, which were now located beyond the Czechoslovak border.[39]

Unlike German banks and industry, which after 1918 opposed foreign penetration,[40] the Viennese banks were anxious to attract capital from the countries of the Entente. The bankers and Austrian government officials assumed that the shrunken Austrian economy would not be viable without external support.[41] During the inflation of the early 1920s industrial demand for credit rose steeply and was met by the banks, but at the price of plunging the Austrian financial sector further and further into foreign debt. This eventually dire situation arose because a prerequisite for the expansion of bank advances to industry was lending to the Viennese banks from Western Europe and the United States. With respect to only the short-term foreign indebtedness of the biggest Viennese banks, this lending increased approximately threefold from 1924 to 1930, rising from 370 million to 980 million Schilling.[42]

As compared with the pre-1913 period, industry became dependent to a much higher degree on bank loans while, in turn, the banks increased their share ownership of dependent client companies. Bank financing became increasingly marked by financial institutions borrowing short and then relending the funds on a longer-term basis. This was in no way altruistic; to sustain their own credit-worthiness, the banks had to keep their industrial debtors afloat. An illusion of prosperity was created to cover industrial losses and sustain industrial dividends. Although such desperate procedures were not unknown in other countries, the extent of such camouflaging in persistent crisis conditions was, in my opinion, specific to Austria. The banks were encouraged by expectations of an economic revival, but this proved to be illusory and, moreover, Vienna never regained its regional leadership in finance and trade.

As in other economies, bank mergers in Austria took place from the mid-1920s, but to a much greater degree. Fusions of the Viennese banks occurred after rampant speculation that marked the period until 1924 and had been unchecked in the absence of effective banking legislation. In the chaos of hyperinflation, the Austrian government established a Banking Commission in 1922 and charged it with preparing legislation both to control banking practices and restrict fraudulent dealing on the stock exchange. However, its work was stymied and, eventually, the Commission was disbanded in 1926 without result.[43] Crashes and financial crises continued and led to more amalgamations. In 1929 only four out of the eight great Viennese banks remained. As a result of merger and consolidation, each surviving bank had a greater number of dependent industrial enterprises and more packets of unsaleable shares. In addition, the remaining institutions were faced with an increasing demand for credit. The merger movement, which arose largely from the need to salvage ailing banks, peaked in 1929 when the Credit-Anstalt für Handel und Gewerbe absorbed the Boden-Credit-Anstalt, after previously digesting the Anglo-Österreichische Bank in 1926. Yet it was no solution as the Credit-Anstalt itself crashed spectacularly in May 1931.[44] This, as is well known, sent out shock waves and exacerbated the international banking crisis of that summer. The whole Austrian economy, already strained by general depression, was plunged ever more deeply into crisis conditions.

The Austrian government and the Austrian National Bank mounted a rescue operation for the Credit-Anstalt,[45] which by 'socializing' the bank's enormous losses, both satisfied the foreign creditors and, after the fusion with the Wiener Bankverein, led eventually in 1934 to the creation of almost a *one-bank system*. As in Germany this state support was a state-aided reconstruction exercise, not the application of a conscious policy designed to nationalize the banking system. Under it, the debt burden of the insolvent banking system was shouldered by the government. Government financial guarantees indirectly also rescued the bank's industrial enterprises, as most of their debts were written off.[46] The state became the majority shareholder in the Credit-Anstalt, which continued to function as the leading universal bank, although at a much reduced level. It headed a system that from 1934 was composed of three banks; the Viennese branch of a Czechoslovak institution, the strong filial of the Prague Živnostenská banka, and the Länderbank, which was controlled by the Banque des Pays de l'Europe Centrale of Paris.

With its reconstruction, the Credit-Anstalt's management had to decide which of its enterprises to liquidate and which to finance with further credit.[47] The subsequent shrinkage of the banking system has been termed 'Austrification', because the domestic industrial holdings were slimmed down and all the foreign holdings of the Credit-Anstalt were transferred to its foreign creditors.[48] Unlike in Germany, the bank was not reprivatized; the majority of its shares continued to remain in the hands of what ultimately became the Austrofascist state. By the time of the *Anschluss*, the Austrian banking system had resumed profitability, but was by then fully integrated into the German Reich.[49]

III

Without a 'lender of the last resort', universal banks were unable to cope with the crisis of the 1930s. The Great Depression marked an end to the form of mixed banking that had functioned since the 1880s. Across central and eastern Europe, the state was forced to intervene and mount rescue actions. Everywhere the losses of the big credit banks and their large industrial clients were 'socialized' by direct state takeover, outright or through majority shareholdings. This did not, however, usher in socialism as Hilferding had expected; on the contrary, these actions succeeded in rescuing capitalism and buttressed highly concentrated structures within banking and industry.

In the case of Austria, universal banking had outlasted all changes. While banking organization after the *Anschluss* remained essentially unaltered except for the replacement of Jewish by German directors, banking operations were redirected to finance Hitler's war effort.

In the case of Czechoslovakia, the aftermath of the Munich Agreement (30 September 1938) led to the dismemberment of the state and the occupation of the Czech Lands by the army of Nazi Germany.[50] The Czech banking system of the so-called Protectorate of Bohemia and Moravia fell prey to the big banks of the Third Reich during the speedy integration of the Czech economy into the German war economy.[51] In the post-1945 reconstituted Czechoslovak state the Communist regime nationalized the banks after 1948. The central bank as well as the few remaining money institutes became executive organs of official planning policy. The role of the banks was limited to providing evidence of the state of the plan-fulfilment in the individual economic units.[52] Since the demise of Communism in 1989 efforts have been underway in both the Czech and the Slovak Republic to restructure a capitalist banking system. During the Second World War, Austria was recognized as 'the first victim of Nazi aggression' by the Allies (1943) and in the wake of Germany's defeat it recovered its independent status. After a decade of Allied occupation, Austria gained neutrality in 1955. The Credit-Anstalt was nationalized in 1946 to avoid being taken over as German property by the Allies. It has undergone partial privatization since 1957, leaving at least 51% of its equity in the hands of the state. It has functioned effectively as the leading financial institution in rebuilding the mixed economy of the Second Austrian Republic. Since 1989 the Austrian banks have shown vigorous interest in the recently opened investment opportunities in central and south-east Europe where – in historical context – their traditional market has been.

Notes

An essay by Fritz Weber on banking and the development of capitalism in Central Europe was planned but has, to the great regret of the editors, not materialized – the prospective author was taken ill while preparing it.

The author of this contribution is very grateful to Professor David F. Good for granting her permission to draw on her chapter in his edited volume *Economic Trans-formations in East and Central Europe: Legacies from the Past and Policies for the Future* (London and New York, 1994), pp. 63–74. The chapter presented here is a revised and updated version which also draws on recent results of the current research project 'The Economic Role of Austria in Interwar Central Europe' supported by the Austrian Federal Ministry of Science and Research for which the author expresses her gratitude.

1 A. Gerschenkron, *Economic Backwardness in Historical Perspective. A Book of Essays* (Cambridge, Mass., 1965).

2 ' . . . credit is essentially the creation of purchasing power for the purpose of transferring it to the entrepreneur, but not simply the transfer of existing purchasing power. The creation of purchasing power characterises, in principle, the method by which development is carried out in a system with private property and the division of labour.' J. Schumpeter, *The Theory of Economic Development* (repr., New York, 1978), p. 107, cited by H. Lindgren, 'Introduction: The Research Agenda and its Intellectual Setting', in P. L. Cottrell, H. Lindgren and A. Teichova (eds.), *European Industry and Banking between the Wars. A Review of Bank–Industry Relations* (Leicester, London, 1992), p. 3.

3 The research project, 'Bank–Industry Relations in Interwar Europe: Austria, Czechoslovakia, Hungary and Sweden 1900–1939', was conducted from 1986 to 1992. Those involved comprised: Elisabeth Boross (Károli Gáspar Református Egyetem, Budapest); Philip Cottrell (Leicester University); Mats Larsson, Håkan Lindgren, Ragnhild Lundström, Jan Ottosson and H. Sjögren (Uppsala University); Herbert Matis, Alois Mosser, Désirée Verdonk and Fritz Weber (Economics

University Vienna); György Ránki (Historical Institute of the Hungarian Academy of Sciences, Budapest, until his untimely death in February 1988 – he is sadly missed by us all) and A. Pogány (Budapest University of Economic Sciences); Dr Vlastislav Lacina and Dr Jan Hájek (Historical Institute, Czech Academy of Sciences in Prague), Dr Jiří Novotný (Archive of the Czech State Bank, Prague), Prof. Jaroslav Pátek and Dr Jiří Šouša (Charles University, Prague); and A. Teichova (Business History Unit, London School of Economics and Political Science, and Girton College, Cambridge). The author wishes to express her warmest thanks to the Economic and Social Research Council (UK) for generously supporting the project.

4 Friedrich Kleinwächter who, as Professor of the University of Czernowitz (now Cluj in Romania), observed new developments in the industrial world, did not conceive his book *Die Kartelle* as an analysis of cartels as such but as a defence of the institution of private property in face of the demand of socialism for collective ownership. Cf. A. Teichova, 'A Legacy of *Fin-de-Siècle* Capitalism: The Giant Company', in M. Teich and R. Porter (eds.), *Fin de Siècle and Its Legacy* (Cambridge, 1990), p. 15.

5 Cf. D. Good, *The Economic Rise of the Habsburg Empire 1750–1914* (Berkeley, 1984); J. Komlos, *The Habsburg Monarchy as a Customs Union* (Princeton, 1983); and R. Rudolph, *Banking and Industrialization in Austria-Hungary* (Cambridge, 1976).

6 A. Gerschenkron, *An Economic Spurt that Failed* (Princeton, 1977), pp. 45–84, unconvincingly tried to apply his approach to Austria.

7 E. März, *Österreichische Industrie- und Bankpolitik der Zeit Franz Josephs I. Am Beispiel der k. k. priv. Österreichischen Credit-Anstalt für Handel und Gewerbe* (Vienna, 1968).

8 P. L. Cottrell, '"Mushrooms and Dinosaurs": Sieghart and the Boden-Credit-Anstalt during the 1920s', in A. Teichova, T. Gourvish and A. Pogány (eds.), *Universal Banking in the Twentieth Century. Finance, Industry and the State in North and Central Europe* (Aldershot and Brookfield, Vt., 1994), pp. 155–9.

9 R. Cameron *et al.*, *Banking in the Early Stages of Industrialization* (New York, 1967).

10 Cf. Rudolph, *Banking and Industrialization*, p. 104.

11 A. Teichova, 'Banking in Austria', in *Handbook on the History of European Banks* (Aldershot and Brookfield, Vt., 1994), pp. 3–11.

12 E. März, 'Introduction' to R. Hilferding, *Das Finanzkapital* (Frankfurt/Main and Vienna, 1968), 14.

13 R. Hilferding, *Finance Capital. A Study of the Latest Phase of Capitalist Development* (London, 1981), p. 213.

14 *Ibid.*, p. 368.

15 Cf. V. Wellhöner, *Großbanken und Großindustrie im Kaiserreich. Kritische Studien zur Geschichtswissenschaft* (Göttingen, 1989); and H. Wixforth, *Banken und Schwerindustrie in der Weimarer Republik* (Cologne, Weimar and Vienna, 1995).

16 H. Rosovsky, 'Alexander Gerschenkron: A Personal and Fond Recollection', *Journal of Economic History*, 39 (1970), pp. 1009–13.

17 Gerschenkron, *An Economic Spurt*, p. 14.

18 E. März and F. Weber, 'Commentary', in A. Teichova and P. L. Cottrell (eds.), *International Business and Central Europe 1918–1939* (Leicester, 1983), p. 342.

19 R. Tilly, 'German Banking 1850–1914: Development Assistance for the Strong', *Journal of European Economic History*, 15/1 (1986), pp. 113–52.

20 Rudolph, *Banking and Industrialization*, p. 104.

21 H. Matis and K. Bachinger, 'Österreichs industrielle Entwicklung', in *Die Habsburgermonarchie 1848–1918. Die wirtschaftliche Entwicklung* (Vienna, 1973), vol. I,

p. 216; also A. Mosser, *Die Industriegesellschaft in Österreich 1880–1913* (Vienna, 1980), p. 184.

22 Mosser, *Die Industriegesellschaft in Österreich*, pp. 113, 134.

23 Rudolph, *Banking and Industrialization*, p. 159.

24 F. Weber, 'Die österreichischen Großbanken in der Zwischenkriegszeit', *Christliche Demokratie*, 4 (1985), p. 232.

25 Gy. Ránki, 'The Hungarian General Credit Bank in the 1920s', in Teichova and Cottrell, *International Business*, p. 356.

26 W. Layton and Ch. Rist, *The Economic Situation of Austria. Report Presented to the Council of the League of Nations* (Geneva, 1925).

27 P. L. Cottrell and I have discussed the influence of foreign capital in this particular period in several publications: P. L. Cottrell, 'Aspects of Western Equity Investment in the Banking Systems of East Central Europe', in Teichova and Cottrell, *International Business*, pp. 309–47; *idem*, 'Austria between Diplomats and Bankers 1919–1931', in G. Schmidt (ed.), *Konstellationen internationaler Politik 1924–1932* (Bochum, 1983), pp. 292–311; A. Teichova, 'Versailles and the Expansion of the Bank of England into Central Europe', in J. Horn and J. Kocka (eds.), *Law and the Formation of Big Enterprise in the 19th and Early 20th Centuries* (Göttingen, 1979), pp. 366–87. F. Weber finds that, in day-to-day organization, the influence of foreign capital on the big Vienna banks had not been decisive on policy issues, as 'until 1929 the managers of the Viennese banks acted independently of foreign shareholders' and that after the Credit-Anstalt crisis the role of foreign capital in the banking system of Austria had declined. Cf. F. Weber, 'Central European Banking between 1850 and 1950', in M. M. G. Fase, G. D. Feldman and M. Pohl (eds.), *How to Write the History of a Bank* (Aldershot and Brookfield, Vt., 1995), p. 139.

28 Ch. Natmeßnig, 'The Establishment of the Anglo-Czechoslovak Bank: Conflicting Interests', in Teichova, Gourvish and Pogány, *Universal Banking*, pp. 97–8.

29 A. Teichova, *An Economic Background to Munich. International Business and Czechoslovakia 1918–1938* (Cambridge, 1974), p. 342; *idem*, 'East-Central and South-East Europe, 1919–1939', in P. Mathias and S. Pollard (eds.), *The Cambridge Economic History of Europe* (Cambridge, 1989), p. 924.

30 W. Nečas, *Na prahu české kapitálové expanze* (*At the Threshold of Czech Capital Expansion*) (Brno, 1987).

31 J. Riesser, *Die deutschen Großbanken und ihre Konzentration im Zusammenhang mit der Entwicklung der Gesamtwirtschaft in Deutschland* (Jena, 1921); and Z. Jindra, 'K rozvoji českého bankovního kapitálu před první světovou válkou' ('The Development of Czech Banking before the First World War'), *Československý časopis historický*, 5 (1957), pp. 506–26.

32 J. Hájek, 'Origins of the Banking System in Interwar Czechoslovakia', in Teichova, Gourvish and Pogány, *Universal Banking*, pp. 22–31.

33 A. Teichova, *The Czechoslovak Economy 1918–1980* (London and New York, 1988), pp. 29, 47.

34 J. Hájek, *Rozvoj národnostně českých bank od konce 19. století do roku 1914* (*The Development of the National Czech Banks from the End of the Nineteenth Century to 1914*) (Prague, 1986), p. 129.

35 Weber, 'Central European Banking between 1850 and 1950', pp. 136–45.

36 V. Lacina, 'Živnobanka a její koncern v letech velké hospodářské krize (1929–1934)' ('Živnobanka and its Concern during the Great Economic Crisis 1929–1934'), *Československý časopis historický*, 3 (1983), pp. 350–77; *idem*, 'Živnostenská banka před a

během první světové války (1907–1918)' ('The Živnostenská Bank before and
during the First World War 1907–1918'), *Československý časopis historický*, 3 (1990),
pp. 276–303.

37 E. Márz, *Österreichische Bankpolitik in der Zeit der großen Wende 1913–1923* (Vienna,
1981), pp. 352–3.

38 *Compass*, vol. I (1919 and 1925).

39 Teichova, *An Economic Background*, pp. 339–40; *idem*, 'Versailles and the Expansion of
the Bank of England into Central Europe', p. 372; *idem*, *Kleinstaaten im Spannungsfeld
der Großmächte. Wirtschaft und Politik in Mittel- und Südosteuropa der Zwischenkriegszeit*
(Vienna and Munich, 1988), pp. 57–63.

40 G. D. Feldman, 'Foreign Penetration of German Enterprises after the First World
War', in A. Teichova, M. Lévy-Leboyer and H. Nussbaum (eds.), *Historical Studies in
International Corporate Business* (Cambridge and Paris, 1989), pp. 87–110.

41 Teichova, *Kleinstaaten*, pp. 87–9.

42 H. Kernbauer and F. Weber, 'Multinational Banking in the Danube Basin', in
A. Teichova, M. Lévy-Leboyer and H. Nussbaum (eds.), *Multinational Enterprise in
Historical Perspective* (Cambridge and Paris, 1986), p. 193.

43 Allgemeines Verwaltungsarchiv, Vienna, BKA, Inneres Präsidium, Karton 67,
Bankkommission: Die Tätigkeit der Bankkommission (1922–6).

44 März and Weber, 'Commentary'; D. Stiefel, *Finanzdiplomatie und Weltwirtschaftskrise.
Die Krise der Credit-Anstalt für Handel und Gewerbe 1931* (Frankfurt/Main, 1989).

45 H. Kernbauer, *Währungspolitik in der Zwischenkriegszeit Geschichte der Oesterreichischen
Nationalbank von 1923 bis 1938, Das österreichische Noteninstitut*, Third Part, vol. 1
(Vienna, 1991), pp. 291–304.

46 Weber, 'Die österreichischen Großbanken', p. 345.

47 A. Mosser and A. Teichova, 'Investment behaviour of industrial joint-stock
companies and industrial shareholdings by the Österreichische Credit-Anstalt:
inducement or obstacle to renewal and change in interwar Austria' in H. James, H.
Lindgren and A. Teichova (eds.), *The Role of Banks in the Interwar Economy* (Cambridge
and Paris, 1991), pp. 122–57.

48 D. Stiefel, 'The Reconstruction of the Credit-Anstalt', in Teichova and Cottrell,
International Business, pp. 415–30; *idem, Finanzdiplomatie und Weltwirtschaftskrise. Die Krise
der Credit-Anstalt für Handel und Gewerbe 1931* (Frankfurt/Main, 1989).

49 H. Matis and F. Weber, 'Economic *Anschluss* and German *Großmachtpolitik*: The
Take-Over of the Austrian Credit-Anstalt in 1938', in Cottrell, Lindgren and
Teichova, *European Industry and Banking*, pp. 109–26.

50 Teichova, *The Czechoslovak Economy*, pp. 82–3.

51 Ch. Kopper, *Zwischen Marktwirtschaft und Dirigismus Bankenpolitik im 'Dritten Reich'
1933–1939* (Bonn, 1995), pp. 315–48.

52 Teichova, *The Czechoslovak Economy*, pp. 140–1.

13 Banking and economic development in Spain

Gabriel Tortella

Introduction

Banking services are by no means consumer goods. Even when one goes to a bank to ask for consumer credit what one hopes to obtain is capital. Unlike the services of a barber or a hairdresser, or the performance of an actor or an opera singer, the services offered by a banker, exactly as those offered by a lawyer, are capital goods: nobody goes to a banker or to a lawyer for pleasure or leisure. Talking to a banker, like talking to a lawyer, is work.

Since bankers' services are capital goods, theirs is a *derived demand*, as that of all capital goods. There is an old dictum (attributed, if I am not mistaken, to Joan Robinson) that 'finance goes where enterprise takes it'. All this implies that banks grow with the *real* economy, and also stagnate when the *real* economy stagnates. Of course, this does not mean that the banking system is a passive agent: it may contribute to the growth of the real economy, or may be an obstacle to it. To determine to what extent different banking systems have contributed to overall growth is one of the main functions of banking history. All in all, the functional relation between the financial sector and the real sector is very close, but if one of the two sectors plays the role of a dependent variable, this is the banking sector. The Spanish case illustrates these ideas very well. Unlike other European countries, where modern banks and their pre-modern antecedents exhibit a continuous evolution, in

Spain there is continuity between medieval and early modern banking institutions, but the economic decline of the seventeenth century brought about a sharp cleavage between the early modern and the modern period in the field of banking.

The medieval and early modern period

As in all of medieval Europe, banking activities in Spain have been closely associated with government finances and private trade since the Middle Ages. Perhaps one of the earliest references we have to money-lending in Spain appears in a literary monument, the *Poema del Cid*,[1] written in the twelfth century and narrating events which took place in the mid- and late eleventh century. The opening passages of the poem tell us how the Cid's conquering enterprises were initially financed by means of a loan of 600 marks obtained from two Jewish moneylenders established in the ghetto of the commercial city of Burgos, and secured by collateral, two coffers supposedly containing jewels and precious metals, although in effect full of sand. The poem even tells us that the bankers paid a commission fee to the Cid's lieutenant who negotiated the loan. The *Poema del Cid* is widely recognized as a realistic epic poem and its depiction of financial activities in medieval Castile has a strong ring of truth which tallies well with scholarly descriptions of the period.

In the late Middle Ages bankers were well established in the main commercial centres of the Kingdoms of Aragon and Castile, and they were originally moneychangers. The words *cambio, cambiador, canvi, campsor* are most frequently used to designate bankers in medieval Spain. They appeared most frequently acting in the trade fairs which developed in northern Castile during the late Middle Ages (notably Medina del Campo), but also, in cities such as Burgos, a stopping point on the pilgrimage road to Santiago, which attracted travellers from all Europe. In Catalonia, where fairs were of minor importance, private changers were numerous in Barcelona, the most active commercial port and the capital of the Catalan Principality (and in fact of the Kingdom of Aragon). Bills of exchange were used in Barcelona in the fourteenth century, and the oldest known *endorsed* bill was endorsed in Barcelona in the fifteenth century. Barcelona also saw the birth of one of the earliest state (municipal) banks, the Taula del Canvi (1401; although a municipal bank, its name – literally 'Table of Change' – eloquently described the professional origins of bankers in Catalonia), whose main aim was to attract deposits to help the city's finances. Some of these deposits were compulsory, but the Taula tried to attract voluntary deposits, and must have been successful, since at some point a quarter of all Barcelona's households had accounts there. Vicens Vives makes a negative assessment of the Taula, which unfairly competed with private bankers, absorbed an excessive share of private savings, and thereby hurt 'the flexibility of the money market'.[2] In spite of its failures, the Taula was imitated in Valencia, Gerona and Saragossa (called Tabla de comunes depósitos in this last city).

The expulsion of the Jews from Spain in 1492 was no doubt a severe blow to its banking system. For social and religious reasons Jews were prominent in the financial world of medieval Spain, as was true in most Christian countries, and their absence left a wide gap in the human resources of the sector. Native Christians could not wholly fill the void ('Spanish merchants, largely due to their own shortcomings, were subject to the competition of foreigners . . . and saw themselves displaced by them in their own country'),[3] and another specialized minority, the Genoese, stepped into the breach. This was especially the case in Seville, the city which became the great commercial centre of trade with the Americas. The growth of this trade and the inflows of silver that the trade originated turned Seville into a financial centre of the highest order during the reign of Charles V (1516–46), but its bankers' close links with the chaotic finances of the Spanish crown were to prevent Seville from developing a banking system of the kind which developed in northern Europe in the early modern period. Genoese and Spanish bankers flourished in early sixteenth-century Seville, usually combining the normal financial activities (deposit taking, giro payment, and lending to private and public borrowers) with commerce and moneychanging. The Sevillian bankers financed the large flows of international trade which passed through its harbour, and lent to the crown, whose continental political and military enterprises required increasing amounts of finance. The most common way of financing the crown was by means of the *asientos*, contracts to supply some specified merchandise (most often specie) at some given point, typical of Italy or Flanders. This involved exporting money, credit, or goods. Both of these activities (lending to the private or the public sector) were extremely profitable, and attracted businessmen from all of Spain and Europe. Their problem was, however, that a considerable proportion of their loans was secured against silver shipments which arrived periodically in Seville, and 'any delay in the arrival of the silver fleets caused such tightness in the money market that the solvency of the bankers was

severely threatened'.[4] A worse problem was the general unreliability of
the crown as a debtor. The crown first fell into the habit of paying in
bonds (*juros*) instead of in specie as convened, and later it suspended payments outright. Several open bankruptcies under Philip II (1557, 1575,
1595) 'almost completely destroyed the Sevillian banking system'.[5] The
powerful houses of Íñiguez, Lizarrazas, Morga and Espinosa, among
others, failed in this way during the second half of the sixteenth century.

The Spanish sixteenth century is a clear example of the state
crowding out private business and destroying a burgeoning financial
sector through persistent budget deficits and a lack of respect for legal
rules and the market system. During the seventeenth century the state
made several attempts to establish an official bank (*Erario*) which would
drain private savings in a semi-compulsory way and free the crown
from the growing demands and guarantee requirements of private
bankers. The Cortes were opposed to these schemes and in the end the
Parliament prevailed.

The nineteenth century

Spanish banking history in the modern era parallels her general
economic history. While benefiting from an early start, and in spite
of some undoubted vigour and achievement during the nineteenth
century, the fact is that both the Spanish economy and her banking
system remained relatively underdeveloped. By contrast, the twentieth
century has been a period of catching up and consolidation, both for the
Spanish economy and for her banking system. In this, Spain has been a
typical Gerschenkronian latecomer, in that its catching-up has been
substantially assisted by the intervention of the state and of the banking
system.

The first modern banks in Spain were official institutions, established
in Madrid, and catering to the needs of the state. Only later modern
private banks were founded in Barcelona and Cádiz, with the aim of
financing private commerce. The foundation of the first Bank of Spain,
the Banco de San Carlos, was closely connected to the growth of public
debt. In the last years of the reign of Charles III Spain joined in the war
France and the British North American colonies were waging against
Britain. To finance the burden of war imposed upon royal finances the
government issued a form of public debt (the *vales reales*). In order to
facilitate the increasingly difficult redemption of the *vales*, the Banco de
San Carlos was chartered in June 1782. In spite of the vagueness of its

charter, the San Carlos remained a viable institution until about 1795. The wars against France (1793–5), against England (1796–1808) and against France again (1808–14) totally disorganized Spanish finances and put the Spanish state into virtual bankruptcy. The payment of interest on the *vales* was suspended and their quotation plummeted. Since the largest part of the bank's assets was in the form of *vales*, from around 1800 on it was almost totally incapacitated for ordinary business. Although the San Carlos formally survived the Napoleonic Wars, it remained a moribund institution until its official liquidation in 1829.

The San Carlos was transformed into a new institution, the Banco de San Fernando, chartered in July 1829. In the previous weeks, the San Carlos had concluded an accord with the government whereby the bank renounced all its credits against the state – which by then reached the figure of some 77.4 million pesetas – in exchange for 10 million pesetas in cash. (The peseta did not become Spain's official unit until 1868, but I am converting other units into pesetas for simplicity's sake.) This sum was distributed among the stockholders of the Banco de San Carlos in the form of shares of the Banco de San Fernando in proportion to their holdings in the old bank; and this was the effective capital on which the San Fernando started operations.

The Bank of San Fernando was conditioned by the stormy history of its predecessor. For several decades (with a few exceptions) the overriding aim of the Bank's managers was to dispel the disreputable memory of the Banco de San Carlos by enhancing the San Fernando's respectability, keeping its assets as liquid as possible, and guaranteeing the convertibility of its bank notes. To these ends nothing was better than to restrict note issue and to be very parsimonious with loans and discounts. The first fifteen years of its life were for the San Fernando ones of intense, growing and absorbing service to the government. Public loans took up the greater part of the bank's liquid assets; operations with the public had a marginal character.

The first modern private bank in Spain was the Banco de Barcelona, chartered in the capital of Catalonia in 1844. It held the note issuing privilege in the city of Barcelona. Its founder and lifelong president was Manuel Girona, aged twenty-seven the year the bank was established, the scion of a family of merchant bankers. The Bank of Barcelona soon became a byword of prudence and respectability, its commercial policies extremely cautious and its note–cash ratio almost invariably below unity. The Banco de Isabel II, although established the same year as the Barcelona followed opposite policies. Its headquarters were in Madrid, it was semi-official, it lacked – but circumvented – the note issuing privilege and its policies were reckless. The Isabel II soon became a fierce competitor of the Banco de San Fernando. Since only the San Fernando was authorized to issue notes (*billetes*), the drafters of the Isabel II's charter had recourse to a semantic trick by empowering it to issue bonds (*cédulas*), which were bank notes in all but name. Competition made the San Fernando abandon all caution and in a few months *billetes* and *cédulas* circulated freely in Madrid and credit became cheaper. Emulation between the two banks soon degenerated into aggressive rivalry. The San Fernando refused to accept the Isabel II's *cédulas*. In retaliation, one of the managers of the new bank tried to embarrass the old by submitting large amounts of notes for redemption. In the end the 1847–8 crisis and the temerity and lack of experience of both banks put them on the verge of suspension of payments. The government then forced a merger; the resulting Nuevo Banco Español de San Fernando was born burdened by the liabilities of the Isabel II, which had lent heavily to insolvent companies, many of them owned by the bank's managers.

Unlike the official banks in Madrid, the Bank of Barcelona weathered the crisis without any serious troubles or government help. Other provincial banks which were established during these years and survived the crisis were the Caja de Descuentos Zaragozana (Saragossa Discount House), the Sociedad Valenciana de Fomento (Valencia Development Company), and the Banco de Cádiz. The birth of these banks obviously responded to the demand for their services in these cities. Saragossa, the capital of Aragón, was an important commercial centre specializing in grain and flour trade. Valencia city played the same role in the prosperous Valencia region: the Valenciana de Fomento became a sort of Crédit Mobilier *avant-la-lettre*, dealing in commercial credit but also financing railroads and urban development projects. Cádiz, the heir of Seville in monopolizing trade with the Americas in the early eighteenth century, was an obvious venue for a commercial bank.

A remarkable but short-lived expansion of the Spanish banking system took place after 1856. In January of that year two banking laws were issued (one on banks of issue, the other on 'credit companies'). The Banks of Issue Law established what may be called a 'plurality of issue' system, which meant that 'in each town only one note-issuing institution will be permitted', and gave the Nuevo Banco de San Fernando its definitive name: Banco de España. The Credit Companies Law was intended to favour the establishment of business banks: it was especially aimed at inviting the entry of branches of the large French credit companies, the Rothschild House of Paris and the Crédit Mobilier Français of the Péreire brothers. In ten years some sixty new banks opened in Spain, most of them in Madrid and Barcelona, but the rest scattered throughout the country in the most active commercial centres. Of these sixty corporations, about twenty were banks of issue and the rest credit companies. This was a remarkable growth, since in 1855 there were no more than six banking corporations. However, this rapid development concealed serious structural weaknesses, foremost among them a dangerous concentration of assets: loans to railroad companies and government bonds made up most of the banks' investments.

Railway construction was very active during those years, but when in 1864 it became obvious that receipts from railroad traffic did not even cover operating costs in most companies, many of those were forced to suspend payments, and the consequences for banks were the logical ones: many suspended payments and in a few years most of them were forced to close, leaving many millions in unpaid debts. There was a grave financial crisis in 1866 and a political revolution in 1868. The number of banks was greatly reduced. In early 1874 there were no more than fifteen, most of them banks of issue; the credit companies, the ones that had invested most heavily in railways, disappeared almost as fast as they had come. The only important one surviving was the Crédito Mobiliario Español, the first and largest of those founded in 1856.

In 1874 the Bank of Spain was granted the monopoly of issue in the whole national territory in exchange for a loan, at a time when the government was in dire straits. From that moment on, the bank made good use of its privilege at the same time as it lent generously to the government. The main activity of the bank became the 'monetization of the public debt': the bank loaned to the government; and the public, in accepting its notes, loaned to the bank. The composition of the money stock underwent a profound change during these years. Although Spain was nominally on a bimetallic standard, in fact the bank soon decided to redeem its notes only in silver, for fear of running out of its gold stock. Thus gold in fact ceased to circulate: silver and notes became the only currency, with deposits about one third of the money supply by 1900. Thus in fact Spain never adopted the gold standard, and since silver depreciated substantially in the last quarter of the nineteenth century, its standard was actually fiduciary.

The number of banks was further reduced, after the Bank of Spain became the leading monopolist, as most of the old institutes of issue chose to merge with the central bank. The growth of the private banking system during the last quarter of the twentieth century was slow: the most important banks during this period were three old banks of issue which had refused to merge with the Bank of Spain (Banco de Barcelona, Banco de Santander and Banco de Bilbao), plus a few others mostly located in Catalonia, the Basque country and Madrid, notably the Crédito Mobiliario.

One could say that the halting development of the Spanish banking system in the nineteenth century reflected her sluggish economic growth. The sudden expansion of the 1850s and 1860s was only a mirage, a sort of banking bubble provoked by a spurt of activity and speculation originating around the building of the railroads. In the long run only in the most active regions there developed solid banking institutions.

The twentieth century to the Spanish Civil War

For Spain this was the formative period of the modern banking system. Although, as we have seen, Spain can boast of having one of the earliest banks of issue in Europe and had a sizeable banking system in the second half of the nineteenth century, it was really during the first part of the twentieth century that its banking system acquired the main traits which have characterized it during most of the period under study.

At the end of the nineteenth century the Bank of Spain was by far the largest of all Spanish banks, holding about three-quarters of all deposits. By 1913 this proportion was down to 60%, and by 1934 it was about 20%. This is a clear indication of how fast the private banking system developed. Another indicator of the growth of the banking system is the banking assets/national income ratio: it stood at 0.38 in 1915, it was around 1.0 in 1934. A simpler figure is the number of banks: this evolved from thirty-six in 1900 to sixty-one in 1914 to eighty-six in 1935, having reached a maximum of ninety-five in 1928.

The main traits of the banking system during this period were as follows. (1) There was considerable *concentration*. The six largest banks (Banco Hispano-Americano, Banco de Bilbao, Banco Urquijo, Banco Central, Banco de Vizcaya and Banco Español de Crédito) had about 40% of paid-up capital and over 50% of all bank deposits. (2) These and a few other large banks practised what is called '*mixed banking*' in the style of the German 'universal' banks: these were commercial banks which also undertook promotional and holding activities. Their portfolio held a large share of private stocks and bonds, as well as government bonds. (3) These activities of the mixed banks had two main consequences. On the one hand, they promoted the *development of industry*, especially 'heavy' industry: they became holding companies, each controlling its own group of firms, typically public utilities, transportation, metallurgy and mining concerns. On the other hand, through their credit activities, they contributed to the expansion of the *money supply* thanks to their special relationship with the Bank of Spain. (4) The big banks also created a close partnership with the government. They co-operated in large government projects, such as the Banco de Crédito Industrial and CAMPSA, the private company which exploited the petrol monopoly instituted in 1927. (5) Concentration was not only individual, but also *geographical*. The main headquarters of all the large banks were located in Madrid or Bilbao. Barcelona, which had been the main private banking centre during most of the nineteenth century, was left behind in an ever-more distant third place, a fact which became evident when the venerable Banco de Barcelona closed its doors in 1920, after years of ill-advised speculation in German marks. (6) Finally, the large banks created *branch networks*, which increased competition in the short run, but also helped the largest few to become national and to reap (probable but as yet unproven) economies of scale.

Most of the new private banks were founded in the early years of the twentieth century. Only the Banks of Bilbao and Santander (at the time one of the largest but not of the 'big six') had been established in the nineteenth century, as we have seen. The Banco Hispano-Americano was founded in 1900, with repatriated capital from Cuba and Puerto Rico after the loss of these colonies in 1898. The Banco de Vizcaya was founded in 1901; the Banco Español de Crédito in 1902, it being the heir of the old Crédito Mobiliario Español. The Banco Urquijo was incorporated in 1918 from an old banking house; the Banco Central was established in 1919, and for a long time it was considered as a latecomer. Other important banks, such as the Banco Guipuzcoano (1900) and the Banco Popular (1926) also appeared at this time.

The addition of this powerful banking group caused not only quantitative but also qualitative changes in the Spanish financial market. As the market grew, there was a greater division of labour. The Bank of Spain could become more of a true central bank by diminishing its direct dealings with the Treasury and with the public, while increasing its rapports with the banking sector. In the nineteenth

century, one of the Bank's main functions had been to monetize the
public debt: it helped finance the deficit by issuing bank notes. In
the twentieth century the deficit was increasingly financed by the private
banks, which purchased government bonds; the bank's role was to lend
to the private banks at low rates with these bonds as collateral. This
lessened the inflationary impact of the deficit, for not all bonds were
monetized. For the private banks the bonds were almost like interest
bearing cash, and they often just held on to them. More than through
the rediscounting of bills of exchange, it was through lending on public
debt bonds that the Bank of Spain became the centre of the banking
system. This situation was given legal status in the Banking Law of 1921,
the first to regulate the relations between the bank and the private
banking sector.

At this time there also appeared a small public banking group. The
Banco Hipotecario had been founded in 1872. The Banco de Crédito
Industrial, and the Banco Exterior were established in 1920 and 1929.
Their respective missions were to lend to industry and to participate in
foreign trade operations. In 1925 the Banco de Crédito Local and the
Banco de Crédito Agrícola were created. The first was supposed to
lend to town halls and municipalities, the second to private farmers.
The Banco Hipotecario, whose original role had also been to help
agriculture, had ended up lending mostly on urban real estate. All these
banks, the Bank of Spain included, were privately owned but under
government control.

As we have seen, Spain was one of the few European countries that
never adopted the gold standard. The depreciation of silver turned the
Spanish monetary system into a *de facto* fiduciary standard. In spite of
this, the money supply increased moderately during the period under
study and, on balance, prices were stable. From the end of the nineteenth century until the First World War money in circulation increased
at a lower rate than national income, an unusual phenomenon. From
the First World War onwards the growth of the money supply was
faster, but only moderately so. During the 1920s and 1930s (until the
Civil War) the money supply seems to have moved at about the right
speed, for prices remained remarkably stable while income grew at a
considerable rate. As to the composition of the money supply, silver
soon became a small fraction, and bank notes, the largest component
around the turn of the century, soon became overshadowed by the
increase in bank deposits.

If this somewhat peculiar monetary system was harmful in that it isolated the Spanish economy excessively, it was beneficial in the critical circumstances of the 1930s. The Spanish banking system was little affected by the Depression: there were almost no bank failures and the general effects of the slump were lighter than in most other European countries. To a certain extent this can be attributed to the flexibility of a fiduciary standard. The government pressured the Bank of Spain to be generous with its credits, and the interest rates, after a sudden increase in 1931 (due more to political than to strictly economic reasons), went down steadily until 1936. The outbreak of the Spanish Civil War created a discontinuity in the normal economic evolution.

The twentieth century from the Civil War

The period from 1936 to 1946 is anomalous in the history of Spanish banking. From 1936 to 1939 the Civil War created a highly abnormal situation for the functioning of all aspects of the economy. After the end of the war, the serious distortions caused by the hostilities, plus the circumstances of the Second World War and the peculiar economic policies followed by the Franco regime in the flush of victory, all contributed to prolong the situation of provisionality. The Banking Law of 1946 was supposed to mark the return to 'normalcy'; in fact it gave rise to a rigid monetary and banking system characterized by pervasive government intervention and loss of power and independence of the Bank of Spain.

One of the most salient features of that remarkable piece of legislation was the consecration of what Spanish specialists called the 'banking *status quo*' (*Statu quo bancario*), i.e. strong government regulation of bank foundations, mergers and absorptions which in fact amounted to a freezing of the number of banks. The control by the state over the Bank of Spain was vastly increased, while all dealings in foreign currency were transferred to the Ministry of Commerce, and the function of supervising the private banking sector and the main levers of monetary policy, especially the regulation of interest rates (which in fact remained nominally frozen) was transferred to the Ministry of Finance. The final effect of all this was that monetary policy ceased in fact to exist, as its levers were scattered among several government agencies, and the Bank of Spain became little more than a bank note issuing agency.

In this situation of *numerus clausus* the lopsidedness of the banking sector was bound to increase: the relative weight of the small number of 'big banks' expanded even further. The government established very low interest rates on deposits, across the board for all banking institutions, in the belief that if banks paid higher rates nobody would purchase government bonds. As a consequence, banks had to compete by means of their branch networks and by absorbing smaller banks, although some illegal higher interest rates (*extratipos*) were paid to large deposits. Thus bank absorptions and branch networks increased spectacularly: between 1940 and 1956 the five largest banks (Español de Crédito, Central, Hispano, Bilbao and Vizcaya) combined absorbed sixty-one institutions, and their combined branch network went from 959 to 1,619. The number of banks, however, remained fairly constant at around one hundred, due to two facts: many of the absorbed institutions remained nominally independent and the government allowed the addition of a few new banks so as to keep the total number at about the same level.

As the government had in fact renounced any effective monetary policy, the money supply increased by leaps and bounds during the 1940s and 1950s driven by the persistent budget deficits and by the demand for credit by the private sector, attracted by the low interest rates. The consequence was a high rate of inflation, which in turn fuelled the increasing demand for money and credit. Although the Spanish economy grew considerably during the 1950s, increasing inflation and balance of payments deficits exhausted foreign exchange reserves: by the late 1950s the Spanish economy was at an *impasse* and a stabilization plan was required.

With the Stabilization Plan of 1959 a measure of market economy rationality was introduced. Government controls over the economy were relaxed considerably although by no means entirely. The Banking Law of 1962 was an attempt to introduce into the banking sector the principles consecrated in the Stabilization Plan. The law made a half-hearted attempt to bring the Bank of Spain back in control of monetary policy: the bank was nationalized (and so were most of the public sector banks, later to be grouped under the direction of the ICO – Instituto de Crédito Oficial, Official Credit Institute). Most of the supervisory powers over private banks were restored to the Bank of Spain, but foreign currency reserves and policy remained with the Ministry of Commerce until 1973. Another distinctive feature of the 1962 law was its attempt to separate investment banking and commercial banking, thus trying to do away with the traditional 'mixed' character of Spanish banks. At this time also the 'special relationship' between the Bank of Spain and the big banks through soft credits with government bonds as collateral was terminated, and restrictions over new bank creations were relaxed. Serious problems remained, however. The government not only kept foreign reserve policy, but also interest rate regulation (and persisted in 'pegging'), while establishing a series of 'privileged credit circuits' for firms and sectors it considered as especially deserving. It also persisted in fragmenting monetary authority, as it retained the Instituto de Crédito a Medio y Largo Plazo (ICMLP, Institute for Medium- and Long-Term Credit – later to become ICO), which, among other roles, was supposed to supervise those privileged credit circuits.

The 1962 law was a step in the right direction. However, as it was vague and incomplete, it had some unwanted consequences. First, the attempt to separate commercial and investment banking failed, as the big banks complied with it by just creating new banks which in fact were little more than their own portfolio departments. Second, although twenty-two new banks were founded in the ten years after 1962, many of these proved unstable and unscrupulous. Since interest rates remained pegged, resources were extremely inexpensive, so many of these new banks developed rash schemes to purchase older banks and branches. In the euphoric climate of the 1960s any investment seemed profitable as long as one had funds to lend. When the business atmosphere changed in the 1970s many of these new banks were in serious trouble. Third, the privileged credit circuits scheme suffered a setback with the MATESA affair.

The MATESA affair was a business scandal which created a political crisis in the last years of the Franco dictatorship. Its ultimate cause was the privileged credit circuit created in order to stimulate exports of capital goods, one of the pet projects of the Francoist governments of the 1960s. For reasons unknown, the administration of these soft loans to exporters was entrusted to the Banco de Crédito Industrial, which had no experience whatsoever in foreign operations. MATESA was a manufacturer of textile looms which created a world network of subsidiaries to which it 'exported' its looms. It thus obtained enormous sums in soft long-term credits with which it could finance its foreign network. Perhaps if given time the company would in the end have sold its machines. But the affair was discovered in 1969, and aired by the Falangist press in order to discredit Opus Dei, the rival faction whose members held most key cabinet posts. The affair became one of the few publicized scandals of the Franco regime and marked a turning-point in politics (it signalled the beginning of the end of the Franco system) and in banking policy. From then on the liberalization of the banking system proceeded slowly but unmistakably. During the 1970s the privileged credit circuits were gradually abolished, the Bank of Spain asserted its role as executor of monetary policy, interest rates were slowly liberalized, and government intervention in general receded.

The 1970s were a crucial decade in Spanish history. They witnessed the end of the Franco dictatorship and the establishment of a democratic system. The political transition entailed the economic transition towards a more liberal, market-oriented society. The liberalization of the banking system was part and parcel of these transitions; it took place in a difficult environment, however, for the international crisis of the 1970s hit Spain belatedly but forcefully. In fact the full impact of the crisis was not felt in Spain until after the end of the dictatorship, for the last governments of the Franco regime did their best to insulate the country from the effects of what they thought would be only a passing disturbance. With this in mind they muffled the oil shocks and were slow in increasing energy prices (this they could do because the state had the monopoly of oil distribution). When the crisis came after 1975 it hit particularly strongly at a few sectors such as tourism, real estate, building and construction, and heavy industry. These were sectors in which many of the new and small banks had invested heavily, for they had been extremely profitable in earlier years. As a consequence of all this, the Spanish banking system underwent a severe crisis from the end of 1977 to around 1985. Of some 110 private banks operating in 1977, more than half, almost 60, were in some sort of trouble during those eight years. Of course, the banks affected were predominantly small, so that the proportion of combined deposits or capital that were hit by the crisis were about 30% of the banking sector by 1980, and the number of employees of the banks in trouble by the same date was 27%. Most banks affected were new and small, but some were old and big, most significantly the Banco Urquijo, which suspended payments in 1981. The crisis reached a peak around 1982–3. The most spectacular moment arrived when in 1983 the RUMASA holding was expropriated by the recently inaugurated Socialist government: it included eighteen banks.

The Bank of Spain had foreseen the crisis and attempted to devise an institutional framework to forestall it. It was soon decided that the bank and the monetary authorities would try to prevent a panic situation by avoiding suspensions of payments and bankruptcies. The guiding principle would be to protect depositors and let managers and shareholders bear the consequences of their decisions. One of the main instruments of this policy would be the Fondo de Garantía de Depósitos (FGD, Deposit Insurance Corporation) in the style of the federal institution created in the United States during the New Deal. The FGD was legally established at the end of 1977, but a series of legal problems prompted the creation of Corporación Bancaria as a stopgap solution. Corporación Bancaria was a private institution financed in equal proportions by the Bank of Spain and by the private banks. Its mission was to help or purchase banks in difficulties. In some cases a loan and some restructuring would suffice to refloat a bank. Most often, however, the bank needed a major intervention and the old managers had to be replaced. In these cases the purchase price was decided on the basis of an appraisal of the bank's assets; once Corporación was in charge, the illiquid assets were sold out and the bank itself was again put up for sale, preferably to a solvent bank. After 1981 the FGD became effectively operative and Corporación was finally liquidated. The FGD operated along the same basic principles. Most of the banks in difficulties were dealt with in this way.

While the crisis was shaking the Spanish banking system, the liberalization process continued: interest rates were gradually freed, the *numerus clausus* principle was abandoned, the legal distinction between commercial and investment banks was abolished, etc. Most importantly, foreign banks, whose activities had been traditionally the object of severe restrictions, were gradually allowed to compete in the Spanish market. One of the earliest opportunities for the establishment of foreign banks was the sale of reconstituted firms by Corporación Bancaria and the FGD. The monetary authorities used the sale of 'convalescent banks' to foreign institutions to break the reluctance of Spanish banks in refloating operations.

Among the latest developments in Spanish banking has been a wave of mergers, generally with government encouragement, among the largest banks in order to achieve the scale that is considered necessary to compete in the European unified market after 1992. Thus the two largest Basque banks (Bilbao and Vizcaya) merged in 1988, the two largest Catalan savings banks merged in 1990, and two large Madrid banks, Central and Hispano-Americano, agreed to merge in October 1991. In December 1993 the Banco Español de Crédito (frequently shortened to Banesto) was intervened by the Bank of Spain on the grounds that it suffered a serious unbalance and heavy losses. The bank was later sold to the Banco de Santander, in what in effect became a new merger of two big banks.

This drastic restructuring of the Spanish banking system is an evident response to the profound changes which are affecting it. These changes are not limited to the radical deregulation which I have tried to summarize above. The *real* economy suffered a parallel process of liberalization and reconversion from the rigidly protected and regulated Francoist framework. By means of strong government intervention the dictatorship had promoted an inefficient heavy industry sector, which could endure as long as the country did not try to compete in international markets. The Spanish banks, as we have seen, were heavily engaged in this sector, and they had to disengage when trade liberalization imposed industrial reconversion from the mid-1970s onwards. This drastic shift contributed to the banking crisis of those years and to the breathtaking changes which have taken place recently. Banks have moved away from close identification with industry and into commercial credit and retail banking, thereby shedding their traditional 'mixed' character.

The Spanish banking system therefore has been a reflection of the whole economy in the twentieth century, as was the case in earlier periods. With the help of a rather original fiduciary monetary system, the banking sector became heavily engaged *à la* Gerschenkron in the financing of industry in the early stages of economic modernization without undergoing the periodic crises which afflicted Italian banks or anything resembling the collapse which affected German and Austrian banks in the 1930s. Under the heavy hand of Francoism the banking system resumed this role. The crisis came when the economy had to reconvert and open. From an oligopolistic system the banking sector has evolved towards competition. The challenge for Spanish banks today is to adapt to the new circumstances.

Notes

1 Anómino, *Poema de Mío Cid*, ed. Angeles Cardona de Gibert, Luis Guarner and Joaquín Rafel (Gerona, 1973).
2 Jaime Vicens Vives, *Manual de historia económica de España* (Barcelona, 1959).
3 Ramón Carande, *Carlos V y sus banqueros. I. La vida económica en Castilla (1516–1556)*, 2nd edn (Madrid, 1965), p. 263.
4 Ruth Pike, *Enterprise and Adventure. The Genoese in Seville and the Opening of the New World* (Ithaca, N.Y., 1966), p. 87.
5 *Ibid.*, p. 96.

14 The role of banking in Italy's industrialization, nineteenth to twentieth century

Luigi De Rosa

Introduction

In the absence of a banking system, capital from commerce provided one of the main financial sources for developing trades and industries in Italy in the second half of the eighteenth century. Such capital, put up by a number of private bankers, many of Jewish origin who were operating in the cities and larger towns, made it possible to keep in work both master and apprentice artisans in the traditional workshops, as well as women and children who were working at home after corporative organization had broken up. Princes and sovereigns interested in the developing industry throughout their dominions provided a further source of capital. One example was the Compagnia reale del Piemonte per le opere e i negozi di seta, which was founded in 1752, under the auspices of King Charles Emmanuel, with 600,000 lire of share capital for the production and sale of silk thread, fabric and silk products in general. Another example was the Reale Fabbrica di Capodimonte for the production and sale of porcelain, founded in what was the then Kingdom of Naples by the Bourbon King Charles. In 1783, Charles's successor Ferdinand built the Real Fabbrica di seta at San Leucio near Caserta.[1]

Given the lack of any financial contribution from the landowners, many of whom were burdened with feudal obligations, other capital contributions to the creation of the modern Italian factory came from abroad. The Swiss, for example, provided capital and input, particularly in the textile industry, above all in the cotton industry, by providing technicians and mechanics. In so doing they introduced the technical skills and know-how that had been spreading to Europe from England. Noted Swiss cases are those of A. G. Kramer who founded a cotton-printing factory in Milan in 1782;[2] Felice Clerici, who, after having built a water-powered spinning mill for camel and goatshair, went on to build a weaving mill for various types of fabrics, which was based on English, French and Dutch models; and Tieffen who built a large woollen mill in Milan with the aid of technicians from England, France and Holland.[3]

Still in the eighteenth century, further capital was brought in by the setting up of joint-stock companies, such as the Ginori and Doccia porcelain factory near Florence and a large silk mill founded in Milan in 1765 by the Pansa, Larla and C. Company.

Continental system

During the period of French rule in Italy (end of the eighteenth century to 1815), the French did not intend to aid the progress of Italian industry: Napoleon was set on making France the industrialized nation of Europe, whereas the other nations under French rule were to provide internal markets and be a source of raw materials. However, despite this aim, and despite the Continental System which halted the importation of raw materials from 1806 to 1815, Italian industry did make significant progress. This was first and foremost because France was heavily involved in wars and was forced to exploit to the full those Italian industries which supplied products connected directly or indirectly to the war effort. French officers and technicians were often called upon, frequently at the request of the Italian government, to manage or to aid production. The state-owned and state-controlled arms factories in the Brescia area, for example, were provided with management and the best machines from France. To overcome the technological gap in the steel industry, the Italian administration turned not only to France but also to Carinthia, investing considerable sums of money to send Italian labourers to learn skills in the steelyards there. In a similar vein, the woollen industry specialized in producing coarse, hard-wearing fabric suitable for clothing the French soldiers; the leather and hides industry and the shoe industry were especially useful as the former produced saddles and horse tackle for the French artillery, and the latter supplied footwear for the soldiers.

In the production of these and other goods, Italian industry benefited in the following ways: (1) from the exclusion of British products from the European market – British production being much more advanced and able to offer goods at a lower price; (2) from France's dependence on Italian industry; this is shown, for example, by the fact that a community of Swiss cotton spinners, and weavers given the favourable conditions offered to them, crossed the Alps to settle in the south of Italy in the area between Salerno and Caserta and set up water-powered mills there; (3) from a series of reforms and policies which the French carried out in Italy: the abolition of the feudal system; the adoption of the civil and commercial Napoleonic code; significant investment in public works; the modernization of the education system and the creation of Polytechnics; the input of technical know-how in various industrial sectors.

In general, apart from the fact that kings and princes now played a minor role, the financing of this industrial growth did not present any major changes with respect to what had taken place in the past.

The 'Risorgimento' and industry

With the fall of Napoleon, Italian industry also regressed. Apart from the lack of available capital and high interest rates, it was the reopening of markets and the inability to withstand foreign competition which caused this regression, affecting the textile industries, including the silk industry, the iron and steel industries and mechanical engineering. The more industrially advanced provinces of the north were hit, alongside the less developed southern and central areas.[4] Nor did industry show any improvement as a result of the introduction of protectionist policies. This was due to the fact that smuggling was widespread and cancelled out any of the positive effects which might have been achieved. The situation gradually improved after 1830, particularly in Piedmont and Lombardy where, unlike in central and southern Italy, a more liberalized customs policy was adopted. However, in spite of this, there was no significant progress.

The scarcity of available capital and an insufficient internal market, split into seven states, each one with its own customs system and duties, its own currency, its own laws, and so on, hindered the development of industry. Thus, in the two most advanced regions – Piedmont and Lombardy – but also in the south which had opened up to international trade after 1846, 'rural and artisan industries prevailed' in the middle of the nineteenth century. Their characteristics were 'extreme smallness and dispersion, even though there were water- and steam-powered factories, with numerous workers – including a good number of children – that used coal and produced goods for export'.[5]

One important fact must be emphasized: alongside the financial sources indicated above, banks also began to promote industry. This phenomenon is evident in Piedmont, where, in Genoa and Turin, joint-stock banks were set up. These banks financed trade and industry, in particular the well-established silk industry. In the south of Italy, too, at the Banco delle Due Sicilie, a discount service (*Cassa di Sconto*) was opened by the government to finance industry and commerce. However, neither before nor after the unification of Italy did these banks resolve the problem of capital deficiency which characterized the internal market and this was 'because the newly formed annual savers had no faith in industrial enterprises'. Moreover, industry could not guarantee returns equal to those that were assured by public savings bonds.[6]

Unification and economic growth

Although the Unification of Italy did not bring about any radical changes in the relationship between banks and industry, the years that followed saw a major development in the banking system: this was now based on six deposit and circulation banks,[7] a sizeable number of savings banks, operating almost exclusively in northern and central Italy,[8] a few ordinary credit institutions, a considerable number of private bankers, the vast majority of whom were of Jewish origin and worked extensively throughout the country, the Credito Mobiliare (an institution which came into being in 1863, and was originally French, but became 'italianized' later) and, a few years after Unification, the first co-operative banks.

The growth and development of industry and the banking system reflected the expansion of joint-stock companies after Italy went from a metal currency to a non-convertible system. The number of issuing banks, co-operative banks and ordinary credit institutions grew from twenty-nine (1863) to forty-four (1867), while bank stock increased from 235 million lire in 1863 to 331 million lire in 1867.[9]

The year 1866 has been singled out because it was the year in which the government abolished the convertibility of the lira and started an inflationary process which acted as a barrier to foreign imports, to the tune of around 10%. In the wake of this, the Italian economy, and in particular industry, which had recovered from the consequences of the economic crisis of 1864 to 1866, was able to aim at greater economic development.

Investments grew until the recession which lasted from 1873 to 1878. They began to grow more conspicuously after the end of this recession. First, the number and the capital of joint-stock companies increased, although the most significant increases took place in banking and transport (particularly in the railways). These two sectors alone accounted for more than 74% of all existing joint-stock companies and around 71% of their total capital. Secondly, there was significant and rapid growth in all kinds of banks: their numbers increased from 44 in 1867 to 260 at the end of the economic crisis in 1880. At the same time, bank capital doubled from 331 million lire in 1867 to 634 million lire in 1880. Industry also benefited from the increase in capital, despite the fact that an industrial inquiry which had taken place between 1870 and 1874 had drawn attention to 'the lack of confidence and dejection which was seeping into the industrial world'.[10] The biggest increase in capital was in the textile industry, in mining, in the mechanical and chemical industries and in paper mills.[11] These investments enabled marked progress to be made which was evident at the various industrial exhibitions/trade fairs held both in Italy and abroad (Naples, 1871; Vienna, 1873; Paris, 1878; Milan, 1881), where Italian production was on show.

The Great Exhibition of Milan in 1881 revealed the serious short-comings which still characterized Italian industry, but it also showed that Italy had increased its energy potential, having doubled it in some sectors. Considerable progress had been made in the mechanical industry; the silk and chemical industries had progressed notably, and progress could also be seen in the pottery and glass industries.

Much of this progress, as well as being due to bank investments, was also due to joint-stock capital or foreign bonds, which were accompanied by valuable investment know-how. French, Belgian and English companies had made sizeable investments in the mining industry in Sardinia and elsewhere. Even more important was the input of English and Belgian companies in the urban and regional transport sector, in aqueduct construction and in gasworks.[12]

As far as the impact of this progress on individual sectors is concerned, agriculture continued to employ more than half of the labour force. This percentage may have been even greater if one

considers the fact that the youth population made up a small proportion
of workers employed in other industries, a mere 12.5%, including
craftsmen and workshop labourers. With regards to geographical
location, however, industry was undoubtedly concentrated in the north
of Italy, with just less than half in Lombardy, a quarter in Piedmont and
the rest in the other regions, with a slight concentration in Veneto,
Campania and Tuscany. Of the 54,000 horsepower produced in Italy's
steam boilers, 33,000 were produced in northern Italy, the rest being
produced in other regions, with a higher percentage in Sardinia, owing
to the existence of a large mining industry on the island.[13]

The growth of a banking system

Given that this industrial development had made use of Italian and
foreign joint-stock capital, as well as bank capital, it also contributed to
stimulate further the growth of the banking system. First, there were
many mergers – involving most of the private bankers – in the areas
where industrial development had been more intense. Merging
intensified after 1879, when economic activity, having overcome the
effects of the 1873 economic recession, began to expand once more.
Secondly, banking structures in the main urban centres expanded.
Milan added some important credit institutions to the well-established
Banca di Credito Italiano. Among these were the Banca Lombarda di
Depositi e Conti Correnti, the Banca di Milano and Credito Lombardo.
In Turin, alongside existing influential banks like the Banco di Sconto e
Sete and the Banco Industria e Commercio, other important banks
were founded such as the Banca di Torino, the Unione Banche
Piemontese e Subalpina, the Banca Tiberina and the Credito Torinese.
Genoa, which despite the annexation of Venice to the Italian state in
1866 had become the main commercial and industrial port, also
expanded its banking system. To the pre-Unification banks were added
the Banca di Genova, Banca Provinciale, Cassa Generale, Cassa
Marittima and Cassa di Sovvenzioni per Imprese. New banks were set
up even in Naples, with the creation of Cassa Marittima, etc. Rome,
which was made the capital city in 1870, saw the establishment of a
group of important banks, like Banca Generale, the Società Generale
Immobiliare di Lavori and the Banco di Roma. In effect, banks grew up
all over the country, even in the smaller cities and towns, although not
always with sizeable capital endowments.

    Not all these banks put industry at the top of their list of priorities.

Many of them, dependent on the local economy, financed public works and facilities. However, although the issuing banks were constrained by their statutes and by government control and were obliged to limit industrial aid to simple, short-term credit, and although the savings banks and the co-operative banks were generally not very interested in financing industry, the other types of banks offered longer-term credit. They also owned shares in the joint stock of the industries they financed and so put their own representatives on the relative management boards of the companies concerned. In this, their forerunner had been Credito mobiliare which had played a key role in industrial growth in Italy.[14] Its methods of financing were later adopted by many other banks, both of Italian and foreign origin, whose representatives were to be found in a large number of industries. In many cases these banks followed the industrial enterprise right from the start, underwriting a considerable number of shares and thus accrediting the company with the banks' own clients, who were urged to underwrite shares. If the operation was successful, as it nearly always was, then they withheld a small stock of shares for themselves which were necessary for placing their own representatives on company management boards. This method can be seen at work at Banca Wagnière in Florence, the Ceriana in Turin and the Banco di Roma.

Growth of industry and banking crisis

The 1880s marked a turning-point for Italian industry. For a brief period there was a return to currency convertibility (1883–5), which encouraged foreign imports and was detrimental to those few Italian industries which had an export trade. However, industry in general benefited by the first protectionist tariff (1878) which had helped some industries and improved conditions in others. Industry benefited even more by the 1887 tariff which extended customs protection to nearly all sectors of industry. Meanwhile, in support of customs policy the government changed its attitude to procurement for the country's defence. Until 1884 there were no shipyards in Italy capable of building large iron vessels, nor were there any large engine factories, large, specialized steelworks or a railway industry (despite hundreds of miles of railway lines). In order to resolve this state of affairs, it was decided to purchase all land and sea defence nationally and not from abroad as had been the case in the past. Therefore certain factories needed to specialize and be equipped for their new role: not only had appropriate machinery to be supplied but also an input of foreign technical know-how had to be provided. This applied above all to naval shipyards. With regard to iron-built steamships for the merchant navy, it was decided that Italian shipowners, who had their ships built in Italy, should be given various subsidies, including financial contributions, proportional to the tonnage of the ship. For the army, the government subsidised, amongst other things, the construction of a large, modern steelworks at Terni. These customs and industrial policies were responsible for considerable progress in Italian industry. It suffices to say that between 1876 and 1890, the number of steam boilers doubled, and the amount of horsepower they produced almost tripled, while water power rose from 451,000 to 496,000.[15] On the whole, industry reached a level where it had at its disposal an energy potential vastly superior to that of the railways.

The change to a protectionist policy between 1878 and 1887 was in response to the great depression in Italian agriculture, especially in the wheat sector, which was responsible for the migration of both capital and labour from rural areas to the cities and/or abroad. The seriousness of this migration was not fully realized in that the masses of migrant agricultural labourers found work in the building industry which was expanding in the big cities. Construction was taking place above all in Rome, where there was a desire to restore the city to the splendour of its imperial and Renaissance past. Naples too had a vast building programme, promoted by the government to clear the areas that had been hit by the cholera epidemic of 1884, when over 10,000 people had died.

Two factors contributed to the recession that shook the Italian banking system between 1888 and 1894, a recession that was to hit industry a few years later: the first was the agricultural depression, made more acute in the south by the customs breakdown with France, which banned the import of Italian fruit, vegetables and wine; the second was the building recession which was seen in Rome and other cities because there were no buyers to be found for those houses that had been built or were being built.

The years 1893 to 1894 greatly influenced the history of Italian banking. In 1893, a banking law – the second after the 1874 law which had regulated the circulation of the six issuing banks – reduced the number of issuing banks to three: the three joint-stock banks Banca Nazionale, Banca Nazionale Toscana and Banca Toscana di Credito merged into one which became the Banca d'Italia and had to liquidate

Banca Romana (which had gone under after being at the centre of a major scandal), while the two southern banks – Banco di Napoli and Banco di Sicilia – were left intact. Although these three banks maintained the privilege to issue, none of them was in a condition to play a decisive role in financing productive activity, industry included, because all three of them were burdened with outstanding credit bills and dead loans, and as such they were making considerable losses. Where was industry to turn to in order to find the means necessary to continue development now that highly protectionist tariffs had assured the domestic market, which had increased due to population growth?

Some of the banks that had played a fundamental role in Italy's industrialization, like Credito Mobiliare and Banca Generale, had become insolvent. Many other banks, like Tiberina, for example, were very close to bankruptcy. Other banks that had been seriously hit by losses, like Banco di Roma, for example, had been forced to reduce their capital and undergo auditing and belt-tightening measures.

Credit financing of industry by banks

In these conditions and intent on providing industry with adequate financial means for its further development, the government called on the intervention of German finance, after the breakdown in relations with France. Between 1894 and 1895, two Italo-German banks were formed in Italy: Banca Commerciale Italiana and the Credito Italiano. The former was ex-novo, with Italo-German, Swiss and Austrian capital, and German management. The latter was formed around a Genoan bank, also with Italo-German capital and German management. Both these banks were of a mixed type, that is they offered both short- and long-term credit.

These two banks were fortunate in that they began to operate in a favourable economic situation. According to the data provided by Gerschenkron,[16] the index of Italian industrial production, which had previously registered continual fluctuations and had never gone beyond 74, showed no decline after 1896. Rather it grew rapidly to 100 (1900), to 109 (1902), to 139 (1906), to 174 (1911) and to 184 (1913).

Again according to Gerschenkron, after moderate development from 1881 to 1888, and stagnation between 1888 and 1896, there was rapid development from 1896 to 1908: the average annual growth rate was 6.7%, whereas from 1881 to 1888 it had been 4.6%, and from 1888 to 1896 to a mere 0.3%. In other words, a rhythm of industrial development was reached that was on a par only with that reached during the years of economic self-sufficiency and the Fascist war of 1936 to 1942, although it was to be greatly exceeded in the years of the so-called 'Italian economic miracle' after the end of the Second World War. In effect, in the years that preceded the First World War, i.e. 1908 to 1913, although there had been development, the average industrial growth rate had never risen above 3.8%.[17]

Despite numerous difficulties resulting from the tariffs and legislation that were in effect at the time, the greatest progress was to be seen in the metallurgical, the mechanical and the chemical industries. The average growth rate in these sectors was even double that of the general average. However, in this development, as Gerschenkron has pointed out, 'the importance of the role played by the big Italian banks must be stressed',[18] and in particular by two banks that had been recently formed: Banca Commerciale and Credito Italiano in effect took the place held until the year before by the Credito Mobiliare and Banca Generale, but they were more fortunate in that they entered the Italian economy at a time when the electrical, mechanical and chemical industries were gaining ground. By assisting them from the start as promoting partners of the industries that were being set up in each sector, they could gain credit as the industries' main credit suppliers.

These were the years, moreover, in which joint-stock companies – an indication of the size of the newly formed companies, and of the revolution that had taken place in savers' attitudes – no longer met with difficulties. Between 1895 and 1900, the capital of joint-stock industrial companies increased enormously, to the point that whilst from 1894 to 1895 it had never provided more than 18% of the total capital of joint-stock companies, by 1900 it had grown to about 31%.[19] The number of industrial enterprises had not only increased, but continued to do so very rapidly. Between the two official surveys of 1903 and 1911, the number of enterprises included in the survey rose from 117,000 to 244,000, and the number of people employed rose from 1,275,000 to 2,304,000, whilst the number of available machines (water-powered, steam-powered and electric), which in 1903 had produced 734,000 horsepower, by 1911 were producing 1,229,000 horsepower.[20]

The banks had benefited from the ease with which industrial growth was taking place and from the concurrence of other factors. These were as follows. (1) A marked upswing in agriculture. Mass emigration, that had begun during the last decade of the previous century, had eased the burden of a surplus agricultural labour force. Agriculture began to be modernized even in those regions – like the south – where there had been stronger resistance to the adoption of machinery, chemical fertilizers and new cultivation techniques. (2) Surplus public finance, which freed the financial market from pressure from the state, and left it exclusively for the demands of production. (3) The return to currency convertibility, due to an equilibrium in the balance of payments, which had benefited from lower transportation costs and the fall in passive interest, from migrants' remittances and receipts from tourism and overseas investments. (4) The marked improvement in the conditions of the three issuing banks, which had not only recovered losses made at the end of the last century, but had gradually freed much of the capital that had been previously immobilized. They were thus able to act better as lenders of last resort – a role that they played increasingly.

However, the fact that the banks made profits continuously, profits which grew according to the increase in financial availability, con- tributed to the increase in their numbers, particularly those that offered banker's credit, although there were mergers here and there, as, for example, in 1898 in the case of Società Bancaria Milanese, which was formed when some Milanese bankers joined forces. A few years later, with the participation of other bankers and small banks in other northern Italian cities, it changed its name to Società Bancaria Italiana, whose principal aim was to back industrial development, especially in the northern regions of the country, where development was still on the whole more intense.

The growth in the numbers of ordinary credit institutions continued until 1909, even surviving the recession of 1907. However, perhaps due to the delayed after-effects of this recession, during which rescue operations had to be carried out in order to keep the Società Bancaria Italiana afloat, this tendency was inverted and merging took place. Merging started in the north and soon caught on in the south. Banca Commerciale, Credito Italiano, Banco di Roma and the same Società Bancaria Italiana took over small local banks, establishing their own branches in place of the local banks.

Although stimulated by the changes that were taking place in economic life, the merging process did not meet with the approval of the government or of public opinion, as there was a fear that substituting local institutions with branches of the bigger banks would result in damaging the local economy. People objected that local banks, managed generally by local people, knew their clients better and were able to adapt to their needs and circumstances. Conversely, the branches of the big banks were on the whole governed by general needs and by the pressures that the wider financial market exerted on the central banks. However, the trend could not be halted. Private bankers and small credit companies continued to be taken over. In fact, at the beginning of the First World War, the Società Bancaria Italiana merged with Credito Provinciale to form the Banca Italiana di Sconto. This was the fourth big ordinary credit bank, with branches over almost the whole of the country. The four big banks were led by the Banca Commerciale, followed in order of importance by Credito Italiano, Banco di Roma and, lastly, Banca Italiana di Sconto.[21]

The first two banks, above all the Banca Commerciale and, to a lesser extent, the Banca Italiana di Sconto, were involved in the development of big industry in Italy, while the Banco di Roma was involved in agriculture, and also in the service sector and in minor industries like construction and the cinema. Above all, it operated not only in the various regions of Italy, but also in most of the Mediterranean countries, since it had opened (almost invariably by taking over small local banks) branches in Paris, Spain, Malta, Libya, Egypt and Constantinople.

The Banco di Roma began to internationalize its operations in 1902, but in 1906 the Banco di Napoli opened a promotions' office in New York; three years later this office became a branch. Banca Commerciale and Credito Italiano opened their own branches in London, and, through foreign banks, developed banking operations in South America. Even the Banca Italiana di Sconto opened branches in foreign countries. In the following years these banks continued to open branches abroad.

The influence of the First World War on economic structure

Despite the fact that the Banco di Roma was forced to reduce its capital because of the big losses made in its Libyan, Egyptian and Ottoman branches as a result of the Libyan war, and although the Banca Italiana di Sconto had to absorb the heavy losses of the two banks it had taken over, these four big banks gave the Italian economy its main boost.

When Italy went to war in 1915, the three issuing banks, which were not allowed to give credit to industry, financed the war on government request, and came to the aid of the savings banks that were on the brink of collapse. These three banks became the pivot of the entire industrial system. The demand for goods that were not closely connected with the war (like dispensable goods for both public and private consumption and building materials) gradually shrank, and so the financial means of the four banks – that were growing continually because of the widening of the monetary base – were used to finance the iron and steel industry, the automobile industry and the shipyards and the industries that produced war material. Moreover, since the state was dependent on these industries during the war years, and did not haggle over prices, both the industries and the banks were soon making good profits. Of these banks, the most important, Banca Commerciale, which unlike Credito Italiano had kept close ties with the German financial world, was soon criticized because of fears that it might be colluding with the enemy, and attempts were made to nationalize, and even inter-nationalize, it. It was only when it was able to demonstrate its patriotic loyalty that it was able to continue freely with its business.

There is no doubt that the Italian industrial system expanded as a result of the war, although some industries developed more than others. This development could not keep up with the technical innovations and improvements in management that had been taking hold elsewhere. Consequently, with obsolete machinery and non-competitive prices in the international market, those industries that produced war material were able to continue their production and their growth only for as long as the war lasted. The crisis came at the end of the war, when the entire economy, and so industry too, had to adapt from wartime to peacetime conditions. This was a long and difficult process, made all the more so by the fact that some industries on the verge of bankruptcy tried to raid the banks to secure the cash they deemed necessary for their survival. In short, all the difficulties that industry underwent had repercussions on the banks. Industries lacked orders and so had no means of repaying all or part of the money they had borrowed.

The state and banking under Mussolini

The Consorzio per sovvenzioni su valori industriali (CSVI) had been set up at the beginning of the war to help industries to find funds by depositing the blocks of shareholdings and bills on hand in their possession, but it had hardly been used during the war, insofar as industries had no difficulty in turning to the banks for funding. However, the end of the war, the ensuing demobilization of industry connected to the war, the lack of orders, imminent inflation and ever-increasing unemployment meant that it was no longer possible to turn to the banks. Hence the Consorzio was soon full of paper that was difficult to negotiate and which it rediscounted at the three issuing banks, who in turn protested against the losses imposed on them.

The practice was of no avail in avoiding the sensational failure of the Banca Italiana di Sconto at the end of 1921, and the collapse of other smaller banks, with serious consequences for the market and the public, who expressed a wish to withdraw their money from the other banks. The crisis was particularly acute for the Banco di Roma which risked closure. In order to try to save the Banco di Roma and the other banks that were in a similarly precarious financial situation, as well as to give some relief to industry which was also on the brink of bankruptcy, in 1922 the government, with a grant of 1 billion lire, decided to create an independent section of the Consortium, which, pending authorization, could grant aid on request. Thanks to the first Mussolini government, the Banco di Roma was saved, but, although it was 'fascistized', it was many years before it expanded economically and geographically.

As for the other two big banks – Banca Commerciale and Credito Italiano – which had also been seriously damaged by the post-war recession (1920–1) and had come out of it with a great deal of capital immobilization, the government, in order to meet them half-way, created in 1926 the Istituto di liquidazione to which the Banca Commerciale and Credito Italiano could turn for advances and rediscounts. Again in 1926, the Banca d'Italia became the only issuing bank: the other two issuing banks, the Banco di Napoli and the Banco di Sicilia, became state-owned banks with the task of granting short-term credit.

Mussolini's policy of sustaining credit to avoid further sensational bank failures between 1926 and 1927 lost its effectiveness when, faced with the fall of the lira against the pound, Mussolini declared that the lira was to be defended at all costs. However, instead of stabilising the lira at its value at that time, on average between 120 and 130 lire to the pound, he wanted to fix it at 90 lire, which had been the exchange rate when he came into power at the end of October 1922.

The fixing of the pound at 90 lire ('quota novanta') had a tremendous deflationary effect. Industry, which was just struggling out of the depression, was the first to suffer from the negative effects of this deflation. Then the banks were seriously affected and their position was further weakened. Thus, while the Western world was going through a particularly favourable economic phase, industry and the economy in Italy slipped back into recession. Both industry and the economy picked up slightly towards the end of 1928, but the following year saw the Wall Street Crash and the Italian economy could not escape its consequences.

The position of the two major banks, together with that of the Banco di Roma, weakened further, and in 1931 the government decided to resort to creating the Istituto Mobiliare Italiano (IMI), which was to take on shareholdings weighing heavily on the banks, thus allowing them to go to the aid of industry. However, the recession was much too serious and despite valiant efforts, IMI was unable to solve the situation. Two years later, in 1933, another attempt was made with the creation of another public institution, the Istituto di Ricostruzione Industriale (IRI), which, by issuing bonds, redeemed the blocks of shares held by the above-mentioned three main banks, and with them it also redeemed the blocks of shares of the three banks. The IRI was to reorganize each individual industrial enterprise and put it back on the market, handing industry over to the private sector again. As for the three banks, the government intended that the IRI should keep, as indeed it did, the vast majority of the respective blocks of shares. In this way, through the big banks, it would exercise an effective control over the country's economic development.

In the meantime, during the depression which had begun in 1929, there had been a spate of agricultural bank closures and many savings banks and co-operative banks had merged, to such an extent that the Italian banking scene appeared to have been largely reorganized. However, the whole banking system found stability with the law of 1936.

The 1936 Banking Act changed the Banca d'Italia from a joint-stock company into a state-owned bank, depriving it of the faculty to collect deposits or to make investments, and making it a central bank which would act as a state treasury. However, this law went even further: it divided the banking system according to the length of the period of reimbursement, making a clear distinction between short-term credit banks and medium- and long-term credit banks. It also conditioned the supply of funds in the same way. It did even more and organized the entire banking structure according to size and function, keeping the Banca d'Italia as the central bank above all the others, and establishing that real banking activity was to be carried out by state-owned banks (the Banco di Napoli, Banco di Sicilia, Monte dei Paschi, Istituto S. Paolo di Torino, Banca Nazionale del Lavoro) and by national interest banks (Banca Commerciale, Credito Italiano and Banco di Roma). The IRI, i.e. the public authorities, were to keep almost all the shares of these banks. Regional banks and bankers' credit companies (i.e. savings banks, mutual-saving societies and co-operative banks), small local credit institutions, bankers and private businessmen, agricultural banks and Monti di Pietà were to co-operate with them.[22]

In effect, the history of the 'mixed bank' – and, with it, the close ties between banks and industry – came to an end with the 1936 Bank Act. This law asserted the principle of credit specialization, and so, alongside the other specialized institutions that had appeared over the years – such as the Credito fondiario (1868), the Consorzio di Credito per le Opere Pubbliche (1919), the Istituto di Credito Italiano per le Opere di Pubblica Utilità (1924), the Istituto di Credito Marittimo (1930), the Istituto di Credito per lo sviluppo dell'Italia Meridionale (ISVEIMER) (1938) – the government set about giving Italy institutions which would finance industry with medium- and long-term credit. However, these are pages of history which belong to the Republic of Italy when, through new legislation, there was greater state interference in banking activities with varying degrees of checks and controls. In the end, the 'mixed' or universal bank inevitably made a gradual comeback.

Conclusion

Banks and industry in Italy have been closely interdependent for almost two centuries; and for the whole of that period this relationship gave rise to a number of problems.

(1) Foreign capital played an important role in Italian industrialization both directly or indirectly, i.e. through the opening of banks like Banco italo-britannica, Banca italo-francese, which had a role for a certain period of time, but generally foreign capital tried to be protected by an Italian name, as in the case of Banca Commerciale and Credito Italiano. Moreover, foreign capital made an important contribution to Italian economic development by financing the Italian national debt: this was the case with French capital in 1862–5 and 1883–7; German capital in 1895; French, English and USA capital during the First World War; English and USA capital between 1926 and 1934; USA capital after the Second World War.

(2) Throughout Italian economic history, the number and share capital of Italian banks have always grown during the boom phases, and they decreased during the depression period. This relation became dramatic on several occasions: in 1873–6, 1888–94, 1907–9, 1920–3, 1930–3.

(3) The spread of saving banks since 1824, the creation of mutual loan societies and co-operative banks since 1864 and rural banks since 1887 were all means for collecting small savings and to foster the habit of saving.

(4) Private bankers, who, at the beginning, formed the basis of the Italian banking system, have now almost disappeared. As the Italian economy developed their numbers decreased, above all during the two world wars.

(5) State intervention and control over banks increased after 1874, and was more incisive after the 1888–93 economic crisis, but reached its apogee during the Fascist period, when in 1939 the Ispettorato del credito e del risparmio was created with the task of authorizing change in interest rates and of opening bank branches.

(6) The Italian banking system has been transformed during recent years under pressure from the European Community. Now foreign banks can open branches in Italy and are answerable only towards their central banks. Moreover, a special law in 1992 provided for the privatization of all banks and encouraged mergers in order to face international competition.

(7) Last but not least the banking law of 1936 has been abolished, and now banks can carry on short- and medium–long-term credit provided that certain conditions are observed; i.e. universal or mixed banks have been restored in Italy.

Notes

1 C. Barbagallo, *Le origini della grande industria contemporanea (1750–1850)*, vol. II (Perugia and Venice, 1930), pp. 4 *et seq.*; G. Luzzatto, *Storia Economica dell'età moderna e contemporanea*, part II (Padua, 1960), pp. 186 *et seq.*
2 Barbagallo, *Le origini della grande industria contemporanea*, vol. II, pp. 8–9.
3 Luzzatto, *Storia Economica dell'età moderna*, p. 185.
4 R. Morandi, *Storia della grande industria in Italia* (Turin, 1959), pp. 30 *et seq.*
5 Barbagallo, *Le origini della grande industria contemporanea*, vol. II, pp. 267, 276 *et seq.*
6 E. Corbino, *Annali dell'economia italiana*, vol. I (1861–80) (Città di Castello, 1931), p. 65.
7 The Banca Nazionale nel Regno d'Italia, founded in 1850 on the fusion of the Banks of Genoa and Turin (cf. L. Conte, *La Banca Nazionale. Formazione e attività di una banca di emissione, 1843–1861* (Naples, 1990), pp. 33 *et seq.*, 66 *et seq.*), aimed to be the only Italian issuing bank, but had to abandon this aim due to the opposition of the other five regional banks: the Banca Nazionale Toscana; the Banca Toscana di credito; the Banca Romana; the Banco di Napoli and the Banco di Sicilia. The first three, like the Banca Nazionale, were founded on equity share capital, the two southern banks on a public foundation. Cf. L. De Rosa, *Storia del Banco di Napoli* (Naples, 1989), vol. I.

8 De Rosa, *Storia del Banco di Napoli*, vol. I.
9 Corbino, *Annali dell'economia italiana*, vol. I, p. 332.
10 E. Corbino, *Annali dell'economia italiana*, vol. II (1871–80) (Naples, n.d.), pp. 88 *et seq.*
11 *Ibid.*, pp. 376 *et seq.*
12 I. Sachs, *L'Italie. Ses finances et son développement économique depuis l'unification du Royaume 1859–1884* (Paris, 1885), pp. 745–7.
13 Corbino, *Annali dell'economia italiana*, vol. II, p. 93.
14 M. Pantaleoni, *Studi storici di economia* (Bologna, 1936), pp. 217 *et seq.*
15 E. Corbino, *Annali economia italiana*, vol. III (Naples, n.d.), p. 115.
16 A. Gerschenkron, *Il problema storico dell'arretratezza economica* (Turin, 1965), pp. 71 *et seq.*
17 *Ibid.*, p. 75.
18 *Ibid.*, p. 85.
19 E. Corbino, *Annali dell'economia italiana*, vol. IV (Naples, n.d.), p. 109.
20 *Ibid.*, p. 99.
21 R. Bachi, *L'Italia economica nel 1915* (Città di Castello, 1916), p. 7.
22 S. Cassese, 'La divisione del lavoro bancario. Distribuzione funzionale e territoriale del Credito dal 1936 ad oggi', *Economia Italiana*, 3 (1983), pp. 404 *et seq.*

15 The role of European banks in the Ottoman Empire in the second half of the nineteenth and early twentieth centuries

Elena Frangakis-Syrett

Introduction

European banks appeared for the first time in the Ottoman Empire towards the middle of the nineteenth century and for the next four decades they had a relatively limited presence in the region as a whole and were involved primarily in commercial banking. The exception to this were those banks that were mainly established in Istanbul and which were involved in the financing of the Ottoman government with short- and long-term loans. Of those latter banks only the Imperial Ottoman Bank, established in 1863, maintained a continuous presence in the capital and Empire, until the closing decades of the century when it was joined by a growing number of other European banks. It was in the twenty-five years or so before the First World War that changes in the world economy and in the economy of the region itself led to an important presence of European banks in the Empire. This presence took the form either of the opening of branches of major European banks or the setting up of overseas banks in the capital or the various provincial centres. For instance, in 1875 the Crédit Lyonnais opened a branch in Istanbul and in the early 1890s in Jerusalem and Izmir; the Deutsche Bank established in 1899 the Deutsche Palästina Bank with branches in Jerusalem, Haiffa and Jaffa. It was in this period that the European banks came to play their most important role in the Ottoman economy by dominating such sectors as state financing, banking, infrastructure construction, transportation and energy.

The Ottoman economy

Throughout the nineteenth and early twentieth centuries, the Ottoman economy remained basically an agricultural economy, with commerce constituting the principal sector of monetary activity as well as of interaction with Western capital and the world economy. Moreover, and since European banks emerged in sizeable numbers *only* in the closing decades of the nineteenth century, an informal, private and usually small-scale, merchant-cum-banking sector filled the gap. Indeed, this informal though complex merchant-cum-banking sector continued to function, coexisting alongside the Western banks, right until the early twentieth century and the end of the Ottoman period.

A number of characteristics of the Ottoman economy account both for the existence and resilience of this informal merchant-cum-banking sector as well as for the late development of a banking system along Western lines. One of them was chronic capital scarcity, which at times became acute. This meant that credit was frequently not available and interest rates were high. The rural sector was more affected than the urban sector where credit could be obtained rather more easily. Efforts by the state to alleviate the unavailability of credit in the rural sector, in particular, failed. For instance, in 1888, the Ottoman government established the Agricultural Bank which was to have the twin aim of serving both as a credit institution to the rural sector as well as the financier for agricultural reform. Inadequately funded and over-burdened – it was also periodically called upon to service fiscal needs of the state – the bank was finally unable to eliminate the particularly usurious lending rates, current in the rural sector, for small-scale proprietors who formed the bulk of its population.[1] Moreover, since monetary scarcity remained a feature of the Ottoman economy, to a greater or lesser degree throughout our period, credit remained an important factor in commercial exchange. As the competition among Westerners to export in the Ottoman market intensified, extension of credit to the Ottoman purchaser became at times a ploy with which to gain entry into a competitive market. For instance, over-generous credit terms were offered through their banks by the Germans, who were relative latecomers in the Ottoman market, in order to gain access into it in the third quarter of the century.

In the first half of the nineteenth century, such credit conditions were further affected by the frequent debasement of the currency and a high rate of inflation which, in turn, led to further increases in interest rates. In addition, the circulation of many different coins simultaneously, often debased, with rates of exchange that differed from one area of the Empire to the other, created problems for interregional as well as international commerce, although it also created opportunities for arbitrage without, however, alleviating monetary scarcity. At the same time the concurrent circulation of European currencies, side by side with the Ottoman ones, the former often preferred and used in lieu of Ottoman coins, which were often scarce, led to a lucrative trade in Western currencies. In such a case the latter became commodities to be imported into and exported out of the Empire according to the special circumstances affecting the various economic centres of the Empire at any given point in time.[2]

The need to move funds within a large geographical area had led to an extensive use of bills of exchange within the Empire, among local Ottoman officials and other elite besides merchants and arbitrageurs, well before our period. By the nineteenth century, the multiple and increasing links of the Empire, mainly through trade, with many European commercial and financial markets, meant that the Empire was itself part of a number of different international circuits of bills of exchange which facilitated and increased the circulation of such bills within it. Chronic scarcity of specie in the Ottoman economy further reinforced the widespread use of bills of exchange leading also to a profitable trade in such bills.[3] Such phenomena were themselves the result, to a large extent, of a lack of a fully functioning banking system as well as of a non-unified national economy.

European commercial banking: the early phase

The first bank established by European capital in the Empire was the Ottoman Bank. It was incorporated in London in 1856 as a non-privileged English joint-stock bank; it was active in Istanbul but also had branches in Izmir, Beyrouth and Galatz. The bank carried out mainly commercial banking operations, making early on a personal loan to the Sultan at a lucrative rate though lower than the prevailing rate in the money market of Istanbul. It was conservative in its policies deciding, early on, 'not to engage in any extensive exchange operations' given the very wide fluctuations in the exchange rate between the Ottoman currency and the pound sterling, which ranged in 1856/7 between 117 and 186 Ottoman piastres to the pound! These were also, of course, years of a general economic crisis.[4] The Ottoman Bank was, on the whole, a lucrative enterprise.

European capital also attempted to establish commercial banks in the provinces. Such was the case, for example, with the Bank of Smyrna set up in 1842 as a joint-stock bank, by British merchants established in Izmir, for commercial banking operations. Within a year or so, and before any results could be registered, the bank was closed by the Ottoman government apparently due, at least in part, to local opposition.[5] Between the 1840s and 1860s there were other private European commercial-cum-banking houses active for a time in various centres in the Empire.[6] Their impact could not have been but local. And it remained so until the closing decades of the century when there was renewed activity on the part of European banks in the Ottoman commercial banking sector.

The Imperial Ottoman Bank

By the 1840s, after a period of particularly high inflation and frequent debasement of the currency that marked the first four decades of the nineteenth century – and despite repeated, although unsuccessful, efforts to control the interest rates as well as the rates of exchange by legislative decrees – the Ottoman government took another series of measures in an attempt to resolve the situation. For the increasingly weaker Ottoman currency was not only impeding the smooth functioning of the economy but it was also causing problems in the Empire's international trade as well as worsening the insolvency of the state. The Ottoman government thus issued in *c.* 1840, mainly for circulation in Istanbul, paper money, or bonds for they bore interest, called *kaime*,[7] as a way to alleviate the specie shortage and thus the need for the minting of new, and potentially debased, coins.[8] At the same time, the government also wanted to stabilize its currency, for which aim the formation of a state bank was seen as an important prerequisite.

The Bank of Constantinople was thus set up in 1847 by an Imperial decree and financed by both Western and local capital, the so-called Galata bankers of Istanbul. It had the primary purpose of keeping the exchange rate at par with the British pound, which had become the basis of the Ottoman currency since 1844; exchanging debased coinage at a certain parity, and, periodically, issuing paper money which it was to buy back at a discount rate of 3%. It thus had the task of facilitating trade and the financial operations of the state, besides stabilizing the currency and dealing with the debased coinage – two of the biggest problems facing the Ottoman government at the time. For a number of reasons, among which were the enormity of its task and the nature of its support from the European money markets, the bank only lasted a few years, closing down in 1852 with a large deficit and thus adding to the financial burdens of the Ottoman government with which it had been closely linked.[9]

Whatever possibilities of success the government might have had with such measures, including the introduction of paper currency, these were dashed with the onset of the Crimean War. However, negotiations continued among various groups of European (British and French) and Ottoman capitalists and the Ottoman government for the creation of a state bank. The British and French governments, which for political and economic reasons were interested in the solvency of the Ottoman government and the facilitation of the Empire's international trade, lent their support to such negotiations. There was, indeed, considerable competition amongst the various groups that vied for such a concession from the Ottoman government. Moreover, this competition did not only take the form of British and French banks competing against each other as well as against the Galata bankers of Istanbul, but also took the form of one group, which could include within it British and French banks and Ottoman private bankers, competing against another group of Western and/or Ottoman bankers.

One of the results of such negotiations was the Anglo-Greek Turkish National Bank, proposed by capitalists from London and Istanbul. The bank was virtually established in 1860 when the bank's charter was granted by the Porte. It never quite got off the ground, however. Inadequate backing in the London money market was one of the reasons for its lack of success. The bank folded up a year later in 1861.[10]

Still further negotiations resulted, in 1863, in the formation of the Ottoman Imperial Bank, an Anglo-French concern, represented by the Ottoman Bank referred to above, on the English side, and the Pereire brothers of the Crédit Mobilier heading the French side.[11] The two groups also shared the board of directors, although the British side was initially the stronger of the two. This situation was, however, to reverse itself in the last quarter of the nineteenth century.

Closely linked to the Ottoman government from the beginning – although it never ceased to be an independent European financial institution and to be seen as such in the West – the Ottoman Imperial Bank, initially, acted as *agent financier* of the government. In 1875, as a result of a special convention with the Ottoman government, the bank became *trésorier-payeur général de l'Empire*. It thus had the sole right to issue bills that could be cashed on sight, to handle the revenues of the Empire both in the capital and in the provinces and a preference over all other banks in negotiating treasury bonds. Besides being a *banque d'état*, the Imperial Ottoman Bank had also the right to operate as a commercial bank and to carry on all normal banking operations.[12]

From early on the Imperial Ottoman Bank attempted to regulate the exchange rates amongst the various silver currencies within the Ottoman Empire in order to allow the Ottoman government to receive revenues and pay for its expenses in stable currencies. It also had the task of stabilizing the Ottoman gold lira against the British pound sterling in the international rates of exchange in order to create favourable conditions for the continuation and further growth of the Empire's international trade as well as to allow the government to contract for long-term loans abroad.

In order to stabilize effectively the rates of exchange, the Imperial Ottoman Bank had to influence the exchange rates between the various metal coins in the Empire as well as the parity of silver to gold externally; that is, to influence the bullion markets (silver and gold) of the Empire. The bank achieved this by being able to tie the Ottoman gold lira to the pound sterling in the international rates of exchange: that is, to determine the rate of the lira against the pound sterling, and then set the rate of the lira against the other European currencies on the basis of the rate of exchange of the sterling to them.[13] Moreover, by providing debt service payments abroad as well as by collecting a large part of government revenues and by handling a large part of the commercial banking operations in the Empire – this was so particularly from the closing decades of the century on, by which time the Imperial Ottoman Bank had acquired the most extensive network of branches than any other bank in the Empire – the bank was, in fact, able to influence the parity of silver to gold in the Empire. By collecting government revenues, which depended largely on the level of agricultural output and by, eventually, handling a large part of the Empire's commercial banking operations, the bank had in place a network through which it acquired advance information concerning the expected level of harvests in various parts of the Empire and thus the likely levels of government revenues and of exports, including the likelihood of a deficit for the government in case of bad harvests. With this knowledge, the bank could estimate which way the rate of exchange was likely to go and choose its time for making remittances abroad for the servicing of the debt or for any of its other operations. Furthermore, the bank's close relations with the British and French money markets, through its two committees based in either country respectively, gave it further expert information in deciding its moves.[14]

Although the Empire did not always have a positive balance of trade, rather the contrary, and it certainly did not have a positive balance of payments, the Imperial Ottoman Bank was able to maintain the exchange rate of the Ottoman gold lira to the pound sterling stable basically because of the constant borrowing in the European money markets by the Ottoman state. For such loans resulted in large inflows of gold into the Empire which strengthened the Ottoman gold lira and provided the funds to maintain debt service payments abroad at regular intervals.[15]

Finally, by favouring gold over silver, and external transactions of the Empire over internal ones, the Imperial Ottoman Bank was able to make, along with those involved in international trade, considerable profits. The bank was also able to influence the exchange rates in the silver currencies that continued to fluctuate from region to region within the Empire affected by local conditions and make considerable profits in the process.[16]

The Imperial Ottoman Bank thus influenced the development of the Ottoman economy in many ways. As a state bank, it used its right of issue conservatively issuing, until the First World War, only a limited amount of paper that circulated mainly in or near Istanbul. By doing so it may not have been able to alleviate the specie scarcity that persisted in the Ottoman economy, or contribute towards the unification of the Ottoman market, but the bank was thus able to control the amount of circulating money convertible to gold.[17] And by maintaining the rate of exchange of the lira to the pound sterling stable, it helped the further growth of international trade and thus the integration of certain sectors of the Ottoman economy in the world market.

Ottoman state financing

Another area where the Imperial Ottoman Bank, along with other European banks, played a particularly important role was in Ottoman state financing. Here, the Imperial Ottoman Bank enjoyed, from the beginning, a very strong position. It had a preference over all other banks in negotiating treasury bonds without, however, ever having exclusive rights. Should better terms be offered by other banks, the Porte was no longer bound to give preference to the Imperial Ottoman Bank.

Although the bank was in a strong position in the financing of the Ottoman state, other banks, such as the Banque Austro-Ottomane, established in Istanbul in the 1860s and financed partly by European capital, were capable of competing with it. It was with such establishments, as well as with the local Galata bankers, that the Imperial Ottoman Bank had to share the profits of advancing short-term loans to the Ottoman government in the 1860s and early 1870s. The financial crisis of the early 1870s, however, either seriously weakened or destroyed a good number of these banks leaving the Imperial Ottoman Bank in an even stronger position.[18]

The 'Fisheries Loan' contracted between the Ottoman government and the Deutsche Bank in 1888 put an end to the strong position that the Imperial Ottoman Bank had come to enjoy. This loan signalled the entry of German finance capital in the Ottoman Empire. It also meant that, henceforth, the Imperial Ottoman Bank would have had to compete for the negotiation of or participation in any Ottoman state loan. A compromise was, however, reached that shielded the Imperial Ottoman Bank from what could have been deadly competition. The bank came to an agreement with the Deutsche Bank that allowed a certain percentage participation to the Imperial Ottoman Bank if the loan were negotiated by the Deutsche Bank and its circle of 'friends', and vice versa. Thus the two banks put up most of the time, for there were exceptions to this, a united front when negotiating with the Ottoman government and secured their profit levels in the process: 'Both parties make advances to the Government at high rates of interest, and when it is desired to force the Government to accept the terms of a loan operation by either party, the doors of both are closed to further temporary accommodation.'[19]

In the period 1881–1914, the French money market subscribed the largest share of the Ottoman state loans – the Imperial Ottoman Bank was by then primarily French in capital – to the amount of 70%.[20] Ottoman state financing offered lucrative returns not only to the banks involved but also to the French and other individual Western investors. The Imperial Ottoman Bank subscribed these loans together with its circle of 'friends', which after 1909 did not only include French finance capital but capital from other European banks too. In provisioning the Ottoman state with loans the Imperial Ottoman Bank, along with other banks, came to play a role of great importance, not only in maintaining the solvency of the government's finances but also in the Ottoman economy as a whole.

Take-off of European commercial banking

Despite a right to open branches all over the Empire, the bank followed a conservative policy opening seven branches in the 1860s and six in the 1870s. Moreover, it took the bank until 1914 to acquire a truly Empire-wide presence.[21] Although it can be persuasively argued that the scope for profitable banking operations all over the Empire was rather limited early on, this policy *de facto* restricted the Imperial Ottoman Bank's role, and hence impact, on the Empire's commercial sector in particular. However, this changed in the closing decades of the century.

It was as a result of the pace of growth of the Ottoman economy, that now afforded greater opportunities for investment and profit, as well as of changes in the world economy and in the overseas investment policies of big European banks, that a number of them started in the 1880s and 1890s to open branches or overseas banks in the capital and/or in various provincial centres of the Empire. The process gathered pace at the turn of the century so that by the middle of the first decade of the twentieth century one can speak of a 'rush' of European bank openings in the Empire.[22] They were primarily active in banking operations in the commercial sector although many of them were also active in trade *per se*. They also came to dominate the Empire's banking sector.

Thus, on the eve of the First World War, there were not only British, French and German but also Austrian, Italian, Russian and Greek banks – for instance, the Bank of the Orient, the Bank of Athens, the Wiener Bankverein, the Banco di Roma – that were affording many facilities to those involved in the international and internal trade of the Empire, both importers and exporters, both in the Empire and in the West. For instance, Westerners who exported goods to the Empire on a month's credit, were now able to discount in their bank in Europe their thirty-days bill. When the bill matured the bank, through its branch or corresponding bank in the Empire, collected the money from the Ottoman importer. It was primarily German banks which were credited as the first to offer such services, against a commission and the profit from discounting the bill. They were seen at the time as having given an unduly important advantage to their nationals in the highly competitive Levantine market but this was probably exaggerated. In any case the other banks were soon following suit, so that by the early twentieth century, a number of European banks allowed commercial transactions to be cleared through them, not only for the collection of funds from the Ottoman importer, but also for the sending of invoices and other documents to the Empire.

Banks also gave extensively, for the first time, the option to the importer in the Empire (Ottoman or Western), to pay his Western exporter – if no particular credit were to be extended – by either cash or cheque, the latter usually drawn on London or Paris, with a margin of profit or loss according to the current rate of exchange concerning either specie or cheque. Exporters of Ottoman goods to the West were paid by drafts of ninety days or four months, with bill of lading and other documents attached, against commercial letters of credit on London or Paris furnished by the Western purchaser. The draft was accepted by the banker abroad and then sold in the discount market whenever terms were most advantageous.

Banks further facilitated trade, mainly in the Empire's larger urban centres, by increasing their capital liquidity through offering loans at lower interest rates. One of the effects of the easing of credit, and the lowering of the interest rates, was in fact an increase in activity, in the 1900s, in the futures market of various exports.[23] For, however conservative some of the banks may have been in their lending policies, the fact that they had to compete, sometimes fiercely, against each other meant that they had to offer competitive terms to credit-worthy entrepreneurs for short- to medium-term loans to attract them as customers. Most of their loans were typically short term (up to a year) to merchants who paid them back at the end of the trading season. A usual practice was to open a line of credit with the bank and draw against it as and when the need arose, usually during the export season, with Western and better-off Ottoman merchants being generally involved in such transactions.

However, there was still room for the local private bankers. For instance, banks were reluctant to accept promissory notes with only one signature, whilst the private banker was willing to do business 'at higher rates of interest and commission in one-named paper'.[24] Local private bankers also borrowed money from the banks in order to lend – at a rate that was higher than the banks' rate but lower than what they had themselves previously charged – usually to small-scale entrepreneurs, to whom the banks might not be willing to lend due to insufficient credit-worthiness.

From commercial banks to universal banks

It was as a result of the same changes in the Ottoman as well as in the world economy, referred to above, which led some of the bigger European banks, in particular, to become active in industrial enterprises in the Empire besides commercial banking. Nowhere was this more so than in the case of the Imperial Ottoman Bank, which was still the biggest European bank in the Empire. With an increase in the imperialist rivalries among the major European powers in the Empire, and with the European banks playing an important part in these rivalries, the role of the Imperial Ottoman Bank was forced to change. It was primarily competition from German finance capital, led by the Deutsche Bank, that transformed it from a commercial bank that viewed industrial ventures only from the point of view of a lending institution, to a 'universal' or 'mixed' bank[25] that participated in the setting up and ownership of industrial enterprises. By 1914, through the various companies that it controlled in a varying capacity, the Imperial Ottoman Bank had almost become an informal holding company.[26] In the twenty-five years or so before the First World War, not only the Imperial Ottoman Bank and the Deutsche Bank but a number of other European banks, some of which were already active on the Ottoman economic scene, started to promote, invest in and partly own – usually through concessions – railway, mining, irrigation, land reclamation, harbour construction, energy and urban public transportation, as well as all kinds of public utility companies.

Has the role governments played in the economic activities of their nationals, especially where it concerned large financial institutions, been over-emphasized in the literature of the period and in the subsequent historiography? I would argue it has not. For instance, one of the reasons rightly given as to why the British-financed National Bank of Turkey, established in 1909, was only relatively successful in its industrial undertakings in the Ottoman Empire in the early twentieth century, was because it did not always enjoy the full and active backing of the British government.[27] And, indeed, it would appear that the governments of the major European powers, especially of France and Germany, did play an important role in the winning of concessions for industrial projects or in the participation of large Ottoman state loans for their respective financial institutions.[28] This, of course, necessitated the prerequisite that the financial institutions involved could themselves raise sufficient funds or put together financial combinations that could. Besides capital resources, however, the big European banks also used their expertise, knowledge of the area and the multiple contacts they were acquiring, whilst operating in the Empire, as important assets in their various ventures.

The Imperial Ottoman Bank and the Deutsche Bank were the two largest financial institutions active in the Empire. Their particularly active role was keenly watched, at the time, by British and American diplomats who saw it as crucial in the process of penetration of French and German capital in the region; and, to a large extent, this was so. Fierce competition was characteristic of this sector too, although it often took the form of one group of banks competing against another group. The two largest banks competed against each other but also participated in financial combinations, that included both banks and their 'friends', for a series of large-scale industrial projects.[29] Moreover, their circle of 'friends' did not only include their respective nationals but could also include finance capital from other European economies, such as the Belgian or the Swiss. For instance, the Consortium de Constantinople, established in 1911 in order to carry out a number of infrastructure projects in Istanbul – mainly in public transportation and energy – had as partners French, German, Belgian, Belgo-Hungarian and Swiss capital. Moreover, in the Société des Tramways et d'Electricité de Constantinople, which was one of the companies that the Consortium established, the share of banking to industrial capital, in each of the principal groups, was as follows: French, 68.6% banking, 31.4% industrial; German, 67.2% banking, 32.7% industrial; and Belgian, 44.8% banking, 19.3% industrial and 35.8% mixed.[30] It was in such infrastructure and transportation projects that the European banks, on the whole, became actively involved in and contributed most to the late Ottoman economy.

Conclusion

Thus the European banks did play a role in the economy of the Ottoman Empire, particularly in the closing decades of the nineteenth and in the early twentieth centuries. It was a role borne out of the need of the Ottoman state to stabilize its exchange rate and to maintain solvency in its finances. It was also a role borne out of the need of European financial capital to invest abroad and of the level of economic growth of the Empire that came to offer opportunities for investment and profits. This role was initially manifested in state financing and in stabilizing its exchange rate. It was also manifested in commercial banking operations which were greatly increased in the later period. The banks' impact in this sector was particularly evident in the greater availability of credit in the Ottoman urban centres and in the facilitation of commercial payments and of trade in general. They also came to dominate the banking sector of the Empire. Moreover, by the turn of the century, the bigger European banks in particular, usually in combination with other European financial capital, became instrumental in a series of industrial projects in the Empire, especially in infrastructure, energy and transportation. In so doing, and in conjunction with their role in state financing and in commercial banking, European banks became, by the early twentieth century, a powerful force in the development of the Ottoman economy.

Notes

Research for this work was supported (in part) by a grant from the City University of New York PSC-CUNY Research Award Program.

1 For more information, see D. Quataert, 'Dilemma of Development: The Agricultural Bank and Agricultural Reform in Ottoman Turkey, 1888–1906', *International Journal of Middle East Studies*, 6 (1975), pp. 210–27.

2 For more details, see Elena Frangakis-Syrett, *The Commerce of Smyrna in the Eighteenth Century, 1700–1820* (Athens, 1992), pp. 139–54.

3 For more details, see Edhem Eldem, 'La circulation de la lettre de change entre la France et Constantinople au XVIIIe siècle', in H. Batu and J. L. Bacqué-Grammont (eds.), *L'Empire Ottoman, la République de Turquie et la France* (Istanbul and Paris, 1986), pp. 87–97.

4 *Banker's Magazine*, 16 (1856), p. 533, and *ibid.*, 18 (1858), pp. 418, 755.

5 Public Record Office, FO 195/177, 20 Jan. 1843.

6 L. Farley, *The Resources of Turkey and Profitable Investments* (London, 1862), pp. 80–8; see also C. Issawi, *The Fertile Crescent* (New York, 1988), p. 410.

7 It is not clear exactly when the first issue took place. For more details, see R. Davison, 'The First Ottoman Experiment with Paper Money', in O. Okyar and H. Inalcik (eds.), *Türkiyenin Sosyal ve Ekonomik Tarihi (1071–1920)* (Ankara, 1982), pp. 243, 250.

8 These were finally withdrawn from circulation in the early 1860s with the help of short-term loans, some from the Imperial Ottoman Bank and some contracted before the formation of the bank. J. Thobie, 'Les choix financiers de l'*Ottomane* en Méditerranée orientale de 1856 à 1939', in *Banque et Investissements en Méditerranée* (Marseilles, 1985), p. 59.

9 A. Biliotti, *La Banque Impériale Ottomane* (Paris, 1909), pp. 11, 23, 117, 162–5; see also M. A. Ubicini, *Letters on Turkey* (London, 1856), vol. I, pp. 299, 303.

10 A. du Velay, *Essai sur l'histoire financière de la Turquie* (Paris, 1903), pp. 153–67; see also *Banker's Magazine*, 19 (1859), pp. 750–1; *ibid.*, 20 (1860), p. 81; and *ibid.*, 21 (1861), pp. 592, 663.

11 C. Clay, 'The Imperial Ottoman Bank in the Later Nineteenth Century: A Multinational "National" Bank?' in G. Jones (ed.), *Banks as Multinationals* (London, 1990), pp. 142–4; see also A. S. J. Baster, *The International Banks* (London, 1935), pp. 88–96.

12 E. Pech, *Manuel des Sociétés Anonymes fonctionnant en Turquie* (Constantinople, 1911), pp. 111–13; and C. Clay, 'The Bank Notes of the Imperial Ottoman Bank, 1863–1876', *New Perspectives on Turkey*, 9 (1993), pp. 101–18.

13 'La Banque détermine le cours de change sur Londres et fixe le prix des autres changes en établissant les parités entre le cours de la livre sterling ainsi obtenu et le prix des francs, marks, couronnes . . . sur le marché de Londres.' Biliotti, *La Banque Impériale Ottomane*, p. 181.

14 *Ibid.*, pp. 180–2.

15 *Ibid.*, pp. 166–77.

16 *Ibid.*, pp. 137–8.

17 Thobie, 'Les choix financiers', p. 60; see also S. Pamuk, 'Money in the Ottoman Empire, 1326–1914', in H. Inalcik and D. Quataert (eds.), *An Economic and Social History of the Ottoman Empire, 1300–1914* (Cambridge, 1994), p. 972.

18 Biliotti, *La Banque Impériale Ottomane*, p. 20. In 1874 it absorbed the Banque Austro-Ottomane altogether. Clay, 'The Imperial Ottoman Bank', pp. 145–6.

19 Baster, *The International Banks*, pp. 100–1.

20 Thobie, 'Les choix financiers', p. 63.

21 See C. Clay, 'The Origins of Modern Banking in the Levant: The Branch Network of the Imperial Ottoman Bank, 1890–1914', *International Journal of Middle East Studies*, 26 (1994), pp. 589–614.

22 J. Thobie, 'Banques européennes, finances et industrie au Moyen Orient, 1870–1914', *Annales du Levant*, 3 (1988), p. 50.

23 However, periodic specie shortages still occurred in some areas of the Empire necessitating specie imports. Issawi, *The Fertile Crescent*, pp. 409–10.

24 National Archives, Washington, DC, RG 84, General Correspondence Series, G. B. Ravndal, US Consul General, Istanbul, 5 Sept. 1912, to Secretary of State, Washington, DC.

25 R. Tilly, 'An Overview on the Role of Large German Banks up to 1914', in Y. Cassis (ed.), *Finance and Financiers in European History, 1880–1960* (Cambridge, 1992), pp. 94–5, 97, 110.

26 Thobie, 'Les choix financiers', pp. 72–5. On the role of European banks in industry, see also Ginette Kurgan-van Hentenryk, 'Banques et Entreprises', in *La Wallonie. Le Pays et les Hommes*, vol. II (Brussels, 1976), pp. 45–8.

27 M. Kent, 'Agent of Empire? The National Bank of Turkey and British Foreign Policy', *Historical Journal*, 18/2 (1975), pp. 376–81.

28 In the last decade before the First World War, the Imperial Ottoman Bank, an overwhelmingly French institution by then, had an increasingly closer relationship with the French government.

29 E.g. G. P. Gooch and H. Temperley, *British Documents on the Origins of the War, 1898–1914* (London, 1928–38), vol. V, pp. 175–80.

30 Thobie, 'Banques européennes', pp. 59–61.

16 The role of banks in establishing a community of firms in Russia

Andrei Yudanov

This is not so much a piece of historical research, in the strict sense of the word, as an economist's theoretical reflections on the history of banking in Russia. I myself feel well justified in taking such an approach. My country's development over the past century and a half is a far cry from that of other countries. Russia has always been unique, first, as a great semi-feudal–semi-capitalist empire; then as the metropolis of socialism; and finally as the major post-socialist power. It is not surprising, therefore, that Russia has been habitually regarded as a 'special case' failing to fit into the general set of uniformities and requiring isolated study.

That being so, special interest attaches to the research designed to put the Russian experience into the world-wide context. The most outstanding attempt here in bank–industry relations theory was made by Alexander Gerschenkron, who linked up Russia's specific industrialization with the degree of its economic backwardness.

Hypothesis formulated

Let us recall Gerschenkron's assumption that in England, which first took the path of industrialization, the technical revolution was carried out by small firms acquiring equipment by reinvestment of profits (or, as he himself put it, by means of original accumulation). Consequently, it was the enterprise itself that provided the source both of the capital for industrialization and of the entrepreneurial knowledge required.

Germany lagged behind England and got down to industrialization later, in an altogether different set of conditions. The optimal size of industrial enterprises had by then become so large that it was quite hard to finance such enterprises merely out of reinvested profits. Accordingly, investment banks came on the scene in Germany as the source of capital for the establishment of large enterprises (and often as the actual organizers of new firms).

Gerschenkron believed that not only contemporaries but even their descendants had less than an adequate grasp of the 'mission' of banks in the process of industrialization. Indeed, his view was that those who regarded the coalescence of banks and industry mainly as a factor of growing instability in the banking system were inclined to take too narrow a view of the problem. By contrast, Gerschenkron held that the important thing was not the side-effects, but the fact that the investment banks had helped to generate Germany's large-scale industry, which stood strong in the face of various upheavals, including those provoked by the investment banks themselves (rather, by their practice of placing their capital in industrial shares).

Tzarist Russia was even more backward than Germany: Russia was unable to industrialize not only through natural reinvestment of profits, but even by means of bank financing. The fact is that the country's banking system was weak and was unable to scrape together the money required. The role of organizer of industrialization was performed in the 1890s by the state, which levied from the country's entire population, through taxes, the money it needed to build up industry.[1]

Professor E. H. Carr applied this logic in his explanation of the Stalinist industrialization in the USSR, thereby unexpectedly causing sharp dissatisfaction on Gerschenkron's part.[2] Indeed, Gerschenkron held that the way chosen by Stalin to finance the industrialization of Soviet Russia through the country's resources coercively centralized in the budget was hardly necessary as an objective factor. It was dictated not by the country's backwardness (which had by then been markedly reduced), but by political considerations. Gerschenkron's theory seems to have had some peculiar ups and downs: in the 1960s it became widely known and generally accepted; subsequently, however, it was subjected to crushing criticism, as most researchers rejected the idea of strong dependence between the state of a country's backwardness and the forms of its industrialization. The strange thing is, however, that the conception did not peter out: instead of being merely forgotten as a rejected theory, it has been subjected by the scientific community to unrelenting criticism for over a quarter of a century.

The answer seems to be the lack of any theoretical alternative to Gerschenkron's approach. The need to give a positive explanation of the role of banks in economic history is a compelling factor in researchers' returning to Gerschenkron's works again and again, as the point of departure, if only to keep pointing out the various inaccuracies, shortcomings, etc. An important step in overcoming this unsatisfactory state of affairs was made by H. Lindgren, who noted the similarity between Gerschenkron's theory and Josef Schumpeter's more general views, while emphasizing the incomplete state of the matter: 'Here, for our research agenda on bank–industry relations . . . it is important to note that the crucial role played by bank financing within the Schumpeterian analysis of economic development has generally attracted much less attention.'[3]

Schumpeter's Entrepreneur is an innovator creating 'new combinations' of the factors of production, i.e. implanting new technologies, modes of management, products, types of raw materials, etc. He tends to upset the old routine in the management of affairs for the sake of benefits understood, for the time being, to him alone, but not to the others around him. In the process, the 'invisible hand' of the market tends to resist, instead of helping, the Entrepreneur, since his acts are 'incorrect' from the standpoint of the static optimum which has taken shape on the market. The Entrepreneur is able to overcome the resistance of the market forces only by relying on credit. For him, bank financing is a *sine qua non*, while the routine operations of a firm engaged in habitual business can, in principle, do without any credit at all. Schumpeter says that the bank is an 'ephor (overseer) of the market economy' who stands between the Entrepreneur in need of the factors of production and the owners of these factors. In providing credit, the bank vests the Entrepreneur, on behalf of the national economy, with the powers to perform new combinations.[4]

From this angle, Gerschenkron's mission of the investment banks in the industrialization of Germany appears to be a specific case of providing finance for the Entrepreneur's innovative activity. Meanwhile, the overall problem seems to consist in identifying all (or, at least, the main) spheres in which *real* banks were instrumental in the course of *real* historical development in promoting innovation in the economy. A convenient instrument for concretizing Schumpeter's views of the

interconnection between the activity of the banks and new combinations in the economy is offered by the theory of competitive
advantage, which classifies all the firms operating in the economy under
several heads, depending on their strategy of behaviour.[5]

Ever since the first large-scale corporations made their appearance
over a century ago, the economy of the developed countries has been a
community of firms belonging to four main types. First, there are the
big enterprises conducting a volume strategy, the gist of which is to
mass-produce standard products of average quality at moderate prices.
For the volume producers, the big size of the firm is a vital necessity,
since big size alone helps to keep costs (notably, fixed costs) at a low
level.

As Alfred D. Chandler has shown, in order to win success in the
market, the large-scale enterprise needs to carry out 'three inter-related
sets of investment in production, distribution and management required
to achieve the competitive advantage of scale, scope or both'.[6] That is
the initial stage of activity at which volume producers are very badly in
need of bank credits.

Firms which have selected the second – niche – type of strategy
concentrate their efforts on a narrow segment of the market. They
usually specialize in the production of extra-high-quality goods or
services and/or goods or services which have unusual properties. Firms
of this type are rarely in need of credits which go beyond the framework
of current-operations servicing; indeed, this only occurs in times of
change of specialization or development of new products.

On the other hand, companies of the innovative type of strategy are
altogether unable to exist without credit. Small firms operating in high-
tech business are known to perform the bulk of radical innovations in
the economy, but, as J. W. Wilson aptly put it, at the earlier stages of
their existence they are firms 'with no assets, no products, no sales, and
decidedly no profits'.[7] Profits will appear only when (and if) they score
success. Meanwhile, the costs – and often very high costs at that – need
to be met long before this moment arrives. That is why, a century ago,
T. A. Edison's company without the Morgan group of banks, or E. von
Rathenau's AEG without the Berlin bankers, would have been just as
unenviable as their innovative enterprises in Silicon Valley today,
should they find themselves cut off from the sources of venture capital.
The fourth type of company – the small unspecialized firms – is
committed to customized strategy, which consists in the utmost
adaptation to concrete market requirements existing here and now and

in taking every opportunity for profitable activity. Customized strategy requires utmost flexibility of any firm, ranging from rapid change of offered goods and services to the closure of the enterprise (or, on the contrary, to the founding of a new one). In no other case is routine activity so easily and frequently changed by the need to take entrepreneurial decisions, even if on a local scale in accordance with the small size of the firms concerned. It is now generally recognized that small business has exceptional need of investment credit. No wonder the provision of credit is now pivotal to most state programmes for small-business development.

My hypothesis, therefore, is that Schumpeter's role of the banks as ephors of the economy is realized through their influence on the realization, by each type of firm, of its natural strategy, and the harmonious (or, on the contrary, disbalanced) functioning of the national community of companies as a single whole.

Let me set forth this approach in the context of Russia's banking history.

The first community (backward capitalism)

Tzarist Russia's first joint-stock bank – the Petersburg Private Commercial Bank – began its operations on 1 November 1864, something like a century behind the trail-blazers of the banking business in the West. By 1875, there were thirty-nine joint-stock banks in the country, a figure that subsequently changed little, if at all: throughout the history of the empire, the number of banks never exceeded the modest number of fifty.

The country's rapid industrial development at the turn of the century largely rested on state financing. Thus, virtually all the railways of the gigantic empire were, directly or indirectly (through the provision of guarantees on shares and bonds, and then their redemption) built at the expense of the state, which supplied the basis for the development of heavy industry in Russia and acted as a mighty locomotive of faster economic growth.

We find, therefore, that the general outlines of the situation in Tzarist Russia accord with the scheme proposed by Gerschenkron to explain the mechanism of industrialization in countries of extreme backwardness: there was a combination of a weak banking system and a high profile of the state in the accumulation of capital. But a closer look shows that, along with the 'Russian' way (as Gerschenkron saw it), the

'English' and the 'German' ways had an essential role in the industrialization of Russia as it then was.

The 'English' way of industrialization through the reinvestment of
profits was of substantive importance only in one, but very important,
branch of Russian industry, namely, the textile industry. In 1893, it
accounted for 43.8% of the joint-stock capital of all the industrial joint-
stock companies, although by 1908 the figure had fallen to 28.7%,
which was still a very high level.[8] Neither the state nor the banks had a
major role to play in the industrialization of this successfully developing
industry. Indeed, according to I. F. Gindin, 'the high profits and the
family ownership of enterprises made it possible to put one's own
accumulations into the expansion of production'.[9]

What is more, the absence of the need for external sources of
financing enabled the Moscow group of banks (Russia's second largest),
which operated with textile enterprises, to acquire the features of
'deposit banks', i.e. to concentrate exclusively on current, short-term
operations. Gindin, a major Soviet expert in banking history, had
written some ten years before Gerschenkron came on the scene: 'The
Russian textile industry has been developing in the conditions most
typical for industrial capitalism (i.e. along non-financial lines, not
involving the bank–industry tie-up), . . . and the nature of operations by
the Moscow banks mainly puts one in mind of the major provincial
banks of England.'[10] In other words, the Russian textile industry not
only itself tended to develop in accordance with the 'English' model, but
also to shape, in a similar way, the banks related with it.

But the 'German' way of industrialization was of especially great
importance for Russia. Gindin's calculations, in particular, show that
from 1908 to 1913, the increase in the joint-stock capital of heavy
industry and large-scale enterprises in other industries came to 770
million rubles, while its financing by the banks (through loro and on-call
accounts) was estimated, with the use of different methods, to range
from 440 million to 513 million rubles (i.e. from 57% to 67%).

'An analysis of credit and joint-stock statistics suggests that from 1908
to 1913 heavy industry and large-scale enterprises in other industries
were financed by banks to a point close to the increase in their joint-
stock capital, and that the bulk of the shares . . . came to rest in the banks
by way of direct or indirect financing', says Gindin.[11] In other words, in
some periods of time, at any rate, Russia's industrialization proceeded
predominantly at the expense of banking ('German'), instead of the
state ('Russian') method of financing. We shall subsequently find that

Russian banks had an even greater part to play as the organizers of large-scale enterprises.

Where, then, did the weak Russian banking system obtain its resources? These came most importantly from foreign capital. One should take note, in the first place, that the major Russian banks were themselves largely owned by foreigners. The view taken by official Soviet historiography is that in 1916 and 1917 foreign owners accounted for 44.1% of the capital of Russia's twelve major banks.[12] Considering that the 'Big Twelve' held almost four-fifths of the joint-stock banks' total liabilities, the influence of foreign capital throughout Russia's banking system was obviously exceptionally high. No wonder we are aware of a documented case in which the Minister of Finance of the Russian Empire attempted to ascertain the merger plans of the country's major banks by making inquiries with the bankers of Paris.[13]

The common procedure of financing the establishment or expansion of large-scale Russian enterprises was likewise oriented towards foreign capital markets. Little use was made in Russia of long-term investment credits, which is why enterprises in need of money usually issued shares and handed these over to a banking consortium for placement. The latter most often placed shares on the St Petersburg and the Paris stock exchanges. V. I. Bovykin estimated that the share of foreign investors in the joint-stock capital of Russia's enterprises was as follows: 23% of the value of issued shares and bonds in 1883; 35% in 1900; and 40% in 1908.[14]

The financing of industry by Russia's banks went through several stages. In the 1890s, in the course of which most of the single-plant large enterprises were set up, the banks actively purchased the shares of industrial firms, with the weakness of the national capital market paradoxically promoting especially close ties between banks and industry. Because of the narrowness of the market, the banks organizing the placement of shares were forced to sell these over a lengthy period in small portions. Each new issue of shares tended to settle for a long time on the so-called consortium accounts of banks. It is estimated that the proportion of these accounts in the assets of Russian banks was 3.5 times higher than it was with the German banks famed for their 'missionary' role.[15]

There was a sharp change in the bank–industry relation during the 1900–8 crisis and depression. The banks' initial response to the worsening outlook was to reduce crediting and seek to get rid of the shares of financed enterprises. It was possible to sell large blocks of shares without substantive loss in no more than a few cases, the banks being more often forced to make available to the enterprises closely related with them more and more credit, to keep them out of bankruptcy. But even that failed to bail out all the enterprises.

The fear of losing their investments induced the banks to be involved directly in the activity of industrial enterprises and to force them to unite in syndicates. Professor I. M. Goldstein, a contemporary of those events, wrote: 'Entry into a syndicate reduced the risks and naturally made it easier to obtain credit from the banks, a fact which eventually forced many enterprises, under bank pressure, to give up their too ambitious demands which hampered the establishment of syndicates.'[16]

Thus, in 1902, initiative was displayed not even by the Russian banks themselves, but by the senior shareholders of some of these, namely, those of the French and Belgian banks Société Générale and the Paris Pays Bas Bank, in organizing Prodamet (i.e. 'Sales of Metals'), Russia's major syndicate. In 1905, the French Société Générale and the Comptoir National d'Escompte founded Produgol ('Sales of Coal'), the second most important syndicate. The St Petersburg International Bank (the second biggest Russian bank) acted as the organizer of the oil syndicate Nobmazut, and so on.

Finally, after 1908, in a boom atmosphere which lasted until the First World War, the banks resumed their policy of financial expansion. The purchase of shares and the granting of credits was concentrated mainly within the circle of industrial enterprises within syndicates, which fortified the oligopolistic structure of the market that had taken shape. We find, therefore, that the banks had a significant role to play in financing the build-up of Russia's large-scale industry, and that their influence in organizational terms (the formation of syndicates) on this process should generally be regarded as crucial.

However, two specific aspects of bank activity deserve wider consideration. First, the banks were obviously in no sense deliberate initiators of 'new combinations' in the economy. On the contrary, they tended opportunistically to adapt to each new change in the situation. At first, lured by the fabulous profitability of stock flotations in the early hectic days of Russian business, they found themselves connected with industry. When the business outlook worsened, they tried, like their colleagues in other countries (see, for instance, Alice Teichova's description of the activity of central European banks in the interwar period),[17] to shed the ties which had become burdensome. Having failed to do so, they were forced to apply their influence in industry in an effort to improve the state of the market, and unsurprisingly chose the most obvious way of doing so, namely, that of *reducing supply through collusive agreements between the leading producers.*

Second, the syndicate form of organization of industry established by the banks was, to put it mildly, just about the worst of all the possible forms for the functioning of major enterprises as volume producers.

Industrial syndicates are hardly known outside the boundaries of Russia, and one could assume such syndicates to be the Russian version of cartels. The fact is that legislation in Russia prohibited any collusion between vendors, so making it illegal to set up classical cartels. The letter of the law was followed in this way: in legal terms, Russian syndicates were trading companies whose shares were owned by industrial firms; the latter, each for its own part, concluded with this trading firm bilateral agreements on the marketing of all the products of a given type turned out by them (something that nullified the charge of any collusion with the other participants). Under such a scheme of things, each producer was obviously out of touch with the marketing (distribution) of his own products, to say nothing of his capacity to decide, according to his own lights, on the size of investments in production, since the overall output was subject to a set of hard-and-fast agreements written into the contract with the syndicate's central office. Finally, the system of industrial-firm management turned out to be rigidly set at the stage of single-plant enterprise. At the same time, the syndicate's central office had no powers other than those of marketing and was unable to exercise the functions of a holding company with respect to the firms making up the syndicate. Consequently, all the three basic spheres – production, marketing (distribution) and management – in which the volume producer was to secure for himself economies of scale and scope were necessarily given an inadequate, rickety development.

The Russian banks took a negative attitude to long-term crediting and financing of other types of companies, with the exception of the giant volume producers. Thus, the well-known politician and financier A. M. Bezobrazov wrote:

> The large-scale industrial enterprises have agencies which already provide the finance they need . . . Things are different with the small and medium-size enterprises . . . While the merchant is always assured of credit, the industrialist always seems to be put down. The industrialist will not be able to obtain some 15,000 rubles to finance a copper mine, or 3,000 rubles for a cotton-growing farm, or

1,500 rubles for his wine-making. The state bank will not come forward with the money, and such sums are of no interest to the commercial bank.

Such was the general state of mind at the turn of the century, as will be seen not only from the numerous statements of view to that effect, but also from the steady stream of schemes for the establishment of a bank (usually a state bank) which would, at long last, undertake the functions of providing credits to small and medium-size industry.

Indeed, the 1915 report issued by the Council of the Congress of Trade and Industry also indicated the effects of such a banking policy: 'The exceptional development in Russia of large-scale industry alone is due to the absence of industrial credit organized on the right lines.'[18] Russia had been generally denied the development of entire branches of industry (such as engineering) with a prevalence of medium-size and small enterprises conducting the niche and customized strategy. Credit difficulties were, in fact, one of the key reasons for that state of affairs.

As for the banks themselves, they were loath to provide credits to small and medium-size enterprises for the same old reason: the under-development of the capital market. Bank personnel found it obviously unattractive to engage in risky and labour-consuming operations with small industrial firms in a set of conditions in which the limited supply of capital was confronted with things like (a) the virtually insatiable demand of the state; (b) the merchants' need for rapidly circulating capital; and (c) the lucrative flotation operations involving the shares of large-scale enterprises (as described above). A piece of objective evidence to bring home the point is the virtual absence of any sizeable provincial banks in Russia (with the exception of the Baltic provinces). The bulk of the small and medium-size Russian industry was located outside the two major cities of Moscow and St Petersburg, but no banks tended to crop up in the backwoods, because the business simply was not there.

Finally, the potential founders of innovative firms in Tzarist Russia had only one recourse, namely, request for aid from the state agencies, notably the ministries of the army and the navy. It goes without saying that this bureaucratic way of scientific and technical progress had an extremely low standard of efficiency.

Just after the Second World War, the Stalinist regime instructed Soviet historians of science to discover evidence to show that Russia had priority virtually in all the areas of science and technology. Strange as it may seem, in the course of this thoroughly false campaign, *objective* confirmation was actually found to show that the first (or one of the first) working prototypes of the locomotive, airplane, incandescent lamp, submarine, radio, etc., had indeed been created in Russia, a fact which well accords with the generally recognized high rating of Russian science in the nineteenth and twentieth centuries. However, not a single one of these revolutionary inventions had been commercialized. Russian banks, acting as the ephors of the market economy, failed to give the public sanction for realizing these 'new combinations'.

So, formally speaking, the banks' influence on the formation of the community of companies in pre-revolutionary Russia corresponds to the model developed by Gerschenkron in Germany: Russian banks carried out their historical mission of creating a large-scale oligopolistic industry. A closer look at this idea shows that the situation was not all that simple. First, the banks' pragmatic interests enabled them to give support to far from all the 'new combinations' in the economy. Second, whenever the banks took part in the changes or even initiated these (I have in mind the syndication of industry), the ensuing results did not necessarily yield the best 'new combinations'.

A highly disharmonious community of firms took shape in Russia, not without the support of the banks: it had a clearly underdeveloped small and medium-size business (niche and customized strategies), virtually no innovative sector to speak of, and a hypertrophied large-scale industry. What is more, the large-scale industry was well organized in the form of syndicates and for that reason tended to restrain the formation of the large-scale enterprises' own marketing networks, multi-unit and multi-functional forms of firm organization, and so hemmed in their investment activity. Russia did not discover the economics of scarcity in the Soviet epoch, but on the eve of the First World War, when the syndicates took turns in provoking the coal, iron, oil and other 'shortages'.

The second community (capitalism restored)

The founding of the joint-stock Inkombank in 1988 marked the rebirth of private banks in Russia. In contrast to the Tzarist period, the network of banks in post-socialist Russia grew at an exceptionally fast rate. By early 1992, the country had in operation 1,360 private banks, whose number increased by August 1993 to 1,858. By then the total amount of bank assets was roughly equal to the country's GNP.[19]

We find, therefore, that in a very brief period the market-type banking system was re-established in Russia, but its impressive absolute and relative proportions should not create the impression that the Russian banking business has already become similar to bank business in other countries. On the contrary, the new Russian banks are the offspring of the paradoxical economy of the transition period. First, the tempestuous growth of private banks has proceeded despite the grave economic crisis, whose scale exceeds that of the 1929–33 Great Depression. Thus, by March 1994, industrial production in Russia had dropped to 52.9% of the 1990 figure. Second, throughout the period of reform, the banks have been operating with a negative real interest, and the extent of the 'negativity' is colossal. In 1993, for instance, inflation was up to 960%, while the banks issued credit at an average of 250% interest. Third, even the bank interest rates, which are insignificant as compared with the inflation, are found to be excessive by most producers of goods and services.

The ability to make a profit even in such conditions is evidence of the fantastic flexibility of the banks as an economic institution and of their tremendous reserves of viability, which those who live in more favourable countries even find it hard to imagine.

What, then, are the firms to which the new Russian banks provide credit? There are no official statistics on this score. At the end of 1993, however, the journal *Kommersant* printed a poll of the heads of 46 banks and 245 non-banking firms.[20] The bankers were asked this question: 'What kind of operations do you prefer to credit?' The answers were as follows:

Marketing of consumer goods	42%
Foreign trade operations (notably raw material exports)	33%
Real estate operations	17%
Foreign currency operations	14%
Exchange trading and brokerage	13%
Insurance operations	10%

At the same time, the journal sought to find out the percentage of non-banking firms operating in various branches of the economy that regarded short-term and investment banking credits as acceptable:

	Type of credit	
Area of firm activity	Short-term	Investment
Foreign trade in raw materials	70	69
Stocks and real estate	70	40
Business services	54	45
Marketing office equipment	46	8
Consulting	46	46
Other foreign trade	44	44
Exchanges and brokers	43	43
Marketing consumer goods	38	31
Industrial and agricultural production	27	19
Public services	25	17
All industries	56	25

The two lists show that responses from the two groups are well in accord with each other. The new Russian banking system offers credits for all practical purposes only to trading and financial brokerage firms. From the standpoint of their specific market behaviour, most of these firms can be classified as enterprises conducting a customized strategy. These are, as a rule, small firms employing no more than a few dozen people and not in possession of sizeable producer or marketing (distribution) capacities, unusual know-how or scientific or technical projects ready for commercialization. The older ones began their activity at the early stages of the reform in the production sphere, but (as customized firms are wont to do) later sharply changed their tack to take their place in various links of the much more profitable chain of 'export of raw materials – import of consumer goods – their distribution on the domestic market' or in providing services to the firms operating within the framework of the chain.

The prevalence of this type of private firm in the country's economy was undoubtedly promoted by the fact that the bulk of bank resources was put at the disposal of the wholesale, retail and brokerage companies. While I am unable to put a quantitative assessment on the share of banks in the financing of this 'new combination' in the economy, I am still inclined to believe that it is very high, since the private business which developed virtually from scratch had no other external sources of finance except those of the banks. By April 1993, shares and stakes in trading and brokerage firms alone had absorbed bank investment of an amount equivalent to 24% of their total authorized capital, a fact which even caused RF Central Bank's Chairman V. V. Gerashchenko to express concern.[21]

The general economic advantages of the banks' financing the emergent private sector are obvious: in a country which has always suffered from the inadequate development of small and medium-size firms, such firms have at long last put in an appearance. These are now concentrated in the sphere of trade and services, once the most backward and neglected in the socialist economy.

But there is also a reverse side to this medal. A disharmonious community consisting of one type of firm seems once again to be emerging in Russia, and not without the aid of the banks, except that these are no longer volume producers, but customized enterprises.

Indeed, in 1988 and 1989, a great many innovative-type enterprises appeared in the country: scientific and technical co-operatives, so-called youth scientific and technical creativity centres, and so on. That was something of a response on the part of the creative section of the population to the opportunities for realizing one's inventive potential which were offered after decades of the bureaucratic stifling of technical progress. Today, as V. Firsov, a venture-enterprise expert, puts it, 'most of these have given up their innovation activity or have switched to conventional purchase and sale operations'.[22] One of the main reasons for this state of affairs is the lack of financing, 'sources [of which] are simply non-existent inside the country'.

Something similar appears to have happened with volume and niche producers. Volume producers were acutely in need of credit in order to adapt the sluggish and obsolete production potential of giant Soviet enterprises to the requirements of the market, and also to unfurl the lacking marketing network. Niche producers were, in effect, expected only to appear as a result of a conversion of former military enterprises with their fairly good basic data (namely, well-qualified personnel, precision equipment, experience of high-quality small-batch production) in order to become producers of high-quality and/or narrowly specialized products.

In most cases, neither the former nor the latter were able to obtain any investment credits. According to M. Bazhanov, who is the president of the association of private banks acting as investment agents for the government, 'private banks shun investments in long-term projects, especially those connected with industry, even when it is unrealistic to expect to have dividends within three or six months, and when two, three and more years are required'.[23]

It is not surprising that up to three months credits account for 96.3% of all the credits issued by Russian banks.[24] Indeed, the results of the above-mentioned polls testify to the virtual lack of access on the part of industry to bank resources.

So, bank activity in post-socialist Russia has been an important factor in the shaping of the national community of companies. Banks and customized firms operating on marketing and brokerage lines have acquired the features of the two opposite poles of a closed system, in which the growth of either tends to whip up the growth of the other. Let us note that the flourishing of what could be called a tandem takes place against the background of a deep recession in business activity in all the other sectors of the economy.

Nevertheless, with their tremendous impact on the market community of firms, the banks appear to be rather bent to the force of circumstances than conducting an active and conscious policy. The fact is that in the situation which had taken shape by the end of the first decade of the latest reforms in Russia, the banks simply had no option in choosing the firms to support: business in Russia can be successfully conducted nowadays almost exclusively within the framework of the above-mentioned chain of 'export of raw materials – import of consumer goods – their distribution inside the country'. Virtually all the national producers have been deprived of their mass market (to which, in effect, Soviet industry had always been geared) by two powerful shocks: the disintegration of the USSR and the threefold reduction in public income. The third shock – an external economic one – has deprived them of demand on the part of the new higher classes. Let us take a somewhat closer look at this third shock.

The liquidation of the state monopoly of foreign trade has laid bare the total qualitative uncompetitiveness of Russian products compared with foreign products. At the same time, the sharp differentiation of incomes has given shape in the country to a sizeable sector of well-to-do people who can afford to buy high-quality goods. According to official statistics, 10% of the richest people of Russia have at their disposal 30% of all the incomes; what is more, in 1993 the incomes of this social group went up by 32% in constant prices.[25]

Virtually the whole of this sizeable demand was used by the 'nouveaux riches' to buy import products, and that, strictly, speaking, provided the basis for the success of the commercial companies and caused virtually all the customized firms, whatever the sphere in which they began to operate, to switch to marketing. Meanwhile, the lot of the other types of firms proved to be an unenviable one. The goods turned out by the volume producers are not being purchased by the impoverished population because it is short of money, or by the 'nouveaux riches' because such goods are not good enough. Besides, with the most acute underutilization of capacity (only 30–50% of the potential is being used), there has been a sharp growth in fixed costs. Russian volume producers have also lost their price competitiveness (A. Chandler identifies this as the throughput problem of the major producers). Now and again, products turned out in Russia are found to be not just worse, but also more expensive than import products. The inventions of the innovative firms have also lost their market attractiveness against the background of the uninterrupted flow of goods which are new to the consumer in Russia, but which have already been tried and tested in the West. The best specimens of the goods turned out by niche producers can hardly bear comparison with similar goods offered by foreign makers of elite or specialized products.

It stands to reason, therefore, that the banks' option in favour of the customized firms is largely taken under duress: for all practical purposes, the banks have no other equally reliable group of clients, and in this sense the banks have even become somewhat dependent on the commercial firms. Thus, the shrinking requirement in credit following the switch by some commercial firms to non-banking modes of financing their activity (share issue, acceptance of deposits from customers, introduction of debit cards) led in April 1994 to a disastrous decline in the rate of short-term credit (from 180% to 100% per annum) and confronted up to one third of all the Moscow banks with the prospect of bankruptcy.

In contrast with the pre-revolutionary history of the community of companies, the final chapter of the existing community has yet to be written, and so it is somewhat premature to pass judgement on the role of banks in its development. The economic upswing, which is bound to occur sooner or later, will surely make great changes in their activity. There has already been evidence of the first few attempts to establish closer relations with large-scale industry, in particular, the involvement of banks in solving the most acute problems of the liquidity crisis (Tveruniversalbank's payment bill programme).

Final remarks

There is a span of seventy years of socialism between the two episodes from Russian banking history considered in this chapter. That is surely a very long time and, one could say, concerns two different countries, even if located in one and the same place. Nevertheless, at least three features give a common touch to the developments in both cases:

(1) Banks had a notable role to play in realizing the 'new combinations' in the economy. Commenting on this point, one is inevitably amazed at the remarkable productivity of Schumpeter's approach, which enables one to apply it with good effect even to situations greatly differing from those for which it had been formulated.

(2) The banks' behaviour was a rational response to the situation which had taken shape, without the least suggestion of visionarism. The banks promoted the 'new combinations', but what they did was in a sense forced upon them. This observation may be easily interpreted in the spirit of Schumpeter's theory. In the interaction and counteraction of the routinely functioning economy and the Entrepreneur, the latter may rely on bank financing, but the banks themselves, while accepting the incidental risk, remain a part of the routine system (just as insurance companies remain a part of it, while constantly facing risks in their everyday practice). The banks are able to fulfil the role of ephors and to sift the true 'new combinations' from the chaff simply because the banks themselves retain their purely pragmatic approach to such combinations.

(3) The realized 'new combinations' were, without doubt, useful for their participants (including the banks), but not necessarily so for the economy as a whole. In his description of the Entrepreneur, Schumpeter makes the tacit assumption that the Entrepreneur's activity is always useful for the economy. In a more obvious form, Gerschenkron applies the same to the missionary activity of the banks. My own impression is that in both cases we are faced with a definite romanticization of the 'new combinations'. Their realization, unfortunately, does not depend on whether, in the long term, they bring about the progress of the economy or drive it into a dead end, but on how advantageous they are, in current terms, to the direct participants. Real banks do not always accord with the ideal image of the midwives of progress. However, they do help to change our world. And without changes any progress is impossible.

Notes

1 A. Gerschenkron, *Economic Backwardness in Historical Perspective. A Book of Essays* (Cambridge, Mass., 1965), pp. 6–30.

2 A. Gerschenkron, *Europe in the Russian Mirror* (Cambridge, Mass., 1970), pp. 114–17.

3 H. Lindgren, 'Introduction: The Research Agenda and its Intellectual Setting', in P. L. Cottrell, H. Lindgren and A. Teichova (eds.), *European Industry and Banking between the Wars. A Review of Bank–Industry Relations* (Leicester, 1992), pp. 3–5.

4 J. Schumpeter, *The Theory of Economic Development* (Russian edn, Moscow, 1982), pp. 157–69.

5 The following classification of the basic types of firms is my own and, unsurprisingly, I believe it to be the best one. But the line of reasoning would change little even if we used another classification system, say, the one formed by the highly authoritative views of Michael E. Porter. See M. Porter, *Competitive Advantage. Creating and Sustaining Superior Performance* (New York, 1985).

6 A. D. Chandler, Jr, *Scale and Scope. The Dynamics of Industrial Capitalism* (Cambridge, Mass., 1990), p. 35.

7 J. W. Wilson, *The New Venturers. Inside the High-Stakes World of Venture Capital* (Reading, Mass., 1985), p. 8.

8 V. I. Bovykin, *Formirovanie finansovogo kapitala v Rossii, konets xix v.- 1908g.* (Moscow, 1984), pp. 108–9.

9 I. F. Gindin, *Russkie kommercheskie banki. Iz istorii finansovogo kapitala v Rossii* (Moscow, 1948), p. 301.

10 *Ibid.*, p. 303.

11 *Ibid.*, pp. 341–2.

12 *Bol'shaya sovetskaya entsiklopediya*, vol. IV (Moscow, 1950), p. 195.

13 I. Vanag, *Finansovyi kapital v Rossii nakanune morovoi voiny* (Moscow, 1925), p. 40.

14 Bovykin, *Formirovanie finansovogo kapitala v Rossii*, p. 163.

15 Gindin, *Russkie kommercheskie banki*, pp. 330, 341.

16 I. M. Goldstein, *Blagopriyatna li russkaya deistvitel'nost' dlya obrazovaniya sindikatov i trestov?* (Moscow, 1913), p. 38.

17 A. Teichova, 'Rivals and Partners: Reflections on Banking and Industry in Europe, 1880–1938', in Cottrell, Lindgren and Teichova, *European Industry and Banking*, pp. 20–6.

18 Cited in Gindin, *Russkie kommercheskie banki*, pp. 297–8.

19 *Biznes, banki, birzha*, no. 1 (1994), p. 5; *Kommersant*, no. 39 (1993), p. 14.

20 *Kommersant*, no. 39 (1995), pp. 13–14.

21 V. V. Gerashchenko, 'Tekushche zadachi denezhno-kreditnoi politiki i tendentsii razvitiya bankovskoi sistemy', *Den'gi i kredit*, no. 7 (1993), p. 18.

22 V. Firsov, 'Perspektivi razvitiya venchurnogo predprinimatel'stva v Rossii', *Joint Ventures*, no. 11 (1993), p. 9.

23 N. Bazhanov, 'Kak stat' partnerom prezidenta. MTsPF provodit konkurs investerov', *Joint Ventures*, no. 2 (1994), p. 26.

24 *Biznes, banki, birzha*, no. 1 (1994), p. 5.

25 *Nezavisimaya gazeta*, 3 Feb. 1994.

PART FOUR

The expansion of banking in the American and Asian economies

17 Banking in North America, 1700–1900

Larry Schweikart

Banking in North America followed from the processes of gold extraction by the Spanish in the south and from the financing of military expeditions by the English and French colonists in the north. Spain, which practised mercantilism long before Thomas Mun elaborated the theory in 1607, followed a policy of extracting gold from mines in the New World for shipment back to Spain, there to be coined or formed into bullion. Although the mines provided substantial amounts of ore in Mexico – before 1550 more than 5 million pesos in gold was exported legally from Mexico – the mined ore proved unsuitable for the small amounts of commerce in the New World, and even local military outposts there required money in the form of coin. Spanish merchants conducted business on the basis of consignment with Mexican merchants, with exchange and interest paid in reales. Later, Spain established credit institutions in the New World, such as the Banco del Monte de Piedad (1774). Yet, as one authority on banking in Latin America concluded, 'most credit activities . . . were handled by persons and institutions which, although not banks in the strict sense of the word, engaged in banking operations in professional ways'.[1]

English and French colonies lacked the gold enjoyed by Spanish outposts. They had to rely on coin shipped from England or, ultimately, on other forms of money, including the first official paper in Canada made out of playing cards. A wide variety of coins circulated, with the Spanish milled dollar always treasured. In America, colonial

legislatures, empowered to print money to meet the needs of government, issued their first bills, or forms of paper money, in the late 1600s
to finance military expeditions against the French. Banks, however, did
not appear until the mid-1700s, and then only in the form of land banks,
wherein borrowers offered land as collateral for bills of credit. The
colonies also had permitted their governments to issue notes, mostly to
pay for military expeditions, and as early as 1761 Nova Scotia issued
treasury notes to finance its expenditures.[2] Concerned about the
liberties afforded by such financial authority, the British government
attempted to rescind the privileges of the colonies in 1751 and 1764
by prohibiting further issue of bills of credit and by restricting colonial
note issue. Restrictions on paper money in the specie-scarce colonies
provided one of several economic irritations that contributed to the
American Revolution.

Still, anything resembling commercial banking did not exist. A few
individuals loaned money or converted notes at a profit, and, as
Benjamin Klebaner observed, ' "Crackerbarrel" bankers served many
communities before incorporated banks appeared.'[3] Not until January
1782 in Philadelphia did the first chartered financial institution appear
in North America when the Continental Congress granted a perpetual
charter to the Bank of North America, organized by Robert Morris, a
merchant who had spent much of his own fortune already supporting
the war effort.[4] Intended mainly as a means of supporting the credit
of the young nation, the bank issued paper money convertible into
gold and silver (specie). Within two years, other banks opened in
Massachusetts and New York. Morris had played a role in organizing a
previous institution, the Pennsylvania Bank, which was created for the
sole purpose of supplying money for George Washington's troops in
the field, but it made no commercial loans. The Bank of North America
prospered after the war, although Morris personally did not, dying in a
debtors' prison in 1806.[5]

By 1800, then, more than thirty commercial banks conducted
business in the United States.[6] But the most important institution
chartered during that period appeared in 1791 when the Congress of
the United States, acting on the advice of Alexander Hamilton,
chartered the First Bank of the United States (BUS). Hamilton, a
foreign-born visionary who determined that the most significant
challenge to the young country would be its ability to pay its wartime
debts, sought to tie the business interests of the nation to the political
structure.[7] He devised a plan whereby the national government would

assume all of the debts of the states and pay them with the proceeds from import tariffs. The bank would provide loans, and, with many of its stockholders from England and France, would bring foreign capital to the young nation immediately. The BUS proved divisive – Thomas Jefferson hated it – and was founded on what (at the time) was considered dubious Constitutional authority, namely the 'necessary and proper' clause. Indeed, considerable evidence suggests that Hamilton concluded that a legislative body could not be trusted with debt, and he thus intended to insulate the nation's financial policy from budgetary squabbles through a number of measures, including the BUS. Hamilton also devised a way to make the finances of the nation independent of annual appropriations from Congress through the use of a sinking fund, which essentially required the country to pay off old debt before assuming new.

But Hamilton was not alone in perceiving the necessity for a sound currency: his rival Thomas Jefferson agreed with the New Yorker about the use of the Spanish dollar as the currency standard as a means of preventing Congress from devaluing the money. (Congress, it should be noted, had the authority to 'coin' money and regulate its value, which virtually everyone at the time interpreted as meaning the minting of gold or silver coin and the establishment of a weight value for a dollar's worth of each metal.)[8] Hamilton and Jefferson also departed from the Spanish practice of making all divisions into eights, instead favouring the more convenient fractions of tenths. Regardless of the division, there was not much money: Hamilton estimated that on the eve of the Revolution the nation's money stock of specie and paper money totalled about 30 million Spanish dollars.

However, the most controversial aspect of Hamilton's proposal, a national bank, did not receive Jefferson's blessing. Hamilton expected that the BUS would facilitate the financial flows from the tariffs and would act as a depository for the nation's funds. It served its primary function of lender, however, by disbursing approximately $13 million to the federal government. Only the fact that a large amount of its stock remained in foreign hands troubled most early Americans. The real source of the bank's power, its interstate branch banking authority, did not seem to disturb most observers, although a few statements of concern can be found.[9]

Banking growth in the United States accelerated after 1790, with the capital stock of chartered banks increasing from $3 million to $168 million by 1830.[10] During the first two decades of the 1800s alone, banks multiplied by a factor of twelve, with growth particularly strong in New England, where it grew at a rate of 20% annually. As an increasing number of entrepreneurs pestered state legislatures for charters – with the exception of the federal government and the BUS the only source to obtain a charter – political favouritism in dispensing charters and the sheer number of charters started to overwhelm the state legislatures. At the time, a charter implied special privileges, including (to some) monopoly privileges. Charters endowed banks with exceptional powers and tremendous respectability, giving a bank the blessing of the state and the authority to issue notes backed by specie. Of course, private banks operating without charters printed notes, as did railroad companies and cities, but with only a few exceptions those notes did not maintain their value as well as the notes of chartered banks.[11]

Bankers entered the business often after displaying competence as merchants, blurring the lines between borrower and lender. Nevertheless, whether they issued their own notes or not, financial intermediaries played a key role in supplying credit to antebellum American industrial and commercial development.[12]

The concerns about special privilege were directed more at the First BUS than the state banks, and as a result it was not rechartered in 1811. But quickly the federal government found that it needed a place to lodge its debt: during the War of 1812 the US government tripled its debt by issuing short-term, interest bearing treasury notes that had most of the characteristics of government paper money. In addition, the number of state-chartered banks increased and prices rose to all-time highs. Circulation of bank notes expanded by 50% since the demise of the BUS, and a series of bank runs in 1814 led to calls for some mechanism of control over the bank note issues. Congress thus acted on legislation for a Second BUS, designed in part by Secretary of the Treasury Alexander Dallas and influenced in its role by the powerful Philadelphia financier Stephen Girard. Like the First BUS, four-fifths of the stock of the Second BUS was owned by private individuals (again, many of them, eventually, were foreigners) and it could maintain branches in many states. Headquartered on Chestnut Street in Philadelphia, it had a twenty-year charter and a capitalization of $35 million.[13]

While in sheer size it was a formidable competitor, its true financial muscle came from its interstate branches and its faithfulness in redeeming its own notes, which circulated throughout the nation as an easily recognizable – though certainly not 'national' – currency. It was not accurate that BUS notes maintained par value, for there was a redemption charge on notes from distant branches, just as banks in remote areas would have a discount on their notes. But the BUS started to enforce stability by policing the notes of state banks by presenting them for specie redemption in 'raids', which forced the state bankers to maintain slightly higher specie reserves than they otherwise might have.

An economic downturn in 1819 resulted in a panic, and the BUS, led by South Carolinian Langdon Cheves, tightened credit.[14] The bank received harsh criticism that never entirely dissipated until the Jackson era, when the effort to recharter the bank failed. Nevertheless, the BUS survived a crucial test that later affected all banking in the *McCulloch* v. *Maryland* case (1819) in which Chief Justice John Marshall reiterated Hamilton's reasoning that the 'necessary and proper' clause of the Constitution permitted Congress to charter a bank, ruling the BUS Constitutional, and also prohibiting Maryland from taxing the bank as a federal institution. Cheves only remained president until 1823, when Philadelphian Nicholas Biddle assumed the reins of power.[15] Under Biddle, the BUS proved adept at maintaining stable notes, and its loans facilitated government transactions. Whether the BUS contributed as much to American commercial and economic growth as some suggest remains in question. More than a few studies have shown the BUS to have relatively little impact on the US economy, and certainly it did not attain the status of a 'central bank' if one defines such a bank as a 'lender of last resort', a 'bankers' bank', or a national guarantor of bank note values.[16]

Other than the Great Depression, few events in American financial history have so captured the imaginations of the public and scholars as Andrew Jackson's 'War' on the BUS and the Panic of 1837 that followed. Although most research now suggests that the two events were only tangentially related – and certainly the first did not cause the second – nevertheless, the Bank War went to the heart of debates in the United States about the proper role of banking in economic growth.[17] It also raised again issues of the proper relationship of the state in the economy.

Ultimately, the regulation of virtually all banking rested with the state governments and their powers to issue charters.[18] The founders of banks intended their institutions to provide a source of loans to themselves and their friends – usually directors in the banks – for commercial activities. 'Insider lending' was not only not illegal, it was the precise purpose many early banks were chartered.[19] Those charters frequently included monopoly or quasi-monopoly powers for the banks, and thus were open to charges of partisanship and privilege – fighting words in Jackson's day. So, as the more traditional interpretations went, Jackson destroyed the BUS to strike at the bank's privileged position as the only bank in the nation with a federal charter; the only bank with interstate branch banking powers; and the accessibility to the government, through the bank, by foreign stockholders in the bank.[20]

When Jackson killed the BUS, it unleashed a torrent of notes from the state banks, often operating in the thinly populated areas of the frontier 'where a wildcat wouldn't go', hence obtaining the name 'wildcat banks'. Often, the appearance of the wildcat banks coincided with the emerging free banking laws that allowed banks to incorporate under general incorporation laws by placing bonds as security on deposit with the secretary of state. Without the BUS to restrain them, the chartered banks and, later, the free banks inflated their note issue.[21] Other actions by Jackson, including his Specie Circular and the redistribution of the surplus, supposedly shocked the financial system, provoking the Panic of 1837. Peter Temin, among others, has offered a cogent and persuasive explanation that places the responsibility for the Panic in the sudden end to Mexican silver flows through the US to England that resulted in sharply rising interest rates.

For the students interested in the political developments, however, the result of the Bank War – which the traditional historians had concluded was to *reduce* federal power under the hands of a 'states' rights' Jacksonian Democratic Party – in fact was to *increase* dramatically the power of the federal government at the expense of business, and to increase substantially the power of the presidency over the other branches of government. A useful test of which theory is more accurate can be found in those state governments where the Jacksonians held a consistent, substantial and often overwhelming majority. How did those states handle banking?

Most of those states were located in the American South, and five of them in particular saw the Jacksonians in control – often as virtually a monopoly party – with little opposition. Out of the five states (Tennessee, Mississippi, Alabama, Arkansas and the territory/later state of Florida) the Jacksonian state governments practised anything *but* laissez faire, and the Democratic Party utilized the state government to set up monopoly state banks in two of the five. In two others (Mississippi and Florida) the Jacksonian-dominated government used the state's authority to back the bonds of private banks that they wanted to create.

Only in Tennessee, which had more Whigs in it for a longer period than the others, were the Jacksonian forces restrained, and except for Tennessee, the banking systems of all those states collapsed during the Panic of 1837. Arkansas and Alabama saw their state monopoly banks go broke, with Arkansas, in a temper tantrum of sorts, *banning* banks from the state.[22] More important for an interpretation of the Jacksonians' federal intentions, Jackson himself had proposed a national bank in 1829, and, as David Martin shows, the Jacksonians had a detailed plan for nationalizing the currency under a gold coin standard.[23]

The immediate effect of the destruction of the BUS was a significant expansion in the number of banks, both state-chartered and 'free banks', in the United States. Thus, the 'Jacksonian Era' witnessed a growth in the US economy, sandwiched around the Panic of 1837, which featured the establishment of a state-chartered banking system supplemented by a number of free banks. In most states, unit banking laws prevailed, and only did several Southern states permit branch banking. The North experimented with a variety of insurance schemes or other attempts to diminish the effects of financial instability, the most important of which was the Suffolk System, which commanded a regional network of banks. Started in 1824, the Suffolk Bank System provided a way to hold and clear drafts or notes drawn on 'country banks'.[24] Those banks maintained permanent specie deposits with the Suffolk Bank over and above the amount needed to redeem any of their notes at par. The country bank notes achieved stability through swift and reliable note redemption. Dissenting bankers eventually created a rival that put Suffolk out of business, and whether it had the impact proponents have suggested remains a matter of debate.[25] One effect of the numerous attempts to insulate the Northern banks from instability was that the more inferior unit banking remained the norm in that region.

Canada also had a surge of banks beginning in 1820 when the Bank of New Brunswick received royal permission for a charter, and four more banks received charters the following year. Although Canada never faced the constitutional dilemmas raised by the First and Second Banks of the United States, it did experience problems with note issue by private banks, including note issuing unchartered banks. It also experimented with 'free' banking under legislation introduced in the Province of Canada in 1850, which permitted a bank to begin operations after depositing securities with the Receiver General. Those laws did not allow enough profit margin, and only unit banks could be established, and, therefore, according to one financial history of Canada, 'the system did not work and soon was inoperative'.[26] Canada did maintain a strong tradition of branch banking, and by 1867 the system had 33 chartered banks with more than 120 branches, accounting for 78% of the assets of all the nation's financial intermediaries.[27]

Unlike the United States, however, the Canadian government maintained a strong external influence on the banking system since its inception. Canadian banks were subject to government inspections, with the government requiring banks to submit statements twice a year. Charters, compared to those of many states in the US, contained significant restrictions. But even with government 'oversight' and with branching privileges, Canadian banking experienced a few insolvencies, nor did 'the banking system enjoy unqualified public confidence'.[28] Still, banking in Canada never became the national issue that it did in the United States under Jackson and, later, the Republicans in the Civil War.

American commercial banks continued to increase in number after the early 1840s, with the South growing proportionately faster than the North in numbers of banks and expanding almost as fast. Largely due to branch banking, which proved effective at transmitting information about instability more quickly than the unit bank system in the North, the Southern system scarcely felt the Panic of 1857.[29] Expansion during the 1850s marked the high tide of branching in the nineteenth-century United States, for after the Civil War and the destruction of the Southern system, the unit bank-dominated North remained in almost total control of the American financial system and the investment banking houses of Wall Street witnessed a dramatic expansion of their power.

Wall Street's emergence probably would have occurred without the war. But when the Confederacy required Southern banks to surrender their specie in return for Confederate bonds, it tied the banking system in the South to only one possible outcome, victory. Those bonds proved worthless after the South lost, and the financial system in the one region of the country where branch banking had matured no longer existed.[30] The war, however, had just the opposite effect on the North, allowing the newly created national banks to issue notes and to achieve instant stability to name recognition through the national bank notes.[31] When combined with the phenomenal explosion of securities issues made possible by the federal government's wartime financing, and, after the war, by the government subsidized railroads, investment banking grew into an equal to commercial banking in the financial community. No longer were the bond brokers and deal makers looked down upon; instead, men such as J. P. Morgan and Jay Cooke singlehandedly amassed millions of dollars for projects within short periods of time that previously would have been considered impossible.[32] Morgan, of course, took the opportunity when putting together the financing for such projects to reorganize management into managerial hierarchies, thus forcing railroads and other big businesses to adopt a more efficient management structure.[33]

When the new investment banking houses combined their ability to float securities with the national bank system (created 1863), which required members to hold US securities as a reserve against note issues, a national money market started to develop. At the same time, state bank note issues had been driven out of circulation by a 10% tax placed on non-national bank notes in 1864. To finance the war, the Union government printed a new note issue called 'greenbacks', which were not redeemable in gold immediately but were to be redeemed in the future. A series of subsequent court cases upheld the government's position that the greenbacks were 'legal tender for all debts public and private'. Essentially, then, through the 10% tax government nationalized the money supply during the Civil War, and had made its money legal tender. It represented a monumental shift away from market-oriented competitive money that had existed in the antebellum period. To retire the greenbacks and redeem them in gold required that the government not issue any new greenbacks while it increased its gold supply. In 1879, the government made good on its promise to pay gold for the greenbacks. By that time the nation was in the throes of a significant deflation.

International forces, not government policy, however, caused that deflation.[34] Many Americans, particularly the Populists, blamed the banks and the Eastern (usually Jewish, in their minds) 'Money Power', although they almost never blamed local bankers for instability.[35] The Populists and other groups made considerable noise advocating both reissue of greenbacks and 'free and unlimited coinage of silver at 16:1', both of which represented inflationary policies. Although banks really had little to do with the silver issue, they were villified. Bankers were associated with the gold standard and, for the most part, the Republican Party. Inflationists wanted an easily expanded money supply, and they suspected that the banks had conspired to keep down the money supply.[36]

Naturally, much of the criticism came from the West, where, compared to the North, fewer banks existed or the banks that existed had smaller capitalizations. The West, on the other hand, had an abundance of silver that the Populists thought would remain in their regions to expand the currency. In short, they wanted a rent – a tax-payer subsidy to silver producers that would provide inflation.[37] That movement climaxed in 1896 when William Jennings Bryan, following his passionate 'Cross of Gold' speech, won the Democratic nomination for president and subsequently suffered defeat at the hands of William McKinley, a 'gold standard man'.[38]

While the Civil War centralized the money-creation power in the hands of the federal government, it did not centralize banking (perhaps to the surprise of the framers of the National Bank Act). National bank charters rose relative to state charters at first, but gradually state charters started to exceed in number federal charters, and by 1900 state-chartered banks totalled 9,322, while national banks numbered 3,731.[39] States could offer inducements for banks to incorporate with a state charter, such as lower capital restrictions and no restrictions on branching or mortgage lending, although many states indeed did prohibit branching. Where unit banks established themselves, such as in the American Northeast and Midwest, there was little anyone could do by way of reason, statistics or promises of banking stability to convince the legislators to remove the prohibitions.[40] Where branching took root in the West, as in California and Arizona, for example, it did so before the unit banks could mount organized opposition in the legislature and was presented as a *fait d'accompli*.[41]

At the very time the United States deliberately ignored branch banking, Canada, after Confederation, concentrated its system and increased the number of branches held by its banks.[42] From 1868 to 1890 the number of branches rose from 123 to 426, then almost doubled again by 1900.[43] In part, the Canadian government had permitted greater concentration as a means to strengthen confidence in the banks, and that concentration accelerated between 1890 and 1920.[44]

Ironically, just as Canada was undergoing a concentration of banking assets, and just as the United States had prohibited private note issue by banks, Mexico's banking system emerged with an expansion of individual banks that had note issue powers.[45] Although legislation enacted in 1897 placed limitations on banks through reserve requirements and classified banks as banks of issue (commercial banks), mortgage banks or intermediate-term credit banks, Mexico's bimetallic system worked against its terms of trade, and several financial crises struck the country, the most serious in 1907. After the 1917 constitution gave the Mexican government the monopoly power to issue money, it established the Banco de Mexico in 1925.

Whether in the United States, Canada or Mexico, banks' first obligations had been to extend credit to the agricultural and mercantile economy. To lump the three systems together in other ways, however, would be an exercise in futility, comparing systems with branching, strong central government oversight but no note issue privileges (Canada) to a system of unit banking, weaker central government control and no note issue privileges (the US) to one with note issue privileges and little government oversight (Mexico). Moreover, each system in the nineteenth century was interwoven into the international economy, tied together by the threads of the gold standard, and still bound in important ways to fluctuations in Great Britain's interest rates. Until the First World War, London remained the financial capital of the world, and to that extent it is worth noting that money flowed freely into the United States, where central government interference prior to 1913 remained light. Differences in the degree of development of each economy also dramatically shaped the banking systems, with Canada maintaining a much closer relationship to England than the United States did, and Mexico still tied in many ways to the old European economies.

Neither problems with private note issue experienced by Mexico later in the nineteenth century nor those of the United States in the antebellum period really made much of a case against private note issue or competitive money. Rather, the natural tendencies of governments to aggrandize power unto themselves goes much further toward explaining the trends in abolishing note issue by private banks in the United States and Mexico. Nor did the 'inelasticity' problems in the US necessarily require the massive centralization of the system under the Federal Reserve System in 1913. Indeed, the Panic of 1857 has been shown to have been associated with developments related to slavery in the western territories, while the Panic of 1893 had much to do with the weakness of the banking system caused by the Populists' demand for 'free silver', resulting in the Sherman Silver Purchase Act and the drain of gold out of the US.[46]

A few general conclusions about the development of banking in North America, however, can be drawn. The structure of a nation's banking system had as much to do with political necessity – creating a national bank to extend loans to an infant nation, for example – or pure partisan politics – Jackson's destruction of the Second BUS – as with sound economics. Branching, a much more desirable structure than unit banking, failed to develop in many parts of the US due to vested interests that managed to gain control of the chartering process in the decentralized early state governments. Where branching did take root – in the American South – it died with the rest of the Southern system after the Civil War.

Second, calls for reform often involve perceptions that 'outsiders' were controlling the capital flows. That proved the case with the Jacksonians, the Populists and, to some extent, the western Canadian provinces. Nevertheless, reform movements often had to face the reality that monied interests in other countries or regions were the only ones willing or capable of supplying capital – witness the fact that the French started the first real bank in Mexico, or that agrarians in the American Midwest did not ever blame their own local banks for money shortages, even though on occasion they had more to do with local conditions than Wall Street.

Finally, the temptation for bankers to join with government to 'reform' a banking system, while understandable under some circumstances, almost always left the public with fewer options in money or banking institutions and tended to concentrate power in the hands of the national or state government. Reform by emotion, which characterized the American industrial reform movement of the late nineteenth century, frequently only cartelized industries and reduced consumer choice. It also, ultimately, reduced the authority of the state governments in such matters as banking.

Ironically, in the last twenty years we have moved in some ways back to a competitive money and banking system that existed in antebellum times, thanks to the computer. Money flows instantly across national and state boundaries, ignoring pleas from politicians to halt, responding only to market forces. Although you cannot spend a franc in an American MacDonalds, you can convert it virtually instantly at any bank, at the rate given that instant. More important, the grip of governments over their citizens via the local bank has eroded. To paraphrase Walter Wriston of Citibank, 'Money goes where it is wanted, and will not stay where it is not.' In a 1988 issue of *Foreign*

Affairs, Wriston maintained that 'the entire globe is linked electronically, with no place to hide', with the resulting effect of that technology on government fiscal and monetary policies 'more draconian than the gold exchange standard and a great deal faster.'[47] No doubt that makes the Secretary of the Treasury sleep all the better as an administration plans its latest financial follies!

Notes

1 Frank Tamagna, *Central Banking in Latin America* (n.p. [Mexico City?], 1965), p. 37. See also Mark Burkholder and Lyman L. Johnson, *Colonial Latin America* (New York, 1990), pp. 126–8 and *passim*.

2 E. P. Neufeld, *The Financial System of Canada, its Growth and Development* (New York, 1972), p. 37.

3 Benjamin Klebaner, *American Commercial Banking: A History* (Boston, 1990), p. 4.

4 An overview of banking historiography appears in Larry Schweikart, 'American Commercial Banking: A Bibliographic Survey', *Business History Review*, 66 (1992), pp. 606–61.

5 On Morris, see Clarence L. Ver Steeg, *Robert Morris, Revolutionary Financier, with an Analysis of his Career* (Philadelphia, 1954), and the excellent capsule biography by B. F. Burg, 'Robert Morris', in Larry Schweikart (ed.), *Encyclopedia of American Business History and Biography: Banking and Finance to 1913* (New York, 1990), pp. 351–64.5.5.

6 Klebaner, *American Commercial Banking*, pp. 6–9, provides a useful summary of the banks chartered prior to 1800.

7 Material on Hamilton appears in Forrest McDonald, *Alexander Hamilton: A Biography* (New York, 1979); Broadus Mitchell, *Alexander Hamilton: A Concise Biography* (New York, 1976); and Richard B. Morris, *Witnesses at the Creation: Hamilton, Madison, Jay, and the Constitution* (New York, 1985). Hamilton's genius in the sinking fund is explored in Charles W. Calomiris, 'Alexander Hamilton', in Schweikart, *Encyclopedia of American Business History and Biography: Banking and Finance to 1913*, pp. 239–48. On Revolutionary finances, see E. James Ferguson, *The Power of the Purse: A History of American Public Finance, 1776–1790* (Chapel Hill, 1961), as well as a series of debates about colonial note issues found in Calomiris, 'Alexander Hamilton'.

8 Money in early America is discussed in John J. McCusker and Russell R. Menard, *The Economy of British America, 1607–1789* (Chapel Hill, 1985), pp. 334–7. See also Richard Timberlake, Jr, 'Denominational Factors in Nineteenth-Century Currency Experience', *Journal of Economic History*, 34 (1974), pp. 835–50.

9 Bray Hammond, *Banks and Politics in America from the Revolution to the Civil War* (Princeton, 1957); John Thom Holdsworth, *The First Bank of the United States* (Washington, DC, 1910); and Richard H. Timberlake, Jr, *The Origins of Central Banking in the United States* (Cambridge, Mass., 1978).

10 J. Van Fenstermaker, *The Development of American Commercial Banking: 1782–1837* (Kent, Ohio, 1965), and his 'The Statistics of American Commercial Banking, 1782–1818', *Journal of Economic History*, 45 (1985), pp. 400–13.

11 See, for example, Larry Schweikart, *Banking in the American South from the Age of Jackson*

to Reconstruction (Baton Rouge, 1987); W. K. Wood, 'The Georgia Railroad and Banking Company', *Georgia Historical Quarterly*, 57 (1973), pp. 544–61; Harold Livesay and Glenn Porter, 'The Financial Role of Merchants in the Development of U.S. Manufacturing, 1815–1860', *Explorations in Economic History*, 9 (1971), pp. 63–87; Richard Sylla, 'Forgotten Men of Money: Private Bankers in Early U.S. History', *Journal of Economic History*, 36 (1976), pp. 173–88; and Hugh Rockoff, 'Varieties of Banking and Regional Economic Development in the United States, 1840–1860', *Journal of Economic History*, 35 (1975), pp. 174–6, 179–81.

12 Some of the various ways bankers contributed to the economy are explored in Rockoff, 'Varieties of Banking and Regional Economic Development', pp. 160–81; John Haeger, *The Investment Frontier: New York Businessmen and the Economic Development of the Old Northwest* (Albany, N.Y.: 1981); Harry Stevens, 'Bank Enterprises in a Western Town, 1801–1822', *Business History Review*, 29 (1955), pp. 139–56.

13 Holdsworth, *The First Bank of the United States*; James O. Wettereau, 'New Light on the First Bank of the United States', *Pennsylvania Magazine of History and Biography* (July 1937), pp. 236–85; and Jeffrey Rogers Hummel, 'The First Bank of the United States', in Schweikart, *Encyclopedia of American Business History and Biography: Banking and Finance to 1913*, pp. 181–3.

14 Edwin Perkins contests the generally held view that Cheves was an exceptional president of the BUS. See his 'Langdon Cheves and the Panic of 1819: A Reassessment', *Journal of Economic History*, 43 (1983), pp. 455–61. See also Murry Rothbard, *The Panic of 1819: Reactions and Policies* (New York, 1962).

15 Thomas Govan, *Nicholas Biddle: Nationalist and Public Banker, 1786–1844* (Chicago: University of Chicago Press, 1959); Ralph Catterall, *The Second Bank of the United States* (Chicago: University of Chicago Press, 1903); and Walter B. Smith, *Economic Aspects of the Second Bank of the United States* (Cambridge, Mass., 1953).

16 Economists and historians long have debated the scope of the BUS's power to influence the economy. Both Hammond and Arthur Schlesinger, Jr, (*The Age of Jackson* (Boston, 1945)) ascribed to the view that the BUS carried out 'central banking' activities, defined as maintaining the value of money through its redemption of state bank notes. Hugh Rockoff, 'Money, Prices, and Banks in the Jacksonian Era', in Robert Fogel and Stanley Engerman (eds.), *The Reinterpretation of American Economic History* (New York, 1971), Peter Temin, *The Jacksonian Economy* (New York, 1969), and Timberlake, *Origins of Central Banking*, challenge the notion that the BUS could have affected prices or the money supply very much. Robert V. Remini, *Andrew Jackson and the Bank War: A Study in the Growth of Presidential Power* (New York, 1967), accepted the first view, although later revisions of his multi- and single-volume biographies of Andrew Jackson suggest that he now no longer holds the Hammond/Schlesinger view and comes closer to accepting the Temin interpretation.

17 The authors mentioned in the note above all emphasized the bank's economic power, but several of them also analysed the political economy of the bank war. Hammond, for example, saw the destruction of a 'central' bank as deplorable, freeing the 'wildcat' banks to issue notes freely, while Schlesinger interpreted the destruction of the BUS as freeing a rising class of entrepreneurs, with Jackson using government power to help the less privileged. A more recent crop of historians and economists have looked upon the Jacksonians in a less favourable light, including John McFaul, *The Politics of Jacksonian Finance* (Ithaca, 1972); James Roger Sharp, *The Jacksonians versus the Banks* (New York, 1970); David Martin, 'Metallism, Small Notes,

and Jackson's War with the B.U.S.', *Explorations in Economic History*, 11 (1974), pp. 227–47; and Larry Schweikart, 'Jacksonian Ideology, Currency Control, and "Central" Banking: A Reappraisal', *The Historian*, 51 (1988), pp. 78–102.

18 Carter Golembe, *State Banks and the Economic Development of the West, 1830–1844* (New York, 1978).

19 Naomi Lamoreaux, 'Banks, Kinship and Economic Development: The New England Case', *Journal of Economic History*, 46 (1986), pp. 647–67, and her article with Christopher Glaisek, 'Vehicles of Privilege or Mobility? Banks in Providence, Rhode Island, during the Age of Jackson', *Business History Review*, 65 (1991), pp. 502–27; Larry Schweikart, 'Antebellum Southern Bankers: Origins and Mobility', in Jeremy Atack (ed.), *Business and Economic History* (Urbana, 1985), second series, pp. 79-103, and his 'Entrepreneurial Aspects of Antebellum Banking', in C. Joseph Pusateri and Henry Dethloff (eds.), *American Business History: Case Studies* (New York, 1987), pp. 122–39. Both those authors examined the antebellum period, but the trends still existed in the postbellum period. See Lynne Pierson Doti and Larry Schweikart, *Banking in the American West from the Gold Rush to Deregulation* (Norman, 1991).

20 A good elaboration of this point appears in Remini, *Andrew Jackson and the Bank War*, *passim*. See also Edwin Perkins, 'Lost Opportunities for Compromise in the Bank War: A Reassessment of Jackson's Veto Message', *Business History Review*, 61 (1987), pp. 531–50.

21 Literature on 'free banking' includes Hugh Rockoff, *The Free Banking Era: A Reexamination* (New York, 1975); Arthur Rolnick and Warren Weber, 'Free Banking, Wildcat Banking, and Shinplasters', *Federal Reserve Bank of Minneapolis Quarterly Review*, 5 (1982), pp. 10–19; *idem* and *idem*, 'Banking Instability and Regulation in the U.S. Free Banking Era', *ibid.*, 8 (1985), pp. 2–9; *idem* and *idem*, 'Inherent Instability in Banking: The Free Banking Experience', *CATO Journal*, 6 (1986), pp. 877–90; *idem* and *idem*, 'New Evidence on the Free Banking Era', *American Economic Review*, 76 (1983), pp. 1080–91; *idem* and *idem*, 'Explaining the Demand for Free Bank Notes', *Journal of Monetary Economics*, 21 (1988), pp. 47–71; *idem* and *idem*, 'The Causes of Free Bank Failures', *Journal of Monetary Economics*, 17 (1984), pp. 267–911; and Kenneth Ng, 'Free Banking Laws and Barriers to Entry in Banking, 1838–1860', *Journal of Economic History*, 48 (1988), pp. 877–90. Other refinements of the Rolnick/Weber position have done little to shake the conclusion that unregulated banking had no inherent instabilities. See Andrew Economopolous, 'Free Bank Failures in New York and Wisconsin: A Portfolio Analysis', *Explorations in Economic History*, 27 (1990), pp. 421–41; *idem*, 'The Free Banking Period: A Period of Deregulation?', *New York Economic Review*, 17 (1987), pp. 24–31; *idem* and *idem*, 'The Impact of Reserve Requirements on Free Bank Failures', *Atlantic Economic Journal*, 14 (1986), pp. 76–84; *idem* and *idem*, 'Illinois Free Banking Experience', *Journal of Money, Credit, and Banking*, 20 (1988), pp. 249–64. Also see Iftekhar Hasan and Gerald Dwyer, Jr, 'Bank Runs in the Free Banking Period', *Journal of Money, Credit, and Banking*, 26 (1994), pp. 271–88.

22 These events are recounted in Schweikart, *Banking in the American South*, *passim*, and his 'Jacksonian Ideology'.

23 See Martin, 'Metallism', and Schweikart, *Banking in the American South*, as well as McFaul, *Politics of Jacksonian Finance*, and Sharp, *Jacksonians versus the Banks*, for support of this interpretation. Schweikart, in 'How the Jacksonians Opposed Industrialization', *Reason Papers* (April 1987), develops this article further. An opposing viewpoint – that the Jacksonians were anti-state – appears in Jeffrey

Rogers Hummel, 'The Jacksonians, Banking, and Economic Theory: A Reinterpretation', *Journal of Libertarian Studies*, 2 (1978), although subsequent publications by Hummel and correspondence from Hummel to this author suggests that he has modified his position. Remini, in *Andrew Jackson and the Bank War*, concludes that Jackson *supported* states' rights through his victory over the BUS, even though it came at the expense of state authority and the other branches of government.

24 See Fritz Redlich, *Moulding of American Banking: Men and Ideas*, 2 vols. (New York, 1968); Wilfred Lake, 'The End of The Suffolk System', *Journal of Economic History*, 7 (1947), pp. 183–207; Donald Mullineaux, 'Competitive Monies and the Suffolk Bank System: A Contractual Perspective', *Southern Economic Journal*, 53 (1987), pp. 884–97.

25 J. Van Fenstermaker and John Filer, 'Impact of the First and Second Bank of the United States and the Suffolk System on New England Money, 1791–1837', *Journal of Money, Credit, and Banking*, 18 (1986), pp. 28–40, found that the Suffolk System had no effect on the expansion of the money supply. Charles Calomiris and Charles Kahn, 'The Role of Demandable Debt in Structuring Optimal Banking Arrangements', *American Economic Review*, 81 (1991), pp. 497–513, suggest it did play a role.

26 Neufeld, *Financial System of Canada*, p. 40; R. Craig McIvor, *Canadian Monetary, Banking and Fiscal Development* (Toronto, 1958).

27 Neufeld, *Financial System of Canada*, p. 43.

28 *Ibid.*, p. 89.

29 On the Panic of 1857, see Charles W. Calomiris and Larry Schweikart, 'The Panic of 1857: Causes, Transmission, and Containment', *Journal of Economic History*, 50 (1990), pp. 807–34, compared with Peter Temin, 'The Panic of 1857', *Intermountain Economic Review*, 6 (1975), pp. 1–12, and James Huston, *The Panic of 1857 and the Coming of the Civil War* (Baton Rouge, 1987) and his 'Western Grains and the Panic of 1857', *Agricultural History*, 57 (1983), pp. 14–32.

30 For a detailed discussion on events in the Confederacy, see Douglas Ball, *Financial Failure and Confederate Defeat* (Urbana, Ill., 1991); James Morgan, *Graybacks and Gold: Confederate Monetary Policy* (Pensacola, Fla., 1985); Gary Pecquet, 'Southern Banking during the Civil War: A Confederate Tool and Union Target', in *Money and Banking: The American Experience* (Fairfax, Va., 1995), pp. 133–62; and Schweikart, *Banking in The American South*, ch. 7, as well as his 'Southern Banks and Secession', *Civil War History*, 31 (1985), pp. 118–25.

31 See Bray Hammond, *Sovereignty and an Empty Purse: Banks and Politics in the Civil War* (Princeton, N.J., 1970); Irwin Unger, *The Greenback Era: A Social and Political History of American Finance* (Princeton, N.J., 1964); Robert P. Sharkey, *Money, Class, and Party: An Economic Study of the Civil War and Reconstruction* (Baltimore, 1959); Richard Sylla, *American Capital Markets, 1846–1914* (New York, 1975); Lance Davis, 'The Investment Market, 1870–1914', *Journal of Economic History*, 25 (1965), pp. 355–99; Marie Shuska and W. Brian Barrett, 'Banking Structure and the National Capital Market', *Journal of Economic History*, 44 (1984), pp. 463–77; Helen Hill Updike, *The National Banks and American Development, 1870–1900* (New York, 1985). Milton Friedman and Anna Schwartz, *A Monetary History of the United States, 1863–1960* (Princeton, N.J., 1963), attributed all developments in this era to changes in the money stock rather than to political events.

32 The best biography of Morgan is Vincent Carosso, *The Morgans: Private International Bankers* (Cambridge, Mass., 1987), and his broader work *Investment Banking in America:*

A History (Cambridge, Mass., 1970). Ron Chernow's *The House of Morgan: An American Banking Dynasty and the Rise of Modern Finance* (New York, 1990) provides another effective treatment of this family.

33 Alfred Chandler, *Visible Hand: The Managerial Revolution in American Business* (Harvard, 1977). Also see Arthur Johnson and Barry Supple, *Boston Capitalists and Western Railroads* (Cambridge, Mass., 1967).

34 Charles Calomiris, 'Price and Exchange Rate Determination during the Greenback Suspension', *Oxford Economic Papers*, 40 (1988), pp. 719–90.

35 Pierson Doti and Schweikart, *Banking in the American West, passim.*

36 Material on the Populists and the agrarian unrest over greenbacks, banking and silver appears in Theodore Saloutos, 'The Agricultural Problem and Nineteenth-Century Industrialism', *Agricultural History*, 22 (1948), pp. 156–74; Robert Higgs, 'Railroad Rates and the Populist Uprising', *ibid.*, 44 (1970), pp. 291–7; Charles Calomiris, 'Greenback Resumption and Silver Risk: The Economics and Politics of Monetary Regime Change in the United States, 1862–1900', University of Illinois Working Paper, July 1992; Barry Eichengreen, 'Mortgage Interest Rates in the Populist Era', *American Economic Review*, 74 (1984), pp. 995–1015; John James, *Money and Capital Markets in Postbellum America* (Princeton, 1978); Wesley Mitchell, *Gold, Prices, and Wages under the Greenback Standard* (Berkeley, Calif., 1908).

37 This is discussed in Friedman and Schwartz, *Monetary History*.

38 Walter Nugent, *The Money Question during Reconstruction* (New York, 1967); George Anderson, 'Banking and Monetary Problems', in George Anderson (ed.), *Essays on the History of Banking* (Lawrence, Kans., 1972).

39 Schweikart, *Encyclopedia of American Business History and Biography: Banking and Finance to 1913*, p. xxxi; Eugene White, 'The Membership Problem of the National Banking System', *Explorations in Economic History*, 19 (1982), pp. 110–27.

40 Eugene White, *The Regulation and Reform of the American Banking System, 1900–1929* (Princeton, 1983); Ray Westerfield, *Historical Survey of Branch Banking in the United States* (New York, 1939); and Pierson Doti and Schweikart, *Banking in the American West*, all address the opposition to branching.

41 In addition to Pierson Doti and Schweikart, *Banking in the American West*, see their *California Bankers, 1848–1993* (New York, 1994), and Larry Schweikart, *A History of Banking in Arizona* (Tucson, Ariz., 1982) on the process by which those two western states obtained branch banking.

42 Neufeld, *Financial System of Canada*, pp. 101–2.

43 *Ibid.*, p. 102.

44 See David E. Bond, 'The Merger Movement in Canadian Banking, 1890–1920, Some Preliminary Findings', unpublished paper presented at the Annual Meeting of the Canadian Economics Association, 1969, and A. J. Glazebrook, 'Finance and Banking: Economic Development of Canada, 1867–1921', *Cambridge History of the British Empire* (Cambridge, 1930). On the tradeoff between stability and oligopoly in Canada, see Michael Bordo, Hugh Rockoff, and Angele Redish, 'The U.S. Banking System from a Northern Exposure: Stability vs. Efficiency', forthcoming, *Journal of Economic History*.

45 Dwight Brothers and Leopoldo Solis, *Mexican Financial Development* (Austin, 1966), pp. 5–9. Also, see Patrice Robitaille, 'A History of Early Banking and Banking Regulation in Mexico', draft paper in author's possession.

46 Friedman and Schwartz, *Monetary History*, effectively detail the developments of 1893, while Calomiris and Schweikart, 'The Panic of 1857', explain the Panic of

that year. See also Charles Kindleberger, *Manias, Panics and Crashes: A History of Financial Crises* (New York, 1978). The tendencies of government to expand is discussed in Robert Higgs, 'Crisis, Bigger Government, and Ideological Change: Two Hypotheses on the Ratchet Phenomenon', *Explorations in Economic History*, 22 (1985), pp. 1-28, and his *Crisis and Leviathan* (New York, 1987), as well as Jonathan Hughes, *The Governmental Habit* (Princeton, 1991).

47 Walter Wriston, 'Technology and Sovereignty: Effect of Advanced Technology on Political Relations', *Foreign Affairs*, 67 (1988/9), pp. 63–75.

18 Banking as class action: social and national struggles in the history of Canadian banking

Robert C. H. Sweeny

In Canada, banks play a crucial role. Their primary function is to mobilize the savings of the working classes and the various strata of the *petite bourgeoisie* in a manner consistent with the interests of the country's complex dominant social classes. In terms of the history of capitalism this function and the resulting economic centrality of banks are relatively new. In no advanced capitalist country are they older than the late nineteenth century. In Canada, these changes were related to a qualitative transformation in the relationship between banks and industry. Despite the attention given to this qualitative transformation in banking by contemporary critics of capitalism,[1] the extensive historiography on Canadian banking has denied its importance. Instead, banks are portrayed as having played an essential role from their inception. By according a timeless primacy to banks, historians sanction an analytically abstract treatment of their history. Conceived as institutions which can be understood simply through the construction of narrative chronicles, Canadian banks have not been the subject of historically grounded critical analysis. In short, historians think banks affect society, not the other way around.

Historiography as narrative fiction

The systematic study of Canadian banking started when the industry was in the midst of its qualitative transformation. The timing was not

315

coincidental; themes and associations first developed in these years have proved to be an enduring academic legacy of Canadian finance capital. The founding father, Adam Shortt, was a seminal figure in the Canadian historical profession.[2] He introduced two important and abiding themes: the centrality of merchant credit in a specie poor economy and the importance of ethnicity. Furthermore, he worked closely with both the banks and the federal government in developing his approach. As a result, the bankers' own perceptions of their historical role marked much of the subsequent literature, while the only important external factor considered seriously in the historiography has been the role of the state.

The image of a specie poor and therefore crippled economy has had a long life. Its popularity speaks both to the dearly held illusion that New France and British North America remained for centuries pioneer societies and to the disproportionate influence of Adam Smith's infrequent comments on the colonial situation. In the standard history of the Canadian capital market, this alleged deficiency was presented as not only the reason for the first chartered bank, but was the organizing theme for the entire pre-Confederation period.[3] In the most recent book-length study it remains a major theme.[4] While historians of such diverse societies as Upper Canada, the Gaspé and Newfoundland have all argued that merchant capital was essential because of the absence of an adequate circulating medium.[5]

A product of mid-Victorian, Presbyterian, Southern Ontario, Shortt firmly believed in an ethnically determined history. Scots were good businessmen, while French Canadians were insufficiently pragmatic. In Shortt, the history of banking was little more than a chronicle of great Scottish businessmen in history. This racist stereotype has since become more nuanced; historians now use 'the French Banks' as an analytical category.[6]

While at Queen's Shortt published widely, but his favoured review was the *Journal of the Canadian Bankers Association*, where he wrote the lead article for thirty-six quarterly issues in succession, between 1897 and 1906. This Association was more than just an industry lobby group. Formed in 1890 to assume informal regulatory functions during the qualitative transformation in banking, since 1901 it exercised a state-mandated supervision of the industry. Individual chartered banks and their leading shareholders also played key roles in the early years. Indeed, the Canadian Bank of Commerce's three volume history, to which Shortt contributed, was the first major work to argue for the essentially timeless nature and centrality of banking in Canadian history.[7] Its institutional focus was the model for later works produced by all of the leading banks. The first general survey was based on a combination of these in-house histories and available government statistics.[8] This symbiotic relationship between the academy and the banks also marked the career of the most influential of recent scholars. Following the publication of his ambitious synthesis, E. P. Neufeld left the University of Toronto to assume the position of Chief Economist at the Royal Bank of Canada, where he was influential in having the Canadian Bankers Association publish as a book all of Shortt's *Journal* contributions.[9]

In addition to the sustained influence of the industry itself, one of the principal reasons for the remarkable continuity in this historiography was that Shortt's two central themes were logically consistent with the long dominant 'staples' approach.[10] In this economic determinist model the motor of Canadian economic development was trade in staple commodities, first with Europe and then the United States, but the terms of trade were unequal. Since these trades occupied centre stage, the banks which financed them became the principal private institutions in the making of Canada. Furthermore, by explicitly explaining Canadian development exclusively in terms of external trade, this approach implicitly denied historical significance to internal social and economic dynamics. French Canada was the most prominent victim of this highly selective reading of the Canadian past.

Given this disciplinary consensus, historiographical debates have tended to focus on relatively minor questions – such as the relative influence of American versus Scottish banking practices – or on the more contentious political issue of banking and economic development. Here, social democratic political economists confused the presumed centrality of banks financing staple trades in the nineteenth century with the altogether different role banks would later assume and argued for a direct causal linkage between early staple trades and American branch plants of the 1960s.[11] The explicitly leftist nature of much of this work drew substantial opposition. Most influential was a frontal attack on the idea of 'Merchants against Industry' which compounded the problem by stressing the dynamic industrial role of nineteenth-century merchants and their banks.[12] More limited in nature, albeit richer, was *A Canadian Millionaire*, which did recognize the novelty of the banks' close connections to industry in the early years of this century, but assimilated it into an image of a short golden age for Canadian business.[13] This *Monopolies' Moment* would pass, however, as Dupont Chandler's *Visible Hand* of management crossed the border at York before reaching out to grasp the minds of business historians from Dalhousie to Victoria.[14]

Despite the problems inherent in any brief survey of a century long historiographical tradition, I trust the principal problems left unresolved are clear. Did banks develop to resolve a shortage in the circulating medium? What was the role of the chartered banks in pre-industrial British North America? Did it change in early industrial Canada? How and why did banking develop differently in French Canada than in English Canada? What were the reasons for the qualitative transformation in Canadian banking at the turn of the century? What was the banks' relationship to the high levels of foreign investment since the Second World War? None of these questions can be answered in isolation, for banks are products of their society and not the other way round.

Select problems in Canadian banking history

Specie, currency and the chartered banks: the early years

In their first fifteen years Lower Canadian banks were the subject of three separate investigations by the elected Legislative Assembly. Central to all three was the banks' extensive dealings in specie and the related question of their paper currency. Historians have accepted unquestioningly the banks' defence in the face of this critical public scrutiny. From Shortt to Baskerville, historians have argued that not only did the colonies face a serious shortage in specie, but the banks' most important contribution to economic development was their creation of an adequate circulating medium in the form of their own bank notes. The early history of the first and largest bank would suggest, however, a much more complex set of relationships.

The Bank of Montreal was formed in 1817, as a joint venture between the principal Montréal-based branches of imperial mercantile houses and a limited number of New England and New York merchants. The Americans accounted for 47% of the initial stock subscription[15] and in the early years, through their influential Boston committee of shareholders, directed the Bank's highly lucrative export trade in hard currency.[16] In the first five years of its existence the Bank of Montreal exported to the United States well in excess of half a million

Spanish dollars and at least £37,000 sterling in gold.[17] Thereafter, having drained the colonial economy of a not insignificant part of its specie reserves, the Bank carried on a large export trade to New York in sterling bills of exchange drawn by the Commissariat General and the colonial government, in excess of £670,000 worth by 1830. This was the very best paper in the world and accordingly received a substantial premium on the New York market. The Bank of Montreal monopolized this trade by 1822. It was a classic example of buying cheap and selling dear: the colonial authorities, by accepting the Bank's own notes in payment, substantially increased both circulation and general acceptance of the Bank's currency; while the Bank pocketed the bulk of the premium in New York.

The reason behind this apparent government largesse was the need to complete a discriminatory currency reform. Colonial authorities had since the Conquest been systematically devaluing the currency of account of New France. In 1808, the livre tournois was pegged at a derisory 24 to the Halifax pound. This devaluation seriously affected *Canadien* seigneurial revenues and mercantile fortunes, as both feudal dues and quit rents were most often expressed in livres. It was an under-standable policy for the conquerors, because it both lowered the purchase price of seigneuries, a favoured investment of the new colonial authorities, and weakened the competitive advantage of *Canadien* merchants. The most widely accepted coinage used to pay debts in this currency of account were French half crowns, whose intrinsic value had declined through constant usage. As a condition of its monopoly on government bills, the Bank agreed to remit some of the proceeds of its New York transactions in American 50 cent pieces. The Bank of Montreal attempted to secure acceptance of this new coinage by banning the use of half crowns in its Offices of Discount and Deposit. The Bank's policy met with considerable resistance from both artisans and peasants, who saw this quite correctly as an unjustified devaluation of their savings, and they forced the Bank to accept half crowns, albeit at a discount.[18] The smaller Bank of Canada, much more dependent on the local economy, continued to accept the half crowns at par and there followed an orchestrated campaign against it by its larger rival. It was a telling episode in early banking history, for the Bank of Canada never really recovered. Within two years it was no longer regularly open for business and in 1832 the Bank of Montreal purchased the remaining assets of its erstwhile rival.

As this episode would suggest, bank notes were not the favoured

currency historians would have us believe. In the early years counter-
feiting and alterations might explain the limited circulation, but by 1830
these problems had been largely overcome and it was clear that banks
limited the circulation of notes that could be used in daily life because
this business was not their business. The banks were in the business of
discounting commercial paper. The role of the banks' note circulation
was to profit from facilitating the operation of what were for the larger
merchant firms throughout British North America the real circulating
mediums: promissory notes, drafts and bills of exchange. For the smaller
merchants, retailers and most importantly the peasants and artisans,
who produced the wealth of these pre-industrial colonies, the mediums
which facilitated economic exchanges remained what they had been for
centuries, a combination of diverse coinage, book debt and the firm
shake of a callused hand.

This international currency speculation had an important impact on
colonial economic development. Lower Canada had a negative balance
of payments in the early nineteenth century because artisans and
manufacturers were heavily dependent on imported raw and semi-
manufactured inputs. The systematic redirection out of British North
America of the best commercial paper, while benefiting bank shareholders, certainly reduced the capacity and facility with which colonial
producers could meet their international obligations. So these bank
profits were achieved at the expense of expanding production in the
garment and metal trades. Ahistorical, neo-liberal, advocates of free
trade will find little to object to here, but it is understandable why
popularly elected representatives in a mature pre-industrial moral
economy so repeatedly questioned the wisdom of this systematic
inversion of Gresham's law.

Wages, currency and banking reform: the Industrial Revolution

Between the construction of the first factories on the outskirts of
Montréal in 1848 and the 1873 crisis of overproduction, British North
America experienced the complex and dramatic changes of an industrial
revolution. Although the effects of this relatively early industrialization
were felt unevenly, three general aspects were clearly in evidence in all
of the mainland colonies. First, there was a significant rise in waged
employment. Second, there was a growing concentration of production
in the urban centres. Third, there was a growing disparity between the
means of production sector and the consumer goods sectors.

The enormous increase in waged employment in these years significantly increased the need for a reliable paper currency to meet industrial payrolls. Banks played only a bit-part in meeting this need in the early years, before retiring completely from the stage. In the Maritime colonies, with their early and relatively large waged workforces in the timber, shipbuilding and shipping industries, banks never played an important role. Instead, colonial authorities developed an extensive provincial note issue in the smaller denominations. In the Canadas, banks continued to restrict circulation of small denomination notes and restricted their total note circulation. By 1864, note circulation constituted only 13% of liabilities, down from 25% in 1851, or a miserly 29% of the permitted amount. In 1866, the government of the Canadas followed the example set by the Maritime colonies and started issuing its own notes. The Bank Act of 1871 extended the New Brunswick ban on bank notes below 4 dollars to the rest of the Dominion. So government notes became the only available paper currency to meet expanding payrolls.

Two attempts at banking reform in these years are also revealing. The first in 1850, known as the Free Banking Act, allowed relatively easy access to banking privileges to private firms and individuals. The avowed aim was to imitate the New York experience and thereby resolve the problem of strictly controlled and discriminatory credit policies. Allowed to lapse in 1856, historians attribute the failure of this legislation to the restrictions placed on note circulation. Because free banks operated with less paid-up capital than chartered banks, they had to offer enhanced guarantees, deposited with the government, for their note circulation. Once again the presumption of banking autonomy led historians to deny the significance of the context within which these banks operated.

Discriminatory discounting by chartered banks, with up to a third of discounts the paper of the banks' own directors, was linked to the hierarchical mercantile structures in the larger centres. Merchants in smaller towns faced increased competition in the late 1840s and 1850s and chafed under the difficult terms of credit imposed by their wholesale suppliers. These were ties that bound and in only three small centres, Stanstead, St Thomas and St Catherines did country merchants achieve some relief by opening their own free banks. Two additional banks were created under this legislation, the Zimmerman Bank, run by a prominent railway promoter, and the Molson's Bank owned by the colony's leading industrial family. The scale of industrial activities linked to these bank promoters set them apart from the overwhelming majority of small manufacturers, who financed expansion primarily through retained earnings and had as yet no need for access to bank financing. In both these aspects, the evolution of banking in the Canadas underlines the historical differences with the north-eastern United States. What had been a successful strategy in New York failed in Canada, not because of conservative currency regulations, but because socio-economic structures were so different.

The second major banking reform, while more piecemeal, would have a greater impact over the long term. In 1859 the government of the United Canadas allowed chartered banks to extend credit to ware-housemen, millers, wharfingers and masters of vessels on the security of warehouse receipts or bills of lading for grains, goods, wares or merchandise to be stored or deposited. The government extended this 'pledge' business to include timber and lumber dealers in 1865, pork processors and wool dealers in 1871, malsters in 1872, petroleum and crude oil refiners, saw-mill owners, timber manufacturers, tanners, meat packers and any purchasers of agricultural products in 1880 and distillers in 1888. Finally, in 1890, on the recommendation of the Bankers' Section of the Toronto Board of Trade, it was extended to all those involved in wholesale manufacturing and all wholesale dealers in agricultural products.

The nature and gradual extension of these provisions reflect the changing nature of the country's industrial activities and are certainly not what Shortt described as 'a limited and illogical list of persons engaged in certain kinds of business'.[19] The issuer of the receipt need not be the owner of the goods and yet the claim of the bank took precedence over all others, including the rights of the unpaid vendor of the goods in question. So what in theory was a measure to grant 'additional facilities in commercial transactions' was, in practice, a means of financing the inventories in selected industries at the expense of farming families. The heavily commercial nature of the early provisions allowed the banks to extend loans to clients, whose capital base provided an insufficient guarantee. This extension reflected the growing complexity and increasingly hierarchical nature of mercantile activities stimulated by the Reciprocity Treaty with the United States. The inclusion of milling was significant, however, for this was one of the earliest indus-tries in the Canadas to industrialize and it set the model for industries to be offered these credit facilities over the next thirty years. The early inclusion of timber and lumber dealers, but not yet saw-mill operators or timber manufacturers, meant an extension of these credit facilities primarily to the older staple houses, who were faced with the American revocation of Reciprocity and the potential glutting of the market from the now excessive capacity of timber and sawn lumber producers.

The gradual extension of these facilities to other industries followed upon the development of regional and pan-Canadian manufacturers. It was not merely a question of scale, however, for those selected shared key characteristics with flour milling. Facilities were extended to consumer goods industries where fixed capital requirements were high and where inventory costs were high relative to wages. These particular industries were among the earliest English Canadian controlled manufacturing activities to experience corporate concentration. This early concentration was itself a calculated response to the increasing transfer of value from the consumer goods sector to the means of production sector. This transfer was a growing problem throughout the economy, but, unlike most manufacturers, for these firms their relatively smaller wage bills meant that increasing productivity, through an increase in absolute and relative surplus value extraction, yielded insufficient gains.

Unquestionably this strategic process of change was in part underwritten by the increase in short-term, revolving, lines of bank credit. The dialectical significance of town/country relations in this new business, however, had both regional and national implications. The state-sanctioned displacement by the banks of the property rights of the vendor, who were primarily farming families and small town merchants, was a significant statement about the deteriorating terms of trade between town and country as industrialization took hold. These provisions primarily benefited firms operating in English Montreal and Ontario, rather than the Maritimes where town/country relations were less significant, or in the heartland of French Canada where these relations were much more balanced and the scale of firms remained smaller for much longer. In this the most important contribution of Canadian banks to the industrialization of the country, therefore, the banks continued to play a supporting role, one dependent on broader social and national characteristics which differed across British North America. Nevertheless, this new business did establish for the first time important linkages between certain leading manufacturing firms and the heretofore merchant-dominated chartered banks. These linkages would prove to be important in the development of both finance capital and the ability of certain *moyen bourgeois* to resist the pressures of monopoly capital.

A qualitative transformation in Canadian banking: finance capital,
the early years

Between the building of the Canadian Pacific Railway and the Great
Depression, finance capital became the defining characteristic of
Canadian economic life. This development constituted a qualitative
transformation in the structure of Canadian capitalism. The General
Strikes of 1919 and the success of petty commodity producer-based
political parties in both English Canada and Newfoundland were
eloquent testimony to what millions of working people thought of this
unprecedented concentration of economic wealth and political power.
Historians of banking have largely ignored this sea change in the history
of the country. Instead, they have focused on two quantitative changes:
the development of branch banking and the decline in the number of
independent banks. Admittedly the magnitude of these two changes
make them difficult to ignore. In 1879, when the CPR contract was
signed, forty-eight banks operated 247 branches. In 1928, when the
Prairie's wheat-based economy collapsed, the ten remaining banks
had more than 4,400 branches. Their scale is not, however, why
historians have focused on them. Branch banking and consolidation in
the industry are the central elements in a historical description, which
has served by default as the explanation of twentieth-century Canadian
banking.

The description is simple enough. Servicing the large-scale European
settlement of the West, first along the lines of the CPR and then those of
the Grand Trunk Pacific and Canadian Northern, the banks developed
far-flung branch systems, which integrated this pioneer society into the
national economy. Bank competition and high overhead costs led to a
rationalization through mergers. English Canadian banks were thus
central to the 'National Dream' of an integrated economy from sea to
sea. Having reached maturity and a level of market saturation so early,
these banks then declined in relative importance. So historians' belief in
the autonomy of banking led in practice to a denial of the significance
of changes within banking and a refusal to understand their relationship
to broader social change.

In these years there developed a two-tiered banking structure within
the English Canadian capital market and the basis was laid for a distinct
capital market in Québec. The two-tiered structure in English Canada
consisted of three rival groups of finance capital representing an *haute
bourgeoisie* and four independent regional banks. In Québec a socially

and spatially divided capital market emerged. New joint-stock intermediaries linked to French Canadian banks developed in the heartland,
while simultaneously a Catholic-inspired, co-operative movement
matured in the outlying regions. Strongly influenced by the struggles
arising from the contradictory and historically specific forms of
Canadian capitalist development, these were the changes which defined
the new parameters of banking in Canada.

The most important change in banking during this period was the
emergence of three distinct groups of finance capital each centred on a
chartered bank, the Montreal, the Royal and the Commerce. Each
group included older industrial concerns, major new corporations and
financial intermediaries in brokerage, insurance and trust operations.
Furthermore, all three groups developed important interests abroad:
the Royal in the Caribbean, Central and South America, the Montreal
in Mexico and the Commerce in Brazil. The structure of power within
these groups was unusual. With the exception of their trust company
subsidiaries, the banks did not control associated companies in manufacturing, transportation, finance or utilities. Control remained with the
leading shareholders, who were most frequently particular families.
These bourgeois held equity interests in their respective banks, but their
holdings were never large enough to constitute outright control. This
diffuse structure of power did not mean these groups lacked coherency,
for the bank boards were loci of power administered collectively by
these prominent families.

Central to the success of each group were oligopolies, whose creation
required close co-operation between differing financial intermediaries.
Using operating capital lent by their bank, brokerage firms floated
the stocks of the new corporations, whose extensive watering meant
continued manning of market pumps to keep them afloat and in this
they were aided by the trust companies. The banks assumed medium-
term debt financing, while life insurance companies covered longer-
term debts and frequently took not insignificant equity interests.

The creation of these new corporations had a dialectical impact.
These mergers involved the elimination of numerous firms, which
undermined the viability of regional economies. The numerous small
pools of investment capital created in the wake of these mergers went
primarily into local real estate and service industries. So in English
Canada, the property market has had an inverse relationship to
industrial development: rents have been highest precisely where people
can least afford them.

The expansion of branch banking preceded consolidation. Linked to the increase in waged employment throughout central and eastern Canada, its pace was largely dictated by the spread of salaried employment. As firms developed beyond family-based management structures, the savings of salaried organic intellectuals fuelled the growth in deposit taking institutions. This process coincided with a stronger demarcation between town and country as commercial agriculture for distant markets came to predominate. Thus, the expansion in branch banking was accompanied by increased seasonality in the rhythm of savings and ironically, for the first time in Canadian banking history, bank note circulation became significant and there resulted repeated modifications to regulations governing the ratio of note circulation to paid-up capital.

Bank mergers were not a simple rationalization brought about by higher costs. Federal deregulation facilitated the rationalization of banking in Canada, but it was more a symptom of the changes affecting banking than a cause. The three centres of finance capital did not build branch systems, they bought them: the Bank of Montreal led the way with eight takeovers in Canada and one in Mexico; the Bank of Commerce was close behind in the early years and would take over six Canadian banks by 1928; and the Royal Bank of Canada, born of an English Montreal-based syndicate's takeover of the Merchants Bank of Halifax, engineered five additional takeovers in Canada and three in the Caribbean and South America by 1925.

There were important regional characteristics to this consolidation in Canadian banking. Local control of nine Maritime banks was lost prior to the Great War, while in Western Canada consolidation took place primarily in the 1920s. This timing was important. The effective elimination of locally-based banks in the Maritimes compromised the already problematic competitive position of Maritime-based industrial firms. For the future of many of these firms, faced with increasing corporate concentration in English Montreal and southern Ontario, the loss of an embryonic regional capital market was significant. In the 1920s manufacturing employment was devastated, with job losses of 50% in industrial centres and 15% of all Maritimers took the difficult decision to migrate elsewhere.

In the West it was only after the wheat economy was fully established on the Prairies that finance capital effectively monopolized branch banking. The groups had been major players in the development of this economy, but not as bankers to farming families. They co-ordinated the financing of three continental railways, underwrote the rapid consolidation of Central Canadian manufacturers, who most benefited from this captive market's rapid growth, and supported Winnipeg grain houses. Thus growth of these three banks' business during the wheat boom was due primarily to their roles at the centre of financial and industrial groups, whose members controlled the commanding heights of the Canadian economy. It would only be after they had firmly established their respective groups' positions and entered into a period of relatively slower growth that they would move to eliminate local banking interests in the West.

On the whole regional banks fared better in Ontario. Here mergers took place gradually over the course of the first quarter century: the Bank of Montreal purchased the Ontario Bank in 1906; the Royal Bank bought the Traders Bank of Toronto in 1912; the heretofore regionally-based Bank of Nova Scotia emerged as a national bank with its purchase of the Metropolitan in 1918 and its merger in the following year with the Bank of Ottawa; while the Commerce consolidated its pre-eminence in the industrial heartland of Ontario with its purchase of the Bank of Hamilton in 1923. This left three independent Ontario-based banks: the Toronto, the Dominion and the Imperial. The shareholding patterns and balance sheets of these banks and the Bank of Nova Scotia sheds light on the broader socio-economic factors which enabled these banks to retain their independence.

Each of these banks had firmly rooted regional shareholding patterns. The Bank of Nova Scotia was the most complex, because of its mergers with the Bank of New Brunswick in 1913 and then the Bank of Ottawa. In both cases, regionally important bourgeois families became significant bank shareholders and would remain so for most of the century. Indeed all four banks had significant shareholdings held by regionally prominent bourgeois families, who did not control pan-Canadian businesses. These four banks also had remarkably similar dispositions of their assets over time; with private securities playing a substantially less prominent role than they did for the three majors, but managing much more active short and call loan businesses. There was a cost to banking independence, however, as these banks had a consistently higher proportion of their liabilities in savings deposits than did their larger rivals. Itself a reflection not only of their weaker corporate connections, but also the stronger ties these banks maintained with their predominantly *petit* and *moyen bourgeois* clientele. In short these banks remained institutions of banking capital, which did not make the qualitative leap to finance capital. They were controlled by and served regionally-based strata within the Canadian bourgeoisie. By North American standards all four were good sized banks and, although none were active in the financing of large scale Canadian businesses either here or abroad, they did play active roles in the North American money markets.

In Québec the contradictory factors of the national character of economic development and the hegemonic position of English Montreal made the situation quite complex. The three French Canadian controlled regional banks were among the most profitable in the country. Only one, however, was the subject of a takeover. In 1923, with substantial provincial government assistance, the Banque d'Hochelaga of Montréal purchased the troubled Banque Nationale of Québec and created the Banque Canadienne Nationale. The ability of these banks to maintain their independence contrasted sharply with the fate of three regional banks serving primarily English language communities: the Eastern Townships Bank was bought by the Commerce in 1912; the Bank of Quebec was bought by the Royal in 1917; and the Molson's Bank merged with the Bank of Montreal in 1925.

The French Canadian controlled banks in Québec managed their assets and liabilities in a manner quite similar to their regional counterparts in English Canada; however, they did not participate to anywhere near the same degree in national and international money markets, nor did they build branch systems outside Québec. The clearly *Québécois* focus of these banks was due to the differing path to capitalism that had been followed for more than a century in this part of the country and was most evident in their unique shareholding patterns. Unlike the independent regional banks in English Canada, there were no significant concentrations of share ownership among prominent bourgeois families. Instead, they raised their share capital from an active French Canadian investment community, composed of both traditional and organic intellectuals as well as a minority of *moyen bourgeois* in the industrial towns and cities. In a further marked contrast with English Canadian banking capital, these *petit* and *moyen bourgeois* bank shareholders were heavily involved in the financing of new intermediaries in differing types of insurance and trust company business.[20] The nationalist nature of this endeavour was important, but it should be stressed that it did not include the outlying regions where the co-operative Caisse Populaire Desjardins movement and a large number of principally parish-based mutual insurance companies predominated.

The development of mature industrial economies in North America,

Europe and Japan all led to a quantitative increase in banks' deposit taking business and a corresponding decline in the relative importance of the discounting of commercial paper. These significant changes in banking activity, however, did not necessarily lead to the development of finance capital. In only a minority of these countries would the commanding heights of both the financial and industrial activity of the country become tightly controlled by closely knit groups of capitalists. The Japanese Zaibatsu are certainly the best-known example and the Canadian experience confirms the observation of Takahashi that such extreme examples of fundamentally anti-democratic socio-economic structures are integrally related to the nature of the capitalist developmental paths followed in each country. The strong national and regional characteristics of the Canadian experience were, however, important. They were the product of the uneven and contradictory evolution of differing types of capitalism in Canada. In the Canadian experience, differing town/country relations were of central import-ance, for they influenced the rhythm of the historical differentiation within the popular classes.

The timing of the emergence of the *petite bourgeoisie* appears therefore to be an essential question, because the varying composition of this complex class influenced to a significant degree the nature of the capital market and the role of the state. Within Québec, a predominantly traditional, French Canadian, intelligentsia which had emerged prior to industrialization was successful in the late nineteenth and early twentieth century in articulating a distinct national vision, which mobilized diverse bourgeois elements in the heartland to create a separate national private capital market. The limits of this uniquely successful defence against finance capital's expansion in Canada were both spatial and social. It would not be until the Quiet Revolution of the 1960s that these internal divisions would be largely overcome and an integrated *Québécois* capital market combining the private capital market, the co-operative movement and a dynamic state sector would emerge. In southern Ontario, where the *petite bourgeoisie* was pre-dominantly organic and developed out of the changes wrought by industrialization they could prove to be important allies of the *moyenne bourgeoisie* not only in their struggle to maintain an independent base, but in the limits placed on finance capital's growth by state intervention most notably in the field of hydro-electricity.

As the contrasting experience in English Montreal indicated, however, the dialectical relationships between town and country and the historical basis of the *haute bourgeoisie* could seriously circumscribe any developmental potential of *petit* and *moyen bourgeois*. In Newfoundland and the Maritimes, where differentiation was slowest, the largely organic *petite bourgeoisie* developed too late for there to be successful bourgeois-led alliances in defence of regional interests. Here and in the West, the most important struggles were led by the working class and by farmers' or fishers' organizations. These diverse and contradictory struggles were central to the making of an advanced capitalist society in Canada.

Struggles against national oppression and increasing regional disparities interacted with class and gender to establish the options and constraints within which the complex strata of *petite, moyenne* and *haute bourgeoisies* made their individual and collective decisions. Although none of the long-term aims of the popular classes in these years were achieved, through their parliamentary and extra-parliamentary struggles important limits were placed on the continued growth of what must have seemed to be at the time the almost insatiable appetite and greed of elements of Canada's ruling classes. The significance of this achievement needs to be stressed. In the few advanced capitalist societies where there was a comparable concentration of economic power to that which had emerged in Canada by the early decades of the twentieth century, Fascism would triumph. Here it did not. Instead, the working classes were able to build labour movements which despite their many problems remain far stronger than those of the United States; the economic and political basis for a distinct modern society in Québec were consolidated, while the co-operative organizations formed in these years within both English and French Canada have thrived. Finally, these struggles within a bourgeois democratic state shaped a substantially altered and historically significant role for the public sector in the social and economic life of the country. Thus the underlying dynamics of social and national struggles fashioned the divergent types of capitalism, which created the complex banking and capital market structures in the country. Given their long historical evolution, it is not surprising that these structures would profoundly influence the relationship between the very different advanced capitalist societies of Canada and the United States in the last half of the twentieth century.

Directed foreign investment: finance capital and American imperialism

The distribution of wealth in the first half of the twentieth century in Canada had been extremely unequal. The great strike wave of 1946 challenged the legitimacy of this inequality. With the major advances of industrial-based unions in the 1940s and 1950s and the subsequent massive unionization of public sector employees in the late 1950s and 1960s, there developed for the first time in Canada a large consumer market. At the same time, the increasingly technical nature of mass production and the growing demands on the state in health and social services placed a renewed emphasis on higher education and the *petite bourgeoisie* expanded very significantly. When 'stagflation' in the 1970s threatened these hard-won gains, direct action by organized labour, community groups, students and *petit bourgeois* professional groups transformed the political agenda. A social democratic sovereignist party was elected in Québec and the federal government was forced to adopt a number of measures that would ultimately reshape the structure of capital markets in Canada.

The historical problem which has preoccupied English Canadian scholars in the human sciences over the past quarter century was not, however, directly related to any of these mass movements. The issue of greatest academic concern has been the relationship between Canada and the United States. In terms of the economic aspects of this relationship, there have been two historically specific areas of concern and work. In both areas a social democratic political economy of dependency, based on the staple theory, has been the dominant interpretive framework. In the 1960s and through the 1970s the issue was American direct investment in Canada. The concern was under-standable. By 1970, 70% of the mining industry and 60% of the manufacturing industry of the country were foreign controlled. In this context, the Canadian banks were, it was argued, all too ready to assume a junior partner relationship with American transnationals in their takeover of the country. Since the 1980s, work has focused on the related state policies of deregulation, privatization and free trade.

The assumption of dependency led to a denial of any significant historical autonomy, let alone internal complexity, to the Canadian bourgeoisie. In Canada, according to the leading political scientist of this school: 'nothing approaching a national bourgeoisie with its own political, ideological and economic unity vis-à-vis other national capitals has emerged'.[21] Thus, ironically, given the ostensibly critical nature of much of this literature, it supported the denial of Canadian finance capital by mainstream historians. Both social democratic social scientists and liberal historians of banking agreed that the 'Big Five' English Canadian banks were all essentially the same. Having denied the significance of qualitative change over time, it is not surprising that these scholars failed to analyse American direct investment in Canada historically.

In order to understand American economic imperialism in Canada it is necessary to summarize briefly the post-war evolution in the control and structure of Canadian capital markets. The central element is that of continuity. The two-tiered English Canadian and the distinct *Québécois* capital markets have both survived into the late twentieth century. No new finance capital group emerged in the country in these years, despite the many changes to the country's industrial base. It is against this backdrop of structural continuity at the highest levels of the Canadian bourgeoisie that the drama of American direct investment from the 1950s to the 1980s was played out.

The two groups of finance capital centred in English Montreal emerged from the Depression and the war years as still the largest and most influential groups in the country, but in many ways the writing was already on the wall. In the mid-1930s as the European economies rearmed there was a mining boom in Canada. Toronto rapidly became the prime source for investment capital in mining and its stock exchange became the leading market in the country. By the end of the 1940s a majority of directors of the leading life insurance companies, those responsible for vetting all significant long-term loans and equity positions, were resident in Toronto. The move from Saint James to Bay Street most directly benefited the Commerce group, which substantially diversified its interests in the 1950s and early 1960s. In part this changing face of corporate Canada was due to the emergence of financial holding companies. First pioneered in Canada by Argus Corp., these new corporate forms became a characteristic feature of contemporary Canadian capitalism. Each was controlled by either a family or a very limited number of investors and all save the first were firmly within the ranks of a single finance capital group. Financing these new holding companies while supporting the expansion of older group members has dominated the lending portfolios of finance capital in post-war Canada.

Over time, the internal composition of each of the groups changed, due largely to continued corporate concentration. The majority of the leading Canadian corporations were group members by the 1920s and the same was true in the 1970s. To a significant degree, this group continuity has been ensured by the generational transfer of power within the older families and a selective integration of a very limited number of new members. In my opinion, this reproduction of class power at the highest reaches of the socio-economic structure in Canada has been sufficient to merit the use of the term, first suggested by Lenin, of a financial oligarchy. If, for example, one compares the composition of the boards of directors of the leading financial intermediaries in the immediate post-war period with that of the 1970s, no fewer than eighty-eight sons and two daughters had inherited their father's seat on these boards. In short, organic linkages are more important than institutional persistency in understanding the internal structure of Canadian finance capital.

Since the end of the Second World War, there have also been important changes at the level of the regional banks. The Toronto and the Dominion merged in 1956. Consummating a relationship that dated from the early 1950s, the Commerce and the Imperial merged in 1961. Rationalization of the regionally-based trust companies affiliated with the surviving pools of banking capital was one of the most important corporate changes affecting both the Toronto Dominion and the Bank of Nova Scotia in the 1960s. The composition of the boards of these banks and their associated intermediaries, however, changed remarkably little. In both cases, regionally prominent bourgeois families predominated and no major Canadian corporation allied themselves with either of these banks. Although both grew substantially, through greatly enlarged branch systems, they remained in the sphere of banking capital. With the development of Euro-dollar markets and then the expansion in Third World debt both banks increased substantially their international banking and currency businesses.

What was unusual about foreign direct investment in Canada up to the 1970s was not so much its size, but its distribution. The leading American transnationals in Canada are almost all large players in other advanced economies. In Canada, Japan and Europe these flagship enterprises are in a minority, however, for most of the largest companies in each of the G7 countries are controlled by their own bourgeoisie. The exceptional nature of the Canadian situation did not lie here, but rather in a very significant presence of American firms in the middling ranks, where American branch plants accounted for 40% of all industrials. No other advanced capitalist country experienced such a concentration in the middle range. In terms of the number and relative importance of the companies involved, at its peak foreign direct investment in Canada followed a distinct bell curve.

The tight control exercised over the Canadian capital market was one of the most important reasons for this unusual distribution of American investment. Expansion to meet the rapidly developing consumer market in the post-war period required more than retained earnings; access to the capital market was essential for most businesses. For smaller firms in English Canada, both regional and pan-Canadian, the two-tiered capital market significantly weakened their competitive position in the face of American expansion. Early attempts to redress the capital market inequities through tax reform cost two reform-minded finance ministers, Walter Gordon and Edgar Benson, their jobs. In such a context, it is understandable why so many owners of small Canadian-owned manufacturing firms would have concluded that their best strategy was to sell out to American firms.

The English Canadian banks did not, however, restrict access to credit because they were in a partnership with American imperialism. The post-war economic boom meant substantial new investments for older, larger firms and it was to meet their needs that the savings of the country were directed. The top tier of the Canadian capital market had been developed to serve the interests of families controlling the largest firms in the country. These firms remained Canadian controlled, closely linked and well served by this capital market structure. The much smaller second tier continued to serve regional bourgeois interests and only the Toronto-Dominion, based in the area which had the greatest concentration of American direct investment, would, by the 1970s, develop any significant working relationship with branch plant operations.

Over the 1980s there was a very significant reduction in the relative importance of American direct investment. Nor was this simply a matter of fewer firms, the characteristic feature of a concentration in the middle ranks was eliminated.[22] In part this was the result of continued corporate concentration, the scale of which was very impressive. In order just to maintain its relative position a firm had to post an annual growth rate over the decade of more than 16%. The most important factor was, however, a complex and ongoing process of democratization of capital markets in Canada. This dramatic change was largely made in Canada and, rather than representing a legacy of dependency, the Canadian and *Québécois* bourgeoisies' enthusiastic endorsement of free trade and the resurgence of right wing political forces more generally resulted from the greatly expanded opportunities afforded these bourgeoisies by more open capital markets.

The most visible changes were in Québec and reflected the continued importance of small and medium-size businesses in Québec. The viability of these smaller businesses was due to both the greater decentralization of the Québec capital market, three in five residents of the province bank at a locally controlled credit union, and the nationalist economic policy of the Parti Québécois. The cornerstone of this policy was a tax reform which gave substantial tax credits to those investing in Québec-based equities. This fiscal underwriting of a democratization of the equity market revived the Montréal stock exchange, which increased its share of Canadian trading from 7% to 20% in the first three years of the plan. In addition the province slashed corporate tax rates for small and medium-size businesses and gave a new, more aggressive, mandate to the state-run pension plan.

In response to popular political pressures, the federal government initiated a number of new policies in the 1970s and early 1980s. A National Energy Policy underwrote both expansion of Canadian-controlled integrated oil companies and repatriation of a substantial part of the oil and gas exploration business. A long delayed revision of the Bank Act created an additional tier of chartered banks. Although foreign controlled, the opening up of over seventy new lending institutions significantly increased the options for small and medium-sized businesses seeking commercial loans particularly in Ontario and Western Canada. Most important, however, was the fiscal underwriting of a dramatic decentralization of the private pension business in the country. Instituted to address poverty among the elderly caused by a rigid, sexist and underfunded pension system, the Registered Retirement Savings Plan now allows some 20 billion tax-free dollars to be funnelled every year into mutual funds, largely by the *petite bourgeoisie*. While the banks participate in this new market, they have yet to dominate it and regulations requiring 80% of the funds to be invested in Canada have meant a significant increase not only in the number and variety of institutional investors, but in the ability of smaller firms to gain access to equity markets.

Conclusion

Advanced capitalist countries are few in number and yet quite varied in their internal economic structure and historical evolution. In each country banks play a major role, for if their bourgeoisie could not mobilize the savings of the country then they would be unable to retain their privileged position for very long. Canada represents an unusual case. Created on the basis of violent expropriation of First Nations, conquest of New France and bloody repression of democratic reform forces in 1837–8, it would develop a stable bourgeois democratic form of government. A colonial society, it was among the first countries to industrialize. Never having been a nation state, its *haute bourgeoisie* created one of the most developed forms of finance capital. Having long possessed one of the most concentrated corporate structures of any of the OECD countries, within its borders, in Québec, there has developed one of the most decentralized national economies in the advanced capitalist world. Increasingly threatened by American imperialism, it opted for closer continental economic relations.

The key to understanding these contradictory historical developments lies not in the specific trades, industries or financial institutions, but in viewing these developments in light of the social and national struggles within the country. The historical centrality of these internal dynamics does not mean, however, that international dimensions are insignificant. The wealth and the high standards of living that have characterized advanced capitalist countries since the end of the Second World War are based in no small measure on the systemic transfer of value from other countries. By the early 1980s, each of Canada's three regional banks had loaned more funds to Latin American states than they had to their respective provincial governments. This globalization of capitalist flows has not created one world, but has instead contributed to an accentuation of long-standing social, gender, regional and national inequalities at home and abroad, while at the same time underwriting an unprecedented expansion of the *petite bourgeoisie* within advanced capitalist countries. The global significance of these dialectical changes will undoubtedly have an even greater impact on the future evolution of capital markets in Canada and elsewhere than they have in the recent past. What will not change, however, is the importance of analysing this evolution in light of the broader, historically-rooted, social and political questions which have in the past and will continue in the future to shape the history of banking.

Notes

1 Alongside the standard international texts by Hobson, Hilferding, Lenin and Bukharin were the Canadian texts: Phillips Thompson, *The Politics of Labour* (New York, 1887); Gustavus Myers, *A History of Canadian Wealth* (New York, 1914); and Wat Hugh McCallum, *Who Owns Canada?* (Regina, 1935).
2 Adam Shortt taught political economy from 1891 until 1907, when he joined the

Civil Service Commission, where he played an extremely influential role in the fashioning of the Canadian civil service. While in Ottawa, Shortt wrote the volume on Lord Sydenham in the *Makers of Canada* (Toronto, 1908), was both an editor and a leading contributor to the twenty-three-volume *Canada and its Provinces* (Toronto, 1913–17) and edited two volumes on the history of currency in New France and Nova Scotia (Toronto 1929 and 1933).

3 E. P. Neufeld, *The Financial System of Canada* (Toronto, 1972).

4 Peter Baskerville, *Bank of Upper Canada* (Toronto, 1987).

5 Douglas McCalla, 'Rural Credit and Rural Development in Upper Canada, 1790–1850', in *Merchant Credit and Labour Strategies in Historical Perspectives* (Fredericton, 1990), pp. 255–72; Rosemary E. Ommer, *From Outpost to Outport: A Structural Analysis of the Jersey-Gaspé Cod Fishery, 1767–1886* (Montreal, 1991); Sean T. Cadigan, *Hope and Deception in Conception Bay: Merchant-Settler Relations in Newfoundland, 1785–1855* (Toronto, 1995).

6 Neufeld, *Financial System of Canada*; Tom Naylor, *The History of Canadian Business* (Toronto, 1975); Ronald Rudin, *Banking en Français the French Banks of Quebec, 1835–1925* (Toronto, 1985).

7 Victor Ross and A. St L. Trigge, *A History of the Canadian Bank of Commerce* (Toronto, 1920, 1922 and 1934). Shortt wrote the extended review of state regulation of the industry in the second volume.

8 A. J. Glazebrook, 'Finance and Banking: Economic Development of Canada, 1867–1921', in *Cambridge History of the British Empire*, vol. VI (Cambridge, 1930).

9 *Adam Shortt's History of Canadian Currency and Banking 1600–1800* (Toronto, 1986).

10 For a critical evaluation of the staples approach see my article 'The Staples as the Significant Past: A Case Study in Historical Theory and Method', in *Canada: Theoretical Discourse/Discours théoriques* (Montreal, 1994), pp. 327–49.

11 M. H. Watkins, 'A Staple Theory of Economic Growth', *Canadian Journal of Economics and Political Science*, 29 (1963), pp. 141–58; Kari Levitt, *Silent Surrender, the Multinational Corporation in Canada* (Toronto, 1970); Ian Lumsden, *Close the 49th Parallel* (Toronto, 1970); Gary Teeple, *Capitalism and the National Question in Canada* (Toronto, 1972); Robert Laxer, *(Canada) Ltd. The Political Economy of Dependency* (Toronto, 1973); Wallace Clement, *The Canadian Corporate Elite, An Analysis of Economic Power* (Toronto, 1975); Naylor, *History of Canadian Business*; Wallace Clement, *Continental Corporate Power, Economic Linkages between Canada and the United States* (Toronto, 1977); M. H. (Mel) Watkins, 'The Staple Theory Revisited', *Journal of Canadian Studies*, 12, 5 (1977), pp. 83–94.

12 Larry Macdonald, 'Merchants against Industry: An Idea and its Origins', *Canadian Historical Review*, 56 (1975), pp. 263–81.

13 Michael Bliss, *A Canadian Millionaire: The Life and Business Times of Sir Joseph Flavelle, Bart. 1858–1939* (Toronto, 1977).

14 Christopher Armstrong and H. V. Nelles, *Monopolies Moment: The Organisation and Regulation of Canadian Utilities, 1830–1930* (Toronto, 1988); Graham Taylor and Peter Baskerville, *A Concise History of Canadian Business* (Toronto, 1994).

15 The early stock transactions were recorded in *The First Book Opened by this Bank on June 23 1817*, Archives of the Bank of Montreal.

16 *Book of Resolve of the Bank of Montreal*, 19 December 1817, pp. 35–6, Archives of the Bank of Montreal.

17 We cannot know the full extent of this business, because on three separate occasions the Board Minutes only note that 'all available Spanish dollars' were sent.

Historians have accepted at face value the falsified returns prepared by the Bank which were printed at *Appendix N, JLALC, 1830*. My calculations, based on the Bank's *Book of Resolve* reveal a much larger trade.

18 *Book of Resolve*, 25 January 1820 and 25 August 1820, pp. 150 and 177, Archives of the Bank of Montreal.

19 Ross and Trigge, *A History of the Canadian Bank of Commerce*, vol. II, p. 465.

20 For details see my 'Aperçu d'un effort collectif québécois: la création, au début du 20ᵉ siècle d'un marché privé et institutionalisé de capitaux', *Revue d'histoire de l'Amérique française*, 49, 1 (Summer 1995), pp. 35–77.

21 Leo Panitch, 'Class and Power in Canada', *Monthly Review*, 36 (November 1985), p. 10.

22 American firms dropped from 137 to 93 of the 400 largest industrials; British firms declined from 31 to 20; while firms controlled in other countries rose from 19 to 33. This growth was accounted for mostly by Japanese firms – up from 2 to 14 – of which half were in the top 100 in 1988.

19 Nation building and the origins of banking in Latin America, 1850–1930

Carlos Marichal

This study posits that in the modern era, changes in political regimes often lead to major changes in economic organization and, more specifically, to changes in the financial and banking sector. This hypothesis – which attributes particular significance to the relation between politics and institutional change in the economic sphere – underlies our present aim, which is to explore some of the ways in which politics and the evolution of state structures influenced the early development of banking in Latin America.

To affirm that politics and finance have been (and are) closely intertwined in modern Latin American history is to claim nothing new. But it is worth noting that relatively few studies have made an explicit attempt to link political modernization with the creation and/or development of banks in Latin America.

At the same time this study proposes that institutional policies and innovations in the financial sector can – reciprocally – affect the economic efficiency of state administrations. In this respect, it can be argued that in the process of capitalist development the establishment of banks represents one of the key institutional 'innovations' contributing not only to financial modernization but also to political-administrative modernization. It will be argued here that in the case of Latin America, the forging of a 'modern' banking system in the late nineteenth century accompanied and reinforced the consolidation of national state structures. In fact, the modernization and increasing financial strength of government depended to a considerable degree on the creation of powerful banks which served as key auxiliaries in the task of creating a more efficient and broad-ranging fiscal and financial administration.

A different and much more debatable question is whether the type of heavily 'political' banking structures which emerged in many Latin American countries at the time proved to be economically beneficial in the long run. For this reason, care must be taken to evaluate just what one means by 'modernization'. For in the principal Latin American nations, the rapid advances in the banking sector achieved by the beginning of the twentieth century were not accompanied by a process of balanced economic development or of rapid industrial trans-formation. Furthermore, the extremely close ties between certain large banks and their respective governments could have adverse effects, as can be observed in the widespread financial crises in Latin America in the early 1890s.

Indeed, a review of the evolution of the overall structure of banking systems in the larger Latin American nations demonstrates that contrary to popular belief, the most important banks were those most closely linked to national governments. Several of these big domestic banks began operations in the 1850s, although it was only after the 1880s that their dominance became truly evident. It is well known that a few British banks were established in various cities of the region from the 1860s, but it should be emphasized that they were neither the first banks, nor by any means the largest financial institutions.[1] On the contrary, domestic institutions with close links to government such as the Banco do Brasil, the Banco de la Nación (Argentina) and the Banco Nacional de México became, by the turn of the century, the dominant institutions in their respective Latin American financial markets, and *continue* to be the largest banks in Latin America today.

Given this continuity, it is of interest to explore the historical period when such structural trends originated – that is, the last quarter of the nineteenth century. But in order to place these problems in context we must begin with a few comments on the current historiography of Latin American banking and then proceed to a brief overview of the birth of banking in Latin America in the mid-nineteenth century. This chapter centres, however, on the analysis of developments during the decade of the 1880s – when banking *systems* and modern financial markets began to develop – and during the equally critical decade of the 1890s – when major political and financial crises led to a profound and long-lasting restructuring of national banking structures, establishing trends that would hold at least until 1930 and which, in some ways, can still be perceived in contemporary Latin American banking structures.

Recent trends in Latin American banking history

Banking and monetary history of Latin America has been advancing at a fast pace over the past fifteen years. Testimony to this is the proliferation of monographs and essays in the field. To cite only a few of the most significant contributions to this literature, it may be useful to draw attention, for example, to the recent works of Alfonso Quiroz on the development of Peruvian banking and finance between 1850 and 1950; to the studies of Roberto Cortes Conde on banking and monetary policies in Argentina between 1862 and 1890; to the various publications of María Barbara Levy on the banking history of Brazil and the formation of the Rio de Janeiro stock exchange; to the already classic studies of Carlos Peláez and Wilson Suzigan on Brazilian monetary policies in the nineteenth and twentieth centuries; or to the monographs of Flavio Saes on the origins of banking in São Paulo in the late nineteenth century.[2] In the case of Mexico, a number of monographs and collections of essays have opened up the field of banking history in recent years[3] and – as in the rest of the subcontinent – it may be expected that this trend will intensify in the near future, particularly as the financial sector comes to occupy a more important place in economic history than has hitherto been the case.

In this area, studies on the relation between banks and economic and monetary policies have gained a certain pre-eminence, as the studies on Peru, Argentina and Brazil testify. On the other hand, it is clear that much more work on the history of individual firms and on financial markets is required in order to flesh out the still stark anatomy of Latin American banking history.

It should, however, be noted that economic historians who are working on the banking history of Latin America face a number of problems which differentiate the field somewhat from current trends in research in Europe or the United States. In the first place, in Latin America there is much less preoccupation with the analysis of the relationship between early banking structures and industrialization, since the latter process began quite late in Latin America. Throughout the subcontinent, the first banks emerged largely as a result of the expansion of agro-export and mineral-export economies. A second key feature of the early Latin American banking systems – perhaps not unique, but which must nevertheless be borne in mind – was the intense concentration of banking resources in the hands of a few banks, a fact perhaps linked to the marked concentration of income in the landed, mining and mercantile elites, as well as to the relatively small size of the 'middle classes'. A third and related issue is the dominant role of powerful government banks in most of the larger Latin American countries. Such 'government' or 'national' banks were not necessarily state owned; indeed, *most were not*, but they maintained extremely close links with the state and effectively used that privileged relationship to increase their (generally) dominant role in the financial markets.

Our aim in the present chapter is to emphasize the long-term development of banking structures and, in particular, the key role of the largest banking firms which were closely linked to national governments from the last decades of the nineteenth century. This preoccupation is in good measure the result of consideration of the ideas advanced by two distinguished bank historians who have reflected on comparative problems in banking history: Charles Goodhart and Rondo Cameron.[4]

One key question raised by Goodhart concerns the extent to which government banks in the nineteenth century exercised the functions of central banks. A comprehensive response based on the Latin American experience is not yet available due to the lack of institutional and company histories, although it is sufficiently clear that by the end of the century a few of these banks were fulfilling some of those functions, hence suggesting the importance of further study of the historical antecedents of central banking.[5] In this respect, it should be kept in mind that nineteenth-century Latin American finance ministers, not having a very broad grasp of the principles of central banking, found it necessary to impel a given bank or banks to assume responsibility for the implementation of monetary and debt policies which were essential to the efficient fiscal and financial administration of the state. The increasing complexity of the institutionalization of such policies was thus a major factor in promoting privileged relations between the increasingly strong national governments and a given bank.

A second key issue is that raised by Rondo Cameron and the co-authors of several comparative studies on banking history and economic development in the nineteenth century, respecting the possibly negative effects for an economy in which the commercial banking structure is dominated by one great government bank (with tendencies toward monopoly), as was the case in France or Spain during periods of the nineteenth century.

In the various Latin American nations, the dominance of one or two large banks with close links to their respective governments from the end of the nineteenth century could be observed in the cases of Brazil, Argentina and Mexico, among others. Naturally, it must be asked why this was a common tendency among the principal economies of Latin America. We venture to suggest that it may be attributed to the advantages acquired by those banks which had a monopoly of note issue and dominant control of government financial accounts. Furthermore, such advantages were particularly important in monetary and credit markets which were still relatively underdeveloped.

Alliances with the state were therefore fundamental. A privileged relation with the government (precisely at the time when such governments were consolidating a national administration) would appear to have been considerably advantageous to the banking sector. In this regard, moreover, it seems appropriate to recall the commentary of the great banking historian Jean Bouvier, who insisted on paying special attention to the role of the state in the economy: 'What has the state been in the nineteenth and twentieth centuries but the largest enterprise in the economy? By reason of the mass of its employees, the enormous nature of its business and the great movement of funds . . . the state has always been the most influential of economic agents.'[6]

On the other hand, such alliances could also prove to be the cause of bankruptcy and the origin of political and financial crises of severe impact. The early 1890s were witness to such crises, and major political revolutions in Argentina, Brazil and Chile were in various cases linked to extreme mismanagement of state banks. As a result of the different crises, the relationships between state and banks were restructured – paradoxically, undergoing a strengthening rather than a weakening. Thus the symbiotic evolution of national governments and state banks continued into the twentieth century.

Origins of government banks in Latin America

In Latin America the first half of the nineteenth century was witness to a series of relatively short-lived banking experiments which will only be mentioned briefly as antecedents. Among these experiments stand out the first Banco do Brasil (1808–29), the Banco de Buenos Aires (1822–6) and its successor the Banco Nacional (1826–35), although a number of additional financial institutions were also established in other countries of the region such as the Banco de Avío (1830–40) in Mexico.[7]

It was not, however, until the 1850s and 1860s that banking truly took root in Latin America, and it was during these decades that a considerable number of firms were established in the leading ports and capitals of the vast subcontinent. It was in this period that small financial markets in Rio de Janeiro, Santiago, Valparaíso, Buenos Aires and Lima began to acquire a certain dynamism, manifest in the diversification and early institutionalization of financial activities. These years saw the establishment in these cities (still relatively small urban centres) of primitive but operative stock exchanges, and the proliferation of the first private commercial banks along with a series of insurance and complementary financial firms. By the early 1870s, there were a dozen of these new commercial banks in both Rio de Janeiro and Buenos Aires and half a dozen or more in Santiago and Lima.

Already from this era, those banking institutions most closely linked to national governments began to stand out. The Banco do Brasil – refounded in 1850 – was to dominate Brazilian domestic banking until the end of the nineteenth century.[8] The Banco de la Provincia de Buenos Aires, created in 1854, soon controlled much of local credit for commerce in the Argentine capital and for agriculture and ranching in the rich hinterland of Buenos Aires. Similarly, although perhaps a less dominant force, there was the Banco Nacional de Chile, established in 1865, which soon became a key auxiliary of government finance as well as a dynamic commercial bank.[9]

It was also during this period that debate began on the institutional and legal models held to be most adequate for the development of local banking systems. In most Latin American countries there were already two different schools of thought which corresponded broadly to those in favour of 'free-banking' and limited regulation, and those who were advocates of stricter regulation and of a great state bank in the style of the Banque de France. 'Free-bankers', such as Souza Franco, finance minister of Brazil in 1857, argued that this system allowed for more rapid growth and diversification of the banking sector. Similar arguments were advanced by Juan Bautista Alberdi in Argentina and – as of the 1860s – by the disciples of the influential French economist, Courcelle Seneuil, in Chile.[10]

While the ideologues of free-banking tended to win space in the financial press, in practice the incipient banking structures in Argentina, Brazil and Chile were soon dominated by one or two large government banks, as we have already had occasion to indicate. These banks were not usually owned by the government, although in some cases there was state participation. In the 1870s, for example, the largest Argentine bank was the Banco de la Provincia de Buenos Aires. This bank's capital was largely controlled by the provincial government, but the directors were selected from among the merchant community of Buenos Aires on the basis of their commercial and financial experience. Its new rival, the Banco Nacional (1872), on the other hand, was privately owned but began by tending to operate as an auxiliary to the national treasury. Thus there were many different possible ways of operating these banks, and success depended on a combination of personality, good management and limited government intervention in the daily affairs of such firms.[11]

The growth of Latin American banking was fairly rapid between 1865 and 1873, but in this latter year an international economic crisis stopped short most commercial activity, driving a number of private banks in various cities into bankruptcy.[12] The crisis of the 1870s hit hardest in Lima and Callao, wiping out virtually all the existing banks except the Banco de Londres y Perú and the Banco de Callao. In Santiago, Rio de Janeiro, Montevideo and Buenos Aires a few private banks went under but the major banks linked to government finance were able to weather the storm, albeit with some difficulties.[13] Evidently, the mismanagement of the resources of government banks was not yet common practice.

National banks and national governments: the 1880s

In the 1880s there was a renewed boom in banking in the larger Latin American nations, beginning in the capital cities and by the end of the decade spreading to the more commercially dynamic provincial centres in Argentina, Brazil, Chile and Mexico.[14] Traditional historiography of Latin America sees the 1880s as both the age of consolidation of national government under oligarchic structures, and the golden age of the export economies. It is often argued that it was the new political stability which allowed the expansion of the economies, but it is more rarely observed that it was precisely the turnaround in the economy that allowed a more stable and stronger national administration. In the following pages it will be argued that the expansion of national banks proved to be a key element in facilitating 'national' government, so lacking in previous decades.

In essence, we argue that institutional innovation in the banking sector initially induced improvements in the efficiency of management of the state fiscal and financial administration. But the structure of banking varied from country to country, and not all 'national' banks were similar. Thus, to provide an idea of the relative importance of these banks, a few preliminary descriptive comments are in order. In Argentina, for example, banking was heavily concentrated in the city of Buenos Aires, and, furthermore, was dominated by two 'government' banks, namely the Banco de la Provincia de Buenos Aires and the Banco Nacional: in 1855 these two banks controlled 67% of the capital, 41% of the metallic reserves, 64% of the loans and 89% of the note issue of all banks in the capital.[15]

In Brazil, the predominance of the Banco do Brasil was manifest until the end of the 1880s, as it held sway in the realm of capital, deposits and note issue. It should be noted that the relation between reserves and total note issue was apparently similar to that of the Argentine banks, but the Brazilian banks actually proved (initially) to be more conservative in this regard, since most of the notes were issued by the national treasury rather than by the banks. Nonetheless, the stability of the Brazilian banking system was undermined in the late 1880s when two other banks with special issuing privileges were established. According to Stephen Topik: 'By September, 1890, the three banks, the Banco do Brasil, the Banco dos Estados Unidos do Brasil and the Banco Nacional controlled by means of their privileges – and through other banks which they owned – 95 per cent of all banknotes in circulation.'[16]

The banking system of Chile in the mid-1880s was freer and more competitive from every point of view than its South American neighbours. It is true that in the 1860s the Banco Nacional de Chile dominated the local banking structure, but after the financial crisis of 1873 and the suspension of convertibility of the notes of the Banco Nacional in 1876, its influence declined. By 1885, for example, the Banco de Valparaíso had attained a similar size and surpassed the Banco Nacional in deposits.

The situation in Mexico, the Latin American nation where banking took longest to develop and where – from the start – the banking structure proved most concentrated, was different. It was only in the mid-1880s that a banking infrastructure was established in Mexico City, an infrastructure initially dominated by one great institution, the Banco Nacional de México, which in 1885 held close to 80% of total capital, deposits and loans of the Mexican capital's banking firms. The Banco Nacional de México was a privately owned and managed bank, but at the same time it was put in charge of a large number of government financial affairs: it handled a large account for the finance ministry, provided the service on the internal and external debts of the republic, and made regular medium-term advances to the government when in urgent need of funds.[17]

Similar functions – as government banker – had been carried out by the aforementioned Banco de la Provincia de Buenos Aires, Banco Nacional (Argentina), Banco do Brasil and Banco Nacional de Chile from the 1860s; but it was only in the 1880s that the importance of their activities as government bankers intensified, a fact not unrelated to the steep rise in the income and expenditures of national governments.

That the governments of the larger Latin American nations were able systematically to increase income and at the same time consolidate political, military and administrative control over their relatively vast territories during the 1880s has been considered by many historians as the result of new intra-oligarchic political pacts and, also, as the consequence of capable military and political authoritarianism as represented by such dominant figures as Porfirio Diaz in Mexico or General Roca in Argentina. However, the impact of institutional and economic innovations must also be taken into account.

It is a well-known but little studied fact that the combination of rail and telegraph contributed notably not only to the establishment of incipient domestic markets, but also to a more efficient state and military administration. Much more infrequent, however, are references to the role of 'national' banks, which also played a significant part in this dramatic process of 'modernization'. In my opinion the national banks (some public and some privately owned) contributed in numerous ways to the improvement of fiscal and financial administration by the government, mainly because they were the first banks to establish large networks of offices and agencies throughout the nations in which they operated. It should, however, be understood that the observations in the following pages require verification (or dismissal) by future research – using quantitative analysis – on the relationship between bank administration and public fiscal administration.

Prior to the 1880s, national administrations in most Latin American countries had been relatively weak due to a great variety of factors: lack of modern transport and communications, federalist political trends (and, as a result, frequent local rebellions), inadequate fiscal machinery, chronic deficits and, therefore, wavering military loyalties by officers and soldiers who were often underpaid or paid late. All of these traditional obstacles to political modernization and centralization of national state power began to be eliminated in the 1880s in the larger Latin American nations.

The improvement of government finances and administration went hand in hand with military modernization. Railways, telegraphs and banks reduced military costs substantially and increased efficiency. This was largely due to the fact that now the same or a lesser number of soldiers could be moved more rapidly, and – being well paid and armed – their loyalty and efficiency increased. Not surprisingly, after 1880 there was a sharp drop in provincial revolutions by military discontents (a key figure of early nineteenth-century political instability). And proportionally, military expenditures declined in terms of total public expenses.[18]

If we look more specifically at fiscal administration, it is clear that the creation of national banks – with numerous agencies – led to 'institutional innovations' with important and positive effects upon state finance. For example, the collection and movement of taxes (and government funds in general) proved much swifter and surer in the 1880s as a result of the establishment of bank agencies in many secondary cities and ports. The collection of funds continued to be handled by fiscal agents but they now had more secure places to safeguard such funds. Moreover, finance ministers could now count on more complete and rapid information on how much money was available throughout the nation, and could therefore dispose of it more effectively. In combination with telegraphs and railways, this substantially improved the efficiency of the state fiscal and financial administration.[19]

The improved collection and transfer of funds, the more rapid concentration of funds in key points, the reduced risks and greater punctuality in government payments all substantially reduced the financial costs of government. Indeed, these factors can be defined as 'transaction costs' which had seriously limited the efficiency of previous governments and, therefore, had negative effects upon the private sector. But the establishment of banks with national networks of offices also had other, additional benefits. For example, public accounting methods improved substantially as both private and public managers became more familiar with modern financial administration, allowing for great precision, punctuality and centralization of the movement and register of funds. In addition, finance ministers had greater possibilities of predicting future trends in public finance and of its general relationship with the economy, as banks now published regular information on interest rates, a key variable for the diagnosis of economic cycles. In this respect, it can be argued that information costs (for government finance ministries) related to 'the price of money' (present and future) tended to drop. In the first half of the nineteenth century such costs were quite substantial and had diminished the efficiency of the respective state administrations.[20]

It was not, however, only information costs that declined. The broadening of money markets and the creation of banks brought down the *price of money* (interest rates) generally speaking and, specifically, reduced the costs of money required by the government for short-term overdrafts or medium-term loans.[21] With the creation of national banks, governments opened large accounts which allowed for substantial overdrafts at small cost, facilitating the payment of expenses by all public agencies in any part of the country. This increased flexibility was accompanied by the improved handling of internal debt, with lower interest rates and less dependency on moneylenders. The national banks took charge of service of internal debts and, in addition, provided increased access to foreign funds – external loans – at more reasonable costs, and with regular service in gold.[22]

Hence, both information costs and costs of money for the respective governments tended to fall as a result of the establishment of institutions such as the Banco do Brasil, the Banco Nacional de Argentina and the Banco Nacional de México. Nation building and administrative modernization thus went hand in hand with the broadening commercial networks of these new banking institutions. Nonetheless, the creation of such large banking companies with such close links to governments also posed a series of formidable dangers. Indeed, the financial boom of the 1880s and the consequent phase of prosperity led political and economic elites to fancy that they could do no wrong and impelled them into speculative ventures that were pregnant with catastrophe.

The political and financial crises of the 1890s

While the 'national' banks we have reviewed provided Latin American governments with important instruments for more efficient administration, they also lent themselves to all kinds of speculation, with both public and private funds. Thus – paradoxically – the creation of the state banks strengthened the state's fiscal and financial machinery and, at the same time, encouraged politicians, bureaucrats and well-connected speculators to engage in risky financial deals on a large scale.

Finance ministers of the moment had little grasp of the complexities of managing monetary policy in a time of unbridled bank competition which led to massive issues of paper money by many rival financial institutions. Nor did finance ministers understand the dangers of overheating the economy by implementing policies which tended systematically to lower interest rates. For instance, as a result of massive inflows of foreign capital, and as a result of the establishment of a great number of financial firms (banks, insurance firms, real estate financial agencies, firms specializing in stock exchange speculation, etc.), interest rates in the leading Latin American cities tended to decline somewhat in the early and mid-1880s. These lower rates, in combination with the abundant supply of capital, stimulated two related speculative booms in burgeoning stock exchange markets and in the growing urban real estate markets.

The allure of fast fortunes drew all kinds of speculators – including many politicians – into the financial frenzy. And in numerous cases the larger banks were also drawn into the game, advancing credit to clients who wanted the money basically for speculation. The Argentine state banks were among the most notorious instruments of the financial boom of the late 1880s, just as they would also soon be victims of the subsequent financial panic.

Nonetheless, most Latin American finance ministers of the late 1880s believed that the financial boom was simply a sign of their respective economies' entry into a phase of modern capitalism. Was it not true that – as had occurred in all the great industrial nations, France, Great Britain, Germany and the United States – stock exchange booms and speculation were formidable engines of growth? Indeed, the late 1880s were everywhere a time of general unbridled optimism in the magic of the money markets.

But the crash came soon enough, and in the case of Latin America financial collapse was accompanied by major social convulsion and political crises. In the Argentine case the banking crisis of 1890–1 (which coincided with a foreign debt crisis) lasted a year and a half and was extremely violent. The two largest state banks, the Banco Nacional and the Banco de la Provincia de Buenos Aires, collapsed, as did ten regional banks sponsored by provincial governments.[23] In other words, all the banks closely linked to government went under, an indication of the perils potentially inherent in such relationships. On the other hand, relatively few private bankers went bankrupt, although the number of mercantile firms that did so was quite large.[24] It would not be until the end of 1891 – with the creation of the Banco de la Nación – that the financial situation began to ameliorate. In practice, the success of the new national bank in establishing itself at the heart of the Argentine financial system was quite surprising given the breadth of the collapse of the previous state banks. For in a short time, the Banco de la Nación had not only become the largest bank in the capital, but also proceeded to establish branches in virtually all important provincial cities and large towns. This was due in large part to the export boom of the years 1890–1914, but it also reflected the success of the extremely cautious policies of the new bank's managers who maintained extremely high metallic reserves in order to ensure that a financial crisis like that of 1890–1 would not be repeated.

In Brazil, the late 1880s also witnessed an extraordinary stock exchange boom that culminated in the financial frenzy of 1889–91 known as the 'Encilhamento'. The position of the Banco do Brasil was weakened by increasing competition with two large banks that obtained note issue privileges from the government: the rivalry intensified as of December 1890, when the two rival banks – the Banco dos Estados Unidos do Brasil and the Banco Nacional – proceeded to fuse into one giant financial enterprise called the Banco da República. Nonetheless, the fusion also reflected the increasingly unstable economic situation and the need to pool resources in order to avoid a panic. In 1891 bankruptcies began to multiply in Rio de Janeiro in the midst of an orgy of speculation. A generalized financial collapse came in 1892 as dozens of old and new companies toppled. In order to shore up public and private credit a new restructuring plan was put in force, leading to the fusion of the old Banco do Brasil and the new Banco da República.[25]

In this instance – as in the Argentine case – the Brazilian state assumed rectorship of the banking system, forcing bankrupt firms to close down and thereby accentuating the concentration of bank capital. The objective of such policies was essentially designed to defend and stabilize public finance. But in practice they also deeply affected private finances. Eventually the reforms gave place to the configuration of the Banco do Brasil in 1905, the institution which was destined to dominate Brazilian banking during most of the twentieth century.

In Chile the banking crisis followed the civil war of 1890–1 and the downfall of the Balmaceda administration. In this case too – and in a surprisingly similar fashion – the government intervened to force the fusion of the three largest banks into one dominant institution, the Banco de Chile – which, inevitably, was to assume many of the functions of a government bank, even while continuing as a privately-owned firm.

Finally, in the case of Mexico it may be observed that while the financial crisis of the early 1890s was less severe, it also reflected the dangers implicit in the close links established between a great bank and the government. In 1893 – as a major economic crisis broke in the international arena – Mexican finances began to break down. The Banco Nacional de México had made large advances over various years to the government in order to cover its deficits, and was by now over its head in public debts which, however lucrative, threatened the lifeblood of the bank. Finance minister José Yves Limantour was able to save the situation by negotiating a large foreign loan with the Bleichröder banking firm of Berlin, a loan that was nominally to be used for public works but in practice went to pay the backlog of loans due to the Banco Nacional de México. A few years later, in 1897, Limantour ratified the first comprehensive Mexican banking law which promised to allow for a more federalist financial structure, but in practice the Banco Nacional continued to be the most important bank and the one most engaged in the administration of government finance.

Given the parallels between the financial and banking crises in various Latin American nations in the early 1890s, it seems worthwhile to attempt to summarize the causes of these crises and their effect on banking policies in the immediate decades following. For, indeed, the banking reforms that followed these crises were to shape the basic banking structures and policies of most Latin American nations until the outbreak of the Great Depression in 1929, when a whole slew of new and very different financial reforms began to be formulated.

Among the causes of the financial crises of the early 1890s, it is possible to note a large number of strictly bank-related factors which point to bad management and overly political use of banks, elements which go beyond the collective, psychological behaviour characteristic of financial frenzies and booms.[26]

One dangerous bank policy which tended to be adopted by the managers of Latin American government banks in the late 1880s was excess bank note issue in relation to metallic reserves.[27] This was indicative of the lack of banking experience locally, and proved to be in notable contrast with the few British banks operating in the region, all of which emerged from the crises of the early 1890s with flying colours.[28]

A second bad management policy was the acquisition of risky bonds and stock – much in speculative bonds and real estate paper – which were often registered as part of bank reserves. This was common practice among the Argentine and Brazilian banks in the late 1880s, and exposed them to the perils of bankruptcy when the stock exchange and real estate markets declined. A related weakness of these banks was the adoption of indiscriminate policies of issuing loans to clients with inadequate guarantees: particularly notorious were large loans to capitalists and speculators who offered real estate as guarantees precisely when property values were going through the roof. When prices dropped, however, such guarantees turned out to be virtually worthless.

Another characteristic of much of the banking conducted by banks which were closely linked to national or provincial governments in the 1880s was favouritism: policies of lending money to associates of bank directors, and, more particularly, to politicians and their friends and relatives, were quite common. This practice was particularly notorious in the case of the Argentine state banks.

Bank management problems arose from misunderstandings of monetary and public debt problems. On the one hand, bank directors had an inadequate understanding of monetary inflation with inconvertible currency (as was the Argentine case after 1885) or with monetary systems with inadequate metallic reserves, common in Brazil and Chile too. In Mexico, on the other hand, this pitfall was avoided because of large silver monetary reserves, but major problems did arise as a result of the falling value of silver in relation to gold.

Finally, the accumulation of foreign debts by state banks, which were only payable in gold – a common feature of Argentine finance in the late 1880s – led to perilous situations and the balance of payments situation worsened. As the metallic reserves of banks evaporated and, generally, as foreign currency and gold disappeared from local money markets, there was no way of continuing the service on foreign debts. As a result, a number of banks found their international sources of credit and capital frozen, and they were soon subject to severe international pressure to renew payments despite all the difficulties. In summary, inadequate care in the management of bank balances (overlending, insufficient reserves, low metallic reserves), corruption and a hugely speculative market created the necessary conditions for major financial crashes.

Epilogue

This brief review of the birth of banking in Latin America in the second half of the nineteenth century and of the growing importance of national banks – closely linked to governments – may be of some interest to economic historians insofar as it indicates the existence of certain structural trends which appear to have been common throughout a vast geographical zone. On the one hand, it should be emphasized that in Latin America the 'banking revolution' took place before the 'industrial revolution'. On the other hand, the fact that many of the largest banks were so closely linked to state administrations implied certain advantages, insofar as the rapid growth of government also helped spur the growth of national banks with a network of offices and agencies in each of the larger Latin American countries. Nonetheless, the links with government led to some singular tendencies and certain dangers in the financial sphere – as can be seen in the general financial crashes in Argentina, Brazil and Chile in the early 1890s.

To summarize, there was a fairly close relationship between the institutional development of banks and political evolution during the second half of the nineteenth century. In the 1850s the consolidation of parliamentary government – accompanied by an export boom – led to economic conditions and legislation favourable to the establishment of early banks. In the 1880s the consolidation of national government administrations went hand in hand with the creation of the networks of offices and agencies of the largest national banks in each of the countries here reviewed. Finally, in the 1890s the downfall of many government banks led to a massive process of restructuring and to the creation of even more powerful state banks.

The restructured state banks – the Banco de la Nación de Argentina (1891), the Banco do Brasil (1905), the Banco de Chile (1892) and the Banco Nacional de México (1884) – dominated both commercial and public finance for many years. They also fulfilled – during several decades – several of the functions of central banks. Indeed, their pre-eminent role might help explain why central banking took as long as it did to become formally established in these countries: 1923 saw the first central bank established in Chile, 1926 the first in Mexico, 1935 the first in Argentina, whilst it was not until 1965 that Brazil was to see its first central bank! Clearly, the historical exploration of the banking structures in Latin America can provide some useful insights into the long-term trends of the respective financial sectors in these diverse nations well into the twentieth century.

Notes

1 On British banks in Latin America the best studies are David Joslin, *A Century of Banking in Latin America* (London, 1966), and Charles Jones, 'Commercial Banks and Mortgage Companies', in D. C. M. Platt (ed.), *Business Imperialism, 1840–1930: An Inquiry Based on British Experience in Latin America* (Oxford, 1977), pp. 17–52. The first of these were the Bank of London and the River Plate (1863), the Bank of London and Brazil (1863) and the Bank of London, Mexico and Peru (1864). They were relatively small firms but catered to a wealthy elite including some of the more prosperous local landowners and merchants as well as the leading British import/export firms in the capital cities – Buenos Aires, Lima, Rio de Janeiro and Mexico City – but as yet (1860s) had no offices in secondary cities.

2 Alfonso W. Quiroz, *Banqueros en conflicto: Estructura financiera y economía peruana, 1884–1930* (Lima, 1989); idem, *Domestic and Foreign Finance in Peru, 1850–1950: Financing Visions of Development* (Pittsburgh, Pa., 1993); Roberto Cortés Conde, *Dinero, deuda y crisis. Evolución fiscal y monetaria en la Argentina, 1862–1890* (Buenos Aires, 1989); María Barbara Levy, *Historia da Bolsa de Valores do Rio de Janeiro* (Rio de Janeiro, 1977); María Barbara Levy and Ana María Ribeiro de Andrade, 'Fundamentos do Sistema Bancário no Brasil: 1834–1860', *Estudos Económicos*, 15, special issue (1985), pp. 17–48; Carlos Manuel Peláez and Wilson Suzigan, *Historia monetária do Brasil: analise da política, comportamento e instituçoes monetárias* (Rio de Janeiro, 1976); Flavio Saes, *Crédito e bancos no desenvolvimento da economía paulista, 1850–1930* (São Paulo, 1986).

3 The pioneer was Robert Potash, *Historia del Banco de Avío y Fomento de la Industria, 1830–1841* (Mexico City, 1965), but more recent contributions include Carlos Marichal and Leonor Ludlow (eds.), *Banca y poder en México, 1800–1925* (Mexico City, 1986); Eduardo Turrent, *Historia del Banco de México* (Mexico City, 1988); Abdiel Oñate, *Banca y agricultura en México, 1905–1926* (Mexico City, 1991); Leonor Ludlow, 'La primera etapa de formación bancaria (1864–1897)', in Leonor Ludlow and Jorge Silva (eds.), *Los negocios y las ganancias: de la colonia al México moderno* (Mexico City, 1993), pp. 330–62.

4 Rondo Cameron, *Banking in the Early Stages of Industrialization: A Study in Comparative Economic History* (London, 1967); Rondo Cameron (ed.), *Banking and Economic Development: Some Lessons of History* (London, 1972); and Charles Goodhart, *The Evolution of Central Banks* (Cambridge, Mass., 1988).

5 A good model of the usefulness of such analyses are Rafael Anes, 'El Banco de España, 1874–1914: un Banco Nacional', and Gabriel Tortella, 'Las magnitudes monetarias y sus determinantes', in Gabriel Tortella (ed.), *La banca en la Restauración*, 2 vols. (Madrid, 1974), vol. I, pp. 107–215, 457–251.

6 Jean Bouvier, 'Histoire financière et problèmes d'analyse des dépenses publiques', *Annales ESA*, 5 (1978), pp. 207–15.

7 All of these were government-owned banks except for the Banco de Buenos Aires. On the Banco do Brasil see Carlos Manuel Peláez, 'The Establishment of Banking Institutions in a Backward Economy: Brazil, 1800–1851', *Business History Review*, 49 (1975), pp. 446–72; and María Barbara Levy and Ana María Ribeiro de Andrade,

'A Gestão Monetária na Formaçao do Estado Nacional', *Revista Brasileira do Mercado des Capitais*, 6, 17 (1980), pp. 138–52; on the Banco de Buenos Aires and Banco Nacional, see Samuel Amaral, 'Comercio y crédito: el Banco de Buenos Aires, 1822–1826', *América*, 2, 4 (1977), pp. 9–48, and 'El Banco Nacional y las finanzas de Buenos Aires. El curso forzoso y la convertibilidad del papel moneda en 1826', *Actas del VI Congreso Internacional de Historia de América*, vol. V (Buenos Aires, 1982), pp. 415–29; and O. Garrigós, *El Banco de la Provincia de Buenos Aires* (Buenos Aires, 1873). On the Banco de Avío, see Potash, *Historia del Banco*.

8 A discussion of the banking developments in Brazil in the 1860s can be found in Ana María Andrade, '1864: Conflicto entre metalistas e pluralistas' (Masters thesis, University of Rio de Janeiro, 1987). In the late 1880s and early 1890s the Banco do Brasil went through a series of fusions with two other banks, which together dominated the Rio de Janeiro financial market. Later in 1905 the Banco do Brasil was reorganized and restructured into the banking firm which today is still the largest in Brazil. See Franco Barroso, *Reforma monetária e instabilidade durante a transição republicana* (Rio de Janeiro, 1983); and Stephen Topik, *The Political Economy of the Brazilian State, 1889–1930* (Austin, 1987).

9 For additional information on these early banks see Carlos Marichal, 'El nacimiento de la banca en América Latina, 1850–1873', in Marichal and Ludlow, *Banca y Poder*, pp. 231–65.

10 For the Brazilian debate see Sebastião Ferreira Soares, *Elementos da Estatística comprendendo Theoria da Sciencia e a Sua Aplicaçao a Estatística Commercial do Brasil* (Rio de Janeiro, 1865). For the Argentine debates, see Cortés Conde, *Dinero, deuda y crisis*, who reviews the parliamentary discussions of banking in 1863; on the influence of Courcelle Seneuil in Chile from 1860, see Guillermo Subercaseaux, *Monetary and Banking Policy of Chile* (Oxford, 1922). For an overview, see Carlos Marichal, 'Modelos y sistemas bancarios en América Latina en el siglo XIX, 1850–1880', in Pedro Tedde and Carlos Marichal (eds.), *La formación de los bancos centrales en España y América Latina*, 2 vols. (Madrid, 1994), vol. I, pp. 131–58.

11 Behind most of the major new banks in Latin America it can be frequently found that there was some outstanding personality who was an innovative entrepreneur with a penetrating grasp of financial affairs. The names of the Baron de Mauá (founder of the second Banco do Brasil and of the privately owned Banco Mauá), of Eduardo Tornquist (founder in 1872 of the Tornquist Bank of Buenos Aires and influential adviser to the government and state banks on international finance) or of Edouard Noetzlin (one of the guiding spirits of the Banco Nacional de México, from 1881) are indicative, but only Mauá has found a biographer. See Anyda Marchant, *Viscount Mauá and the Empire of Brazil: A Biography of Irineu Evangelista de Sousa, 1813–1889* (Berkeley, 1965).

12 For some comparative data, see Carlos Marichal, 'La crisis internacional de 1873 en Latinoamerica', *Iztapalpa, Revista de Ciencias Sociales* (1982), pp. 42–71; and Carlos Marichal, *A Century of Debt Crises in Latin America: From Independence to the Great Depression 1820–1930* (Princeton, N.J., 1989), ch. 4.

13 Among the most notorious bankruptcies was that of the famous Mauá Bank which operated in Rio de Janeiro, Montevideo and Buenos Aires. Owned by the foremost Brazilian capitalist of the age, the Barón de Mauá, its fall marked the demise of his multinational business empire.

14 By the end of the 1880s there were at least fifteen important commercial banks in Rio de Janeiro and sixteen in Buenos Aires and smaller numbers in other Latin

American cities. In Argentina there were also some ten official provincial banks and another dozen private banking institutions in various provincial cities. In Brazil provincial banking in the late 1880s was concentrated in the north-east and in São Paulo, although a few small banking firms could be found in other regions. Among the few studies on regional banking in this period see Saes, *Crédito e bancos.*

15 The best statistics on Argentine banking in the 1880s are to be found in the official reports of Pedro Agote, *Informe del Presidente del Crédito Público Nacional sobre la deuda pública, bancos, acuñación de moneda y presupuestos*, vol. IV (Buenos Aires, 1887).

16 Topik, *The Political Economy*, p. 31.

17 See the essays by Batiz, Ludlow and Marichal in Marichal and Ludlow, *Banca y poder*. Also see Ludlow, 'La primera etapa'.

18 This, in turn, helped free public funds for investment in public works (investment in communications infrastructure, etc.), in public education and other activities which were essential to modernization and the forging of a strong state administration.

19 For the consolidation of national administration both telegraphs and railways were essential. Telegraphs provided the means for swift communication of instructions to local agents for payment or transfer of funds, and railways allowed for rapid transfer either of government metallic funds or of the government agents themselves, in the persons of fiscal or military personnel.

20 A particularly notorious example of the negative effects of the lack of adequate information on supply and costs of money can be found in the review of Mexican state finances before 1860. See Barbara Tenenbaum, *The Politics of Penury in Mexico, 1821–1856* (Albuquerque, N. Mex., 1986).

21 In the case of Mexico City, for example, interest rates in the 1870s fluctuated between 10% and 14%, but from the early 1880s, with the establishment of several large banks, they dropped to levels of 6–10%. Obviously, this benefited both the private and the public sectors. For analysis of trends in the 1880s see Carlos Marichal, 'Foreign Loans, Banks and Capital Markets in Mexico, 1880–1910', in R. Liehr (ed.), *The Public Debt in Latin America in Historical Perspective* (Berlin, 1995), pp. 337–74.

22 The Banco Nacional in Argentina, for example, negotiated various foreign loans in the 1880s for the national government, as did the Banco Nacional de México. For details, see Marichal, *A Century of Debt Crises*, ch. 5.

23 For details, see *ibid.*, ch. 6.

24 The most important private bank to collapse was the Banco Carabassa, subsequently absorbed by the Bank of London and River Plate. The other merchant and financial firms that went under suffered as a result of the decline in trade, the fall in real estate prices and the fall of the state banks with which they had conducted business. For details see *ibid.*, ch. 6.

25 For antecedents and details, see Barrosso, *Reforma monetária*, and Topik, *The Political Economy*.

26 On collective financial mentalities and behaviours, see Charles Kindleberger, *Manias, Panics and Crashes: A History of Financial Crises* (New York, 1978).

27 In the case of the Banco Nacional of Argentina these tendencies can be observed in the banking balances: it had among the most expansionist loan policies (the ratio of loans to total resources being close to 90/100) while its metallic reserves were extraordinarily scarce (the ratio of reserves to note issue was extremely low, 12/100). Data can be found in Agote, *Informe del presidente*.

28 It was precisely the success of these few British banks in crisis situations that won
    them their fame within Latin America in the late nineteenth century and,
    subsequently, in economic history texts. See the classic text by Joslin, *A Century of
    Banking*.

20 Banking, trade and the rise of capitalism in Argentina, 1850–1930

Andrés M. Regalsky

Between 1850 and 1930 Argentina underwent a vigorous process of growth, leading to its consolidation as a capitalist economy. This growth, however, was not related to industrialization, as was the case for the US and Western Europe. Rather, it was related to the expansion of an externally-oriented agrarian sector, accompanied by a parallel enlargement of the internal market that later allowed some industrial progress.

Argentina's economic growth was part of the world expansion of capitalism during the second half of the nineteenth century, and, at this time, she was considered one of its most successful followers. The transport revolution and the 'factor migration' (labour, capital) were decisive landmarks in that process, furthering Argentina's access to foreign markets, and providing the necessary resources for the exploitation of her vast prairies.

Economic progress brought about important social and institutional changes: on the one hand, the emergence of the middle classes and of a new breed of entrepreneurs, related to the migratory impact; on the other hand, the organization of a national state, based on the old autonomous provinces, with an exclusive authority over all the territory, which insured the establishment of a modern legal order.

All these changes demanded a great financial effort. Foreign capital brought a very significant percentage (at times the majority) of the resources. Nevertheless, they also required a banking and financial system capable of facilitating the transfer of funds to those sectors demanding them, and capable of securing the right conditions for currency circulation.

Both the monetary and the credit aspects are related to two important fields: the operation of monetary markets in the period of the classical gold standard and the role of banking in economic development. This chapter examines these subjects throughout the evolution of the Argentine banking system and its relationship with the real sector.

The formation of the monetary and banking system, 1854–80

Up to 1880 Argentina lacked a unified monetary system, as a consequence of the obstacles delaying the organization of a national state and the limited circulation of goods. Since the end of the colonial period two great systems had taken shape: that of the provinces, based on low-quality specie coins from Bolivia and Chile, and that of Buenos Aires, where a paper money system had been established, first as convertible (Banco de Buenos Aires, 1822) and later as inconvertible legal tender.

The circulation of paper currency in Buenos Aires was initially caused by the needs of the new independent government, unable to meet the demand for conversion with the available specie resources. The acceptance of the new notes by the mercantile community of this city, who handled most of the country's foreign trade, was a decisive factor for the establishment of that monetary system in Buenos Aires.[1]

The monetary anarchy did not change after 1860, when the organization of the new national state came. The new national government recognized the peso fuerte (hard dollar) as its monetary specie-based unit, and committed itself to accepting the Buenos Aires notes at the market value. Since the suspension of convertibility in 1826, paper peso issues had risen some 140 times, while its market value had fallen to one twenty-eighth of the peso fuerte. The issuing house was the Banco de la Provincia de Buenos Aires (hereafter BPBA), successor to the Casa de Moneda and to the primitive Banco de Buenos Aires, under the rule of the provincial government. After national organization this provincial government undertook adjustment measures in order to reverse the devaluation process. This provoked a sharp contraction in the paper market, which coincided paradoxically with a period of abundant gold arrivals, due to the growth of exports and foreign loans. Whether this gold could have joined the circulation, and counterbalanced the reduction of paper money supply (and credit), is an open question.[2]

However, this process of contraction and revaluation of paper currency was stopped from 1867 onwards by the establishment of an Oficina de Cambios in the BPBA, which converted paper pesos at fixed exchange rate (twenty-five for one peso fuerte). This measure had been demanded especially by the rural producers, damaged in their double condition of debtors and exporters. The gold inflows helped to reactivate the note issue, which in 1872 had risen above the 1863 level by 150%.

This evolution was closely followed by the credit of the BPBA. It started in 1854, when the primitive Casa de Moneda was authorized to receive deposits from the public and use them in discounts to the private sector. The abundance of money in the market and the multiplying effect of the loans encouraged a sharp rise of the deposits, which in 1863 exceeded the paper money stock. Credit itself, after a fall between 1864 and 1866, reassumed its expansion intensely until 1872, when it was five times larger than in 1863 (cf. Tables 20.1 and 20.2).

This expansive link between the gold inflow and the bank notes, deposit and credit supply, can be specially related to the low level of cash reserves of the BPBA, below 20% of deposits. This fact is an indicator of the very heterodox credit policy of that institution. Its special position in the market, as the only deposit bank, and the kind of resources it handled, including interest-bearing deposits of low mobility, determined its business practices.

At the beginning bank regulations only authorized the discount of ninety days' bills of exchange and promissory notes stemming from genuine commercial transactions. Soon innovations started. The loan term was enlarged to 180 days, more commonly used by local commerce. This was complemented with the discount of accommodation bills, issued *ad hoc* and indefinitely renewable. The stated objective was to open the access to credit to other sectors besides commerce, such as cattle raising and other 'industries'.[3]

This was accompanied by a similar policy on interest rates. During the opening period, up to 1866, the bank rate followed market conditions closely and reached peaks of 15–16%. Since convertibility, bank rates were kept at a relatively low level (6–7%), which persisted beyond the following crisis. When in 1873 the market rate rose to 21%, the bank rate was only increased to 9% and for a short time, for the explicit purpose of exercising a moderating influence in the market.

Table 20.1. *Economic and monetary statistics of Argentina, 1852–1928 (million pesos)*

Years	Population (million)	Exports (gold)	Notes issue (paper)	Notes issue (gold)	Deposits (gold)	Credits (gold)	Mortgage credit	Cash ratio	MM
1852			130.5	7.9	0.0				
1863	1.2	30.4	340.0	12.1	14.5	11.3		9.7	2.0
1866			318.8	14.2	25.0	16.0		28.4	1.8
1872	1.8		826.0	33.0	60.3	57.6		25.1	2.0
1875			717.0	28.7	51.4	63.7		18.2	2.2
1880	2.3	59.6	919.5	32.1	48.4	57.0		26.8	1.8
1881			965.9	38.6	60.8	56.7	16.0	24.8	1.9
1884				61.4	122.3	176.0		22.8	2.2
1889	3.6	65.4	172.0	73.8	218.8	273.9	110.0	25.0	2.7
1901	4.7	173.9	296.0	122.8	165.1	129.9		53.8	1.5
1912		497.6	799.8	352.3	652.4	681.1	1,100.0	36.1	2.0
1914	8.2	385.3	803.0	352.2	521.6	543.9		39.2	1.8
1920		970.0	1,352.2	481.5	1,163.9	1,011.7		29.6	2.6
1928	11.9	1,046.0	1,405.9	619.3	1,741.5	1,507.9	1,540.0	22.2	2.8
Increase									
1863/89	3.0	2.1		6.1	15.2	24.2			
1889/1928	3.3	16.0		8.4	7.9	5.5	14.0		
1901/28	2.5	6.0		5.0	10.5	11.6			
1863/1928	9.9	34.3		51.2	120.1	133.4			

Notes: Cash ratio: cash/deposits (in percentage). MM (money multiplier): money supply (M2)/monetary base. Money supply = deposits + notes issue − notes in banks. Population was measured in 1857, 1870, 1880, 1890, 1900, 1914 and 1930; mortgage credits, in 1881, 1889, 1915 and 1925. One gold peso (and one peso fuerte) was roughly equivalent to one gold dollar (one pound = five gold pesos).

Sources: Pedro Agote, *Informe del Presidente del Crédito Público Nacional sobre la deuda pública, bancos, y emisiones de papel moneda*, 5 vols. (Buenos Aires, 1881–9); Roberto Cortés Conde, *Dinero, deuda y crisis. Evolución fiscal y monetaria en la Argentina, 1862–1890* (Buenos Aires, 1989); Carlos Díaz Alejandro, *Essays on the Economic History of the Argentine Republic* (New Haven, 1970); Octavio Garrigós, *El Banco de la Provincia* (Buenos Aires, 1873); T. Halperín Donghi *et al.*, 'Evolutión del comercio exterior argentino. Exportaciones' (unpublished); Instituto de Estudios Bancarios, Universidad de Buenos Aires, *La economía bancaria a través de sus índices más significativos 1901–1935* (Buenos Aires, 1973); Zulma R. Lattes and Alfredo Lattes, *La población en Argentina* (Buenos Aires, 1975).

Table 20.2. Deposits and credits in Argentine banks, 1863–89 (million of paper pesos)

Years	Exchange rate	Deposits				Credits			
		BPBA	BN	Others	Total	BPBA	BN	Others	Total
1863	28.0	406.1	0.0	0.0	406.1	317.1	0.0	0.0	317.1
1866	22.5	445.5	0.0	117.0	561.4	235.8	0.0	126.0	360.9
1872	25.0	1,192.5	0.0	315.0	1,507.5	1,165.7	0.0	275.0	1,440.0
1875	25.0	990.0	40.0	252.5	1,282.5	1,167.4	140.0	285.0	1,592.5
1880	28.6	966.7	17.2	400.4	1,384.2	1,182.2	80.1	368.9	1,630.2
1881a	25.0	1,200.0	20.0	300.0	1,520.0	1,035.0	77.5	325.0	1,417.5
1881b	1.00	48.0	0.8	12.0	60.8	41.4	2.3	13.0	56.7
1883	1.00	63.9	11.7	23.4	99.0	69.5	33.6	30.5	133.6
1884	1.00	76.6	19.1	26.6	122.3	82.3	57.7	36.0	176.0
1887	1.45	98.3	40.1	122.0	260.4	109.5	110.6	160.0	380.1
1889	2.33	138.4	151.3	220.0	509.7	164.4	193.8	280.0	638.2
Increase									
1863/81		2.95		18.67	3.74	3.26			4.47
1881/9		2.88	189.1		8.38	3.97	84.26	21.54	11.25
1863/89		8.54		31.41	12.94			50.25	

Notes: **Paper pesos:** pesos 'moneda corriente' (1863–81a), and pesos 'moneda nacional' (1881b–9).
Sources: see Table 20.1; Banco Español del Río de la Plata, *Memoria y Balance* (Buenos Aires, 1887–9); Banco Francés del Río de la Plata, *Memoria y Balance* (Buenos Aires, 1887–9); Banco de Italia y Río de la Plata, *Memoria y Balance* (Buenos Aires, 1872–89).

It may be asked to what extent this sort of anti-cyclical policy was globally beneficial to the market or discriminated in favour of a minority with access to BPBA credits. Contemporary references underline the bank's support of rural production, and its large credit distribution in small individual amounts. The role of branches was remarkable. Founded between 1863 and 1872 in little towns and rural areas, their share of the total portfolio rose from 8% in this last year to 20% in 1880. It has been suggested that branch debtors were mainly small and middle rural producers. The largest producers and the city merchants usually resorted to the bank headquarters. There they had access to much larger credits (up to 100,000 pesos fuertes, against an annual average of 10,000 pesos for the larger credits of the branches).[4]

Up to 1880 the BPBA enjoyed, therefore, a central role in the financing of commercial and agrarian sectors in the most dynamic region of the new Argentine capitalism. By then, however, its position as the only deposit and credit bank had ended because of the appearance of new establishments.

New official banks had been created. In 1872 the national government associated with private capitalists founded the Banco Nacional. Its role was to act as the government's financial agent and, with branches in all the provinces, to contribute to the unification of the banking and monetary system. This aim was far from being reached, as neither by the size of its deposits nor by the amount of notes could it compete with the BPBA. Furthermore, the governments of the neighbouring provinces of Santa Fe and Cordoba created two small banks issuing notes convertible into Bolivian coins.

Private banks had even greater importance, the London and River Plate Bank being the main one. Established in Buenos Aires since 1864, its portfolio and deposits averaged 25% of those of the BPBA. Founded by English bankers and merchants with interests in the region it applied, from the beginning, a conservative policy, accepting only 'good' bills corresponding to foreign trade transactions. After 1873 this was reinforced with a high level of cash reserves of over 40% of deposits.[5]

The commercial sector was also supported by commission and mercantile houses, which had slowly turned into banks. The most important, Carabassa, remained, until 1890, a personal partnership, like the British private banks. Others became the basis for the new joint-stock banks at the beginning of the 1870s, with the participation of national and metropolitan capital. Their credit policy was less conservative and the interest rate more moderate than those of the London

Bank, even during the 1873 crisis. Only one of them, the Banco de Italia y Río de la Plata, linked to the large Italian colony of Buenos Aires, survived.[6]

The working of this banking and monetary system, with rather similar patterns to the gold standard, was seriously affected by the crisis which began in 1873. In May 1876, after three years of large gold withdrawals, the Oficina de Cambios of the BPBA (and subsequently that of the Banco Nacional), was forced to close its operations, putting an end to convertibility.

This event has been variously interpreted. Contemporaries tended to explain it by the excess of the previous expansion, including the notes issue. Later, Prebisch emphasized the incidence of structural, not monetary factors: the decrease of exports caused by the international crisis, and that of the foreign capital inflows, which financed a great part of the foreign goods, would have brought about these gold withdrawals (something that showed the limits of the gold standard system in peripheral countries).[7] More recently, Cortés Conde has taken up the argument of the overissue, not so much during the phase of the rise as during that of the decline, which would have prevented the automatic mechanism from working: currency would not have contracted proportionally to gold withdrawals, thanks to the new paper money issued without a gold basis, outside the Oficina, called notas metálicas.[8] Now, the issue of these notas in the years of larger withdrawals (1873–5) was only equivalent to 40% of the paper money taken out of circulation. Therefore, the contractive effects continued, which can be seen in the impressive commercial and financial crisis that hit the local market. On the other hand, the deficit of the balance of payment and trade was not significantly diminished, nor was that of the public accounts.

Towards 1876–8 an adjustment was reached in the last two items, not because of the automatic mechanism of the system, but because of explicit decisions by the government (tariff increase, currency devaluation and a drastic reduction of public expenditure). These measures were not free from conflicts, and brought about the removal of several finance ministers and even of the board of the Banco Provincia.

In spite of the new commercial and fiscal balance, the devaluation of the currency was not immediately reverted to. This could have been due to the great increase in currency after 1876, because new notas were issued after the Oficina was closed, overtaking the level of 1872 (cf. Table 20.1).

The private credits of the BPBA were reduced in those years due to the high incidence of arrears (more than 20% in 1880). This was in contrast with the sudden increase of the public sector credits, hitherto of little relative importance. Based essentially on the new issues of gold notes, they reached the same level as that of the private sector. If, before the crisis the whole of the public and private portfolio was equivalent to the deposits, these were exceeded in 1880 by more than 80%.

This period cannot be closed without a reference to a new kind of operation, mortgage credits. They were developed by the Banco Hipotecario de la Provincia de Buenos Aires, founded in 1872. Some years before, the BPBA had tried its hand at this but gave up because of the excessive immobilization of the portfolio. The new establishment worked in an indirect way, handing in 'cedulas hipotecarias', mortgage-backed securities, which had to be placed in the financial market by the borrowers. Their cost was higher than that of discounts, but was not subject to the variations of the renewals. Towards 1875 their amount was equivalent to almost half the private portfolio of BPBA, and mainly encumbered urban properties in Buenos Aires. The financial crisis interrupted their growth until the beginning of the new decade.

Boom, crisis and depression: from promotional banking to orthodoxy (1880–1900)

Towards 1880 a new period of economic expansion began. The nationalization of the city of Buenos Aires and the end of the frontier war with the Indians were two favourable institutional factors. The national government, with the support of the provincial elites, tried to promote development on the basis of foreign loans, new railways and the unification of the currency circulation.

The new monetary system, sanctioned at the end of 1881, established a return to convertibility on the basis of a new peso, its value was equivalent to that of the old peso fuerte replacing notas and the old issues in bolivianos and in pesos corrientes. Convertibility was in fact very ephemeral. Established at the end of 1883, it was over in January 1885.

When discussing this failure, some authors have stressed the role of the balance of payments.[9] The affluence of foreign capital brought about an enormous increase in imports, when by 1884 total foreign commitments exceeded the actual income and had to be liquidated with a large export of gold. The influence of the note issue was not considered by Williams, although currency increased by 20% during

Table 20.3. *Notes issue and monetary base in Argentina 1881–9 (million pesos)*

Years	Exchange rate	Notes issue BPBA (in paper pesos)	BN	Others	Total	Total (in gold pesos)	Gold reserves (in gold pesos)	Monetary base (gold pesos)
1881	1.00	33.8	2.4	2.4	38.6	38.6	13.6	52.3
1883	1.00	31.8	15.4	3.5	50.7	50.7	23.2	73.5
1884	1.00	32.1	27.0	2.3	61.4	61.4	18.2	79.6
1887	1.45	33.5	46.8	12.0	92.3	63.7	30.9	94.6
1889	2.33	50.0	55.1	66.9	172.0	73.8	25.2	99.0

Notes: Exchange rate: quotation of 1 gold peso in paper pesos. BPBA: Banco de la Provincia de Buenos Aires. BN: Banco Nacional.
Monetary base = notes issue (in gold pesos) + gold reserves.
Sources: see Table 20.1

convertibility (compensated partially by an enlargement of the cash reserves).

For Cortés Conde, the problem was again that the demand for gold from the public was not matched by currency contraction. As no issuing department was created in the banks, the paper money could return to the market through new loans. This had already been suggested by Hansen, who stressed the credit expansion as a cause of the crisis.[10] In our view, this can be attributed not so much to a 'technical' omission but to a 'political' decision not to hinder economic growth, convinced that it would bring about in the short term a new basis for stability and that, in any case, it should not be sacrificed for its own sake.

The suspension of convertibility did not alter the rising movement of currency creation. Until 1887, the issue was allowed to increase 50% by successive authorizations, mainly by the Banco Nacional, that had now become the most important issuing bank. After 1887 a greater increase took place under the new regime of Bancos Garantidos. This system, imitating the United States 'free banking', authorized the incorporation of new issuing houses. The requisite, to make a gold deposit equivalent to the amount to be issued, was supposed to aid a quick return to convertibility. In spite of this, between 1887 and 1889 the notes increased by 90%, mostly issued by a host of new provincial banks, on account of a new foreign indebtedness. At the same time, the paper currency value fell to reach 0.43 gold pesos in 1889 (cf. Table 20.3).

In this context, the evolution of the credit supply shows a spectacular increase: it was multiplied almost twelve times between 1881 and 1889, or four and a half times discounting depreciation. The Banco Nacional experienced the greatest expansion, reflecting the strengthening of the government whose treasury it represented, and a sharp rise of its notes issue. Its portfolio increased from 4% to 30% between 1881 and 1889. Between 1887 and 1889 this growth was due to deposits which quadruplicated in nominal terms. Its branches in the provinces experienced an increase too, amounting to two-thirds of the Bank's credit. This achieved two functions: to lead the spread of bank notes towards regions hitherto obstinately opposed to its circulation, and to provide long-term credits with interest rates scarcely higher than those of Buenos Aires.

The BPBA developed in a very different way. Its share of total credit fell from about two-thirds in 1881 to a fourth in 1889. The shortage of resources, due to slow-growing deposits and to the restrictions on the notes issue imposed by the national government, led after 1884 to an increase lower than the currency depreciation. Its credit policy, after a short orthodox period, was favourable to large individual requests, very often used in speculative operations, and in financing of the provincial political machinery, which was also practised by other official banks.[11]

The private banks experienced great growth, especially after 1884. The national ones increased their loan volume seven times until 1887, or five times in gold pesos. Most of them were sponsored by the main foreign communities (Italy, Spain and France), and reached then their highest growth period. Greater concurrence promoted changing policies, and even the London Bank was to relax its orthodox rules. On the other hand, several national bank portfolios were frozen in real estate and stock exchange business, and became more vulnerable when the crisis broke out in 1890.[12]

During this period mortgage credit greatly expanded. The issue of the Buenos Aires cedulas was increased seven times in gold terms; including those of the other new official bank, the Banco Hipotecario Nacional, they represented more than half the commercial bank credits. Most of them were placed in European markets, where they became directly linked with the local financial and currency market. Unlike the previous decade, most of the loans were placed in the countryside of the province of Buenos Aires. The main destinations of the loans were investments in the building of the new provincial capital, La Plata, in real estate and equipment.

In 1890, an unprecedented financial and monetary crisis took place, which triggered a wave of bankruptcies, money shortage and external deficit. Currency depreciation was accelerated, as were note issues. The country, after having received an enormous amount of foreign capital, showed itself unable to meet its external payments and the London financial market was thereby greatly affected (the Baring crisis). The credit chain was broken by the fall of real estate and stock exchange prices in the local market and led to a massive withdrawal of bank deposits, which reached its climax in 1891.[13]

Many establishments, including the largest (the Banco Nacional and the BPBA) fell on account of the bank panic of 1891, which led to a brutal contraction of the money supply due to the loss of availability of deposits. Banks were definitely deprived of issuing rights, which were transferred to an *ad hoc* establishment, the Caja de Conversion. For the time being the amount of currency was not to be increased. The surviving banks adopted a strictly conservative policy. At the beginning of the new century the credit volume was still half of that estimated for 1889. This situation can be explained by the low level of deposits and the high cash ratios, of more than 50%. Conditions for interest, terms and guarantees became more severe. The new state-owned Banco de la Nación Argentina (hereafter BNA), organized on the basis of the dissolved Banco Nacional, kept to this pattern. Although it created branches in all the provinces including Buenos Aires, neither its number nor its capital was comparable to those of its predecessors.

In these circumstances, informal credit among private individuals seems to have greatly increased. The land and cattle sector which, in those years, experienced a remarkable expansion, had to develop a system whereby the sectors with a surplus – large landowners and rural merchants – lent money to the other producers. They were allowed to act as informal redistributors due to their access to the restricted bank credit, when this was being re-established. In this way financial costs of credit increased but lenders assumed a share in the risks.[14]

The last great expansion, 1900–30: towards a modern banking system?

At the beginning of the new century, the country entered a new stage of accelerated growth. New regions had started to produce during the previous decade, transforming the country into one of the world's main meat and cereal exporters. Once again, the affluence of foreign capital acquired importance. The value of the paper peso started a steady rise, and already towards the end of 1899 the government decided to re-establish conversion at a fixed exchange rate. This new convertibility was, like three decades before, intended to protect the exporting sectors, and was extended until 1914, when it had to be suspended due to the outbreak of the First World War.

New note issues from the Caja de Conversión were made possible by the gold inflow, as a result of the positive balance of payments, and the currency stock was increased by 170% between 1901 and 1912. Bank deposits grew by almost 300% and credits, no less than 400% (cf. Tables 20.1 and 20.4).

This expansion, led by the national private banks, was characterized by a greater flexibility and the development of new lines of credit (advance payments on merchandise and securities, including those of joint-stock companies). The Banco Frances, perhaps the most advanced in this field, added to all that the promotion of enterprises (electricity, railways, food industry), which so far had only been tried by private firms like the Tornquists and Bembergs.

Table 20.4. *Deposits and credits in Argentine banks, 1901–30 (million of paper pesos – moneda nacional)*

Years	Exchange	Deposits				Credits			
		BNA	NaBanks	FoBanks	Total	BNA	NaBanks	FoBanks	Total
1901	2.41	111.4	142.3	144.3	398.0	88.3	112.0	113.0	313.3
1908	2.27	246.2	348.2	281.4	875.8	253.7	378.3	213.0	845.0
1912	2.27	478.3	674.3	328.3	1,480.9	432.8	803.0	309.8	1,545.6
1914	2.28	552.7	365.4	271.2	1,189.3	540.6	478.4	220.5	1,239.5
1920	2.83	1,412.3	1,190.4	691.2	3,293.9	1,162.0	1,066.2	634.8	2,863.0
1928	2.27	1,748.9	1,490.6	713.7	3,953.2	1,348.1	1,231.9	843.1	3,423.1
Increase									
1901/12		4.29	4.74	2.28	3.72	4.90	7.17	2.74	4.93
1912/28		3.66	2.21	2.17	2.67	3.11	1.53	2.72	2.21
1901/28		15.70	10.48	4.95	9.93	15.27	11.00	7.46	10.93

Notes: BNA: Banco de la Nación Argentina, NaBanks: national banks (private and mixed). FoBanks: foreign banks. The BNA deposits have been reduced in order to exclude the Camara Compensadora funds.

Sources: Instituto de Estudios Bancarios, *La economía bancaria*, pp. 6–62 and 100–4; Banco de la Nación Argentina, *El Banco de la Nación Argentina en su cincuentenario* (Buenos Aires, 1941), pp. 250–7.

These innovations were made possible by the new long-term resources, obtained by these banks through issues on European markets. The fall of the Banco Frances enterprises in 1914, and the bankruptcies brought about by the changed situation, dissuaded others from following this path. Even so, their support continued through short-term credits to the industrial sector, and helped in the emergence of some related entrepreneurial groups (Banco de Italia). In other cases, the bulk of the loans and the difficulties of repayment ended in new formal partnerships during the twenties (Banco Español).[15]

In 1912–14 a severe crisis hit the local market which culminated in the outbreak of the First World War and, as in most other countries, caused the suspension of the gold standard. Against official fears the value of the peso on foreign exchanges was largely favourable in the succeeding years. Only during the post-war period some difficulties were experienced as the currency depreciated somewhat. At the end of 1927, much later than other countries, the government restored convertibility. The new experience was short-lived: in November 1929, under the impact of the Wall Street crash, convertibility was discontinued and never restored.

The currency indicators of the twenties reverted to the expansive character of the pre-war period. The volume of currency in 1928 reached 70% above the 1912–14 level and bank deposits increased 170%. The money multiplier was coming close to the values of the most sophisticated monetary systems (cf. Table 20.1), although it was still low when considering current accounts only (1.24). This showed the limits in the use of cheques as means of payment, which prevented the system from creating its own money supply. Furthermore, this was connected with the large growth of other categories of deposits, due to savings among the middle and popular classes. They were mainly channelled through the BNA, now in the very important position that the BPBA held before.

The rise of credit was also resumed under the influence of the growth of deposits, but with a certain delay. Towards 1928 it exceeded, by 120%, the 1912 levels, and by 1,000% those of 1901 (cf. Table 20.4). The BNA was the only bank that had not been affected by the 1914 crisis; since then it had become the most important institute and its deposits represented between 40% and 50% of the total. Its nationwide branch network (233 branches) was equivalent to more than half of the whole system. Its reserves were higher than those of all the other banks together, because it performed a stabilizing role in the gold exchange

Table 20.5. *Banco de la Nación Argentina: credit distribution between commerce, livestock, agriculture and industry, 1894–1928 (in million of pesos moneda nacional and percentages)*

	1		2		3		4			
	Commerce	(%)	Livestock	(%)	Agriculture	(%)	Industry	(%)	Total	(%)
1894	50.2	52.3	21.1	22.0	11.7	12.2	13.0	13.5	96.0	100.0
1905	87.2	43.5	69.8	34.9	24.0	12.0	19.4	9.7	200.4	100.0
1914	286.0	44.0	218.7	33.6	71.9	11.1	73.8	11.3	650.4	100.0
1928	588.9	45.5	377.1	29.1	129.5	10.0	200.1	15.4	1,295.5	100.0

Note: Total: 1 + 2 + 3 + 4 (other items excluded).
Sources: Banco de la Nación Argentina, *El Banco de la Nación*, p. 257.

market. Nevertheless, its credit distribution still had conservative features. In 1928, as in 1913, nearly 50% of its credits were assigned to commerce. Another well-established activity, ranching, was in second place (cf. Table 20.5). Its branches in the Provincia de Buenos Aires, as those of BPBA (reopened since 1906), favoured these two activities to the detriment of agriculture and industry.[16]

During the third decade of the century, Argentine banking showed a mixture of contradictory features. There was a remarkable expansion of the range of depositors allowing operations to be carried out on a scale comparable to the Anglo-Saxon system. However, quite different to the practices of those markets, the use of 180 days' automatically renewable loans was widespread. This was accompanied by the important role played by middlemen, merchants in the countryside and brokers in the city, who mediated in the relationship with their customers, and in a certain way provided a distribution of risks. The system lacked any sort of a central bank, regulating the activity and playing the role of lender of last resort. In 1914 the BNA was authorized to make rediscounts to the others, but the scarce funds assigned to it and its disconnection with the issuing mechanism ruined the attempt. The official bank, therefore, continued behaving as just one more competitor.

Mortgage credit began to expand again since the first years of the century. It was channelled through the Banco Hipotecario Nacional and many local and foreign companies. By 1915 its magnitude was estimated as double the commercial bank credit. This declined during the war, but in 1925 it was still above the level of bank credits. Foreign capital showed a decreasing tendency, and on the eve of 1930 financial resources were mainly drawn from national savings. As in the previous period, the rural sector was the main borrower. Only those industrialists who owned buildings or land had access to this type of credit.

Conclusion

The banking system performed an important role in the consolidation of the capitalist economy in Argentina, though in different ways at different periods. In this sense, the first 'heroic' age appears in the mid-nineteenth century when, in the Gerschenkronian style, the banks directly promoted economic activity especially in the agrarian sector. This period closes with the great crisis of 1890, although in the most dynamic region, the province of Buenos Aires, this role had been achieved before 1880.

After 1890 a more conservative or 'orthodox' policy as far as credits are concerned was pursued, in spite of some short-lived attempts at business partnerships. The influence of the banks over the productive sectors was exercised in an indirect way, through commerce, in accordance with the 'British' model. Their main contribution was to generate a growing money supply compatible with stability, through the enlargement of bank currency.

One of the main questions concerns the fact that stability and a large money supply appear to have been irreconcilable except for certain special occasions. To opt for the second one, implied breaking with orthodoxy and facilitated the appearance of banks of promotion, which contradicted the rules preached for commercial banking. The system's reorganization after 1890 indicated the success of the commercial banks and the monetary doctrine of the gold standard at a time when the agrarian expansion had been consolidated, and when the other kind of establishments tended to be regarded as disturbing instruments. It was necessary to wait until the crisis of the 1930s to implement agrarian and industrial credit policies, which resembled those of the first period, but in the context of a new period of Argentine capitalism, that of import substitution.

Notes

The author is indebted to Dr Samuel Amaral and to Raquel Mallar for their valuable comments and the translation.
1 Samuel Amaral, 'El descubrimiento de la financiacion inflacionaria. Buenos Aires, 1790–1830', *Investigaciones y Ensayos*, 37 (1988), pp. 379–41.
2 This position was sustained by Roberto Cortés Conde, *Dinero, deuda y crisis. Evolución fiscal y monetaria en la Argentina, 1862–1890* (Buenos Aires, 1989). Some doubts remain about the real dimensions of specie circulation and the monetary character of gold deposits.
3 Andrés Lamas, *Estudio histórico y científico del Banco de la Provincia de Buenos Aires* (Buenos Aires, 1886); Octavio Garrigós, *El Banco de la Provincia* (Buenos Aires, 1873).
4 Samuel Amaral and A. Harispuru, 'El Banco de la Provincia de Buenos Aires y la conquista del desierto (1867–1880)', in Academia Nacional de la Historia, *II Congreso Nacional y Regional* (Buenos Aires, 1983), pp. 237–46; Hilda Sábato, *Capitalismo y ganadería en Buenos Aires, 1850–1890* (Buenos Aires, 1989).
5 C. A. Jones, 'The Transfer of Banking Techniques from Britain to Argentina, 1862–1914', *Revue Internationale d'Histoire de la Banque*, 26–7 (1983), pp. 251–64.
6 Pedro Agote, *Informe del Presidente del Crédito Público Nacional sobre la deuda pública, bancos y emisiones de papel moneda*, 5 vols. (Buenos Aires, 1881–9), vol. II, pp. 319–24.
7 Raúl Prebisch, 'Anotaciones sobre nuestro medio circulante', *Revista de Ciencias Económicas* (Buenos Aires, 1921–2).
8 Cortés Conde, *Dinero, deuda y crisis*.

9 John Williams, *Argentine International Trade under Inconvertible Paper Money* (Cambridge, Mass., 1920); Alec Ford, *The Gold Standard, 1880–1940: Britain and Argentina* (Oxford, 1962).

10 Emilio Hansen, *La moneda. Estudio histórico* (Buenos Aires, 1916).

11 Sixto Quesada, *Historia de los bancos modernos. Bancos de descuentos; la moneda y el crédito* (Buenos Aires, 1901).

12 Andrés Regalsky, 'La evolución de la banca privada nacional en Argentina (1880–1914). Un introducción a su estudio', in Pedro Tedde and Carlos Marichal (eds.), *La formación de los bancos centrales en España y América Latina*, 2 vols. (Madrid, 1994), pp. 35–60.

13 For the Baring crisis, A. G. Ford, 'Argentina and the Baring Crisis of 1890', *Oxford Economic Papers*, 8, 2 (1956), pp. 127–50. The monetary aspects, in Cortés Conde, *Dinero, deuda y crisis.*

14 Jeremy Adelman, 'Agricultural Credit in the Province of Buenos Aires, 1890–1914', *Journal of Latin American Studies*, 22 (1990), pp. 69–87. The deflationist policy is discussed in Gerardo Della Paolera, 'Monetary and Banking Experiments in Argentina: 1861–1930', Universidad Torcuato di Tella, Working Paper No. 11 (Buenos Aires, 1994).

15 A. Gancedo, *Porqué fracasaron los bancos de negocios en la Argentina?* (Buenos Aires, 1932); Andrés Regalsky, 'El Banco Francés del Río de la Plata y su expansión en el Paraguay', *Boletín del Instituto de Historia Argentina 'Dr. Ravignani'*, 3, 2 (Buenos Aires, 1990); Paul Souweine, *L'Argentine au seuil de l'industrie* (Paris, 1927).

16 Banco de la Nación Argentina, *El Banco de la Nación Argentina en su cincuentenario* (Buenos Aires, 1941); Universidad de Buenos Aires, Instituto de Estudios Bancarios, *La economía bancaria a través de sus índices más significativos 1901–1935* (Buenos Aires, 1937).

21 International banking in China, 1890–1913

Shizuya Nishimura

I

The period, 1890–1913, was a watershed in the history of China, both politically and economically. Economically, China's incorporation in the world economy was just about completed in this era. This is shown by the almost fivefold increase in her foreign trade, which increased from Haikwan taels (hereafter Hk.tls) 214 million (£55.4 million) in 1890 to Hk.tls 973 million (£147.0 million) in 1913 (one Hk.tl is equivalent to 583.3 grains of pure silver).[1] There were only 225 kilometres of railway lines in 1892, but in 1913 there were 9,854 kilometres.[2] In 1890 China's indebtedness to foreign countries amounted to about £4 million,[3] but by 1914 foreign investments in China, including direct investment, are estimated to have reached US$1,610.3 million (£331 million).[4]

Both Chinese nationalists and Marxists viewed this development in the light of imperialist aggression and exploitation. Western intrusion in China was said to have caused destruction of the traditional agriculture-based economy, and yet hampered the rise of modern industrial society by impoverishing the Chinese populace, by depriving China of tariff autonomy and inundating the Chinese market with Western products.

These allegations have never been fully established by rigorous factual studies and there are researchers who contend that there was respectable economic growth in the last decades of the Ch'ing dynasty.[5] But here I am not concerned with this controversy. This chapter aims to explore the actualities of international banking in China and the relationships between international banks and the *ch'ien chuangs*, traditional Chinese banks, in Shanghai (old-style spelling for Chinese words are used throughout this chapter).

The international or multinational banks in China too were condemned as spearheads of imperialist aggression. Whilst they were undeniably profit-seeking capitalist institutions, and as such not particularly concerned with the well being of the Chinese nation, an objective analysis of their role in the development of the Chinese economy is required in order to make a judgement on whether their operations were beneficial or detrimental to China.

II

The main function of international banks, such as the Hongkong and Shanghai Banking Corporation (hereafter referred to as the HSBC) in China was to purchase export bills on Europe and the US. They also provided means of remittance to Europe and America by selling drafts and telegraphic transfers on their offices in Europe and the US. These represented payments for China's imports and servicing of foreign debts as well as reparation payments. China's principal exports consisted of agricultural products, which were subject to prominent seasonal fluctuations. The major items of her exports and imports are shown in Tables 21.1 and 21.2. China registered large deficits in her balance of trade. However, no sizeable outflow of precious metals resulted. This is remarkable in view of the fact that China had to pay huge reparations to the Western powers and to Japan. She had also to meet service charges on her growing foreign debts. Although no accurate balance of payments statistics exist for this period, H. B. Morse of the Chinese Maritime Customs made an attempt to estimate the current balance of payments for 1903.[6] According to him, the exports of goods (f.o.b.) amounted to Hk.tls 236.2 million, while imports (c.i.f.) came to Hk.tls 310.5 million. Gold bars and coins exported amounted to Hk.tls 33.0 million, while those imported were Hk.tls 37.0 million. Thus, the balance of trade including gold showed a deficit of Hk.tls 70.3 million. On top of this, China had to meet reparations and debt service payments of Hk.tls 44.2 million. Home remittances by foreigners were estimated at Hk.tls 16.0 million. There were other minor items like freight and

Table 21.1. *Principal items of China's exports (Hk.tls million)*

Years	Raw silk	Tea	Soybean/ soybean products	Cotton	Fur	Wool	Vegetable oil	Foodstuff/ beverages	Total
1890	24.5	26.5	0.4	3.0	1.2	0.9	0.5	2.8	87.1
1900	39.7	25.4	5.5	9.9	6.9	4.0	2.8	7.4	159.0
1910	80.3	35.9	36.7	28.4	20.3	13.8	13.2	26.6	380.8

Source: Yan Pei Huang and Sung P'ang, *Chung Kuo Su Shu Nien Hai Kwan Shang Wu T'ung Chi Tu Piao (Statistics of Foreign Trade of China during the Past Forty Years)* (Hong Kong, 1916; repr. Hong Kong, 1974).

Table 21.2. *Principal items of China's imports (Hk.tls million)*

Years	Cotton goods	Opium	Rice	Sugar	Metals/ metal products	Petroleum	Coal	Dyestuffs	Seafood	Total
1890	25.7	29.0	11.4	10.8	6.9	4.1	2.0	1.2	4.9	127.1
1900	45.6	31.0	11.4	6.4	9.2	14.0	6.4	2.5	5.1	211.1
1910	69.2	55.4	31.3	22.3	18.9	21.7	8.4	9.0	12.1	463.0

Source: see Table 21.1

insurance, tourist expenditures abroad and so on amounting to Hk.tls 16.1 million.

However, there were items to the credit of China, the largest of which was home remittances by Chinese abroad. This was estimated to amount to Hk.tls 73.0 million. Then, there were disbursements of the proceeds of foreign loans and investments by foreigners. This was taken to amount to Hk.tls 27.0 million. Various other minor items which included expenditures by foreign military forces stationed in China, expenditures by foreign ships and warships, those by Christian missionaries and schools and by tourists. These amounted altogether to Hk.tls 51.5 million.

Thus, according to Morse, China's current balance was more or less in equilibrium. This can be confirmed by taking the sum of the balances of trade in gold and silver to represent the overall balance of payments of China (see Table 21.3). Thus, throughout the period, the net outflow of gold persisted. The silver balance, however, experienced a turnabout from net inflow to net outflow during the years, 1901–8, and thereafter net inflow of silver returned. The yearly average figures of the overall balance, however, are not very great. In 1901–8, it is minus Hk.tls 14.5 million, which is very small compared with average deficits on commodity balance of trade of Hk.tls 135.0 million. Thus, we may probably say that the current balance of payments of China was on the whole in equilibrium. However, within each year there must have been pronounced seasonal fluctuations in the current balance of payments, because exports exhibited marked seasonality, while imports were more or less evenly distributed over a year.

The exporting season commenced each year in April and lasted till November. Between August and June was the season for exports of silk and tea. July was an off-season. From August to November exports of cotton and other miscellaneous goods reached a peak. In the exporting season, the international banks had to purchase large amounts of export bills and send them to their offices in London. Buying these bills depleted the banks of their silver holdings. In order to replenish their silver holdings, they had to sell drafts or telegraphic transfers on London. However, the export bills had usance of four months. Drafts sold by the banks were mainly sight drafts. Telegraphic transfers had no usance. By selling these means of remittance the Chinese offices increased their debts to the London office, because the London office had to pay sterling to the payees or transferees, for which the London office debited the inter-office accounts of the overseas branches.[7] When the bills sent to the London office by the Chinese offices came to maturity, the proceeds would be used to offset the liabilities of the Chinese offices. Thus, during the export season from spring to late autumn the Chinese offices overdrew their accounts at the London office. But in winter and early spring the export bills came to maturity and their overdrafts were progressively diminished by the proceeds. A simple T form can exemplify these relationships. During the export season, a Chinese office purchases export bills and sends them to London, at the same time selling telegraphic transfers to the residents in China. Suppose the amount involved were £200.

The Chinese office		
Bills purchased and sent to London 200	Overdraft debt to London	200

The London office		
Bills receivable	200	Bills receivable	200
Overdraft by the Chinese office	200	Deposits and current accounts 200

In winter, bills mature and the proceeds are used to offset the overdraft.

The Chinese office		
Bills purchased	0	Overdraft debt	0

The London office		
Cash (proceeds of the bills rec.)	200	Deposits and current accounts 200

Thus, deposits and current account credit balances received in London were used to finance the seasonal imbalances of payments of overseas countries. If an overseas office became a net creditor of the London office, the balance, of course, would be held as credit balances of the inter-office accounts in London, earning appropriate interest.

These were nothing but accommodating short-term capital flows, but without this mechanism overseas countries will suffer fluctuations in exchange rates, particularly when they were on the silver, and not on the gold, standard. In other words, these accommodating short-term capital exports from the UK served as the lubricating oil of international trade.

Unfortunately, we do not have enough data to show these seasonal variations. I have only balance sheets of the London office and of the Shanghai branch of the HSBC. Still they might give us a glimpse of the actual operations of these offices. Therefore, Table 21.4 shows the

Table 21.3. *China's overall balance of payments, 1892–1913 (Hk.tls million)*

Years	Balance of trade of gold (a)	Balance of trade of silver (b)	Overall balance (a) + (b) (c)
1892	−7.3	−5.4	−12.7
1893	−7.5	9.8	2.3
1894	−12.8	25.8	13.0
1895	−6.9	35.9	29.0
1896	−8.1	1.7	−6.4
1897	−8.5	1.8	−6.7
1898	−7.7	5.0	−2.7
1899	−7.6	1.4	−6.2
1900	−1.2	15.4	14.2
1901	−6.6	−6.1	−12.7
1902	−9.4	−13.8	−23.2
1903	0.1	−6.0	−5.9
1904	8.4	−13.6	−5.2
1905	7.1	−7.2	−0.1
1906	3.8	−18.7	−14.9
1907	2.5	−31.2	−28.7
1908	−11.5	−12.3	−23.8
1909	−6.8	6.8	0.0
1910	−1.0	21.8	20.8
1911	1.5	38.3	39.8
1912	7.5	19.2	26.7
1913	−1.4	36.0	34.6

Note: a minus sign denotes a net outflow.
Source: Takeshi Hamashita, *Chuugoku Kindai Keizaishi Kenkyuu (Studies in Modern Chinese Economic History)* (Tokyo, 1989), pp. 448–9.

balance sheet of the London office on 30 September 1911. Table 21.5 shows the balance sheet of the Shanghai branch. From the two tables we can see that the London office was lending to the branches a sum of £3,875,000. We must, however, take into account the fact that the credit balances on the current account of the branches may have reached £1,312,000 (current account balances £3,840,000 minus £2,528,000, which was held by foreign governments). Moreover, the bills receivable here were just bills purchased by the other offices and sent to London for collection. As such, they appear on both sides of the

Table 21.4. *The balance sheet of the London office of the HSBC, 30 September 1911 (£000)*

Cash in hand	3	Fixed deposits	4,374
Balances with other banks	23	Call and short notice deposits	93
Securities: London office a/c		Current accounts*a*	3,840
(31 Oct.)	710	Bills discounted	31
Sundry loans to constituents	180	Bills receivable	9,406
Overdrawn current accounts	159	Branch drawings on the London	
Short loans to brokers	135	County and Westminster	
Bills discounted	31	Bank	230
Bills receivable	9,406	Branch drawings on the	
Bills purchased and remitted		London Office	197
to branches	2,751	London Office acceptances	915
London Office acceptance	915	Suspense a/c	32
Branch accounts overdrafts	3,875	Marginal deposits	4
Provision for bad debts a/c	3		
Extended bills	73		
	18,394		19,122

*a*This includes £2,528,000 of foreign governments' balances.
Source: HSBC, Inspector's Report on London office, 6 November 1911.

account. But, as has already been noted, when they matured, the proceeds were used to offset the branches' debit balances and, if any surplus balance remained, their current accounts would be credited. On the other hand, bills purchased by London and remitted to branches appeared as bills receivable in their accounts.

Table 21.5 shows that on 31 March 1911 the Shanghai branch had purchased bills on Europe and the US to the amount of £3,707,000. Of this amount, £3,058,000 were bills in pound sterling and the remainder in French francs and US dollars. The £3,707,000 was equivalent to about Shanghai taels (hereafter Sh.tls) 30,611,000. This amount of silver money must have been raised by selling drafts and telegraphic transfers on London and so on. In other words, the Shanghai branch incurred debts in gold in order to purchase bills on gold standard countries. These debts would appear as branch overdrafts at the London office.

Another important function of the overseas offices of the

Table 21.5. *The balance sheet of the Shanghai branch of the HSBC, 31 March 1911 (Sh.tls 000)*

Cash and bullion	7,601	Bills receivable	6,655
Bills receivable	6,655	Reaccepted bills	381
Reaccepted bills	381	Bills for collection	1,044
Bills for collection	1,044	Cover for London acceptances	2,184
Cover for London acceptances	2,184	Branch loans for collection	3,311
Branch loans for collection	3,311	Loans for collection	206
Loans for collection	206	Bills discounted	31
Past due bills	137	Notes in circulation	1,655
Bills discounted	31	Fixed deposits	8,700
Overdrafts	10,345	Current accounts	17,850
Loans	7,369	Savings bank	1,058
Advances upon shares	2,673		
Dollar overdrafts	89		
Short loans to native banks	462		
Bills purchased			
(+ £3,707,000)	30,611	Inter-office debts to London	30,611
	74,925		73,686

Note: conversion at the rate of £1 = Sh.tls 8.258.
Source: HSBC, Inspector's Report on the Shanghai branch, 2 May 1911.

international bank was to receive deposits of local residents (including expatriate foreign merchants, officials, missionaries and others). With these deposits the overseas offices performed ordinary banking functions: the provision of loans, overdrafts and discounts for such residents. Most of the recipients of such credit seem to have been the nationals of the respective banks' home countries. Currently I have the relevant data only of the HSBC.

In the case of the HSBC's Shanghai branch the depositors were predominantly Europeans. For instance, during the eight months from January to August 1908, thirty-seven new accounts of fixed deposits of upwards of 10,000 taels each were opened, the total amount of which was Sh.tls 612,000, but of these only three (total amount, Sh.tls 62,000) belonged to the Chinese.[8] As for current accounts, the Inspector's Report on the office working at the Shanghai branch, 18 January 1912, notes that 'A separate ledger is also kept for Chinese accounts which have been increasing very rapidly of late.' However, there were only 174 Chinese accounts out of the total of 3,490 accounts at this date.

A totally different picture emerges from the accounts of the Tientsin Agency of the HSBC. Here fixed deposits were by far the bigger item compared with current accounts, and most of the fixed deposits were those of Chinese individuals and firms as well as Chinese government agencies. In 1896 only about 10% of fixed deposits seem to have been those of Europeans.[9] Perhaps the same holds for the Peking Agency.

Yet the Shanghai branch was a giant among the various offices of the HSBC in China (except, of course, the head office in Hong Kong). Therefore, we can safely say that the majority of the depositors of the HSBC in China were Europeans.

The money received on deposit and current accounts was employed in granting loans and advances principally to European residents in China. Loans were chiefly given on the security of the imported goods and goods waiting shipment for export. An explanation of the nature of loans is given in the Inspector's Report on the Shanghai branch, 5 October 1908, as follows: 'In most cases when a Loan is taken out against goods, the goods related to Bills Receivable which passed through our hands and have been retired and the value is usually based on the Invoice cost, the invoices being shown to the Loan Department.'[10] However, on 31 March 1911 loans amounted to Sh.tls 7,370,000, of which only Sh.tls 2,191,000 related to imported goods.

Overdrafts were mainly covered by shares, property and other securities.[11] Advances to municipal councils of the foreign settlements and to public utilities such as the Shanghai Gas Co. Ltd, Shanghai General Hospital, Shanghai Waterworks Co. Ltd, were included here.

Then, there were advances against shares, which were given to investors and speculators of shares as well as to the *ch'ien chuangs* or merchants who used the money to finance collection of export goods in the up-country.[12] These were the so-called 'packing credits'. In 1910 there was a great speculative boom, and subsequent collapse, in rubber shares. The market valuation of twenty rubber companies reached a height of Sh.tls 61,738,000 on 7 April 1910 but fell to Sh.tls 19,448,000 on 8 April 1911.[13] This must have brought huge losses to the international banks.

On 31 March 1911, the sum total of advances given by the Shanghai branch was Sh.tls 20,476,000. The breakdown of these by security was as follows.[14]

Sh.tls (000)		(Sh.tls (000)	
Shares and bonds	4,895	Exports and local produce	985
Property	6,100	Authorized by the Chinese government	3,893
Imports	2,310	Clean and guaranteed advances	2,113

International banks also gave short-term loans to the *ch'ien chuangs* against their '*chiao p'iaos*' (promissory notes), which were called chop loans. We turn to the operations of these native banks in the next section.

III

There were thousands of *ch'ien chuangs* in Shanghai and in other cities of China. The smaller of these were nothing but moneychangers, pawn-shops or outright usurers. But the biggest among them were essentially no different from private banks in European cities. They were private undertakings or partnerships and did not issue bank notes, but, judging from the existing records, their deposits far surpassed their equity capital. In Shanghai they had their own clearing house called Hui Hua Tsung Hoi, and those *ch'ien chuangs* which were its members were termed *hui hua chuangs*. Foreigners called them native banks with no derogatory connotation. There were forty-one of them in 1897,[15] and their number increased to 115 in 1908, but an abrupt reduction occurred with the collapse of the speculation in rubber shares, their number falling to only fifty-one in 1911.[16] No overall statistics of their assets and liabilities remain, but those for just three of them were published by the People's Bank of China in 1960 (see Table 21.6).

As can be seen from Table 21.6, *ch'ien chuangs* received deposits, which far surpassed the amounts of own capital. Most of the deposits were current accounts, on which customers could draw cheques (*chi p'iao*). But more commonly they requested the *ch'ien chuangs* to supply them with the banks' promissory notes (*chuang p'iao*), either payable on demand or with terms up to ten days. They were used just like bank notes. The holders tendered them into their accounts, which would be credited. The *ch'ien chuang* which received the notes would present them to the issuing bank through the clearing house and demand payment. The clearing balance was settled by delivery of silver sycee (sycee is silver alloy case in a form

Table 21.6. *Principal accounts of three ch'ien chuangs (Sh.tls 000)*

Years	Capital	Reserve plus profits carried forward	Deposits	Loans and advances			Loans to other banks	Borrowings from other banks	Of which from foreign banks
				Unsecured	Secured	Total			
Fu Kang									
1896	20	19	103	135	—	135		133	41
1900	20	21	398	216	168	384		72	
1904	20	45	489	356	562	918	195	535	
1907	20	44	817	539	501	1,041	97	252	103
Shun Kang									
1905	20	16	283	289	164	453	102	113	
1907	20	3	287	469	20	489	202	338	122
1909	20	5	237	623	366	988	124	859	297
1911	20	12	492	112	348	460	32	94	
Hang Sing									
1905	30	10	557			402	93	239	
1907	30	3	483			527	103	83	
1909	30	15	639			597	95	89	
1911	30	11	540			113	301	155	150
1913	100	22	582			408	44	6	

Source: Chung Kuo Jen Min Yin Hang Shang Hai Shi Fen Hang (The Shanghai Branch of the People's Bank of China), *Shang Hai Ch'ien Chuang Shi Liang (Archival Materials on Ch'ien Chuangs in Shanghai)* (Shanghai, 1960), pp. 775–837.

which looked like Chinese ladies' shoes and hence counted as shoes of sycee. A shoe of sycee had a value of Sh.tls 53,469).

Chuang p'iaos were the standard means of payment among Chinese merchants in Shanghai. Even European trading firms received them in payment for goods they sold to Chinese merchants. These were paid into their accounts at international banks, which presented them to the issuers through the *ch'ien chuang* with which they were in close contacts. The payments here were again made by delivery of sycee. However, *ch'ien chuangs*, taken together, did not have much silver on hand. Thus, they had to borrow the necessary sycee from international banks by taking chop loans, when imports exceeded exports.

Another limit to circulation of credit money like *chuang p'iaos* was that in inland China almost all transactions were settled in silver cash. Here, the standard means of payment was Mexican dollars, British trade dollars, Japanese yen and other dollar coins. Thus, when export goods, such as tea and silk, were collected inland, the money used was silver dollars, which were either drawn from deposit and current accounts at native banks in Shanghai or borrowed from them. Thus, the *ch'ien chuangs* had to find silver dollars to supply to merchants trading with the inland. This, too, caused them to borrow silver money from international banks.

Thus, the amount of chop loans outstanding experienced regular seasonal fluctuations, which were very pronounced, as can be seen from Table 21.7, where the seasonal index of their amounts is also shown. The extremely low index for January is chiefly due to the habit of settling every account before the lunar new year.

The interest rates on these loans were based upon inter-*ch'ien chuang* loan rates, which were termed *yin ch'ai* in Chinese and 'native interest rates' by foreigners. They were very volatile, although the average level was not high.

The HSBC seems to have been cautious in giving such loans to *ch'ien chuangs* and their average chop loans in 1908 came just to Sh.tls 1,165,000. But some of the international banks, particularly the Yokohama Specie Bank and the Banque de l'Indochine, were very eager to lend to the native banks, the average for the former in 1908 being Sh.tls 2,505,000 and for the latter Sh.tls 2,999,000.

The next question concerns the importance of this type of loan in the business of the *ch'ien chuangs* as a whole. In the case of the three banks shown in Table 21.6, these did not bulk large, but we must be aware of the eternal trap for business historians: that is, we are dealing with those

Table 21.7. Amounts of chop loans[a] (Sh.tls 000)

Years End of month	1898	1905	1906	1907	1908	Averages for 1905 to 1908	Seasonal index
Jan.	450	290	815	2,270	2,030	1,351	15.4
Feb.	1,200	2,556	2,460	5,041	6,970	4,257	48.4
Mar.	3,600	4,040	4,300	11,775	13,487	8,401	95.6
Apr.	3,300	3,340	1,960	9,435	16,414	7,787	88.6
May	5,100	6,377	6,460	7,300	18,400	9,634	109.6
June	4,100	6,615	3,550	15,235	18,690	11,023	125.4
July	4,200	7,670	3,780	15,570	19,750	11,693	133.1
Aug.	4,000	11,208	7,690	16,310	21,020	14,057	160.0
Sept.	4,000	10,255	12,450	15,500	17,780	13,996	159.3
Oct.	3,000	8,510	12,480	8,820	10,100	9,978	113.6
Nov.	3,400	8,260	14,905	6,980	2,300	8,111	92.3
Dec.	1,200	6,900	8,200	5,425	100	5,156	58.7

[a]Does not include loans in Mexican dollars, but the amount of such loans was minimal.
Source: for 1898, Yuuki Yamakawa (Yokohama Specie Bank), Shinkoku Shuccho Fukumeisho (Report of the Business Trip to China) (Yokohama, 1898), pp. 55–7; for other years, 'Memo of Stock of Sycee, Dollars and Loans to Natives', in HSBC, Shanghai branch manager's letter to J. R. M. Smith at the head office, 24 December 1908.

undertakings which have successfully survived the vicissitudes of decades and which, therefore, must have been pursuing exceptionally prudent business practices. We do not, unfortunately, have any overall statistics covering all the native banks. There is, however, an estimate by the compradore of the HSBC of the total deposits at the native banks. The manager of the Shanghai branch of the HSBC in a letter to the head office dated 7 August 1908 quotes his compradore as follows: 'There are over 100 Native Banks in Shanghai all registered at the Bankers' Guild. The Compradore estimates total deposits at an average of say Tls 8 Lacs [800,000] each, or say Tls 800 Lacs [80 million], and their total advances he puts at tls 800/900 lacs [80/90 million].'[17] Chop loans reached a maximum of Sh.tls 21,020,000 in August 1908. This is equivalent to 25% of deposits of the 100 native banks.

As for the nature of these loans, 'it is the custom of the Native Banks to grant clean overdrafts to Merchants, who buy Rice, Tea, Piece Goods

Table 21.8. *Native interest rates (inter-*ch'ien chuang *loan rates) in Shanghai, 1908 (%)*

End of:											
Jan.	Feb.	Mar.	Apr.	May	June	July	Aug.	Sept.	Oct.	Nov.	Dec.
2.125	3.625	8.375	3.625	4.5	2.5	4.0	4.0	4.0	5.0	3.25	1.5

Source: 'Memo of Stock of Sycee, Dollars and Loans to Natives', in HSBC, Shanghai branch manager's letter to J. R. M. Smith at the head office, 24 December 1908.

&c., which they distribute to different parts of the country.'[18] Thus, chop loans were an indispensable source of finance for the native banks. However, many *ch'ien chuangs* were involved in the rubber boom of 1909–10, and suffered from its collapse. Then, the Revolution of 1911 halted all business temporarily. In this sequence of events more than half the native banks failed, and chop loans became largely irrecoverable. Their fingers burnt, the international banks mutually agreed to stop making chop loans, but very soon the practice revived under the name of dollar loans. In this case, however, it was customary to demand security for the loans, whereas chop loans were mostly unsecured.

The international banks did not on the whole deal directly with the Chinese, for whom the *ch'ien chuangs* served as payments mechanism. The lending of these native banks was primarily to finance commodity transactions and goods in transit. As such, they were essentially commercial banks for short term financing of business dealings. There was no reason why the international banks could not directly participate in this business and compete with the native banks. The Shanghai branch of the HSBC had deposits and notes in circulation of Sh.tls 29,263,000 in 1911, while Fu Kang Ch'ien Chuang had only Sh.tls 817,000 in 1907 (see Table 21.6). Nevertheless, the international banks did not attempt to penetrate the market for loans and advances to the ethnic Chinese. One of the obstacles in the way must have been the language barrier. Another may have been the guild system among merchants. However, even the Chinese modern banks, which proliferated during the interwar years, could not compete with the *ch'ien chuangs*. They were more or less dependent upon *ch'ien chuangs* for day-to-day business.[19] The reasons are said to be as follows. (1) The *ch'ien chuangs* permitted their customers to overdraw without any prior arrangements and without any security or surety. The only precaution they took was that they did not open a new account without an introduction from an existing trustworthy client, who was held responsible for any misdemeanour of the new customer. (2) As has been said, the native bankers' guild had a clearing house, so that a *chuang p'iao* (promissory note) of any one *ch'ien chuang* could be paid into another *ch'ien chuang*. (3) A *ch'ien chuang* handled even the smallest transactions without any disinclination. (4) *Ch'ien chuangs* opened their offices until late in the night and on Sundays.[20] In East Asia shops used to be open until near midnight and Sundays were the major shopping days. Banks which closed their doors at 5 p.m. and on Sundays could not be competitive. However, *ch'ien chuangs* were always in close touch with their clients. One of their important functionaries was what was called *p'ao chieh*, which literally means street-runners, but in actual fact they were something like canvassers who regularly visited the banks' customers and gathered market information.[21] Compradores of foreign banks could have fulfilled the same function, but surely could not have reached tens of thousands of indigenous merchants.

Thus, there was a division of work between international banks and native banks. The former were specialized in foreign exchange business and also served as bankers to European or Japanese residents of foreign concessions. They were also bankers to the Chinese government, although this role began to change after the establishment of the Bank of China in 1905 (first as Hu Pu Yin Hang – Bank of Treasury – and then renamed Ta Ch'ing Yin Hang – Bank of Great Ch'ing). The *ch'ien chuangs*, on the other hand, served as bankers to Chinese traders. The interface between these two sorts of financial intermediaries was (1) the chop loans given by international banks to native banks; (2) settlement of *chuang p'iaos* paid into international banks by foreign traders, who received them from Chinese merchants; (3) 'packing credits'.

Thus, the international banks were suppliers of cash (silver money) to the native banks. This does not necessarily mean, however, that the former were exploiting the latter. The power relationship between them must have changed according to the supply–demand conditions in the market. The international banks ordinarily held in their coffers huge amounts of silver sycee and dollars, which they had to employ as remuneratively as possible. Thus, the manager of the HSBC's Shanghai branch reports his compradore as saying that 'The Market Rate is kept low to squeeze the Foreign Banks and the Native Banks are encouraged in this by the anxiety of some of the Banks to lend them any surplus funds they may have from time to time.'[22] He further says that 'Some of our neighbours seem very keen on lending to Native Banks. Our own advances, which as a rule are much under tls 20 lacs [2,000,000 tls], are spread over about 40 Banks.'[23] According to him, the Yokohama Specie Bank was lending to the native banks at market rate, while the Russo-Chinese Bank often spoilt the market by offering to lend at very low levels. On the other hand, 'The Chartered and German get the same rates as we do, which has never been lower than 4% and is at present 4½% (Market rate to-day 2½%).'[24] Thus, it seems that there was a hierarchy among the international banks. When the market tightens, of course, the native banks could not 'squeeze' the international banks, as is evidenced by very high rates which occasionally prevailed in the market. But certainly the relationship was not that of one-sided domination by the international banks.

IV

The stereotyped picture of poor China being subjected to exploitation and extortion by imperialist Western powers seems subject nowadays to some revision among academic circles. One notable example is Jerry L. S. Wang's paper. His conclusion is that

> there are no grounds for arguing that British traders were able to manipulate prices at the expense of their Chinese counterparts in the Anglo-Chinese trade. On the contrary, in many cases, particularly in the export trade, it was the Chinese who manipulated prices. Consequently, Anglo-Chinese trade was more profitable to Chinese rather than British merchants. In fact, losses rather than profits were more frequently made by the latter. And this is why so many British firms trading with China ended in failure. The reason why some enterprises [like the Swires] carried on trading is, first, that they were often also engaged in other businesses in China, and trading was only part of their activities.[25]

We may also quote such researchers as Chi-Ming Hou, Loren Brandt, Barbara Sands, Albert Feuerwerker and others,[26] whose studies reveal that there was quite respectable economic growth in China during the last decades of the Empire. As has been said, growth of foreign trade of China registered remarkable rates of growth from 1890 to 1913. That is, imports grew from Hk.tls 127 million in 1890 to Hk.tls 570 million in 1913, while exports grew from Hk.tls 87 million to Hk.tls 403 million during the same period. These are nominal amounts in silver taels, and the exchange rates of silver taels to pound sterling fell markedly from 62¼d. per Haikwan tael in 1890 to 37¼d. in 1900. But thereafter exchange rates stabilized and were 36¼d. in 1913.[27] As there was a revolution in 1911, it may be better to observe the behaviour of trade during 1900–10. During the period, Chinese imports grew from Hk.tls 211 million to Hk.tls 463 million or by 8.2% per annum. Exports increased from Hk.tls 159 million to Hk.tls 381 million or by 9.1% per annum (both are compound rates of growth).[28] These rates are comparable with the growth rates of Japanese trade, where imports grew by 8.3% per annum and exports by 8.4% during the same years.[29] The international banks were material in facilitating this growth of foreign trade by utilizing the funds obtained in London at comparatively low interest rates.

There certainly was imperialist penetration and exploitation of the Chinese economy, particularly by those latter-day imperialists like the Russian and the Japanese. But the Chinese economy seems to have been more resilient than the traditional stereotyped theses seem to suggest.

Notes

In this chapter the source material in the Hongkong and Shanghai Banking Corporation, kept at the Group Archives in Hong Kong, was used. This material has now been moved to the Midland Bank Group Corporation Affairs, Mariner House, Pepys Street, London EC3N 4DA. Only those works directly cited in this chapter are listed here. For a detailed bibliography of works on modern Chinese economic history, see Frank H. H. King, *The Hongkong Bank in Late Imperial China, 1864–1902* (*The History of the Hongkong and Shanghai Banking Corporation*, vol. I) (Cambridge, 1989). See also Takeshi Hamashita, *Chuugoku Kindai Keizaishi Kenkyuu* (*Studies in Modern Chinese Economic History*) (Tokyo, 1989), and Albert Feuerwerker, 'Materials for the Study of the Economic History of Modern China', *Journal of Economic History*, 21, 1 (March 1961).

1 Yen P'ei Huang and Sung P'ang, *Chung Kuo Su Shu Nien Hai Kwan Shang Wu T'ung Chi T'u Piao* (*Statistics of Foreign Trade of China during the Past Forty Years*) (Hong Kong, 1916; repr. Hong Kong, 1974), pp. 170–3.

2 B. R. Mitchell, *International Historical Statistics, Africa and Asia* (London, 1982), p. 504.

3 Hamashita, *Chuugoku Kindai Keizaishi Kenkyuu*, p. 75.

4 C. F. Remer, *Foreign Investments in China* (London, 1933; repr. New York, 1968), p. 69.

5 For example, see Chi-Ming Hou, 'Economic Dualism. The Case of China, 1840–1937', *Journal of Economic History*, 23, 3 (September 1963); Chi-Ming Hou, 'Some Reflections on the Economic History of Modern China (1840–1949)', *Journal of Economic History*, 23, 4 (December 1963); Albert Feuerwerker, 'Handicraft and Manufactured Cotton Textiles in China, 1871–1910', *Journal of Economic History*, 30, 2 (June 1970); Loren Brandt and Barbara Sands, 'Beyond Malthus and Ricardo: Economic Growth, Land Concentration and Income Distribution in Early Twentieth Century Rural China', *Journal of Economic History*, 50, 4 (December 1990).

6 China, the Maritime Customs, *Trade Reports and Returns*, 1904, xvi (quoted in Hamashita, *Chuugoka Kindai Keizaishi Kenkyuu*, p. 139).

7 King, *The Hongkong Bank*, p. 320.

8 HSBC, Shanghai branch manager's letter to J. R. M. Smith at the head office, 31 August 1908.

9 HSBC, interest at credit of depositors at the Tientsin Agency, December 1895 to May 1896 (SHG LEDG 896).

10 HSBC, Inspector's Report on the Shanghai branch, 5 October 1908, p. 12.

11 *Ibid.*, p. 6.

12 King, *Hongkong Bank*, p. 505.

13 HSBC, Inspector's Report on the Shanghai branch, 2 May 1911, p. 6.

14 *Ibid.*, p. 5.

15 Yuuki Yamakawa (Yokohama Specie Bank), *Shinkoku Shuccho Fukumeisho* (*Report of the Business Trip to China*) (Yokohama, 1898), p. 50.

16 Chung Kuo Jen Min Yin Hang Shang Hai Shi Fen Hang (The Shanghai Branch of the People's Bank of China), *Shang Hai Ch'ien Chuang Shi Liang* (*Historical Materials on Ch'ien Chuangs in Shanghai*) (Shanghai, 1960), p. 94.

17 HSBC, Shanghai branch manager's letter to J. R. M. Smith at the head office, 7 August 1908, pp. 1–2.

18 *Ibid.*, p. 1.

19 Gaimusho Tsuushoukyoku (Department of Trade, Ministry of Foreign Affairs, Japan), *Shina Kinyuu Jijou* (*A Factual Study of Banking and Monetary Conditions in China*) (Tokyo, 1925), pp. 1048–9.

20 P'an Chun-Hao, *Chung Kuo Ch'ien Chuang Kai Yao* (*An Overview of Chinese Ch'ien Chuang*) (Shanghai, 1929; repr. Taipei, 1970), p. 214.

21 Yang Yin P'u, *Shang Hai Chin Jung Tsu Chi Kai Yao* (*An Overview of the Financial System of Shanghai*) (Shanghai, 1929), pp. 66–8.

22 HSBC, Shanghai branch manager's letter to J. R. M. Smith at the head office, 7 August 1908, p. 2.

23 *Ibid.*, p. 2.

24 *Ibid.*, p. 2.

25 Jerry L. S. Wang, 'The Profitability of Anglo-Chinese Trade, 1861–1913', *Business History*, 35, 3 (July 1993), p. 59.

26 See n. 5.

27 Hamashita, *Chuugoka Kindai Keizaishi Kenkyuu*, p. 447.

28 Huang Sung, *Chung Kuo Su Shu Nien Hai Kwan Shang Wu Tung Chi Tu Piao*, pp. 170–3.

29 Mitchell, *International Historical Statistics*, p. 391.

22   The role of banking in Japan, 1882–1973

Kanji Ishii

Introduction

One of the reasons for the high growth rate of the economy of modern Japan is its high rate of savings. Even in the 1980s the rate of savings of the household economy was around 17% which was twice as much as those in the Western advanced countries. The main subject of this chapter is to investigate how this high amount of savings were invested in the industries of Japan or other Asian countries and to examine the role of the Japanese banks in such investments.

The orthodox view on this subject in Japan has been that, until the high economic growth ended in 1973, the main part of the funds of the industrial enterprises was not procured directly from the capital market but supplied indirectly through various kinds of banks, and the Bank of Japan which was established in 1882 provided these banks with funds abundantly if necessary.

To such an orthodox view, however, criticisms by the revisionists have appeared recently. In this chapter I would like to examine the propriety of these revisionisms and present my new view.

Direct finance or indirect finance?

The first point that the revisionists presented was about the origin of the indirect financial system. They say that before the Second World War

396

Table 22.1. *The increase of the private savings (million yen)*

	1901–5		1906–10	
Long-term domestic bonds	511.1	(25.1)	303.2	(15.9)
Long-term foreign bonds	872.8	(42.8)	476.8	(25.1)
Short-term securities	99.0	(4.9)	−89.0	(−4.7)
Local government bonds	19.8	(1.0)	105.9	(5.6)
Domestic corporate bonds	—		200.2	(10.5)
Stocks and shares	184.6	(9.1)	538.6	(28.3)
Total (A)	1,687.3	(82.8)	1,535.6	(80.8)
Securities held by banks (B)	104.8	(5.1)	183.3	(9.6)
Loans secured by stocks (C)	0.8	(0.0)	315.2	(16.6)
Total (D) = (A) – (B) – (C)	1,581.7	(77.6)	1,037.2	(54.6)
Deposits (E)	361.0	(17.7)	688.7	(36.2)
Insurance (F)	12.8	(0.6)	32.1	(1.7)
Currency (G)	82.5	(4.0)	143.3	(7.5)
Total (D) + (E) + (F)+ (G)	2,038.1	(100.0)	1,901.3	(100.0)

Source: K. Emi, M. Ito and H. Eguchi, *Savings and Currency* (Tokyo: Toyo Keizai Shinposha, 1988).

the main part of the industrial funds of Japan was supplied directly from the capital market and the system of the indirect finance was created during that war.[1] If it is true, the role of banking before that war must not have been so important as argued in the orthodox view.

The data which were presented by M. Okuno and T. Okazaki as the evidence of the predominance of the direct finance at the beginning of the twentieth century were that the proportions of the amount of the investment in securities to the total amount of the private savings were 77.6% (1901–5) and 54.6% (1906–10), and they were far higher than those of the deposits which were 17.7% and 36.2% respectively. According to their opinion, it was after the latter half of the 1920s that the amount of the deposits exceeded that of securities investment.

The problem with this opinion is that the contents of the securities were not examined. As shown in Table 22.1, most of the securities investment at that time consisted of long-term bonds issued for the expenditure of the Russo-Japanese war from 1904 to 1905. The total proportion of the domestic corporate bonds and stocks and shares, which means the weight of the direct finance, was only 9.1% in the first half of the 1900s. It is true that in the latter half of the 1900s such a total

Table 22.2. *The increase of savings (billion yen)*

	(1) Bonds and stocks of corp. excluding banks	(2) Deposits and stocks of banks	(2)/(1) (%)
1891–1900	0.337	0.704	209
1901–10	0.766	1.207	158
1911–20	6.887	7.954	115
1921–30	8.511	6.407	75
1931–40	18.741	30.085	161
1941–50	389.700	1,317.800	338
1951–60	4,176.800	11,955.800	286
1961–70	14,837.000	61,708.400	416

Sources: Emi, Ito and Eguchi, *Savings and Currency*: Statistics Department of the Bank of Japan, *Hundred-Year Statistics of the Japanese Economy* (Tokyo, 1966).

proportion increased to 38.8% which is nearly the same proportion of the deposits. But if we classify the increase of the stocks of banks by 113.6 million yen (6.0%), which is included in the stocks and shares shown in Table 22.1, to the indirect finance, we can regard the latter half of the 1900s as the period of the dominance of the indirect finance.

In order to compare the weight of the direct finance with that of the indirect finance, Table 22.2 shows the increase of the amount of the bonds and the stocks of corporations excluding banks (= direct finance), compared with those of the deposits and the stocks of banks (= indirect finance).

As the results of the stock boom which took place in the First World War and continued until the outbreak of the economic crisis in 1920 and the debenture boom in the 1920s, the direct finance seemed to have overcome the dominance of the indirect finance. In the 1930s, however, the rapid increase of deposits revived the dominance of the indirect finance which continued until the 1960s. So we should look at the situation of the 1920s as an exceptional one caused by the long depression.

Since the outbreak of the first oil shock and the introduction of the floating exchange rate system in 1973, the dominance of the indirect finance in Japan has gradually weakened. The decline of the rate of economic growth decreased the demand for industrial funds so that the role of banking has been changing.

Table 22.3. *The proportions of the balance of loans and discounts of the BOJ to those of all other banks at the end of the years*

Average	%
1888–90	16.2
1891–1900	20.5
1901–10	9.8
1911–20	5.7
1921–30	6.1
1931–40	6.8
1941–50	18.5
1951–60	9.6
1961–70	7.8
1971–80	2.2
1981–90	1.8

Note: before 1888 the data of all other banks are unknown.
Sources: Statistics Department of the Bank of Japan, *Hundred-Year Statistics*; Research and Statistics Department of the Bank of Japan, *Economic Statistics Annual (1991)* (Tokyo, 1992).

What was the role of the Bank of Japan?

The Bank of Japan (hereafter BOJ) played an important role at the top of the indirect financial system mentioned above. Usually the BOJ has not supplied funds directly to the industrial enterprises. The financial institutions, such as the city banks, regional banks, trust banks and so on, mediated between the BOJ and the industrial enterprises.

It is apparent that the role of the BOJ changed often reflecting the situation of the economy in Japan. Table 22.3 shows the rough weight of the finance of the BOJ in each period. The activity of the BOJ was energetic from 1888 to 1910 and from 1941 to 1970. The former period is that of Japanese industrial revolution and the latter period covers the periods of the Second World War, the economic reconstruction after the war and the high economic growth. In contrast to these periods, the periods of the First World War and the interwar period (1911–40) and that of the low economic growth (1971–90) are characterized by the inactivity of the loan and discount business of the BOJ.

According to the orthodox view the BOJ supplied the strategic industries and the Yokohama Specie Bank with the so-called growth money (the bank notes needed for the economic growth) abundantly in its active periods.[2] To such an orthodox view, however, the revisionists presented a new opinion that the most important objective of the monetary policy of the BOJ had been always the stability of the value of currency.[3]

If such a new opinion is right, the level of the Japanese economy before the industrial revolution must have been much higher than the level we have supposed. Professor Tsurumi's recent work tried to prove the development of the private financial system which restricted the activity of the BOJ.[4] It is true that his work succeeded to some extent in proving the existence of the developed private financial system, but it must be also noted that he sometimes confused idea with reality. For example, he classified the advance of capital to the filatures by Yokohama raw silk merchants, which were supported by the BOJ, as a kind of commercial finance because he observed that a bureaucrat of the Ministry of Finance had proposed to introduce commercial bills to the transaction between filatures and silkworm raisers. But such a proposal had not been realized at all. So we should classify the advance mentioned above as a kind of industrial finance which proves the supply of growth money by the BOJ.

As for the active policy to supply the growth money by the BOJ after the Second World War, the authors of the above-mentioned history of the BOJ insisted that it had not been the bank's real intention. But it is an undeniable fact that Hisato Ichimada, the governor of the BOJ from 1946 to 1954, regarded the inflation caused by the supply of the growth money as unavoidable in order to reconstruct the post-war economy.

The positiveness of the monetary policy of the BOJ after the Second World War is well shown in the dominance of the bills of special treatment. The bills, which were authorized by the BOJ as necessary for the reconstruction of the economy, could be rediscounted by the BOJ freely and cheaply. The proportion of the amount of such kind of bills to the total amount of loans and discount of the BOJ were 38.7% in 1948, 77.1% in 1950 and 77.4% in 1952.[5]

Therefore we have come to the conclusion inevitably that the orthodox view that until 1973 the BOJ, as a central bank of a latecomer in the advanced capitalistic countries, provided the Japanese economy with the growth money is basically correct. It was after the hyperinflation from 1973 to 1974 that the BOJ selected price stability as the most important objective of the monetary policy.[6]

Postal savings and the Ministry of Finance

We should not, however, limit our views to the private banks and the BOJ. There existed a group of public financial institutions which promoted strongly the expansion of the Japanese economy before the Second World War and the economic growth after the war. The core of these institutions were the Postal Savings System of the Ministry of Communication and the Deposit Bureau (the Trust Fund Bureau, since 1951) of the Ministry of Finance which employed the postal savings together with other funds. Although the Postal Savings System is not a bank because it cannot create a credit by issuing the bank notes or opening the current accounts, we have to investigate the history of the Postal Savings System in Japan.

The Postal Savings System in Japan was opened in 1875, following those in the United Kingdom (opened in 1861), New Zealand (in 1867) and Belgium (in 1870). As shown in Table 22.4, the amount of the postal savings increased along with the deposits of all banks. Through the rapid increase of postal savings in the depression of the 1920s and in the wartime economy of the first half of the 1940s, the proportion of the outstanding postal savings to the deposits of all banks went up to 40.5% at the end of 1945. Although the proportion fell in the periods of the economic reconstruction and the high economic growth, it rose again in and after the 1970s.

The power of the postal savings is strengthened by the concentration of the savings to a bureau of the Ministry of Finance. All of the postal savings collected by a large number of post offices were entrusted to the Deposit Bureau (Trust Fund Bureau) which was often called 'the Second Central Bank' and the financier for 'the Second Budget of the Government'.

Before analysing the operation of the postal savings by the Deposit Bureau, we will examine the depositors of them. As shown in Table 22.5, nearly 90% of the depositors of the postal savings deposited less than 50 yen respectively, depositing in all only 20% of the total savings. On the other hand, the proportion of the total savings of the big depositors who deposited 500 yen and over amounted to 32%, though they represented only 1.2% of all the depositors. In the case of the savings bank, the situation of the depositors was similar to that of the postal savings.

Table 22.4. *The postal savings outstanding compared with the deposits of all banks (billion yen, %)*

End of year	Postal savings (A)	Deposits (B)	(A)/(B)
1890	0.0195	0.0627	31.1
1900	0.0240	0.5758	4.2
1910	0.170	1.649	10.3
1920	0.883	8.829	10.0
1930	2.397	11.546	20.8
1940	8.142	34.284	23.7
1945	48.548	119.829	40.5
1950	157.2	1,048.5	15.0
1960	1,134.6	8,872.2	12.8
1970	7,772.8	41,308.8	18.8
1980	62,096.9	154,909.4	40.1
1990	136,673.5	454,485.4	30.1

Sources: as in Table 22.3.

As for the pre-war period, the data of the time deposits by rank of value of all banks were not given. According to the data of the time deposits of the Hachiman Bank quoted in Table 22.5 from Professor S. Asajima's article, 30% of the total number of depositors and 81% of the total value of deposits were concentrated in the class of big depositors who deposited 500 yen and over. Considering the fact that 23% of the total number of depositors and 82% of the total value of time deposits of all banks were concentrated in the class of big depositors who deposited 100,000 yen and over in 1961,[7] the example of the Hachiman Bank can be regarded as a typical one.

It has been said that the purpose of the postal savings system was to encourage thrift and savings among workers and collect their small-scale deposits.[8] As already pointed out, however, the small quantity of the postal savings is very doubtful.[9] We should classify the depositors of the postal savings into numerous small and medium depositors and a few big ones.

Promoted by the campaign sponsored by the officials to encourage thrift and savings at the beginning of the twentieth century,[10] the number of depositors which was 1,883,262 in 1900 increased to 11,017,588 in 1910, and 23,781,640 in 1920. In the latter half of the 1910s the number of the depositors of the postal savings of Japan

Table 22.5. *The postal savings and the deposits by rank of amount at the end of 1918 (%)*

Rank of value	Postal savings		Savings deposits[a]		Time deposits[b]	
	Depositor	Value	Depositor	Value	Depositor	Value
>1,000 yen[c]	0.4	15.6	0.4	23.7	16.3	66.3
>500 yen	0.8	16.2	0.8	15.9	13.5	14.4
>100 yen	6.0	38.2	4.8	31.7	47.5	17.7
>50 yen	5.1	10.8	5.3	11.8	13.0	1.3
<50 yen	87.7	19.2	88.7	16.9	9.7	0.3
Total	17,737,154 accounts		11,026,710 accounts		1,101 accounts	
(100%)	581,148,032 yen		338,213,326 yen		628,824 yen	
Value/depositor	32.8 yen		30.7 yen		571.1 yen	

[a]saving deposits of saving banks
[b]time deposits of the head office of the Hachiman bank.
[c]in the case of the postal savings, 900 yen and over.
Sources: Saving Bureau, *Statistics Annual (1919)* (Tokyo, 1923); Banking Bureau, *Annual Report of the Banking Bureau* (1918) (Tokyo, 1920); S. Asajima, 'The Analysis of the Time Deposits of the Hachiman Bank in the Taisho Era', *Kinyu Keizai (Journal of Finance)*, 202 (1983).

exceeded that of the United Kingdom and became the greatest in the world.[11] Needless to say, the majority of the numerous depositors were small depositors.

As for the big depositors, there existed the restriction of maximum deposit for single individuals although in the case of public bodies such as schools, temples and so on, no maximum existed. The maximum fixed at 500 yen in 1892 increased to 1,000 yen in 1905, and 2,000 yen in 1920. Table 22.6 shows the proportion of the number of depositors by occupation in each rank of value. From this table it is clear that the most important occupations of depositors of the postal savings were agriculture and commerce, and the postal savings deposited by employees and pupils are specially inclined to smaller-scale deposits less than 100 yen. According to the investigation in 1921, the average monthly income of the white-collar workers in Tokyo was 123 yen and that of the blue-collar workers was 93 yen.[12] Therefore it was not easy even for the white-collar workers to become the big depositors who saved 500–2,000 yen. Some of the white-collar workers could have been the medium-scale depositors who saved 100–500 yen. It should be noted that the big or medium-scale depositors of the postal savings, who were also the depositors of banks, were very sensitive to the rate of deposit interest and the degree of reliability of the financial institutions.

After the economic crisis of 1920 and the financial crisis of 1927, the number of savings banks and ordinary banks which totalled 1,983 at the end of 1920 decreased drastically. At the end of 1945 there existed only four savings banks (exterminated by 1949) and sixty-one ordinary banks. The Savings Bank Law enacted in 1921 and the Banking Law enacted in 1927 played the decisive role in the decreasing process. At the meeting of the House of Lords held on 15 March 1921 which discussed the Savings Bank Bill, Minister of Finance, Korekiyo Takahashi, admitted the possibility of the disappearance of the savings banks because all the small-scale savings could be collected by the postal savings system.[13] On the other hand, at the meeting of the Committee for Financial System Research held on 26 October 1926, the representative of the Ministry of Finance, Akira Den, rejected the claim of bankers that the merger of regional banks by city banks should be approved, saying that an approval would increase the complaints of country people about the concentration of funds in the big urban area as had been the case with postal savings.[14] Thus the development of the postal savings in the interwar period was an important background for the extermination of the savings banks and the formation of the dual system of ordinary banks composed of city banks and regional banks.

Activity of the Deposit Bureau (Trust Fund Bureau)

The use of the postal savings collected by the Ministry of Communications has been entrusted to the Ministry of Finance. The Deposit Bureau which used the postal savings together with other funds was at first only one of the accounts of the Ministry of Finance to which its minister had full authority. At the end of the fiscal year of 1924, the total amount of the funds of the Deposit Bureau was 1,656 million yen, 69% of which was the postal savings. In 1925 the Law of the Fund of the Deposit Bureau was enacted in order to establish the Deposit Bureau as one of the bureaus and to restrict the power of the financial minister. By this reform the investment of the funds had to be approved by the Committee on the Investment of the Deposit Bureau.

Until 1945 the most important operation of the Deposit Bureau was the finance of wars and foreign investments. Among the wars fought by

Table 22.6. *Occupation of the depositors at the end of 1918 (%)*

	Total	>500 yen	<500 yen	<100 yen	<50 yen
Agriculture	31.4	33.3	35.1	33.0	31.0
Commerce	11.4	16.8	14.8	14.2	10.9
Industry	5.2	5.7	5.8	5.5	5.2
Fishery	1.8	2.6	2.6	2.1	1.7
Miscellaneous	3.5	6.3	5.6	5.3	3.3
Official	7.1	7.9	7.6	7.8	7.0
Employee	7.5	4.3	6.4	7.9	7.6
Pupil	19.7	4.2	5.9	8.5	21.5
Without job	4.0	5.4	5.1	5.2	3.8
Group	0.8	3.3	1.7	1.5	0.7
Unknown	7.5	10.3	9.3	9.1	7.2
Total	100.0	100.0	100.0	100.0	100.0

Source: Saving Bureau, *Statistics Annual (1919).*

modern Japan, those which cost several times as much as the entire monthly budget of the government were the Sino-Japanese War (1894–5), the Russo-Japanese War (1904–5) and the China Incident and the Second World War (1937–45). The main parts of the expenditure of these wars were naturally procured by issuing government bonds.[15]

The government bonds issued for the Sino-Japanese War, however, were bought mainly by Japanese people and banks in co-operation with the Bank of Japan, and the Deposit Bureau did not have to buy many bonds for the war. As for the Russo-Japanese War, about half of the government bonds for the war were issued in London and New York, and all of the remaining half were bought by Japanese people and banks. Therefore the Deposit Bureau which had been using most of the funds for the government bonds did not have to buy the new bonds for the war. In contrast to these cases, the Deposit Bureau played the most important role among the financial institutions in accepting the government bonds for the China Incident and the Second World War. At the end of 1945 the government bonds amounted to 139.9 billion yen of which 45.5 billion yen were held by the Deposit Bureau, 18.0 billion yen by the Regional Banks, 17.2 billion yen by the City Banks, and 7.2 billion yen by the Bank of Japan respectively.[16]

From the end of the Russo-Japanese War (1905) to the outbreak of the China Incident (1937), the activity of the Deposit Bureau was diversified. Table 22.7 shows the main contents of the investment of the funds just before the reform of the Deposit Bureau in 1925.

Loans for local development began to increase after the First World War responding to the claims from the local communities to return the funds of postal savings. The most problematic investment was special loans to the special banks and others in order to promote foreign investment to China or give financial support to the big companies which expanded their business excessively during the First World War and were on the verge of bankruptcy.

Now let us focus our analysis on the special loans for foreign investment in order to clarify the background of the Japanese 'modern' imperialism in China. After the Russo-Japanese War Japanese capitalists and government, which had begun to invest their capital in Taiwan and Korea after the Sino-Japanese War, paid attention to China as a new area of investment. At that time, however, the capital accumulation of Japanese enterprises were insufficient for such a new activity. As stated before, Japanese enterprises had to borrow large sums from banks which were provided with money by the Bank of Japan if necessary. The biggest Japanese foreign investment in China was that of the South Manchurian Railway Co. which was established in 1906 with the capital of 200 million yen. It was virtually the inheritance of the investment made by Russia, and the Company had to borrow money from the United Kingdom by issuing debentures four times at London from 1907 to 1911 amounting to 14 million pound sterling (= about 140 million yen). It was in the first half of the 1920s that the main Japanese cotton spinning companies began to invest directly in Shanghai and Tsingtao, using their own funds.

It should be noted, however, that before the First World War Japanese investment in China started being supported by the funds of the Deposit Bureau. The first example was the investment in 1907 to the Kiangsi Nanshun Railway Co. which was undertaken by Chinese officials and merchants in Kiangsi province in 1904 and was constructing the Nanchang–Kiukiang (Nanshun) Railway. Having obtained the information on the shortage of funds of that Company, the Foreign Ministry of Japan ordered the Industrial Bank of Japan to make a loan of 1.5 million yen to the Company through a Chinese merchant in Shanghai using the funds of the Deposit Bureau. In 1909 the Toa Kogyo Kaisha (the East Asian Development Co.) was established in order to mediate Japanese investment in China. When it made a loan of

Table 22.7. *Investment of the funds of the Deposit Bureau at the end of 1924 (million yen, %)*

Government bonds	309	(18.7)
Loans to the government account	163	(9.8)
Loans for local development	339	(27.1)
Special loans	343	(20.7)
to the Industrial Bank of Japan	137	
to the Bank of Korea	53	
to the Bank of Taiwan	50	
to the Yokohama Specie Bank	38	
to the Oriental Colonization Co.	35	
to the others[a]	30	
Others	392	(23.7)
Total	1,656	(100.0)

[a] 20 million yen was loaned to the Industrial Bank of Korea and the Bank of Taiwan for the Nishihara Loans.
Source: K. Shimura, 'The Significance of the Funds of the Deposit Bureau in the Financial Market', *Kinyu Keizai* (*Journal of Finance*), 63, 1960.

5 million yen to the Nanshun Railway Co. in 1912, the Deposit Bureau accepted the bonds of the Industrial Bank of Japan for the loan amounting to 3 million yen at the low interest of 4.2% which enabled the Toa Kogyo Kaisha to defeat the Western rivals. Although the whole railway line between Nanchang and Kiukiang opened in 1916, that Railway Co.'s business was too poor to refund the various Japanese loans amounting to 10 million yen of which the Deposit Bureau accepted 7.5 million yen.[17]

Among foreign investments using the funds of the Deposit Bureau, loans to the Hanyehping Coal and Iron Co. Ltd, in order to secure the materials of iron and steel for the government-owned Yawata Ironworks in Japan were the biggest and most important investment. The Hanyehping Co. was established in 1908 by Sheng Hsuan-huai amalgamating his three enterprises, namely, the Hanyang Ironworks, the Tayeh Iron Mines and the P'inghsiang Coal Mines. Sheng took over the government-owned Hanyang Ironworks and the Tayeh Iron Mines in 1896 and developed the P'inghsiang Coal Mines borrowing 4 million marks (tls 1.5 million) from the German firm of Carlowitz and Co. The Yawata Ironworks, which had concluded a contract with Sheng for the shipment of 50,000 tons of ore to Japan annually in 1899, offered a loan of 3 million yen (tls 2.18 million) to Sheng in 1904 through the Industrial Bank of Japan at 3% for thirty years to be repaid by the sale of ore to Yawata at a fixed price. The fund of this loan, which had been at first supplied by the government special account, was replaced by the money of the Deposit Bureau in 1908. After 1907 the Yawata Ironworks offered many loans to the Hanyehping Co. through the Yokohama Specie Bank using the money of the Deposit Bureau. The Hanyehping Co., which had to continue to supply ore and pig iron to the Yawata Ironworks at a fixed low price during the First World War, could not finish the repayment of the loans. At the end of March 1929 the balance of the loans including the interest was 51.27 million yen which could not be collected and was refunded by the Japanese government.[18]

While the loans mentioned above were closely connected with the Chinese economy, the so-called Nishihara Loans amounting to 145 million yen which were negotiated secretly between the Chinese government in Beijing and Mr Kamezo Nishihara, the personal representative of Prime Minister Hisaichi Terauchi of Japan, were mostly used for political purposes. The Nishihara Loans were granted to the Chinese government from 1917 to 1918 through the Industrial Bank of Japan, the Bank of Taiwan and the Bank of Korea. Of the total amount of the Loans, however, only 5 million yen was supplied by the three banks mentioned above, and 40 million yen was supplied by the Deposit Bureau, the remaining 100 million yen being supplied by the group of eighteen private banks for foreign investment by way of accepting 100 million yen of government guaranteed bonds issued by the Industrial Bank. As the Chinese government was unable to pay the interest of the Nishihara Loans after 1921, the three banks mentioned above which had to pay the bond bearers the interest encountered difficulties and had to ask the Japanese government for support. Finally, the Nishihara Loans also were liquidated by drawing on taxes imposed on Japanese people.[19]

There were many other examples of the investment in China which were supported by the funds of the Deposit Bureau. According to an investigation at the end of October 1923, the total amount of Japanese loans in China was 488 million yen, of which 108 million yen was provided by the Deposit Bureau.[20] Compared with 1,540 million yen of the balance of the funds of the Deposit Bureau at the end of 1923, the share of 108 million yen was only 7.0%. But most of the Japanese loans in China supported by the funds of the Deposit Bureau were very risky and not repaid at all. Such a careless operation of the Deposit Bureau was one of the main reasons for its reform in 1925.

Since the end of the Second World War, the objectives of the operation of the postal savings have changed drastically. The operation of those funds for wars or foreign investments disappeared. The Trust Fund Bureau was organized in April 1951 as the successor of the Deposit Bureau and was to operate all the postal savings together with other funds for the reconstruction and development of the post-war economy of Japan.

From 1945 to 1973, the funds of Japanese enterprises were mainly supplied by banks, which were supported by the Bank of Japan, because the enterprises could not issue stocks or debentures easily on the capital market. For the ordinary banks, however, it was a burden to provide enterprises with long-term funds.

In order to solve such a problem, the public or private banks which concentrate their operations on making long-term loans were established at the beginning of the 1950s and began to provide credits for industrial equipment to the enterprises. The biggest public bank of this kind is the Japan Development Bank which was established in April 1951 by the government in place of the Reconstruction Finance Corporation. On reflection it is obvious that the Reconstruction Finance Corporation, established in 1947, caused a hyperinflation not only because its bonds were accepted by the Bank of Japan but also because it extended unsecured loans on the basis of favouritism (as, for instance, the Showa Denko Scandal). The Japan Development Bank tried to maintain its independence from government by supplying funds for industrial equipment from their own resources and from money borrowed from the Trust Fund Bureau.

In addition to the Japan Development Bank, the Industrial Bank of Japan and the Long-Term Credit Bank of Japan were organized in December 1952 as the private banks specialized in long-term loans under the Long-Term Credit Bank Law. In contrast to their pre-war predecessors, which had operated on the basis of special laws and had been strictly controlled by government, these were completely private banks. They could, however, issue the financial bonds in order to collect the funds for the long-term loans. The Trust Fund Bureau was at first the main acceptor of these bonds.

Table 22.8 shows the balance of industrial equipment loans supplied by the various kinds of banks. According to the data on loans, including short-term credits, the proportion of loans made by ordinary banks (city

Table 22.8. *The balance of industrial equipment loans (billion yen)*

End of year	Japan Dev. Bank	Long-term credit banks	Ordinary banks	Trust accounts[a]	Total
1950	89.9[b]	46.9[c]	50.4	0.9	188.1
1955	373.2	232.8	153.5	68.9	828.4
1960	537.7	802.0[d]	542.5	466.5	2,348.6
1965	927.2	1,923.1	1,371.2	1,663.9	5,885.4
1970	1,705.1	3,907.8	4,431.2	4,014.9	14,059.0

[a]Trust accounts of the trust banks and the Daiwa Bank.
[b]Data of the Reconstruction Finance Corporation.
[c]Data of the former special banks.
[d]The Nippon Credit Bank was organized in April 1957, originally as the Japan Realty Finance Bank.
Sources: Statistics Department of the Bank of Japan, *Economic Statistics* (1961); Statistics Department of the Bank of Japan, *Economic Statistics Annual (1974)* (Tokyo, 1974).

banks and regional banks) amounted to 75.4% of the total amount supplied by all banks at the end of 1955. Concerning the long-term industrial equipment loans shown in Table 22.8, however, the Japan Development Bank provided 45.1% and the long-term credit banks 28.1% of the total amount supplied by all banks at the end of 1955. Such a dominance of the banks which were mainly specialized for long-term loans continued until the middle of the 1960s.

At the end of March 1961, the Japan Development Bank and the long-term credit banks made industrial equipment loans amounting to 1,495.5 billion yen of which 472.3 billion yen was made to the electric power industry, 235.4 billion yen to the marine transport industry and 160.8 billion yen to the iron and steel industry.[21] These industries were most important for the reconstruction and high growth of the Japanese post-war economy.

As mentioned before, the activities of the Japan Development Bank and the long-term credit banks were closely connected with the Trust Fund Bureau. Table 22.9 shows how much these banks depended on the Trust Fund Bureau. The funds provided by the Trust Fund Bureau (A) were the second largest part of the funds of the loans made by the Japan Development Bank (B) from 1953 to 1958, while the former funds (A) became the largest part of the latter funds (B) from 1959 to 1964. On

Table 22.9. *Supply of funds by the Trust Fund Bureau (billion yen)*

	1953–5	1956–8	1959–61	1962–4
(1) Funds of loans made by the Japan Development Bank				
Trust Fund Bureau (A)	54.0	76.2	138.5	250.0
Government	49.2	—	6.8	32.4
Bank's own funds	87.3	92.2	71.3	106.9
Total (B)	190.5	168.4	216.6	389.3
(2) Purchasers of the bonds of the long-term credit banks				
Trust Fund Bureau (C)	109.1	118.5	48.9	104.6
Ordinary banks	119.3	227.1	324.6	578.4
Individuals	91.9	242.3	792.6	1,267.3
Total with others (D)	339.1	614.4	1,218.4	2,078.6
(A) + (C) = (E)	163.1	194.7	187.4	354.6
(B) + (D) = (F)	529.6	782.8	1,435.0	2,467.0
100 × (E)/(F)	(30.8)	(24.9)	(13.1)	(14.4)

Sources: Twenty Five Years of the Japan Development Bank (Tokyo, 1976); Wakanabe and Kitahara, *Banking.*

the other hand, among the purchasers of the bonds of the long-term credit banks (D), the proportion of the Trust Fund Bureau (C) decreased from 1959 to 1964 due to the rapid increase of the proportion of the ordinary banks and individuals. Consequently, though the whole supply of funds for the long-term loans by the Trust Fund Bureau (E) tended to increase, its proportion to all the long-terms loans (F) gradually decreased.

As already shown in Table 22.8, at the end of 1950 nearly half of the loans for equipment were supplied by the Reconstruction Finance Corporation and the share of loans supplied by the former special banks such as the Industrial Bank of Japan, the Nippon Kangyo Bank and the Hokkaido Takushoku Bank was a quarter of all the loans. But the bonds issued by the Reconstruction Finance Corporation were accepted by the Bank of Japan, and it was in December 1950 that the Deposit Bureau began to accept the bonds issued by the Industrial Bank of Japan. After 1960 the main objectives of the fiscal investment and loan programme of the government began to shift from big business and industrial infrastructure to small and medium business, agriculture and livelihood infrastructure. While the former portion decreased from 54.9% in 1955

to 47.2% in 1965 and 35.9% in 1975, the latter proportion increased
from 45.1% in 1955 to 52.8% in 1965 and 64.1% in 1975.[22]

Therefore we can say that it was in the 1950s that the role of the funds
of the Trust Fund Bureau was essential for the reconstruction and high
growth of the Japanese post-war economy.

Conclusion

It can be concluded that the postal savings were invested by the
Japanese government in foreign loans to China in the 1910s, and in
long-term loans to the big business in Japan in the 1950s. Both types of
investments could not have been made to a sufficiently large extent
by private enterprise of banks. The expansion of Japanese 'modern'
imperialism in China after the Russo-Japanese War and the 'miraculous'
reconstruction and high growth of the Japanese economy after the
Second World War were not only supported by the activities of banks
headed by the Bank of Japan, but also promoted by the functions of the
Deposit Bureau (later, the Trust Fund Bureau) which used the huge sum
of postal savings.

Notes

All of the books and articles except for Y. Suzuki (ed.), *The Japanese Financial System*
(Oxford, 1987); K. Ishii, 'Japan', in Rondo Cameron and V. I. Vovykin (eds.),
International Banking, 1870–1914 (Oxford, 1990); and K. Ishii, 'Japanese Foreign Trade
and the Yokohama Specie Bank, 1880–1913', in Olive Checkland, Shizuya Nishimura
and Norio Tamaki (eds.), *Pacific Banking, 1859–1959* (New York, 1994) are written in the
Japanese language.

 1 M. Okuno and T. Okazaki (eds.), *The Origin of the Contemporary Economic System of Japan*
   (Tokyo, 1993).
 2 S. Watanabe and K. Kitahara (eds.), *The Industrial History of Modern Japan*, vol. XXVI:
   Banking (Tokyo, 1996); K. Ishii, 'The Industrial Finance of the Bank of Japan',
   Shakaikeizaishigaku (Socio-Economic History), 38, 2 (1972); K. Ishii, 'Japan', in Rondo
   Cameron and V. I. Vovykin (eds.), *International Banking, 1870–1914* (Oxford, 1990);
   K. Ishii, 'Japanese Foreign Trade and the Yokohama Specie Bank, 1880–1913', in
   Olive Checkland, Shizuya Nishimura and Norio Tamaki (eds.), *Pacific Banking,
   1859–1959* (New York, 1994).
 3 Bank of Japan (ed.), *Centennial History of the Bank of Japan*, 7 vols. (Tokyo, 1982–8).
 4 M. Tsurumi, *The Establishment of the Japanese Credit System* (Tokyo, 1991).
 5 K. Yagi, 'The Monetary Policy of the Bank of Japan after the Second World War',
   Seikei-Kenkyu (Journal of Politics and Economics), 55 (1988).
 6 Y. Suzuki, *The Monetary Policy of Japan* (Tokyo, 1993).
 7 Statistics Department of the Bank of Japan, *Economic Statistics of Japan (1961)* (Tokyo,
   1962).

8 Y. Suzuki (ed.), *The Japanese Financial System* (Oxford, 1987).
9 J. Teranishi, *The Economic Growth of Japan and the Finance* (Tokyo, 1982).
10 S. Sugiura, 'The Development of the Postal Savings and Savings Promotion Policy in Japan 1905–1914', *Shakaikeizaishigaku (Socio-Economic History)*, 56, 1 (1990).
11 Saving Bureau, *Sixty Years of the Economic History of the Postal Savings* (Tokyo, 1935).
12 H. Takeda, *Imperialism and Democracy* (Tokyo, 1993).
13 Teikokugikai (Imperial Diet), *The Minutes of the Proceedings of the Committees of the House of Lords* (Tokyo: Tokyo University Press, 1982).
14 T. Tsuchiya (ed.), *The Historical Materials of the Finance in Japan, Meiji and Taisho Era*, vol. XVIII (Tokyo, 1956).
15 Ministry of Finance, *The History of the Public Finance in the Showa Era*, vol. IV (Tokyo, 1955).
16 Statistics Department of the Bank of Japan, *Economic Statistics (1961)*.
17 K. Ikegami, 'One Pattern of the Loans to China', *Ikkyo Ronso*, 71, 6 (1974); Kokkashihonyushutsu-kenkyukai (Research Group of the Capital Export by the Government), *The Capital Export of Japan. A Study on the Loans to China* (Tokyo, 1986); K. Murakami, 'Japanese Concession in the Yangtze Valley', in H. Ando (ed.), *Modern Japan and China* (Tokyo, 1989).
18 S. Sato, 'A Note on "Loan for Iron Ore" with Special Reference to the Finance of State Works', *Tochiseidoshigaku (Journal of Agrarian History)*, 32 (1966); B. Nagura, *A Study on the Iron and Steel Industry in Japan* (Tokyo, 1984).
19 T. Suzuki (ed.), *A Study on the Materials of the Nishihara Loans* (Tokyo, 1972).
20 Ikegami, 'One Pattern of the Loans to China'.
21 I. Denda, *Political Finance in Japan* (Kyoto, 1990).
22 *Ibid.*

Index